Black Atlantic Crossings

The Lives and Anti-Racist Tactics
of Booker T. Washington
and Manuel R. Querino

Sabrina Gledhill

Editora **Funmilayo Publishing**

funmilayo.co.uk

© Helen Sabrina Gledhill 2025

This publication is in copyright. Subject to statutory exemption and to the provisions of relevant collective licensing agreements, no reproduction of any part may take place without the written permission of Editora Funmilayo Publishing.

First published 2025

Book cover and interior design: Miriã Araújo
Vector/Texture: Freepik

ISBN: 978-1-0686064-5-8 Paperback

Editora Funmilayo Publishing has no responsibility for the persistence or accuracy of URLA for external or third-party internet websites referred to in this publication and does not guarantee that any content on such websites is, or will remain, accurate or appropriate.

Au milieu des découragements, des hésitations, des apostasies qui nos assiègent, que du moins notre voix et notre vie restent d'accord avec notre passé.

Manet immota fides.[1]

---

[1] Conclusion of J. Teixeira Barros's foreword to a biography of Manuel Querino, quoting the French historian Charles Forbes René de Montalembert, Count de Montalembert, Deux-Sèvres (1810-1870): "Amidst the discouragement, hesitation, and apostasies that besiege us, may at least our voices and our lives remain in harmony with our past. Faith remains unshakable" (in Pereira 1932, ii).

CONTENTS

FOREWORD BY JEFERSON BACELAR i
ON PEOPLE, IDEAS, AND CROSSINGS, BY FLAVIO GOMES xi
PREFACE TO THE ENGLISH EDITION xv
ACKNOWLEDGEMENTS xix
INTRODUCTION 1
1. EXPANDING THE BLACK ATLANTIC 21
2. SELF PORTRAITS AND "THE EYES OF OTHERS" 59
3. REVISION AND RECLAMATION 129
4. BRAZILIAN READINGS OF BOOKER T. WASHINGTON 179
5. PORTRAYALS AND PUSHBACK 233
BY WAY OF A CONCLUSION 289
APPENDIX I. TIMELINES 297
APPENDIX II. "THE EDUCATION OF FREEDMEN" 305
APPENDIX III. REVIEW OF *UP FROM SLAVERY* 319
APPENDIX IV. "THE BLACK MAN WITH THE WHITE FACE" 373
APPENDIX V. MENTORS AND ROLE MODELS 375
BIBLIOGRAPHY 385
ILLUSTRATIONS 427
ABOUT THE AUTHOR 429

FOREWORD

It is a great pleasure to write this foreword for Sabrina Gledhill's book, as her invitation was based on a strong friendship established over the course of many years, firmly based on mutual affection and intellectual respect.

I will begin by saying that, in addition to her merits, Gledhill possesses tremendous academic courage. First, due to the choice of two authors marked by lives and ideas that are, at the very least, complex, as well as filled with antagonisms, in life and after death. Secondly, because without adhering to all-too-easy political correctness, she comes to the defence of Manuel R. Querino, and particularly Booker T. Washington. For me, this makes her work all the greater, because it will certainly be the subject of healthy debates. Thirdly, because she does not follow the lines of classic biographies, preferring to traverse through aspects that have not been sufficiently addressed—when they have been addressed at all— in the literature on these two figures.

As he was not a proponent of the ideals of the Civil Rights movement, Booker T. Washington was largely erased by academia and Black activists in Brazil. This was a huge injustice, given the prestige he enjoyed in the United States in the late nineteenth and early twentieth centuries. In the US, Rebecca Carroll has edited a compendium in which Black Americans with different outlooks reflect on the life and work of Booker T. Washington (including "Up from Slavery, 100 Years Later"), entitled *Uncle Tom or New Negro?* (2006). Now, Gledhill brings us an important analysis of that author, who, although still debated in the twenty-first century in the United

States, is largely unknown to the Brazilian public. Not to mention that this book also deals with the similarly controversial Manuel Querino, who is now legitimised by academia and generally accepted by Brazil's Black movement, although he is largely unknown to Euro-Americans.

But let's get down to the subject at hand: her work. As the title, *Black Atlantic Crossings*, indicates, Gledhill moves away from the essentialist view of Black people, which is generally based on illusory unity and sectarian and totalitarian perspectives. In the introduction, Sabrina Gledhill sets forth the main concepts that will guide the progress of her book. She then discusses the context in which the two protagonists lived—societies marked by slavery and racism, but with very different histories, characteristics, and outlooks. It is one thing to live in a society based on the "one-drop" rule and open segregation, and quite another to live in a multiracial society where miscegenation is legitimized. However, this does not mean there are no connections. These include the influence of the theories and authors of pseudoscientific racism, or racialism, and the outbreak of two wars in which Blacks played a major role, and in which Washington and Querino were indirectly involved, each in their own country—the Civil War in the United States, and the Triple Alliance War, which pitted Brazil, Argentina, and Uruguay against Paraguay.

A highlight of the book is the second chapter: "Self-Portraits and the 'Eyes of Others.'" Perhaps the author is ironically using Du Bois's concept of "double consciousness" in the title as a metaphor: "One ever feels his two-ness, an American, a Negro; two souls, two thoughts, two unreconciled strivings; two warring ideals in one dark body, whose dogged strength alone keeps it from being torn asunder." For Gledhill, Washington and Querino shared common ground: they lived in the same period, were born poor, had White mentors and allies, believed in education as a means of advancing Black people, and, each in their own way, engaged in a fierce struggle against racialism and racism. Manuel Querino knew of Booker Washington, whom he deeply admired; the Black American probably never heard of Querino, but he knew of Bahia, as he tried unsuccessfully to recruit a Black US consul for that state. From that point on, Gledhill outlines the two protagonists' different trajectories. I will leave to the reader the details of their lives which the author presents, based on abundant research and a consistent bibliography. Booker T. Washington was born into slavery in 1856, and with the support of his White "father," Samuel Chapman Armstrong, the founder and director of the Hamilton Institute, as well as wealthy patrons, he founded the Tuskegee Institute in Alabama in 1881. From that time on, he achieved growing success and prestige. His speech at the Atlanta Exposition in 1895 brought him nationwide fame. In it, he said that Blacks and Whites could live apart but work together. He received a letter praising him for his performance in Atlanta from the man who would become his nemesis: W. E. B. Du Bois. His future enemy later asserted that Washington avoided confrontation with Whites, accepted segregation, wanted Blacks to limit themselves to industrial education, and kept silent about civil and political rights. Du Bois believed that the "Talented Tenth," the elite group of Black intellectuals born in the North, of which he was a member, should lead the mass of Blacks who had been freed from slavery. Booker T. Washington had a utilitarian vision, believing in vocational education, but not only that—he also trained teachers to multiply his project.

Far removed from Du Bois's ideas, Washington consolidated his fame among Blacks and Whites with the publication in 1901 of his autobiography *Up from Slavery*. That same year, he was invited to dine at the White House with President Theodore Roosevelt and his family. This assured him, according to one of his biographers, "his position as virtual monarch of the Black people in the United States" (Harlan 1975b, 304). His influence made the Tuskegee Institute reach as far as Africa, although the projects there were not successful. He was called upon to assist the Americans in Liberia by asking for the intervention of the United States. He was even an advisor to two US presidents. One of his publicists, Robert Ezra Park, the director of public relations for the Tuskegee Institute between 1905 and 1914, and the ghostwriter responsible for producing three of the most important books in Washington's bibliography, became an eminent sociologist. Washington received an honorary master's degree from Harvard (1896) and an honorary doctorate from Dartmouth (1901). However, in 1906, following the riots in Atlanta and Brownsville, his once-majestic stature began to wane. His downfall reached its nadir in 1911, when he was the victim of violence in New York City, requiring 16 stitches for a head wound and being placed under arrest. The charge was that, while in a White residential area, he allegedly flirted with a White woman, the mistress of a janitor, also White. It was a humiliation that his enemies tried to exploit, and from which he never recovered. Towards the end of his life, beginning in 1912 (probably because of the incident in New York), he began to change his stance: he started contesting Black disenfranchisement and openly opposing segregation. But it was too late: he was always known for his previous positions. He died at Tuskegee in 1915 and was buried in the small cemetery on the Institute's campus.

Manuel Raymundo Querino was born in Santo Amaro da Purificação, in the Bahia Recôncavo (bay region) in 1851. A note on his death certificate states that he was the "illegitimate son of Maria Adalgisa," which contradicts the baptismal records showing that he was the son of the carpenter José Joaquim dos Santos Querino and Luzia da Rocha Pita. Although his parentage is in doubt, we do know that the cholera epidemic of 1855 left Santo Amaro, a relatively populous hub of sugar production, virtually uninhabited. Officially orphaned, Querino was taken to Salvador and handed over to a guardian, Manuel Correia Garcia, a cultivated man who was educated in Europe and helped establish Bahia's first teacher training school. Unfortunately, the only future the retired teacher, politician, journalist, and lawyer saw for young Querino was in manual labour, as a worker and artisan. Nevertheless, our protagonist had different aspirations. He went to the state of Piauí in 1868, probably to escape being forcibly recruited to fight in the Triple Alliance War, but to no avail. He was enlisted there and taken to Rio de Janeiro for military training. Fortunately, because he could read and write, as well as being endowed with intelligence and education in a country of illiterates, he stayed in Rio to work as a battalion clerk. By the time the war ended in 1870, he had reached the rank of corporal and was demobilised through the influence of his political "godfather," Manuel Pinto de Sousa Dantas.

After returning to Bahia in 1871, Querino devoted himself to work and study. He was a founding student of the Liceu de Artes e Ofícios (School of Arts and Crafts), where his mentor and teacher was the Spanish artist Miguel Navarro y Cañizares. When his mentor left the Liceu and founded the School of Fine Art, Querino followed him. He was hired as a painter and became a founding student of that institution. Later, Cãnizares would also leave the School of Fine Art, but Manuel Querino stayed on, obtaining a certification as a teacher of Geometric Drawing in 1882. There, he also experienced one of the greatest frustrations of his life: he enrolled in the Architecture course because he wanted to be a "Doctor,"[2] but he was thwarted because, according to his biographers, he was unable to finish the course due to a lack of lecturers. He taught at the Liceu de Artes e Ofícios and the Colégio dos Órfãos de São Joaquim (São Joaquim Orphans' College)—institutions for the humbler echelons of society. As a civil servant, he did not attain important posts. He was also an abolitionist and republican, without gaining prominence in either movement. He went into politics as the Worker's Party's candidate for Federal Deputy in 1890, but the oligarchic groups that dominated the political scene in Bahia dissolved that organisation—and with Manuel Querino's approval. Without establishing a causal relationship, he must have been compensated with an appointment—between 1890 and 1981—as an Intendent (now City Councilman) and held that post until 1893. He would only return to the Council in 1897 as a first alternate, replacing an Intendent who

---

[2] Author's note. In Brazil, not only physicians but people with a university degree or who are simply being kow-towed to (especially in a business organization) are called *doutor* or *doutora*. People with a PhD are called *"professor doutor"* or *"professora doutora."*

resigned. He stepped down in 1899, having been defeated in the election to fill the post he had occupied temporarily. Humiliated, he left political life. He took part in several associations, including the Sociedade Protetora dos Desvalidos (Society for the Protection of the Destitute, SPD) and the Afoxé Pândegos da África (Revelers from Africa Afro-Carnaval Group). He had problems within workers' associations and other organisations, which made him numerous enemies. His greatness would only appear through his publications as a member of the Instituto Geográfico e Histórico da Bahia (Geographical and Historical Institute of Bahia, IGHB). He was a traditionalist, because he did not accept the new lifestyles and changes in Salvador's urban landscape, and a modernist, because he was the first mixed-race intellectual in Brazil to recognise the important contribution that Africans and Blacks had made to the development of Brazilian civilization. In short, through his work, he became respected and legitimised in the "city of letters." He passed away in 1923.

As we can see, the life stories of our protagonists are very different. Both were successful, but Booker T. Washington came to be considered "the virtual monarch of the Black people in the United States" and gained worldwide fame, while Manuel Querino did not have a major impact on society. His importance lies in the way he revolutionised the interpretation of Brazilian society, giving Black people the status of active agency and visibility in the development of our civilisation.

In the third chapter, "Revisionism and Reclamation: The Posthumous Trajectories of Washington and Querino," Gledhill analyses how the two protagonists' reputations fared after their deaths, doing so through different prisms. Manuel Querino was overlooked at the Second Afro-Brazilian Congress, held in Salvador in 1937; treated with paternalism and considered unscientific by Artur Ramos in 1938; accused of plagiarism by Carlos Ott in 1947, and dismissed as authority on the History of Art by academia. Today, however, Querino is valued in Brazil and abroad.

Booker T. Washington had already lost prestige in life, following the "Brownsville Affray," and even more so after the incident in New York City. However, the factor that most affected Washington's posthumous reputation was the longevity of his former rival, Du Bois, who died in 1963. Even so, the thousands of students and teachers who have passed through Tuskegee, and its transformation into a university, do not indicate posthumous defeat—after all, his work has taken material form and cannot be forgotten. He was controversial but remembered.

The obituaries and death notices on Querino published in the newspapers were all positive. A street was named after him, and his portraits were hung in the Liceu de Artes e Ofícios, the Centro Operário (Workers' Centre), the Sociedade Protetora dos Desvalidos, and the IGHB. As for Booker T. Washington, Gledhill has found dozens of newspaper clippings from the United States, the overwhelming majority of which, beginning with *The New York Times*, praised "Dr Washington" and mourned his death. In contrast, Du Bois penned a devastating critique of Washington for *The Crisis*, the official magazine of the NAACP, published on November 14, 1915.

In life, Booker T. Washington saw the publication of several biographies, co-authored with or written by ghostwriters in his employ, and after his death, others were written by friends and admirers. All of them aimed at creating the legend of a self-made man. However, he was not spared by his White enemies or Black adversaries. Manuel Querino was very fortunate in his biographers, but less so in the authors of introductions to his works. Today, those introductions are generally criticised, while Manuel Querino enjoys esteem and legitimacy, both in academia and among Black activists.

In the following chapter, the author discusses "Brazilian Readings of Booker T. Washington." *Up from Slavery* made him world famous, but Gledhill has been unable to ascertain precisely when Brazilians first heard of Washington and his work as an educator. It was certainly before his dinner at the White House and the publication of *Up from Slavery*. However, she does know that a review of that book by "Th Bentzon" was serialised between March and April 1902, including long extracts from *Up from Slavery*. Gledhill has transcribed, translated, and annotated the review, and included it in an appendix. Bentzon, the pen name of a French journalist, gives a positive view of the controversial Black American's life story. Except for a critique of the creation of a "University for Blacks" in the *Gazeta de Notícias* in Rio de Janeiro in 1903, and an article by Raymond Postgate, a socialist, in *Correio da Manhã* in 1937, calling Washington an "Uncle Tom," in her study of the Brazilian press, from 1901 to 1957, the author found nothing but praise for Booker T. Washington and his great work as an educator. As for Brazilian Portuguese translations of *Up from Slavery*, Sabrina Gledhill finds that there is only one, published in 1940 by the renowned Brazilian writer, Graciliano Ramos. Gledhill demonstrates that the translation was disastrous, fuelled by racism and disrespect for the author and the text. Not without justification, Graciliano Ramos's grandson defends it, attacking Booker T. Washington. However, Abdias Nascimento, the great Brazilian Black leader, praised Washington twice in his *Quilombo* newspaper. In short, Du Bois, Graciliano Ramos, and some recent Brazilian intellectuals failed to destroy the positive image built up around Booker T. Washington.

Instigating and provocative, the final chapter of the book deals with the use of imagery by both protagonists. However, Sabrina Gledhill goes beyond what the reader might think from the title of the chapter—"Portrayals and Pushback: Deploying Images as an Anti-Racist Tactic"—by approaching the subject of imagery and especially photography from various angles, from the historical to the philosophical. She begins by situating Querino regarding the use of photography, but it seems what she intends to do is to denounce the disappearance, since the IGHB's 1970 inventory, of the most important individual portrait of that illustrious figure. In the section entitled "Being Seen" vs. "Making Themselves Seen," she begins with the philosopher, semiologist, and literary critic Roland Barthes as a step towards discussing the history of the use of photography in Britain and the United States, to reach slavery Brazil, especially along the paths forged by Agassiz. As Boris Kossoy observed, it was

Foreword by Jeferson Bacelar

"nationhood constructed from the outside in," proving, among other things, the supposed inferiority of Blacks. Gledhill notes that photography since the late nineteenth century was already being used as a tool for propaganda, self-promotion and brainwashing. The irony is that there was no one better than Booker T. Washington in the use of photography as an element of publicity for Black people and their self-promotion. It was a preview of "modern media identity." Gledhill goes on to analyse "derogatory images," revealing that photographers were at the forefront of the dissemination of images of Blacks as exotic, animalistic, inferior beings. And she adds an adequate bibliography, illustrating, in a unique way, the stereotypes about Black people.

With these significant introductory propositions, Gledhill goes into the authors' perspectives on the use of imagery. She starts with Booker T. Washington, "creating a new Black American iconography," as a strategy to create a positive image in the eyes of Whites. He hired photographers, White and Black, some of whom enjoyed tremendous prestige, to produce images of his Tuskegee Institute, as well as himself—images that were far removed from the stereotypes of Blacks as lazy, savage, and lecherous. The danger is that the photos could suggest—through the sitters' clothes, expressions and modernity—that the "separate but equal" system of racial segregation was working well. Gledhill shows that Washington became a patron of Black photographers, even hiring five of them, two of whom were official photographers for the Tuskegee Institute. Gledhill also points out another essential detail: Washington controlled the use of images and their production.

When addressing Manuel Querino's use of images—without the power and money of the Black American—Gledhill observes that the Afro-Brazilian sought to confront the negative images of Blacks in Brazil in *A raça Africana e os seus costumes na Bahia* (The African Race and its Customs in Bahia). And his strategy was to publicize his image, looking assertive and well-dressed, as well as presenting respectful and dignified images of Africans and Afro-descendants. In Querino's portraits, he is thoroughly modern, smartly dressed in suits in the European style. However, perhaps already more adept in the use of photography, he knew that the sitter's clothes should preferably be dark, hence, unlike one with a light-coloured suit, his missing photo was considered the best of his portraits. However, Sabrina Gledhill intends to demonstrate that, unlike Lindemann, Querino's images of Blacks are not intended to exoticize, but rather to present an ethnographic record. Manuel Querino foresaw the importance of photography as a portrait for posterity, a memory that would not be forgotten. And, if the difference between his group of *ganhadores* (slaves-for-hire) and Lindemann's could be debatable, what is striking are the women of Candomblé who went to a studio to be photographed, revealing the importance of the image to be remembered in the future, demonstrating their pride in their African roots. Finally, Manuel Querino generally left us an historical document, evidenced by the important figures of the African and Afro-Brazilian world he selected. Unfortunately, as Gledhill observes, despite the advances made through the struggles of Black people, racism and negative stereotypes and images about Black Americans and Afro-Brazilians persist in the twenty-first century.

The lives of Washington and Querino, especially that of the Black American, will continue to be controversial, especially because of the roles they played in their respective countries. Therefore, in this well-written, engaging book, the result of consistent research and an appropriate bibliography, Sabrina Gledhill's choice of subject matter is spot on. It will be indispensable for everyone, academics or otherwise, who is interested in the history and politics of Black people in Brazil and the United States.

Jeferson Bacelar

Former director of the Universidade Federal da Bahia (UFBA) Centre for Afro-Asian Studies (CEAO); Researcher at the CEAO; Post-Graduate Lecturer in Ethnic and African Studies at UFBA

ON PEOPLE, IDEAS, AND CROSSINGS

In recent decades, social scientists have been studying connections, links and dialogues involving intersecting ideas, people and circuits. Transnational perceptions of intercultural movements have been revealed. At different times and in different spaces, from the fifteenth century to the first half of the twentieth, the populations of diasporic societies and their social, political and economic structures were linked in the four corners of the Atlantic. Using pieces of what was invented as Europe and designed as Africa, the parts called Cuba, Brazil, Jamaica, Puerto Rico, Colombia, Haiti, Martinique, Mexico, Guadeloupe, the USA, Barbados, and others were linked together and redefined. Fundamentally, experiences and people produced events that were transformed into narratives.

Above all, intellectual constructs and the elaboration of ideas were processed in different contexts, reconnecting different projects and expectations. We can see the emergence of ideas around modernity and liberalism, engaging in dialogue with racism, forced labour, exclusion and vectors of citizenship under construction.

In this complex process, we can think about intellectual roots, their agents, and the circulation of ideas, reframing ideologies and bringing together colonial, slavocratic, post-colonial and post-emancipation societies.

Today, however, it is the people involved in these processes who are mobilizing scholars and research the most. How did ideas circulate? What were the vectors? And what were the levels of reception, transformation and influence? We still need to take a careful look at the literate circulation and oral unfolding of Atlantic ideas. Books and translations came into people's hands. International news abounded in the nineteenth-century press. Since the 1830s, debates on emancipation in the British Caribbean and its consequences were closely followed, gaining shape in the mid-nineteenth century in the French and Dutch Caribbean, Spanish America and, after the US Civil War, Puerto Rico, and Cuba.

How did Black intellectuals—albeit immersed in slavocratic societies—interpret and re-elaborate these processes? Not just by receiving ideas, but by producing and circulating them in an elaborated way. Sabrina Gledhill's research, presented in this book, opens paths for us to get to know this adventure of ideas and its Black Diaspora characters. It begins with Manuel Querino, an outstanding intellectual and working-class leader at the turn of the twentieth century. Born on the fringes of the Bahian hinterland, amid slavery and the cholera epidemic that made him an orphan, Querino crossed some boundaries of exclusion. He learned to read and write at a very young age. This guaranteed him a brief military career—during the Triple Alliance War (1865-70)—as a clerk. Still pursuing his studies, he entered the School of Fine Arts, studying geometric design, architecture, and later working as a teacher at the Liceu de Artes e Ofícios (School of Arts and Crafts) and the Colégio dos Órfãos de São Joaquim (St. Joachim Orphans' College) in the city of Salvador. In the 1870s and 1880s, he was active in the abolitionist movement, joining anti-slavery societies and founding at least two newspapers. His political life was extended at the end of the century when he joined the Workers' Party. He produced technical writings on geometric drawing and the arts, as well as humanist essays on Africans and the Black presence in Bahia.

Some of the highlights of Querino's life and work, which are explored in Gledhill's study, are precisely the Afro-Atlantic dimensions of his thinking, particularly his dialogues and interlocution with the ideas of Booker T. Washington (1856-1915). Thus, this is both a biography and an intellectual history with an Atlantic perspective. Receptions, appropriations, translations and resignifications reveal different roots of the Brazilian social thinking that was emerging in the first decades of the twentieth century. Urban development, exclusion, access to education, trade unions, elections, political parties, African scenarios and debates on race and colonization are the subjects of intersecting elaboration and dialogue that this pan-Africanist Bahian intellectual established.

However, we also need to know more about the intellectual landscapes framed by Querino. We will certainly find generations of Black intellectuals and literati who tried to turn skills, education and expectations of mobility into weapons in a society that was still aristocratic in Bahia, amid tremendous arrogance due to the social invisibility and economic exclusion of the Black population. More than learning about his life and chapters of tremendous personal determination, it is essential to read Querino himself. The subjects he analysed and the intellectual worlds he expanded demonstrate the Black social thinking that was made invisible at the dawn of the twentieth century.

We know that these processes of intellectual erasure were recurrent. It is not a matter of being absent, non-existent or invisible. Silencings have been verified. But not only that. We have identified other Black Diaspora thinkers among Manuel Querino's interlocutors. Not just W. E. B. Du Bois, Marcus Garvey, and even other non-Americans with similar backgrounds. In Brazil, we know very little about the activities and legacy of Booker T. Washington. Why is that? On what basis did Querino establish the dialogue? What were the universes of the influences he saw? Making these connections and dialogues emerge takes us on an Atlantic voyage to the intersecting circuits of ideas and people. It is important to use stronger lenses in our observations. Querino and his work were guided by religious expressions with African roots, political parties, elections, representations, workers' conferences and intellectual affirmation.

More than pointing out the shores of the Black Atlantic from analytical ships on calm seas, we must disembark, locating unstable and improvised territories. Gledhill's study not only offers a safe haven, but, above all, charts the way forward.

Flavio dos Santos Gomes
Professor of History
Universidade Federal do Rio de Janeiro (UFRJ)
Co-author of *The Story of Rufino: Slavery, Freedom, and Islam in the Black Atlantic*

PREFACE TO
THE ENGLISH EDITION

This is an updated and expanded translation of *Travessias no Atlântico Negro: reflexões sobre Booker T. Washington e Manuel R. Querino*, released by the Editora da Universidade Federal da Bahia (EDUFBA) in 2020. That year also saw the birth of my grandson John Benjamin, the COVID-19 pandemic, and the beginning of the global Black Lives Matter movement, which transformed what was once considered "niche" research into a highly relevant study. I now see this book as a weapon against historical erasure and a staunch defence of affirmative action and diversity, equity, and inclusion (DEI), which are facing unprecedented assaults in the USA.

According to Florida's "Stop WOKE Act," any book (fiction or nonfiction) that makes White people feel uncomfortable about their country's slaveholding past should be suppressed. Florida's State Academic Standards—Social Studies (2023) even recommend teaching middle-school students how enslaved people benefited from slavery because, "in some instances," it enabled them to learn useful skills.[3] Also, as I was translating the original Portuguese edition, the

---

[3] Florida's State Academic Standards—Social Studies, 2023. SS.68.AA.2.3 "Examine the various duties and trades performed by slaves (e.g., agricultural work, painting, carpentry, tailoring, domestic service, blacksmithing, transportation). Benchmark Clarifications: Clarification 1: Instruction includes how slaves

Supreme Court of the United States effectively gutted affirmative action in that country.

On January 21, 2025, President Donald J. Trump issued an executive order dismantling DEI initiatives across federal agencies, urging similar action in the private sector. This resulted in the removal of references to Black, Brown, LGBTQ+ individuals, and women, from government websites. That decree, followed by criticism of the Smithsonian Museum's efforts to debunk pseudoscientific racism, further amplified this book's relevance.

In Brazil, former president Jair Messias Bolsonaro attempted to gut higher education—particularly the Humanities—and expressed hostility towards Black civil rights and affirmative action. As a result of his policies, many Black Brazilian students dropped out or simply stopped aspiring to a university degree. Now that Bolsonaro is out of office and may even go to prison for an alleged coup attempt, the Lula administration is undoing some of the damage wrought during Bolsonaro's time in office. Nevertheless, there is still a long way to go.

The landscape of Brazilian academia and publishing has changed substantially since I defended my PhD in Salvador, Bahia, in 2014. Initially, researching Booker T. Washington in Brazil posed considerable challenges, requiring reliance on international sources and archival research at the US Library of Congress. However, my thesis and the Portuguese edition of this book have helped establish Washington's presence within Brazilian scholarly discourse, as demonstrated by their increasing citation and use in post-graduate programmes. Graciliano Ramos's bowdlerised translation of *Up from Slavery, Memórias de um negro* (retitled *Memórias de um negro americano)*, is back in print for the first time since the 1940s, although Washington's best-known autobiography merits a new and more objective rendering.

Efforts to reverse the erasure of Black people from history should never abate, and sometimes, they are rewarded. I wish I had made a

---

developed skills which, in some instances, could be applied for their personal benefit." https://www.fldoe.org/core/fileparse.php/20653/urlt/6-4.pdf

Preface to the English Edition

note of the date, but the moment I felt that Manuel Querino had finally regained his rightful place in Brazilian history was when Lula—then a presidential candidate—mentioned his name along with the usual pantheon of illustrious Black Brazilians, such as Machado de Assis, Teodoro Sampaio, and Luiz Gama.

The year 2020 saw two publications on Querino—a book on his studies of Bahian cuisine by Jeferson Bacelar and Carlos Alberto Dória, published in Brazil, and *Manuel Querino (1851-1923): An Afro-Brazilian Pioneer in the Age of Scientific Racism,* an anthology of essays by several authors which I edited and published in Portuguese and English in Brazil (through the Sagga Editora publishing house) and the UK.

The Afro-Brazilian polymath's profile was raised significantly in 2022 by the Projeto Querino podcast. Inspired by *The New York Times*'s 1619 Project, it follows in Querino's footsteps by increasing awareness of Black people's role in Brazilian history—including Querino's own contributions.[4] Gláucia Maria Costa Trinchão and Suely dos Santos Souza published the edited volume *Os saberes em desenho do professor Manuel Raymundo Querino,* on his geometric design textbooks, in 2021. It includes reproductions of those illustrated works—an invaluable contribution, as the original editions are extremely rare.

In 2023, the 100th anniversary of his death, Querino received several tributes. My daughter, Isis Gledhill, produced a documentary on his life, including interviews with leading Querino scholars, and the organisers and presenters of the Projeto Querino podcast, the journalist Tiago Rogero and the historian Ynaê Lopes dos Santos. The conductor and composer Fred Dantas wrote a piece for brass band called "Dobrado Manuel Querino" that was first performed during the celebrations of the bicentennial of Bahia's Independence on the 2nd of July, a date that was particularly dear to Querino's heart.

---

[4] https://www.theguardian.com/world/2022/oct/06/brazil-history-african-brazilians-tiago-rogero-querino-project. The podcast is available (in Portuguese) at https://projetoquerino.com.br/podcast/

In 2024, I edited and published more two edited volumes inspired by Querino and including translations of his work: *The Need for Heroes: Black Intellectuals Dig Up Their Past,* and *Heroes Sung and Unsung: Black Artists in World History.* Along with *Manuel Querino (1851-1923)* and this monograph, they form part of Funmilayo's Unsung Heroes in Black History series.

Although I began researching this book in the early 2000s, and some of its contents date back to my MA studies on Brazilian race relations in the 1980s, its message feels more urgent than ever. I hope this comparison of the lives and anti-racist tactics of Booker T. Washington and Manuel R. Querino will point up the fact that reparations are still due to the descendants of enslaved Africans in the United States and Brazil. Affirmative action remains a crucial tool for addressing the enduring legacy of racial injustice.

Sabrina Gledhill
April 2025
Crediton, UK

ACKNOWLEDGEMENTS

This work would not have been possible without the financial support of the CAPES (Coordination for the Improvement of Higher Education Personnel). I am also deeply indebted to my PhD advisor, Jeferson Afonso Bacelar, whose insightful guidance proved invaluable. He challenged me to question assumptions, pursue rigorous investigation, and delve deeper into the complexities of my research. Through stimulating discussions, thought-provoking book recommendations, and constructive criticism, he played a crucial role in shaping my ideas, refining my hypotheses, and ultimately, transforming my doctoral dissertation into this book.

From the moment I conceived my PhD proposal, Flavio dos Santos Gomes was a wonderful mentor, encouraging the development and publication of my work and enriching it with suggestions and the results of his own research on Abdias do Nascimento. His generosity extended even further with a contribution to the English edition that is, in essence, a second foreword.

Jaime Oliveira do Nascimento has made a major contribution to the cause of restoring Manuel Querino to his rightful place in Brazilian history. His persistence and determination in organising, lectures, courses, and seminars and editing and publishing books about and inspired by Querino, are a role model and inspiration.

I would like to thank the past directors of the UFBA Centro de Estudos Afro-Orientais (CEAO) Ethnic and African Studies Graduate Program (Pós-Afro), including Jocélio Teles Santos (until 2012),

Valdemir Zamparoni, and Cláudio Furtado, and the current director, Jamile Borges, for their unfailing support.

The members of the Pós-Afro faculty improved and polished my research project during the optional classes taken as a special student and mandatory PhD classes. In addition to Jeferson Bacelar, my deepest thanks go out to Luís Nicolau Parés, Elisee Soumonni *(in memoriam)*, Paula Cristina Barreto, and Jocélio Teles Santos. Marcelo Bernardo da Cunha and Cláudio Luís Pereira showed me the path of studying imagery, encouraging and supporting the production of chapter 5 of this book.

From the bottom of my heart, I would also like to thank all the teachers, mentors, colleagues, and friends—some of whom are no longer with us—for their attention, care, support, advice, constructive criticism, and tips from the beginning, among them (in alphabetical order according to first names, in the Brazilian fashion):

Ana Lúcia Araújo, Antonio Sérgio Alfredo Guimarães, Ana Flávia Magalhães Pinto, Antonia da Silva Santos, Antonietta d'Aguiar Nunes, Ayodele Oshunlade Mason, Barbara Benham, Barry Stinson, Beatriz Mamigonian, Charles Daniel Dawson, Christianne Vasconcellos, Cleidiana Ramos, Consuelo Novais Sampaio, Consuelo Pondé de Sena, Courtney J. Campbell, Edivaldo Boaventura, Graham Haynes, Hendrik Kraay, Hugo Gama, Ivette Wilson, João José Reis, Joceneide Cunha, John Mason, José Marcos Rodrigues, Karin Barber, Luci Nascimento, Luis Guilherme Pontes Tavares, Luis Henrique Dias Tavares, Luiz Alberto Ribeiro Freire, Mano Jhomp, Maria das Graças de Andrade Leal, Mariângela Nogueira, Mário Cravo Neto, Meire Lúcia Alves dos Reis, Michele Washington, Monique Sochaczewski Goldfeld, Myriam Fraga, Nádia Cardoso, Nila Rodrigues Barbosa, Paulo Dourado, Paulo Farias, Marc Herold, Pedro Alexander Cubas Hernandez, Scott Alves Barton, Sergio Guedes, Sidney Chalhoub, Simone Trindade, Urano Andrade, and Wilson Roberto de Mattos.

Acknowledgements

My thanks to the staff at the Biblioteca Manuel Querino, the Biblioteca Central da Bahia newspaper archives, and the staff and interns of the Manuscript Division of the US Library of Congress. I am especially grateful to Laiala de Araújo Félix dos Santos and Zita Matalhães Alves, director of the archives of the Geographical and Historical Institute of Bahia (IGHB), for their help in finding manuscripts related to Querino that greatly enriched this updated edition. Laiala, in particular, went above and beyond.

To my Iyás (all in the *orun):* Maria Stella Azevedo Santos, Mãe Stella de Oxossi, Odé Kayode, who approved, encouraged, and made my work possible; Mãe Georgete, Eyn Oxum, Ojubonã; Valdete Ribeiro da Silva, Detinha de Xangô, Obá Gesin, the wisest, dearest, and most affectionate *ebomi*. Modupe!

To my esteemed colleague and dear friend, Lisa Earl Castillo, whose unstinting generosity merits much more than a footnote. I am deeply grateful for her support and friendship.

I extend my heartfelt gratitude to Miriã Araújo, whose creative brilliance has graced my book covers since the very first Brazilian publication of *Travessias no Atlântico Negro* by Editora da Universidade Federal da Bahia (Edufba). Her artistry has consistently captured the essence of my work, and I'm delighted to collaborate with her once again on this edition.

To my beloved daughters, Isis Gledhill, who produced and directed the documentary on Querino, and Barbara Almeida, who helped me transcribe the review of *Up from Slavery*; my son-in-law, the actor, screenwriter, and teacher Wendel Damasceno, who portrayed Booker T. Washington in the short video Isis made to promote the Portuguese edition of this book; and, representing the next generation, my nephew, Thomas Gledhill, who learned capoeira in Manhattan, and my grandsons Gabriel Nunes Almeida de Figueiredo and John Benjamin Gledhill Damasceno, who was doing capoeira moves before he could walk. Finally, my thanks go out to my partner, David Pett, who cast a much-needed critical eye on the English edition.

INTRODUCTION

This book presents and reflects on the lives, tactics, and posthumous trajectories of Booker Taliaferro Washington and Manuel Raymundo Querino, two Black educators who combated racism in the Black Atlantic world between 1851 and 1923.[5] Introduced by the art historian Robert Farris Thompson (1983), and popularised by the sociologist Paul Gilroy (1993), among others, the concept of the "Black Atlantic" as a transnational space of cultural construction is used here because this study seeks to compare the lives and works of two intellectuals of African descent whose worlds were very different, but far from unconnected. The racist tides and currents which Washington and Querino battled in that diasporic ocean obliged them to use similar tactics, which included valuing the education and professional training of Black people, particularly recently emancipated captives; forming alliances with Whites who held positions of influence and power; and combating racist

---

[5] These dates correspond to Querino's lifetime, as Washington was born after him and died before him. When referring to "tactics," I am using the terminology introduced by the French sociologist Michel de Certeau, who draws a distinction between the strategies of the "strong" (major institutions and nations) and the tactics of the "weak" (1984, xix). According to Certeau, most "ways of operating" are tactical: "victories of the "weak" over the "strong" (whether the strength be that of powerful people or the violence of things or of an imposed order, etc.), clever tricks, knowing how to get away with things, 'hunter's cunning,' manoeuvres, polymorphic simulations, joyful discoveries, poetic as well as warlike" (Ibid.).

stereotypes in two ways: using dignified images of Black people, producing biographies of illustrious Black men [sic], and presenting their own portrayals and example as successful individuals who started from nothing–in other words, "self-made men."

A Black/mixed-race Brazilian[6] who was born in Santo Amaro da Purificação, Bahia, in 1851, Querino has been studied and praised by non-Brazilian scholars, chiefly E. Bradford Burns (1974 and 1993),[7] and, more recently, Kim Butler (2000) and Henry Louis Gates, Jr. (2011), but has only been "re-rediscovered" in Brazil in the past decade. Previously, he was still little known in that country. Many of those who were aware of his life story believed that he was "self-taught"[8] and "intuitive," and that his publications were limited to just a few "pamphlets." Some Brazilian scholars have even denied that Querino was one of the inspirations for Pedro Archanjo, the protagonist of Jorge Amado's novel *Tent of Miracles*, due to a supposed lack of documentary evidence. As we will see in Chapter 3,

---

[2] Querino self-identified as "mulatto" or "mestiço" – at least in his works – but was described as "Black" by commentators of his works and others, including Artur Ramos and Edison Carneiro. He has even been described as a "mulatto journalist" by Wlamyra de Albuquerque (2009, 39). This is due to the fluidity of Brazilian racial classifications but also raises questions about Querino's parentage.

[7] Burns was the first scholar outside Brazil to study the life and work of Manuel Querino. He analysed the biography and bibliography of the intellectual from Santo Amaro in his "Bibliographical Essay: Manuel Querino's Interpretation of the African Contribution to Brazil," published in the *Journal of Negro History* in 1974, which includes an English translation of the conclusion of *O africano como colonizador* (original title: *O colono preto como fator da civilização brasileira*), which Burns translated as "The African Contribution to Brazil." Burns also included a significant discussion of Querino in his book *A History of Brazil* (originally published in 1972, and now in its third edition [1993]), which was one of the most widely used textbooks on the History of Brazil in undergraduate courses in the United States at the time of publication.

[4] The effort to "rehabilitate" Querino's reputation involved contradicting the persistent belief that, presumably due to his race and class, Querino had received no formal education and was even quasi-illiterate.

Amado himself laid that argument to rest in his "non-memoir" *Navegação de cabotagem* (Coasting), originally published in 1992.

Prior to 1930, the focus of the first ethnographic studies in Brazil was on Amerindians. According to the eminent historian and Brazil scholar Thomas Skidmore, none of the major research centres in Rio de Janeiro, São Paulo, and Belém do Pará, "devoted any attention to the African in Brazil.... The African 'immigrant' and his Afro-American progeny aroused no scientific interest among their staffs" (1974, 57).[9] Querino refused to believe that the presence of Africans and their descendants in Brazil was "one of the factors underlying our [Brazilians'] inferiority as a people," according to the coroner, psychiatrist, and ethnologist Raimundo Nina Rodrigues (2004, 20). The mere fact of recognizing the contributions of Africans and people of African descent to the Brazilian identity, culture, and even "race," demonstrated phenomenal independence of mind. Similarly, Querino stood out for another stance–combating and even co-opting the scientific racism propagated in the US and Europe. The first Brazilian to publish a book on the African contribution to Brazilian civilization that debunks scientific racism was a White physician from Sergipe, Manoel Bomfim, the author of *A América Latina, males de origem* (Latin America: Original Ills, 2005), first released in 1905. Later, the supposed superiority of "Aryans" postulated by Gobineau, Vacher de la Pouge, and others, was also rejected by another White intellectual, the Rio de Janeiro politician Alberto Torres, in *O problema nacional brasileiro* (The Brazilian National Problem, 1914,

---

[9] Skidmore observes that there was one exception – the work of Alexandre José de Melo Moraes Filho, who "performed pioneering work in collecting Afro-Brazilian folklore" (1974, 57). Melo Moraes Filho's most important work was *Festas e tradições populares do Brasil*, published in Rio de Janeiro in 1901. It is interesting to note that in *Black into White*, Skidmore describes Querino as a little-known "doctor from Bahia" (1974, 185 and note 40). E. Bradford Burns's article (1974) was still forthcoming, with the provisional title "Black on Black: Manuel Querino's Interpretation of the African Contribution to Brazil" (Ibid., note 40).

50 *et seq.*).[10] Most of the Brazilians who studied "the Black question" at the time, such as Euclides da Cunha, Braz do Amaral, Sílvio Romero, and, particularly, Nina Rodrigues, bowed to the prevailing European thinking on race and were influenced by the fact that they belonged to an elite of predominantly European descent in a slavocracy that endured until 1888 (Rodrigues 2004, 20 and passim).[11]

All these scholars sought a scientific or historical basis for creating a "founding myth" for Brazilian nationality and culture. In their pursuit of a characteristic that would give their country and people a unique identity, all of them identified cultural and biological miscegenation–the famous mixture of the "three races": Europeans, Amerindians, and Africans. All except Querino, Bomfim, and Torres were clearly confused when they attempted to create that myth while accepting the doctrine of the inferiority of the African and the weakness of the *mestiço*. According to Octávio Ianni, that sort of confusion was common in Brazil:

Without a doubt, the racial situation in Brazil has always been characterized by major contradictions, including: ...the plastic exoticism of religious cults such as Candomblé, Batuque, Umbanda and Quimbanda and the classification of Blacks as African, descendants of slaves or other characterizations with negative connotations; the myth of racial democracy and the doctrine of the

---

[10] I would like to thank the anonymous peer reviewer of the Edufba edition for suggesting that I include Torres among the Brazilian intellectuals who rejected scientific racism.

[11] Supervised by the late E. Bradford Burns, my MA research focused on these scholars as well as Querino. I am grateful to Professor Burns for suggesting that I make Querino the lynchpin of my study. It should be noted that Querino knew at least two of these men personally – Nina Rodrigues and Braz do Amaral, who was not only a fellow member of the Instituto Geográfico e Histórico da Bahia (IGHB) and director of the School of Fine Art, but is included in the lists of recipients of free copies of two of Querino's books – the second edition of *Artistas baianos* and *O colono preto como fator da civilização brasileira*. The lists are housed in the archives of the IGHB.

inferiority of the *mestiço*.... In a way, these contradictions are at the base of research into the social realities of the country.[12]

As for the United States, according to Roberto DaMatta:

> The system does not permit gradations that could threaten those who have the full right to equality. In other words, ... there is no "triangle of races," and it seems to me essential to consider how that triangle was maintained as a key datum for understanding Brazil by the Brazilians. Furthermore, how that ethnic triangulation through which they geometrically establish the fable of the three races has become a dominant, sweeping ideology capable of permeating the outlook of the people, intellectuals, politicians and academics from the left and right, occasionally shouting in favour of *mestiçagem* and using "Whites," "Blacks" and "Indians" as basic units that explain the exploitation or redemption of the masses (1981, 63).

Another characteristic that distinguishes the racialist realities of the United States and Brazil is the type of prejudice directed at people of African descent: according to Oracy Nogueira (1985), in a concept the Brazilian sociologist introduced in 1954, in the United States, Blacks suffer from "prejudice of origin," and in Brazil, they endure "prejudice of mark." That is, in Brazil, the distinction between "Blacks," "Browns" *(pardos)* and "Whites" is based on the individual's appearance. That distinction can be arbitrary, as Brazilians discovered when attempting to decide who qualified for affirmative action. Even identical twins were placed in two different "racial" categories in 2007. One was considered "Brown" and the other, "White"—later overturned on appeal.[13]

However, the criteria for determining who is African American are very different. According to the French sociologists Bourdieu and Wacquant:

---

[12] All translations are mine, unless otherwise noted.
[13] https://brasilescola.uol.com.br/educacao/sistema-cotas-racial.htm

Americans in the USA are alone in defining "race" strictly on the basis of descent, and this only in the case of African Americans: one is "Black" in Chicago, Los Angeles or Atlanta, not by skin colour but for having one or more ancestors identified as Blacks, that is to say, at the end of the regression, as slaves. The USA is the only modern society to apply the "one-drop rule" and the principle of "hypodescent," according to which the children of a mixed union find themselves automatically assigned to the inferior group–here the Blacks, and only them (1999, 45).[14]

Racial mixture was so common in the US before Emancipation in 1865 that some of the enslaved were as "White" as their slaveholders, and many freed and free people considered and self-identified as Black who could "pass" as White on the basis of their skin colour, features, and hair, were included in the photographic portraits in W. E. B. Du Bois's contribution to the 1900 Paris Exhibition. Thomas Skidmore has debunked the myth that there was no racial mixture between Whites and Blacks in the United States (1993).[15]

---

[14] While this is no longer true in many parts of the world for people who self-identify as "biracial" or completely reject such categories, this was the case in the US in Booker T. Washington's time. Although he was sometimes considered a "mulatto" because his father was White, he was still "assigned to the inferior group" then called Negroes. And of course, "biracial" people may still be stigmatized and "trolled" by those who insist on considering them members of an inferior group. This was made clear when Prince Harry's relationship with Meghan Markle—now the Duchess of Sussex—first became known and he issued a public statement in her defence in 2016.

[15] In literature, the enslavement of Black people who could "pass for White" was a trope used by American and Brazilian abolitionists alike. The Brazilian novelist Bernardo Guimarães wrote *A escrava Isaura* (Isaura, the Slave Girl) in 1875, thirteen years before Princess Isabel signed the law abolishing slavery in Brazil. The main character is an enslaved woman who is so pale she is "almost White," which was intended to make White readers empathize with her and stir up abolitionist sentiments. The US equivalent of Isaura is Eliza, the light-complected captive from Harriet Beecher Stowe's *Uncle Tom's Cabin* (2003).

Introduction

The group created by the principle of "hypodescent" or the "one-drop rule" is in the minority in the United States (the "non-Hispanic" Black or African American population represented about 12.4 percent of the total population in 2020, according to official census data, making it the second-largest minority after Latinos), but if the same rule were applied in Brazil, that group would be in the majority. Unlike the United States, "*mulatos*" and "*mestiços*" fall into a different racial category from Blacks in that country. People of African descent with lighter complexions, straighter hair and more European features can escape the stigma and stereotypes associated with being "*preto*" or "*negro*," using the phenomenon that Carl Degler calls the "mulatto escape hatch." However, that "way out" may induce mulatos and mestiços to distance themselves from anything that might identify them as "preto." This was the case with the mulato scholars who had a strong intellectual and academic interest in Afro-Brazilian culture, such as the Brazilian anthropologist Edison Carneiro. For that reason, among others, a "Black nation" never formed in Brazil, being replaced and undermined by the ideology of "racial democracy" (Degler 1971, 109-110).[16] Further on, we will look at the factors that can lead to the formation of a community of Afro-descendants–even an "imagined" one, according to Benedict Anderson (1991)—like the one defined by the "one-drop rule" in the United States.

The life and work of Booker T. Washington (1856-1915) are even less known in Brazil than those of Querino, although his autobiography *Up from Slavery* was the main focus of a review serialized in several issues of the newspaper *Diário da Bahia* in 1902 (see Appendix III). It was later (mis)translated by the renowned Brazilian author Graciliano Ramos as *Memórias de um negro* (Memoirs of a Black Man), published in São Paulo in 1940. (We will

---

[16] According to Saunders, the myth of racial democracy assigns responsibility to Blacks for their social status, since race and racism were supposedly not an obstacle, while exempting the White elites from troubling themselves with a problem over which they claim to have no control (1972, 61).

follow the trajectory of Washington's fame, infamy, and ultimate erasure in the Brazilian press in Chapter 4.)

There are strong parallels between the "posthumous trajectories" of our two protagonists. In both cases, they were individuals who were renowned in their time whose images were distorted and tarnished after their deaths. In the case of Washington, the process began during his lifetime, due to the efforts of W. E. B. Du Bois and his fellow members of the "Talented Tenth," as the Black intellectual elite in the United States called itself at the time. Unfortunately, the negative image of Washington as an "accommodationist" and even a "Judas" persists to this day, despite the efforts of writers who have sought to rehabilitate that image, such as the Black poet and polymath Ishmael Reed (2000) and the White historian Robert J. Norell (2009). Both insist that Washington's work should be seen within the context of his time–racial violence that could be considered ethnic cleansing (Jaspin, 2007). Far from being a "sell-out" or "Uncle Tom," Washington dedicated his life to moulding the masses of former captives–approximately four million who were emancipated after the American Civil War–into the bedrock of a future Black middle class. He faced a major challenge from the outset–most freedpersons were illiterate, because the laws of the slaveholding states forbade their Black captives from learning to read and write.

William Edward Burghardt Du Bois (1868-1963) attended Fisk University, Harvard College, and the University of Berlin, before obtaining a PhD in History from Harvard in 1896–the first Black man to receive a doctorate from that university. Although he was born relatively poor, his education, connections, and friendships gave him entry to the Black elite that had formed in the United States since the 1860s (Graham 2000).[17] His opposition to Washington's conciliatory

---

[17] Du Bois was one of the first members of "Sigma Pi Phi," better known as "the Boulé," an exclusive all-male African American social group. Once secret, it "admits professional men once they have distinguished themselves in society" (Graham 2000, p. 15).

ideals made him a nationally known figure in the United States, because he believed that the future of Black people would be assured by activism, political participation, and the education and prioritization of the "Talented Tenth" to lead the "masses." Later, he would become the staunchest enemy of another Black leader, the Jamaican Marcus Garvey, who took an even more aggressive stance towards Black activism.

Du Bois joined the Communist Party, declaring that Socialism was the "only viable hope for Black liberation and world peace,"[18] and died in self-imposed exile in Ghana at the age of 95 in 1963. Amid Cold War tensions, the US government refused to reissue his passport due to his travels to Communist countries, including China. To ensure his right to come and go in the world, he became a Ghanaian citizen in the year of his death (Holt 2009, 169). According to his biographer David Levering Lewis:

> In the course of his long, turbulent career, Du Bois attempted virtually every possible solution to the problem of twentieth-century racism–scholarship, propaganda, integration, cultural and economic separatism, politics, international communism, expatriation, Third World solidarity First had come culture and education for the elites; then the ballot for the masses; then economic democracy; and final all these solutions in the service of global racial parity and economic justice (Lewis 2001b, xiv).

Du Bois began to change his thinking towards the end of his life, increasingly aligning himself with Washington's more pragmatic approach (Moses 1993, 140-141).

In contrast with Du Bois's decades-long opposition to Washington, in an autobiographical essay with the fiercely ironic title, "The Negro's Greatest Enemy," Marcus Garvey wrote that reading *Up from Slavery* had changed his life and made him realize his "doom...of

---

[18] https://hutchinscenter.fas.harvard.edu/web-dubois.

being a race leader" (Garvey 2004, 3). He had wanted to meet Washington personally, but the principal of Tuskegee passed away before Garvey arrived in the US in 1916 (Blaisdell 2004, v).

Washington believed that a good education was the path for a prosperous future for Black people, both individually and collectively, but before learning Greek and Latin, they should concentrate on vocational education. Du Bois and other leaders of the NAACP asserted that Washington espoused manual labour and mechanical trades as the only possible and desirable future for Black people[19]–however, whether deliberately or otherwise, they overlooked the most important function of the Tuskegee Institute: a teacher training college. A more detailed analysis of the institute's curriculum makes it clear that in addition to training teachers who would become multipliers by establishing "mini-Tuskegees" in several parts of the US South, Washington wanted to produce what Antonio Gramsci called "organic intellectuals" who, according to the Italian sociologist, represent "a more advanced level of social organization, characterized by a certain managerial and technical (that is, intellectual) capacity." Antonio Gramsci decried the "duality between classical education and technical education that reflects the social division between intellectual labour and manual labour" (Monasta 2010, s.p.).

Washington was also accused of preferring to avoid confrontations with Whites by seeking "accommodation." However, the principal and founder of the Tuskegee Institute responded that, since Blacks were the minority in the US, the best tactic was to form alliances with Whites who were sympathetic to their cause. Although Du Bois and civil rights activists of the 1960s censured Washington's

---

[19] In 1978, Donald Spivey published *Schooling for the New Slavery* in which he accuses Washington of perpetuating a paternalistic system of education that aimed at keeping Black people "in their place" and describes the Founder of Tuskegee as follows: "His role was like that of the black overseer during slavery who, given the position of authority over his fellow slaves, worked diligently to keep intact the very system under which they both were enslaved (Spivey 2007, 62).

tactics, in the analysis of Anthony D. Smith (1986) he was following a practice adopted by many *ethnie*, particularly minority ethnic groups, in the mid-nineteenth century.

According to Smith, due to what he called the "triple revolution," changes in commerce and trading patterns, the nature of administration, wars and interstate relations and the emergence of a secular intelligentsia, mass culture and education, ethnie—or their intellectuals—increasingly saw their communities as "would-be nations" (1986, 155). At the same time, referring to the ethnie of Central Europe, Smith observes:

Most of the ethnie in question had adopted, as part of the cost of self-preservation, a quietist sentiment and outlook. Except in crises, communal leaders aimed to accommodate their communities to wider social and political frameworks and dictates. Acceptance and a spirit of resignation was often bred in these circumstances, particularly among the smaller ethnie, whose situation was often precarious (Ibid.).

Therefore, if Washington was an "accommodationist," he was following a tactic adopted by many other small ethnie in similar situations.

Smith posits that there are two very different types of "nation"— territorial and ethnic. The first is geographical and based on a "sense of territory" and the interactions that take place within clearly established boundaries (1986, 135). This was the type of nation Benedict Anderson had in mind when he put forward the concept of an "imagined community" (1991).[20] It was this basic idea of nationhood that served as the logic for forming many nations in modern times, including in Africa, bringing together groups with different cultures and attempting to forge a nation state along those lines (Smith 1986, 135).

---

[20] According to Anderson, "It is *imagined* because the members of even the smallest nation will never know most of their fellow-members...yet in the minds of each lives the image of their communion" (1991, 6).

The formation of a nation based on pre-existing ethnic ties was a matter of "'transforming' ethnic into national ties and through the processes of mobilization, territorialization and politicization" (Ibid., 137). This generally produced a very different concept of nationhood, emphasizing factors such as "genealogy, populism, customs and dialects, and nativism" and assigning more importance to presumed bonds of shared descent. Smith gives the examples of three African ethnie—the Ibo, Zulu, and Kikuyu cultural groups, among others (Ibid.).

The concept of the "Black nation" in the United States

How can we associate the two concepts of nationhood Smith provides–the territorial and ethnic nation–with the formation of the "Black nation" in the United States, a concept that never took root in Brazil to the same extent? Although Black consciousness is on the rise in Brazil, particularly among the intelligentsia that has grown since affirmative action made it possible for more people of colour to attend tuition-free federal universities—once the closely guarded province of the White elite—the Black "majority" in that country is still nowhere near achieving the political clout of the Black minority community in the USA. Brazil has never had a Booker T. Washington, much less a Barack Obama.

How is it that a minority community defined by its African ancestry could come to be considered a "nation within a nation" in a country that, in the nineteenth century, was already a paradigm for the concept of the western nation state on the global stage? We can point to several factors, starting with the system of racial segregation known as "Jim Crow"; violence against Blacks inflicted with impunity by Whites through lynchings, other forms of terrorism, and ethnic cleansing; and the geographic concentration in the South of the country after the end of the US Civil War in 1865–at least until the "Great Migration" of Blacks from the rural South to cities and industrialized areas in the Mid-West, Northeast and West of the

Introduction

United States in the early twentieth century. The formation of all-Black neighbourhoods and even towns helped provide a sense of territoriality. Although the laws were imposed by the nation state, which was controlled by the White majority, those Black communities had a sense of citizenship and belonging to their own "nation" which, according to Anthony D. Smith, "conveyed the sense of solidarity and fraternity through *active social and political participation.*" For example, Blacks voted for Black candidates and, until the last decades of the nineteenth century, when virtually all the political advances of the Reconstruction were eliminated, they elected congressmen from their ethnie to represent them in the Federal government in Washington, DC (Smith 1986, 136, emphasis added).[21]

However, while racial segregation provided the ideal conditions for developing their own "customs" and "dialects," the shared history of African Americans–the vast majority of whom are descendants of enslaved Africans who were taken to North America over the course of centuries of forced migration—provided the "genealogy" required for the formation of a racial and ethnic "nation" according to the concept Smith postulated, even by people who were phenotypically more European than African.

This aspect of Black identity in the US became clear during Barack Obama's first campaign for the presidency in 2009. On one hand, his "racial purity" was questioned because his mother was White, and on the other, his legitimacy as a representative of the African American community was put in doubt because his father

---

[21] Regarding the elimination of advances which Black Americans made after Emancipation: "Virtually all the political advances afforded freedmen during Reconstruction were rolled back and eradicated during the years after 1890. In the South, the races were separated even more systematically and rigidly than during slavery. Many Blacks were reduced to a suppressed citizenship that was repeatedly exploited for political and economic purposes. As C. Vann Woodward writes, Jim Crow laws 'did not assign the subordinate group a fixed status in society. They were constantly pushing the Negro farther down'" (History, Art & Archives, US House of Representatives 2008).

was from Kenya, and therefore his Black ancestors had not shared the trauma of slavery. The fact that his wife, Michelle, had a perfectly suited genealogy bolstered his credibility as a leader of the Black community in the United States.

Biographies of Black people—real and imagined

Both in Brazil and the United States, Black people and the "Other" are nearly synonymous. In "the eyes of others"—that is, Whites—Black people in the nineteenth and early twentieth centuries were viewed as a mass of enslaved or freed persons who were marginalized, illiterate, and idle. The Brazilian historian, Célia Maria Marinho de Azevedo poses the following question:

>...to what point did an inert, disjointed, uneducated mass that was of no great historical importance at the time, as it had just left slavery as a marginalized group, not arise from the core of racially based formulations that would seek precisely to justify the need for European immigration to replace the Blacks? (2004, 19).

The existence of Black intellectuals, artists, and scientists in Brazil during the period in question puts paid to that stereotype. Thanks to Law no. 10.639, of January 9, 2003, which requires Brazilian schools to teach Afro-Brazilian and African history, we can now find a growing number of role models and studies–particularly "folk" biographies about that important portion of the population of African descent. The Brazilian journalist, lecturer and "cultural thinker" Sergio Vilas-Boas underscores the impact of biographies of people with whom readers can identify:

> People read and continue to read biographies...for the pleasure of projecting themselves into other lives, different times, other destinations, and returning to the present after the journey. Biographies suggest the universal embedded in the particularity of an individual. It is as if the reader delights in the fact of not

being alone in the world, of being able to share his own story with another person, no matter from what time (2002, 37).

In "A Talk to Teachers," James Baldwin observes: "If, for example, one managed to change the curriculum in all the schools so that Negroes learned more about themselves and their real contributions to this culture, you would be liberating not only Negroes, you'd be liberating white people who know nothing about their own history" (1963).

When researching the life of Afro-Brazilian actor Mário Gusmão for his PhD dissertation in the 1990s–later published as *Mário Gusmão: um príncipe negro na terra dos dragões da maldade* (A Black Prince in the Land of the Dragons of Evil, 2006), Jeferson Bacelar compiled a list of biographical studies of Blacks that includes very few intellectuals. One of the highlights is the biography of the physician and politician Alfredo Casimiro da Rocha, *Negro político, político negro* (Political Black Man, Black Politician), by Oracy Nogueira, published in 1992, but there was a dearth of biographies of Afro-Brazilian scientists and artists who lived in the nineteenth century or earlier–the best-known names are the novelist Machado de Assis, the military engineer André Rebouças, the sculptor Aleijadinho, the poet Luis Gama, the writer José do Patrocínio, the engineer and geographer Teodoro Sampaio, and the poet Cruz e Souza.[22] Rebouças, Gama, and Patrocínio were also prominent abolitionists. In 2019, Flávio Gomes, Jaime Loriano, and Lilia Moritz Schwarcz published the *Enciclopédia Negra—Biografias afro-brasileiras* (Black Encyclopedia: Afro-Brazilian Biographies) with over 550 entries on Black Brazilians from colonial times to the

---

[22] The "Personalidades Negras" (Black Personages) collection published by Editora Garamond offers biographies of the sculptor Aleijadinho, the poet Cruz e Sousa, the abolitionist José do Patrocínio and the novelist Machado de Assis. For children, Editora Callis offers in its collection *A Luta de cada um*, a biography of Luiz Gama by Myriam Fraga (2005)— the other Black character included in this collection of six titles is Zumbi dos Palmares.

present, including lawyers, physicians, healers, activists and revolutionaries, and religious leaders such as Mãe Aninha, the founder of the Ilê Axé Opo Afonjá *terreiro* (Candomblé religious community).

As we will see in Chapter 1, the nineteenth-century authors who pointed out the contributions (and very existence) of Black intellectuals included the White abolitionist Wilson Armistead and the Black abolitionist, physician, and writer Martin R. Delany. In addition to being the subjects of biographies, Manuel R. Querino and Booker T. Washington also helped publicize the lives of illustrious Black men. They believed that doing so was key to shattering stereotypes and mitigating the prejudices of non-Blacks. In addition to combating negative stereotypes and, consequently, racism itself, such biographies are also highly significant for Black people, as they provide positive role models and bolster self-esteem. Such works were also part of the illustrious tradition of "Black Vindicationism."

In his last published article, Querino listed the names and achievements of illustrious Black men (2009a). There is a notable absence of women. One response to the lack of heroic Black women in Brazilian history has been to imagine them. Maria Felipa (or Filipa) de Oliveira, a legendary hero of Brazil's struggle for Independence in Bahia, more specifically the Island of Itaparica, is the most recent example.[23]

Maria Felipa, as she is called, is a controversial figure. During the bicentennial celebrations of Bahia's Independence in 2023, professional and amateur historians took to the radio and television to give their versions of her story. Jaime Nascimento–who has for decades been one of the leading figures in the campaign to restore Manuel Querino to his rightful place in Brazilian history–thoroughly debunked the idea that Portuguese soldiers could be lured into the bushes by the promise of sex, thrashed with *cansação* (stinging nettle-like plants) when they were at their most vulnerable, and

---

[23] Wikipedia entry on Maria Filipa de Oliveira https://en.wikipedia.org/wiki/Maria_Filipa_de_Oliveira

Introduction

captured or killed. In the debate that followed, Nascimento (who is Black) was accused of being a misogynist and racist for denying Maria Felipa's place as the only Black woman recognized as a hero of Independence (the other women—Maria Quitéria, who disguised herself as a man to join the Brazilian army, and Joana Angélica, a nun who died defending her convent from the Portuguese soldiers— were considered White).

Other scholars have pointed out that there is no archival evidence of Maria Felipa's existence. Although her date of death was given as July 4, 1873 in *A Ilha de Itaparica*, by the writer, historian and politician Ubaldo Osório Pimentel, no record of it has been found. Nevertheless, some historians still believe that Maria Felipa did exist, although they admit that aspects of her story are farfetched. She is now included as a real, historic figure on websites devoted to teaching Brazilian history, and a monument in her honour was unveiled in the city of Salvador on July 27, 2023.[24]

In addition to Black Vindicationistm, Chapter 1 also covers the background and historical and intellectual context of the period between 1851 and 1923. In it, I describe the social (class), historical, political and racialist juncture that both protagonists encountered. This chapter also provides information about the specific contexts in which Querino and Washington lived. Instead of engaging in a North-South comparison, the focus will be on the realities of the Black Atlantic. Following the approach used by Micol Seigel (2009), it looks at specific links and interconnections between Brazil and the United States. For example, Querino and Washington worked to educate and value Blacks during the post-abolition periods in their countries when the policies of domination practiced during slavery were evolving into different forms of control, particularly measures to combat "vagrancy."

---

[24] https://ensinarhistoria.com.br/as-heroinas-baianas-da-independencia-do-brasil/. I would like to thank Augusto Albuquerque for sending me newspaper clippings on the most recent developments in this debate.

The section on the ideology of pseudoscientific racism or racialism emphasizes Count de Gobineau, whose influence was (and still is) present in the United States and Brazil. Other ideologies include Social Darwinism, which was prevalent in both countries, and Positivism, which predominated in Brazil.

In Chapter 2, the autobiographies Washington commissioned from ghost writers, and the biographical and autobiographical data Querino supplied show how these two intellectuals built up their self-images as Black role models, and how these writings formed part of their Anti-Racist strategies–demonstrating through their own life stories how Black people could "rise up" from humble beginnings through hard work and education. In Washington's case, his first autobiography was semi-fictionalised (following a strategy also used by Barack Obama in *Dreams from My Father*) to emphasise his qualities as a "self-made man" with the specific aim of setting an example for his readers.

This chapter also highlights another tactic Querino and Washington shared: forming alliances, partnerships and "mentee-mentor" relationships with Whites from the intellectual and political elites. In this regard, Querino's guardian, Manuel Correia Garcia, his political patron Manuel Pinto de Sousa Dantas, who rose to become prime minister of the Imperial government, and his best-known teacher, the Spanish artist Miguel Navarro y Cañizares, were prominent figures in his life.

Washington's first White mentors were Viola Ruffner, for whom he worked as a servant for four years, and Colonel Samuel Chapman Armstrong, the principal of the Hampton Institute. The African American educator's White allies included a president of the United States, Theodore Roosevelt, whose invitation to dine at the White House sparked a major controversy (Norell 2009, 245). Some of America's leading philanthropists also financed the Tuskegee Institute, thanks to Washington's tireless efforts to raise funds for his institution. In addition to being the patron of Black photographers, the employer and protector of one of America's greatest scientists, the Black botanist, George Washington Carver, and a client of the

Black architect, Robert R. Taylor, Booker T. Washington also hired talented White men and women such as the sociologist Robert E. Park and the photographer Frances Benjamin Johnston.

Regarding solidarity with fellow Blacks, Chapter 2 also analyses Manuel Querino's works defending Africans and people of African descent and his (often turbulent) relationship with the Sociedade Protetora dos Desvalidos. As for Booker T. Washington, we will see how he played a double game to make it seem that he supported the "Jim Crow" system while using stratagems to defend Black people's rights and even their lives (Smock 2009, 139-143).

In Chapter 3, obituaries form the basis for following and analysing the high and low points in the remembrance and reputations of Querino and Washington in Brazil and the United States. According to the permanent secretary of the Instituto Histórico e Geográfico da Bahia (Historical and Geographic Institute of Bahia, IGHB), Bernardino J. de Souza, their contemporaries considered Querino and Nina Rodrigues the greatest authorities on Afro-Bahian culture (Souza 1932, 34). However, the validity of Querino's work as a creditable source began to be questioned in the 1930s, culminating in an accusation of plagiarism levelled by the German-Brazilian art historian Carlos Ott (1947).

The negative view of Washington presented by the "Talented Tenth" persisted due to the writings of Du Bois and other Black activists in the United States during the civil rights struggles of the 1960s. Washington's chief biographer, Louis Harlan, made his contempt for his subject clear, partly because he considered him a traitor to the South because he accepted money from the "carpetbagging" millionaires who exploited the region after the US Civil War (1988). Even so, thanks to Ishmael Reed (2000) and more recently, Robert Norell (2009), among others, the African American educator's life and work are being reinterpreted in the context of his time in the United States.

Chapter 4 follows shifting perceptions of Booker T. Washington in Brazil since the early twentieth century, and the process of re-introducing his life and work in that country's newspapers. After the publication of *Up from Slavery* in the United States in 1901, a seven-part review by a French journalist was serialized in the newspaper *Diário da Bahia*, in 1902. The reports published after that in other Brazilian newspapers and magazines–including Abdias do Nascimento's *Quilombo* in 1950–kept Washington in the public eye for decades. Today, however, few Brazilians are aware of Washington's story, and the scholars and Black activists who do know about him have based their impressions on Du Bois's scathing criticism of his "accommodation" and see him as a "race traitor" at a time when his legacy is being reanalysed and reinterpreted in his own country.

In Chapter 5, I assess the anti-racist tactic of using positive imagery in response to anthropometric photographs used to justify the ideology of supposed White supremacy in the United States and Brazil. In some cases, such as those of Washington and Querino, Black intellectuals and leaders produced and disseminated portraits of themselves in which they are well-dressed and striking assertive poses. Consciously or not, they used the same technique as the famous photographer Mathew Brady when he created an album that portrayed the icons of "American" nationality (Smith 1999, 65). To different degrees, portraits of free and enslaved Blacks that emphasized their "personhood" contradicted images that accompanied discourses about race and national identity constructed by ideologies based on pseudoscientific racism.

CHAPTER 1
EXPANDING THE BLACK ATLANTIC:
Contrasts and Connections between the US and Brazil

This chapter covers the background and historical and intellectual context of the period between 1851 and 1923. In it, I describe the social (class), historical, political and racialist juncture that Washington and Querino encountered and the specific contexts in which they lived. Instead of engaging in a North-South comparison, the focus will be on the realities of the Black Atlantic. Following the approach used by Micol Seigel (2009), I present and examine specific links and interconnections between Brazil and the United States. For example, Querino and Washington worked to educate and value Blacks–also known as Black Vindicationism–during the post-abolition periods in their countries when the policies of seigneurial control practised during slavery were evolving into different forms of dominance. The section on the ideology of pseudoscientific racism, or racialism, emphasizes the thinking of Count de Gobineau, whose influence was (and still is) present in the United States and Brazil. Other ideologies prevalent in both countries include Social Darwinism and Positivism, which has been particularly influential in Brazil, as evidenced by the words "Order and Progress" on the national flag.

Considering the settings in which Booker T. Washington and Manuel R. Querino lived and worked, one might think they inhabited separate worlds—the United States, in the North, and Brazil, in the South. However, that notion is misguided, as in many respects, they were closely linked (see Seigel 2009; Horne 2010). There was a varied range of connections and exchanges between the two countries and their inhabitants, on the political, intellectual, cultural, and economic levels, to name a few. Washington and Querino confronted similar and sometimes identical racist ideologies, as they lived in a globalized world when it came to intellectual and cultural influences. They frequently used similar Anti-Racist tactics and strategies along with many other Black educators, scholars and leaders, wheresoever they were based—above or below the Equator in the Black Atlantic.

In addition to similar experiences and influences, and the "grapevine telegraph" that spanned the Black Atlantic, there were other factors, including one as fundamental as transportation. Before the Transcontinental Railway linked the East and West coasts of the USA in 1869, and particularly before the Panama Canal connected the Caribbean and Pacific in 1914, many American seafarers had to stop in Brazil–particularly in the ports of Recife, Salvador, and Rio de Janeiro–to sail from one coast of their own country to the other. That flow of travel increased considerably during the Alaska Gold Rush between 1896 and 1899. When they visited the US, many Brazilians, both unsung and renowned, faced different situations and receptions depending on the colour of their skin.

According to the Brazilian sociologist Antônio Sérgio Alfredo Guimarães (2004, 1), who proposed comparing Querino and W. E. B. Du Bois, "such a comparison would reveal, first, a major contrast between the way in which the formation of ethnic and racial identity transpired among Blacks in the United States, and how it occurred [in Brazil]." Indeed, there are major differences between the realities that shaped the ethnic and racial identity of Black Americans and Brazilians of African descent (among others, hypodescent, the "<u>one-</u>

drop rule" which, until recently, eliminated the racial categories of "Brown" and "mixed-race" people in the United States[25]). Even so, racial mixture occurred–both Booker T. Washington and Frederick Douglass, were the children of enslaved Black women and White men. Racialists used the "White blood" of their fathers to justify the eminence both men achieved (as we will see in Chapter 3, that argument and a counterargument were even presented in Washington's obituaries).

In his analysis of census data from several countries, Petruccelli notes that

> The development of nineteenth-century racialist doctrines led to the inclusion of the category "mulatto" in racial classification for the first time in 1850, and it was kept the same until the 1920 census. Polygenism and its inherent essentialism, then in vogue in the USA...took a special interest in the "scientific" study—depending on the time—of miscegenation and the supposed consequence of infertility or, at least, reduced reproductive capacity of racial differences considered permanent in relation to the ancestors of "pure" races and of the apparently higher mortality of the population of African origin (2002, 537).

In the United States, "mulattos" and other mixed-race people of African descent were considered Black based on their African ancestry. Even so, there was a persistent idea that "White blood" influenced characteristics that were considered superior, such as intelligence and courage, and even prevented a [White] individual from commingling with other races. White men who had children with or–even worse–cohabited with Black women were viewed as social outcasts, and a mixed-race person could therefore be considered handicapped by their White parent's degeneracy. Ironically, we now know that Thomas Jefferson had six children with

---

[25] Today, terms like "biracial" are frequently used in the US and elsewhere.

an enslaved Black woman, Sally Hemings. She was also the product of elite miscegenation, as she was the half-sister of Jefferson's wife and could therefore be considered his sister-in-law.[26]

Although White supremacists considered "mulattos" to be superior to Blacks, there was no "mulatto escape hatch" in the USA.[27] According to Robert E. Park, a co-founder of the Chicago School of sociology and erstwhile assistant to Booker T. Washington (1950, 380):

> ...when Negroes interbreed with other races, the offspring of such unions do not have the same freedom of choice [as the offspring of Christians and Jews]. The mixed bloods are either, as in the case of the mulattos of the United States, incontinently classed as Negroes, irrespective of the degree of the racial mixture, or they occupy, as half-castes and mixed bloods, a position somewhere between the two.

Park also observes, "It is, in fact, the rôle which the mulatto plays, and the position that he occupies in relation to the black man and the white, that determines in every case the character of the existing race relations and the local race problem" (1950, 381).

---

[26] Thomas Jefferson believed that Back people were inferior to whites, and their social status was due to their supposedly: "The improvement of the blacks in body and mind, in the first instance of their mixture with the whites, has been observed by every one, and proves that their inferiority is not the effect merely of their condition of life" (Jefferson 1784, 9). This negative view of Black people is expressed in his essay *Notes on the State of Virginia* (1781), https://docsouth.unc.edu/southlit/jefferson/jefferson.html.

[27] Coined by Carl Degler (1971), "mulatto escape hatch" means that the racial category of "mulatto" supposedly allowed people classified as such to escape the "stigma" and prejudice suffered by Black people. At the same time, it created an intermediate category that impeded the development and awareness of a "Black nation" in Brazil. Some see it is a "trap door."

Although described by some as "mulatto," even by Park himself (1950, 381),[28] Booker T. Washington always self-identified as Black. He was considered the legitimate successor of the abolitionist and diplomat Frederick Douglass, who died in 1895. Washington thus became the "president" of the "Black nation" in the United States.

In Brazil, racial mixture among Whites, Indigenous people, and Blacks began with the first contact between this "triangle of races" and became part of the country's founding myth. Miscegenation was so widespread that the identification of "Blacks, Browns, and Whites" is still based on appearance, on a continuum ranging from "pure African" at one extreme and "White European" at the other (Gledhill 1986).[29]

In the United States, the "one-drop rule" prevailed, requiring official papers and witnesses to attest to an individual's racial status, as a Black American with a pale complexion, blue eyes, and straight hair could "pass for White" in places where they were not known to be Black–a tactic that is viewed as a tragic betrayal by the Black community.[30] The fact that this tactic was possible demonstrates that the idea that Americans always practiced strict apartheid is a myth, as racial mixture was always a reality–albeit strictly curbed and repressed. As Skidmore observes, the greatest difference between miscegenation in Brazil and the United States during the period in

---

[28] In a lecture given in 1929, Park categorized Washington and W. E. B. Du Bois, "the two most eminent figures among Negroes in the United States," as "mixed bloods" (1950, 381).

[29] The best examples of the extremes of this continuum are the late Pelé and his former long-term girlfriend, the children's presenter Xuxa Meneghel, who is of German descent.

[30] This tactic has been the subject of novels such as *Passing*, by Nella Larsen (first published in1929), the basis for a film of the same name released in 2021, and *The Vanishing Half*, by Britt Bennett (2021). Philip Roth's tragic novel *The Human Stain* was made into a film in 2003, starring the Black American actor Wentworth Miller and the White British actor Anthony Hopkins as the younger and older selves of a Black university lecturer who is passing for White and accused of racism against Blacks.

question was not whether it occurred, but "what happened to the offspring" (1993, 377).

For example, in Brazil, we find several examples, including Manuel Querino, a Black man who self-identified as *mestiço*, or mixed-race, and was raised by a White guardian, Manuel Correia Garcia, who may have been his biological father. The outcomes could be radically different. The Afro-Brazilian polymath Teodoro Sampaio was raised by a White priest who was supposed to be his father, while the poet and abolitionist Luis Gama's White father sold him into slavery. Even so, in the United States, cases like Booker T. Washington's were commonplace–the White man who sired him left his mixed-race son to live in bondage. Impregnating enslaved women–often by force–became a relatively economical way to increase the enslaver's "capital" (Ibid.).

The huge disparity between the dates when the transatlantic slave trade was officially abolished (1808 in the US and 1850–for the second time–in Brazil)[31] explains the powerful resistance and influence of African culture in Brazil, particularly Bahia. However, we should not forget that enslaved persons continued to be trafficked to the US illegally until as late as 1870 (Du Bois 2007a) and to Brazil, with the help of American slave traders, for years after the Eusébio de Queiroz Law was enacted in 1850. After their defeat in the Civil War, former Confederates dreamed of continuing their slavocracy in the "deepest South." That dream would only die when Brazil finally abolished slavery in 1888 (Horne 2010).

The United States and Brazil share the "original sin" of slavery. Before that institution was abolished in both countries, one control strategy used by enslavers was to prevent their captives from obtaining even the most rudimentary education. In the case of the US, this policy was reinforced after the revolt led by Nat Turner, an

---

[31] Under pressure from the British, Brazil originally banned the transatlantic trade in 1831. Abolitionists later used the 1831 law to claim that all Africans brought into the country after it was enacted were illegally enslaved, and therefore free (see Mamigonian 2017 and 2023).

enslaved man who had learned to read and write. Several slave states followed the example of Virginia, the site of the revolt, and passed bills banning literacy among the enslaved.[32] According to Mattoso (1982, 113), "The education of enslaved people was completely banned in Brazil, and even freedpersons were not allowed go to school. This prohibition was maintained throughout the period of slavery, even in the second half of the nineteenth century, when the slave system was being dismantled." The fear of literacy among the enslaved was so great that the discovery and translation of Arabic writings found in the possession of alleged conspirators were an important part of the investigation that followed the short-lived uprising led by enslaved Muslims in Bahia, known as the Revolt of the Malês, in 1835 (Reis 2003, 260).[33]

The outbreak and suppression of revolts against slavery were events that attracted the attention of all slaveholders in the North and South. According to Horne,

> ...Brazil's legation in Washington analysed extensively Nat Turner's slave revolt in Virginia, seeking signs of whether this contagion might spread, even in faraway Buenos Aires, where slavery was hardly prominent, note was taken of this chilling revolt.

---

[32] Frederick Douglass learned to read from a female slaveholder while he was still enslaved. The woman later regretted teaching him and stopped his lessons, but it was far too late. From that point on, the young man could learn on his own. Douglass (2004) declared that after he learned to read, he never accepted his enslaved status again. Solomon Northup, the author of *Twelve Years a Slave*, was forced to hide the fact that he was literate during his years in bondage. Born free in New York State, according to his narrative, he was kidnapped and enslaved in the Deep South (Northup, 2012).

[33] Although the rebels were betrayed and the uprising quickly suppressed, the Revolt of the Malês sparked panic among slaveholders, leading to serious repercussions for enslaved and freed Blacks in Brazil. (For a detailed account and analysis, see Reis 1995.)

Likewise, a few years later the US legation in Bahia, Brazil analysed extensively a slave revolt in this province, seeking signs of whether this contagion might spread (2007, 11).

Horne does not mention the year or provide any further details about the revolt in Bahia, but based on the date of the despatch from the US consul to the Secretary of State, John Forsyth–February 11, 1835–he was clearly referring to the Revolt of the Malês (2007, 12., note 75). As Horne observes, "The Brazilian elites could not be indifferent to slave revolts in the US, just as US elites could be affected by slave revolts in Brazil" (2007, 12).

In addition to requiring illiterate and, therefore, more controllable, captives, slavery was an institution that reduced workers to the status of currency, merchandise, or chattel.[34] This tended to undermine the work ethic, as it made work synonymous with slavery, thereby obstructing the development of a market for free labour. According to Kowarick, in Brazil:

> As the material and ideological parameters essential to society had always been closely linked to the spectre of slavery, for the free and the poor, working for someone else meant the most debased form of existence. Over the centuries, this caused a massive increase in the number of individuals of various origins and social backgrounds who did not become a workforce, as disciplined and regular production was carried out by slaves (1994, 12).

In the United States, the "peculiar institution" was concentrated in the southern states until the end of the Civil War in 1865, but in Brazil, it extended throughout the country. As we will see, the phenomenon of "vagrancy" would become the target of specific laws in both countries. Adding to the challenge of replacing the workforce

---

[34] In *A Fistful of Shells*, Toby Green (2020) demonstrates how the currency used in West Africa shifted from objects like shells, cloth, and gold to human beings.

eliminated by the general emancipation of the enslaved, many free Blacks and freedpersons saw work as degrading, because prior to abolition:

> For those who were not slaveowners, work was pointless, and instead of dignifying those who engaged in it, on the contrary, the effort of doing [work] tended to bring them closer to the rules of dominion and submission prevailing in the captive condition of existence.... Those who were not forced to would only work when strictly necessary (Kowarick 1994, 56).

After the abolition of slavery, one result of this inverted work ethic was the rise of vagrancy and laws to combat it.

These and other considerations led to strategies for controlling people emancipated from slavery which were applied in similar ways in both the US and Brazil after abolition. In the case of Brazil, these strategies included repressing expressions of Afro-Brazilian culture, particularly the worship of Afro-Brazilian divinities known as Candomblé (in most parts of the United States, traditional African religions had been effectively suppressed, except for the state of Louisiana, where Vodun, a religion of Ewe/Fon origin, resisted and is still practiced to this day, particularly in New Orleans).

The US Civil War was followed by the Reconstruction period, during which the winners from the North exerted control over the South, and the infamous carpetbaggers and robber barons exploited the defeated southerners, leading to bitter and enduring resentment. At least, that is the commonly held view of what transpired. Naturally, the real situation was much more complex and nuanced. The term "carpetbagger" dates back to 1846, when it meant "any suspicious outsider." It was even used to describe any northerner who migrated to the South during the Reconstruction period. Carpetbaggers were even accused of plotting to "Africanize" the country. According to the Black American intellectual John Hope

Franklin, the image of carpetbaggers as interlopers, adventurers and vagrants of the worst kind impugned

> the integrity and good intentions of thousands whose motives were otherwise.... Even more important, perhaps, is the fact that such descriptions show no understanding of the variety and complexity of the motives underlying the migrations and no appreciation for the economic and political relationships that grew out of such motives (1994, 94).

At the end of the US Civil War, Black captives were freed by the Emancipation Proclamation of 1863, followed by the 13th Amendment, which abolished slavery in 1865. They also received the protection of the 14th Amendment (1868), which guaranteed the privileges and immunities of citizenship (such as the right to a fair trial), and the 15th Amendment (1870), which established the right to vote for all men, without discrimination based on race, colour, or prior enslavement (women would only gain that right in the United States when the 19th Amendment was passed in 1920). Freedpersons were given a promise—never fulfilled—of "40 acres and a mule" to establish their own farmsteads. Several schools were set up to educate the emancipated masses, the vast majority of whom–due to the slaveowners' policy of keeping their captives uneducated–could barely sign their own names. Between 1865 and 1877, around 2,000 Blacks were elected or appointed to federal and state offices in the South, including senators, representatives, and judges (Foner 1996).

"Black Codes" and vagrancy laws

Soon after the war, in 1865 and 1866, the defeated enslavers enacted state laws called "Black Codes" with the aim of controlling freedpersons and attempting to restore slavery in a different guise. According to Franklin (1994, 47), these laws "forecast, to a remarkable degree, the future attitude of former Confederates toward the place of Blacks in the South and in American life." Although they recognized that Black people had the legal right to own property, sue, be sued, marry, and have legitimate offspring, they ordered that Blacks could only testify against other Blacks, and marriage between Blacks and Whites became a felony (Ibid.).

However, the most important restrictions for the former slaveowners were the laws that turned work contracts into mechanisms of re-enslavement. For example, in the state of Mississippi, if a Black person left a job before their contract expired, they could be arrested by "any person" and returned to their employer (Ibid., 48). In Florida, Black people who broke work contracts could be whipped and sentenced to forced labour for up to a year (Foner 2011). Finally, the Black Codes included laws against vagrancy. Any Black person who was arrested and convicted of that crime in Mississippi and could not pay the $50 fine would be hired out to someone who could, and forced to work for them to repay the debt (Franklin 1994, 48).

South Carolina enacted even harsher and more discriminatory laws. In that state, Black people, whether born free or enslaved, were barred from any occupation except farm hands or domestic servants. Any Black person who wanted to practice a profession would have to pay an annual fee that ranged from $10 to $100. In addition to unemployed Blacks, the vagrancy law in that state also applied to "'persons who lead idle or disorderly lives,' and even travelling circuses, fortune tellers, and thespians" (Foner 2011).

After the Compromise of 1877, also called the "Bargain" or even the "Great Betrayal," the Federal Government withdrew its troops from the South, marking the end of the first Reconstruction (Woodward 1966). The White supremacists of the South had resisted all the efforts of the radicals and the Federal government to enforce the constitutional amendments that guaranteed Black people's rights. Now, they reacted by removing all Black officials from their posts–including congressmen and senators–resorting to stratagems and violence to prevent Black American voters from going to the polls.[35]

---

[35] For an in-depth analysis of this period and its aftermath, see Franklin 1994, Foner 2011, and Richardson 2004.

The first version of the Ku Klux Klan had been banned since the early 1870s by the Enforcement Acts–Federal laws enacted by Congress to protect Black people's rights. Nevertheless, other groups with similar aims and methods, such as the Red Shirts and the White League, continued their reign of terror against Black communities. Lynchings of Black people became commonplace, motivated by spurious allegations and suspicions, including the claim that the victim had not known their "place" and was being "uppity." However, the most frequent charge was that the victim had "disrespected" a White woman or even tried to rape her, since Black men were considered "savages" who could not control their basest impulses, particularly lust. (As we will see in Chapter 2, Booker T. Washington was attacked and nearly lynched in New York City in 1911 for allegedly addressing a White woman as "sweetheart.") Lynching only became a federal hate crime in the US when President Joe Biden signed the Emmett Till Antilynching Act into law on March 29, 2022.[36]

In addition to the ways and means the White supremacists used to prevent Blacks from exercising their constitutional rights, other strategies were employed. Instead of receiving the promised "40 acres and a mule," many emancipated individuals were forced to work as sharecroppers, accumulating debts they could never repay. The peonage system created by this situation is now seen as a new form of slavery. "Jim Crow" segregation laws began to be enacted in southern states in 1876, based on a system that would be created to keep Blacks and Whites "separate but equal" in hotels, schools, universities, theatres, restaurants, trains, and even at drinking fountains and in public toilets. In reality, the facilities reserved for Blacks were always inferior. Ending segregation on the railways was a cause that united Black leaders like Washington and W. E. B. Du Bois, who often used that means of transportation.

---

[36] https://www.congress.gov/bill/117th-congress/house-bill/55

In Brazil, Abolition in 1888 was followed by a coup that overthrew the Imperial government, which historians consider to be a direct consequence of emancipation. Of course, the factors that led to the introduction of the First Republic in 1889 were complex, and as we will see in the case of Manuel Querino, abolitionism and republicanism went hand in hand. However, as the American historian E. Bradford Burns observed (1993, 229), "Abolition of slavery in Brazil precipitated the fall of the monarchy, just as abolition in Cuba foretold the end of Spanish dominion there."

Historians concur that, as Luís Henrique Dias Tavares (2008, 300) noted, "The monarchy fell throughout Brazil without the slightest resistance." Even so, there were monarchist uprisings in several parts of the country, the best known being the tragic misunderstanding that led to the Canudos War.[37]

One of the most unusual–and inexplicable–episodes of violence involved a group of foreigners, including five Americans, who joined forces under the leadership of a Brazilian from Rio Grande do Sul, Sebastião "Magali" Magalhães, to attack the city of Ilhéus on November 25, 1907. Its objective, in the words of Magali himself, was "to establish an honest state government" (Tavares 2008, 318). According to a note published in the *New York Herald*, penned by the then Minister of Foreign Affairs of Brazil, José Maria da Silva Paranhos Júnior, Baron of Rio Branco, Magali was a "madman" who organized an expedition of 100 men in New York to stage a coup in Minas Gerais. Magali was tried and sentenced, but as Tavares (2008, 320) observes: "More than ninety years later, this incident remains mysterious and obscure."

After overthrowing Emperor Pedro II and sending him into exile, Deodoro da Fonseca's provisional government issued a decree on June 28, 1890, that upheld the ban on Black immigration introduced by the Eusébio de Queirós Law in 1850 (Nascimento 1978, 71; Skidmore, 1974, 155). The First Republic's Positivist philosophy called

---

[37] The subject of Euclides da Cunha's classic work *Os sertões* (translated as *Rebellion in the Backlands*).

for eradicating everything that could make the country "backward," particularly Afro-Brazilian cultural expressions such as *batuques, lundus,* Candomblé, and capoeira.[38] The latter two were banned by law, and would only be legalized in the 1930s, under Getúlio Vargas.

Vagrancy laws–which also included people accused of *capoeiragem* (practicing the then-illegal Afro-Brazilian martial art capoeira)—decreed that "failing to exercise a profession, trade, or occupation in which they earn a living, not having means of subsistence and a certain domicile in which to live; providing for subsistence by means of occupation prohibited by law, or manifestly offensive to morals and good customs" would be punishable by "imprisonment for fifteen to thirty days" (Brazil, 1890). Anyone over the age of fourteen would be "held in industrial disciplinary establishments," and in the event of a repeat offence, "the offender will be imprisoned for one to three years in penal colonies on sea islands or on the borders of national territory, [and for] this purpose, existing military prisons can be used" (Brazil, 1890).

As for capoeira, the penalty for "performing exercises of agility and corporal dexterity known as capoeiragem in the streets and public squares; going about with weapons or tools capable of causing bodily harm, causing riots or disorder, threatening a specific or non-specific person, or instilling fear of harm" would be punishable by "imprisonment for two to six months." If a capoeira practitioner belonged to "a band or gang," this was considered an aggravating factor, and the penalty would be doubled for the "chiefs, or heads" (Ibid.).

As in the US, "vagrancy" in Brazil arose from a mindset that equated work with subjugation:

---

[38] According to Boris Fausto (2008, 138), Positivism during the First Republic originated from republicans in Rio Grande do Sul, led by Júlio de Castilhos: "It is possible that the military tradition in that area and the fact that the republicans were a minority there, seeking a strong, unifying doctrine, contributed to this."

The free, insofar as bondage was the reference of the productive process, could only conceive of the organized worker as the most degraded form of existence. In turn, as the masters' parameter for work was based on slavery, which the free did everything they could to avoid, the perception that they were the least desirable would crystallise: they were seen as true "idlers," useless for work (Kowarick 1994, 43).

Carvalho (1991, 18) demonstrates that the category of "vagrants" was vast in Brazil. It included:

Thieves, prostitutes, rogues, deserters from the Army, the Navy and foreign ships, gypsies, street vendors, ragpickers, domestics, servants in public offices, rat catchers, streetcar receivers, shoeshine men, cart drivers, flower sellers, bookies, gamblers, fencers, pickpockets. And, of course, the typically Carioca [Rio de Janeiro] figure of the capoeira, whose fame had already spread throughout the country and whose numbers were estimated at around 20,000 on the eve of the Republic. Living, acting and working, for the most part, in the central streets of the Old City, these were the people who most frequently appeared in the crime statistics of the time, especially for misdemeanours such as disorderly conduct, vagrancy, drunkenness, and gambling. In 1890, these misdemeanours were responsible for *60 percent of arrests* of people sent to the Penitentiary (emphasis added).[39]

While clamping down on "vagrancy" and arresting "vagrants," the First Republic continued the Empire's policy of encouraging Europeans to settle in Brazil, attracting an immigrant workforce that

---

[39] According to the same author, "In concrete terms, the republic's preventive measures against poor and Black people was expressed by Sampaio Ferraz's persecution of capoeiras, the fight against the bookmakers, and the destruction by Mayor Barata Ribeiro, an ally of [then-president] Floriano Peixoto, of Rio's most famous tenement, Cabeça de Porco [Pig's Head] in 1892" (Carvalho 1991, 30-31).

competed with the emancipated population. At the same time, the government did nothing to help Blacks and the poor acquire the skills they needed to enter the formal labour market. As we have seen, in the United States, the formerly enslaved people who were emancipated in 1865, after the Civil War, faced numerous obstacles to obtaining civil rights, such as lynchings, political exclusion, segregation, and peonage. Nevertheless, several educational institutions, mainly teacher training colleges and vocational institutes, were created for freedpersons by paternalistic, philanthropic Whites such as General Samuel C. Armstrong, founder of the Hampton Institute, whose most eminent student was Booker T. Washington. There was also a Black elite, the "Talented Tenth,"[40] made up of men like the Harvard-educated W. E. B. Du Bois, PhD.

In his book *As artes na Bahia* (The Arts in Bahia, 1913), Querino– by then a repentant Republican–praises the cultural initiatives carried out during the Imperial period (1822-1889). He observes that the Liceu de Artes e Ofícios and the Academy (later School) of Fine Art were founded during that time in the province of Bahia: "During the Imperial era, it is only honourable to confess, the presidents of the Province did not disdain to protect and enliven artistic culture," underscoring that the Liceu and School of Fine Art "were also viewed as instruments for educating the people, whose noble intentions were respected" (Querino 1913, 26). Referring specifically to

---

[40] According to Du Bois (1903, 33-34), "The Negro race, like all races, is going to be saved by its exceptional men. The problem of education, then, among Negroes must first of all deal with the Talented Tenth; it is the problem of developing the best of this race that they may guide the mass away from the contamination and death of the worst in their own and other races. If we make money the object of man-training, we shall develop money-makers but not necessarily men; if we make technical skill the object of education, we may possess artisans but not, in nature, men. Men we shall have only as we make manhood the object of the work in the schools – intelligence, broad sympathy, knowledge of the world that was and is, and of the relation of men to it – this is the curriculum of that higher education which must underlie true life."
https://archive.org/details/negroproblemseri00washrich/page/n41/mode/2up.

vocational education, he reports that the Navy and War arsenals had produced "outstanding workers, whose skills showed abundant evidence, during the war with Paraguay, when the general government removed them to Rio de Janeiro in order to work in shipbuilding, let alone the works performed here" (Ibid., 27).

The advent of the "republican regime" changed this situation dramatically—for the worse. According to Querino, artists and artisans lacked commissions, and teachers went unpaid: "a professor of sculpture and another of painting at the School of Fine Art left for Europe, abandoning teaching with a heavy heart, due to lack of payment. If one well-intentioned governor favoured the arts, another would withdraw that favour" (Querino 1913, 28). This may well have been the reason why Querino failed to complete his degree in architecture at the School of Fine Art. Nevertheless, his harshest criticism fell on the closing of the arsenals. Due to that measure:

> Young apprentices, future workers, were abandoned to the practice of vice; far from being an economic measure, it became a sordid speculative convenience of a few *hardworking* and *diligent* individuals to whom all the work of the army and navy was delivered, so that the Rio de Janeiro firm "Lage & Companhia" could exploit, with the greed of that time, that which should have been distributed to many and at a reasonable price. And it was through this process that perversity is flaunted and mocks the unfortunate heroes of labour, casting true artistic vocations into oblivion (Querino 1913, 29, emphasis in original).

Having been an ardent Republican, Manuel Querino was profoundly disillusioned with the outcome of that movement. In the public sphere, the First Republic (1889-1930) bolstered the power of the regional oligarchs, maintaining the "model of political and sociocultural exclusion" of the Empire in a republic "without democratic citizenship." The new regime neglected education and the arts, and did nothing to include the enslaved people emancipated in 1888 in the free labour market (Querino 1913, 24). On the contrary, it continued the drive to "whiten" Brazil begun towards the end of the Empire, by encouraging the immigration of European workers (Skidmore 2003, 112). In the private sphere, Querino faced the wrath of the Bahian oligarchy and was forced to leave politics and the civil service. According to Pereira (1932, 13), "He did not know how to curry favour with the politicians, and so he paid dearly for his boldness and independence."

Pseudoscientific racism

In addition to the ebb and flow of people and goods between the United States and Brazil, the two countries shared ideals and ideologues (particularly Europeans with racialist notions that were deemed scientific) which influenced their established concepts of race and nation. Positivism and Social Darwinism influenced both countries, and two Europeans, the French racial theorist Count de Gobineau and the Swiss-American zoologist Louis Agassiz, who both visited Brazil, also had a strong impact on the United States. These "scientific" notions bolstered the generalized racist thinking which both Washington and Querino had to confront.

Gobineau and his followers

During the period covered in this book, the predominant racialist ideologies in both Brazil and the United States included the pessimism of Joseph Arthur Compte de Gobineau (1816-1882) (Ortiz 1985, 14; Biddiss 1970; Meréje 1934). Better known as the Count de Gobineau, he had a major impact on intellectuals in both countries. His theories directly targeted Brazilians because the French aristocrat addressed the situation of racial mixture in their country in his writings, produced during and after an extended stay in Brazil. He was also a close friend of Emperor Pedro II, whom Gobineau considered to be the only Brazilian who did not suffer from the "taint" of miscegenation.[41] The author of *Essai sur l'inégalité des races humaines* (Essay on the Inequality of the Human Races), he saw Brazil as "living proof" of his theory on Aryan supremacy (Skidmore 1974, 30). According to that theory, wherever a White community was found, it would become the centre of gravity of the intellectual world (Meréje 1934, 17). In Gobineau's view:

From a moral standpoint alone, it is accurate to argue that, in addition to all patriotic concerns, the centre of gravity of the social world has always hovered on western shores, without ever leaving them, having, according to the time, two extremes, Babylon and London from east to west, Stockholm and Thebes in Egypt from north to south; beyond it, [there is] isolation, limited personality, inability to excite general sympathy, and, finally, barbarism in all its forms.[42]

Gobineau believed that the Brazilian people had been "irretrievably sullied" by racial mixture, and he was disgusted by a population that was, for him, totally mixed, corrupt, enfeebled, and ugly. He also declared that miscegenation was so extensive that "the nuances of colour are infinite, causing a degeneration of the most

---

[41] Gobineau and the emperor corresponded for 11 years, between 1870 and 1882. Most of their letters have been collected in a 624-page book edited by Georges Raeders (1938). Pedro II disagreed with Gobineau (1884 in Ianni 1970, 268), at least, in principle. In one letter, he declared that racial prejudice did not exist in Brazil: "Here, democracy means the absence of any prejudice regarding origins, faith or colour."

[42] The original French reads : "En se plaçant au seul point de vue moral, qu'il y a de l'exactitude à soutenir que, en dehors, de toutes les préoccupations patriotiques, le centre de gravité du monde social a toujours oscillé dans les contrées occidentales, sans le quitter jamais, ayant, suivant les temps, deux limites extrêmes, Babylone et Londres, de l'est à l'ouest, Stockholm et Thèbes d'Égypte du nord au sud; au delà, isolement, personnalité restreinte, impuissance à exciter la sympathie générale, et finalement la barbarie sous toutes ses formes" (Gobineau 1884).

depressing type among the lower as well as the upper classes" (Skidmore 1974, 29-30).

In an article aimed at encouraging European emigration to Brazil, Gobineau writes that "the vast majority of the Brazilian population is mixed race, the result of mixtures between indigenous peoples, blacks and a small number of Portuguese" (1884, 368). To reassure future White settlers, he guarantees that mulattos could only produce a limited number of generations: "Infertility does not always exist in marriages, but their offspring gradually become so weak, so unviable, that they disappear before bearing children or bear children who cannot survive" (Gobineau 1884, 369). Gobineau calculated that the "descendants of Costa-Cabral [sic]" (Skidmore 1974, 30) would disappear from Brazil in less than 200 years, due to the increasing degeneration caused by miscegenation, and predicted that the alliances formed with Europe's "superior races" would revitalize Brazil: "The race will be restored, public health will improve, the moral temperament will be renewed, and the happiest changes will be introduced in the social state of this admirable country" (Gobineau 1884, 369).

In the United States, his influence took a different path. He never set foot in that country, but criticized its "decadence" in general, and the slavocracy in particular. Although defenders of that "peculiar institution" used a translation of his *Essai* to back their positions, Gobineau disapproved of their version. In no way did he see his book as a recommendation for the institution of slavery, much less a way of reinforcing "the myth of a great American future" (Biddiss 1970, 147). Even so, his *Essai* was translated into English by Henry Hotze, a Swiss-American propagandist for the Confederacy during the US Civil War, according to the ideology of his client, Josiah Nott, a slaveholder who was seeking arguments against abolitionism. Soon after its original publication in Paris, France, in 1853, Gobineau's best-known work was little read and even disparaged by his countrymen–his own mentor, Alexis de Tocqueville, the author of the classic work *Democracy in America*, criticized the *Essai* because its insistence on racial determinism eliminated free will and would therefore lead to "spiritual lassitude." As he observed in *Democracy in America*, Tocqueville considered racialist explanations to be the result of laziness on the part of historians.[43] He asked Gobineau:

> What advantage can there be in persuading base peoples living in barbarism, indolence or slavery that, such being their racial nature, they can do nothing to improve their situation or to change their habits and government? Do you not see inherent in your doctrine all the evils engendered by permanent inequality–pride, violence, scorn of fellow men, tyranny and abjection in all their forms?[44]

Nott, Hotze and others were more interested in using the scientific means of their time to prove that Africans and "Aryans" belonged to different species, thereby demonstrating that there was no conflict with the statement in the American Declaration of Independence that "all men are created equal" (Burnett 2008, 4-5). In Gobineau's work, translated into English in 1865 as *The Moral and Intellectual Diversity of Races: With Particular Reference to their Respective Influence in the Civil and Political History of Mankind, from the French of Count A. de Gobineau*, Nott added a polygenist appendix which he penned himself, presenting the anthropometric data produced by Samuel George Morton. These came from Morton's vast collection of human skulls, classified according to his own racialist taxonomy–with Whites at the top and Blacks at the bottom. Gobineau denounced Nott's appendix as a distortion of his thinking (Burnett, 2008; Painter, 2010).

---

[43] Regarding "historians who live in democratic ages," Tocqueville observed: "Most of them attribute hardly any influence to the individual over the destiny of the race, nor to citizens over the fate of a people; but, on the other hand, they assign great general causes to all petty incidents" (Tocqueville 1848, v. 2, chap XX).

[44] Tocqueville (in Biddiss 1970, 149; Painter 2010), letter to Gobineau, November 17, 1853.

Gobineau's followers came forth with other racialist theories, including Gustave Le Bon and Georges Vacher de Lapouge. Like Morton, Le Bon ranked the human races according to their level of superiority, with Whites at the top. Le Bon also believed that each race had a "soul" and ended up developing a different psychology or character, ideas that influenced the imperialist thinking of American leaders such as Senator Henry Cabot Lodge (1850-1924) and his close friend, Theodore Roosevelt (Dyer 1980, 10).

Burns (1993, 316) observes that "Of particular concern to the Brazilians, Le Bon asserted that miscegenation produced offspring inferior to either parent," including the more "evolved" progenitor. Lapouge (1896, 182) stated that, in Brazil and the United States, mulattos had a lower life expectancy than Blacks, despite better living conditions. The French anthropologist believed that "crises" of miscegenation were "accompanied by a sharp drop in the birth rate. Populations tend to disappear, spontaneous extinction occurs for no appreciable reason" (Lapouge 1896, 187).[45] In the same chapter, entitled "Croisements–Métissage," Lapouge (1896, 187) discusses the racial situation in several countries in the Americas, including Brazil and the United States, demonstrating the ancestry of the "great replacement theory":

> Social selection aside, Nature often disembarrasses herself. In Mexico, in Peru, the European element has been almost eliminated: the Creoles are almost like the mestizos, the mestizos are no longer different from the natives. The population of Haiti has already returned to the Negro type and to the psychology of its race, and the progress of the disease is very swift in the Lesser Antilles and in Jamaica. Brazil is following the same path and will undoubtedly constitute within a century an immense Negro state, unless it returns, which is probable, to barbarism. The situation

---

[45] Original French: "Ces crises sont accompagnées d'une forte diminution de natalité. Il arrive que des populations disparaissent, que l'extinction spontanée se produise, sans raison appréciable" (Lapouge 1896, 187).

of the Southern States of the Union is more and more worrying: the mulattos are dying out, whites and negroes [sic] are still present, the latter with a tendency to eliminate the former completely.[46]

The Brazilian author João Rodrigues de Meréje discusses the theories of Gobineau and Lapouge in his book *O problema da raça* (The Problem of Race). In a chapter entitled *Gobinismo*, he describes Lapouge's theories as Gobinism taken to the extreme and combined with Social Darwinist theories of natural selection and evolution. For Lapouge, there were two human "races" in Europe: Aryan conquerors (*homo europaeus*) and the conquered and enslaved, whom he called "Celts" or "Alpines" (*homo alpinus*). Lapouge believed that these two "races" were physically and morally distinct, and that the Aryans were always preordained to dominate the others, wherever they might be found. In contrast, the Alpines were supposedly submissive and passive, inclined towards vice and vulgarity Another characteristic that defined the "Alpines," according to Lapouge, was devotion t the family (the concept of devotion to the State was far beyond their comprehension). They were said to be lazy, but thrifty, and when they were intelligent, they accumulated more ideas than they produced (Meréje 1934, 18-19).

Gobineau and Le Bon concurred that racial mixture resulted in the decline of humanity, but Lapouge believed that, much worse, it was a factor that was harmful to the "superior race": because Aryans

---

[46] Original French: "Abstraction faite des sélections sociales, la nature se débarrasse souvent d'elle-mème. Au Mexique, au Pérou, l'élément européen este presque éliminé: les créoles ne sont plus guère que des métis, les métis ne different plus des indigènes. La population de Haïti est déjà retournée au type nègre et à la psychologie de sa race; le progrès du mal est très rapide dans les petites Antilles et à la Jamaïque. Le Brésil suit la mème voie et constituera sans doute d'ici un siècle un immense état nègre, à moins qu'il ne retourne et c'est probable, à la barbarie. La situation des Estats du Sud de l'Union est de plus en plus inquiétante: les mulâtres s'éteignent, blancs et noirs restent en présence, ces derniers avec tendance à éliminer entièrement les premiers" (Lapouge 1896, 187).

were supposedly courageous and warlike, they would have a higher mortality rate because they fought and died in wars; their religious fervour was more intense, which might induce them to embrace celibacy, thereby reducing their birth rate. Lapouge believed that the most efficient way of exterminating the "inferior" peoples was to encourage their vices, particularly lust and drunkenness. Since both Gobineau and Lapouge saw Africans as the most decadent race, this seemed to them the perfect solution to the "black problem." The two Frenchmen maintained that, by selecting human beings deemed the fittest to procreate due to their physical and moral characteristics, eugenics would have a victorious outcome for the "Aryan race" (Meréje 1934, 20-21, 24).

Louis Agassiz[47]

Jean Louis Rodolphe Agassiz (1807-1873) was a Swiss-American zoologist and geologist who studied under Georges Cuvier and Alexander von Humboldt in Paris. The German botanist Carl Friedrich Philipp von Martius chose Agassiz to take over his expedition partner Johann Baptist von Spix's research on Brazilian freshwater fish, following Spix's death in 1826. Agassiz arrived in the United States in 1846–by then a renowned naturalist–and soon delved into the controversy about the origins of the human races, rejecting Darwinism and the concept of evolution and siding with the polygenists (Hofstadter 1992, 17). Later, he embraced the theory of degeneration–that is, he believed that racial mixture led to the degradation and infertility of the races (Machado and Huber 2010, 21). Agassiz was one of the pioneers of anthropometric photography

---

[47] Several natural features around the world have been named after Agassiz, including the Agassizhorn in Switzerland, Agassiz Island in Canada, and a rock formation in Rio de Janeiro (Furnas de Agassiz). The Swiss-Haitian-Finnish artist Sasha Huber has begun a project to rename them after the enslaved people he had photographed in the US to prove the "inferiority" of Africans and their descendants (see Chapter 5). For example, the Agassizhorn should become the Rentyhorn (Sealy and Verna 2022).

in Brazil, having conducted an infamous experiment involving enslaved Africans and their descendants on a US plantation (see Chapter 5).

Agassiz led an expedition to Brazil, arriving in 1865, the year slavery was abolished at the end of the US Civil War. In his view, Brazilians saw abolition as being inevitable in their country. In the section of the book he co-authored with his wife entitled "Effect of Emancipation in the United States upon Slavery in Brazil," the zoologist (or his wife) observes that Black people were so "primitive" that freedom would be wasted on them, and their very presence was a threat to White people's quality of life:

> The negroes [sic] were continuing their dance under the glow of a bonfire. From time to time, as the dance reached its culminating point, they stirred their fire, and lighted up the wild group with its vivid blaze. The dance and the song had, like the amusements of the negroes in all lands, an endless monotonous repetition. Looking at their half-naked figures and unintelligent faces, the question arose, so constantly suggested when we come in contact with this race, "What will they do with this great gift of freedom?" The only corrective for the half doubt is to consider the Whites side by side with them: whatever one may think of the condition of slavery for the blacks, *there can be no question as to its evil effects on their masters* (Agassiz 2017, n.p., emphasis added).

Further on, in footnote no. 85, Louis Agassiz make it clear that, in his view, the worst of these "evil effects" was miscegenation:

> Let anyone who doubts the evil of this mixture of races, and is inclined, from a mistaken philanthropy, to break down all barriers between them, come to Brazil. *He cannot deny the deterioration consequent upon an amalgamation of races, more wide-spread here than in any other country in the world, and which is rapidly effacing the best qualities of the white man, the negro, and the Indian, leaving a mongrel nondescript type, deficient in*

physical and mental energy. At a time when the new social status of the negro is a subject of vital importance in our statesmanship, we should profit by the experience of a country where, though slavery exists, there is far more liberality toward the free negro than he has ever enjoyed in the United States. Let us learn the double lesson: open all the advantages of education to the negro, and give him every chance of success which culture gives to the man who knows how to use it; but respect the laws of nature, and let all our dealings with the black man tend to preserve, as far as possible, the distinctness of his national characteristics, and the integrity of our own.— L. A. (Ibid., emphasis added).

Agassiz saw the Brazilian experience as a dangerous precedent for any slavocracy:

At a time when the new social status of the negro is a subject of vital importance in our statesmanship, we should profit by the experience of a country where, though slavery exists, there is far more liberality toward the free negro than he has ever enjoyed in the United States. Let us learn the double lesson: open all the advantages of education to the negro, and give him every chance of success which culture gives to the man who knows how to use it; but respect the laws of nature, and *let all our dealings with the black man tend to preserve, as far as possible, the distinctness of his national characteristics, and the integrity of our own.*— L. A. (Ibid., emphasis added).

Thus, the polygenist sets down the principles that governed the system of racial segregation that was established in the United States after the Civil War and would persist until the first half of the twentieth century. Later, the Brazilian forensic pathologist and psychiatrist Raimundo Nina Rodrigues (1862-1906), who is considered the "father" of anthropology in Brazil,[48] would point to the success with which the Americans implemented this form of apartheid as a factor underlying the economic superiority of the United States and the inferiority of his own country. But first, he made a point of distinguishing the science that had decreed the inferiority of Black people from the "peculiar institution" which used that science to justify its own existence:

> The scientific criterion of the inferiority of the black [sic] race has nothing in common with the revolting exploitation made of it by the slave interests of the Americans. For science, this inferiority is nothing more than a phenomenon of a perfectly natural order, a product of the uneven progress of the phylogenetic development of humanity in its various divisions or sections.... (Rodrigues 2004, 19).

He goes on to reiterate his rejection of the horrors of slavery while expressing sympathy for Black people, but makes it clear that he believes their very existence condemned Brazil to inferior status in the world:

> *The black race in Brazil, however great its undeniable services to our civilization may have been, however justified the sympathies that surrounded it due to the revolting abuse of slavery, however great the generous exaggerations of its sycophants may be, must always constitute one of the factors of our inferiority as a people.* In the trilogy of the intertropical climate inhospitable to Whites,

---

[48] Manuel Querino and Nina Rodrigues have been depicted as adversaries, because their views on Africans and race were polar opposites. As we will see, in Jorge Amado's novel *Tent of Miracles* (2003) two of its main characters – Nilo Argolo (Nina) and Pedro Archanjo (Querino) – are mortal enemies. However, in his introduction to *A raça Africana e os seus costumes na Bahia* (first published in 1916), Querino observes that his study of Africans and their customs was a continuation of the studies of the "ill-fated" Nina Rodrigues – describing his own book as "merely a sketch, an attempt" (Querino 1955, 19-20).

which plagues a large part of the country; of the black, who is barely civilized; of the routine and non-progressive Portuguese, two circumstances give the second salient pre-eminence: the strong advantage against the Whites, which the tropical climate lends him, the vast proportions of the miscegenation that, *handing over the country to the mestiços, will end up depriving it, for a long time at the very least, from the supreme direction of the White race. And this was the guarantee of civilization in the United States* (Rodrigues 2004, 20-21, emphasis added).

We can see here that his pessimism regarding racial mixture–a fait accompli in Brazil—and acceptance of climatic determinism and the supposed inferiority of both Africans and Portuguese—led Nina Rodrigues to believe that America's pre-eminence was due to factors which his own country could never achieve: a society established in regions with a temperate climate which had completely eliminated (or at least markedly reduced) miscegenation between Blacks and Whites.

Herbert Spencer

The father of Social Darwinism, Herbert Spencer (1820-1903) had followers in Brazil and the United States, but, as we have seen in the case of the Gobinists, they cherry-picked the ideas that best suited them. Spencer's own view of Darwin's theory was positive: "evolution means progress" (Mainzer 1996, 333). However, in his book *As raças humanas—a responsabilidade penal no Brasil* (The Human Races–Criminal Responsibility in Brazil), Nina Rodrigues takes a pessimistic view of Spencer's theories:

What is the effect of the mixture of races on the nature of the mind, asks Spencer *(Essais scientifiques,* Paris, 1879), as one of the great problems of the comparative psychology of mankind? In the entire animal kingdom, we have reason to believe, every crossing of varieties makes them very different from each other, in the physical producing nothing that is good; on the contrary, the union between slightly different varieties gives, physically, good results. Is it the same for the mind? Judging by certain facts, the mixture of races of very dissimilar men seems to produce a worthless type of mind, which is no good for the way of life of the superior race, nor for that of the inferior race, which, in short, is not suitable for any kind of life.... (Rodrigues 1894, 92-93).

And the Brazilian medical examiner concludes that "racial mixture in Brazil confirms and exemplifies these predictions" (Rodrigues 1894, 93). Spencer also influenced one of Booker T. Washington's greatest patrons, Andrew Carnegie, who devoted an entire chapter of his autobiography to the English philosopher (Carnegie 2010, 170-174).

Raised as a Calvinist, Carnegie says he set theology and superstition aside when he discovered the works of Darwin and Spencer. Enlightened by the concept of positive evolution, he adopted the motto "all is well since all grows better." But, as his own words demonstrate, Carnegie did not dismiss theology altogether:

Humanity is an organism, inherently rejecting all that is deleterious, that is, wrong, and absorbing after trial what is beneficial, that is, right. If so disposed, the Architect of the Universe, we must assume, might have made the world and man perfect, free from evil and from pain, as angels in heaven are thought to be; but although this was not done, man has been given the power of advancement rather than of retrogression (Carnegie, 2010, 173).

According to his biographer David Nasaw, Carnegie saw Spencer as his "intellectual hero and model" (Nasaw 2006, 273), and had a passion for–even an obsession with–the author of the phrase "survival of the fittest" (Nasaw 2006, 225-226).[49] For Carnegie, the most important thing about Spencer's philosophy was not the inevitability of evolutionary progress or the triumph of industrialism

---

[49] Spencer coined the phrase and used it for the first time in his book *The Principles of Biology*, inspired by Darwin's theory of natural selection (Foner, Introduction to Hofstadter, 1992, xiv; Stucke, 2008, n. 31, 973).

over pre-industrial societies, but the fact that the advances Spencer predicted would be both moral and material (Nasaw 2006, 227).

War and citizenship

In *O colono preto como fator da civilização brasileira* (The Black Colonist as a Factor in Brazilian Civilization) and other works, Querino stressed the contribution made by Black people to the defense of Brazil and the preservation of its national integrity. During his time in the army–and he remained in the reserves–he was in an ideal position to witness the contributions of Black men, including capoeira fighters, Zuavos Baianos and volunteers who fought in the Triple Alliance War against Paraguay (1864-1870).[50] As we will see, the emphasis of this contribution to Brazilian history by Africans and their descendants is part of the tradition of Black Vindicationism and had precedents in the United States. A Black American Civil War veteran, George Washington Williams, stressed the contribution of Black people in his book *History of the Negro Race in America from 1619 to 1880*, a two volume work including, *Negroes as Slaves, as Soldiers, and as Citizens*, published in 1882, followed in 1887 by *A History of the Negro Troops in the War of Rebellion, 1861-1865 (The North's Civil War)*.

In 1894, in an essay entitled "The White Problem," which inverts the conventional focus on the "Black problem," Richard Theodore Greener, the first Black American to graduate from Harvard University, gives several examples of unknown and known Black soldiers and fighters, including (without mentioning his name), Crispus Attucks, killed during the Boston Massacre in 1770:

> He was on the Heights [sic] of Abraham with Wolfe; in the French and Indian wars with Braddock; the first martyr of the

---

[50] Proportionately, this war is considered the most destructive in the history of the modern world, having taken the lives of ninety percent of Paraguay's male population (Alix-Garcia et al. 2022, 131).

Revolution; is seen in Trumbull's picture retreating with the patriots from Bunker Hill, musket in hand; Washington did not disdain to share a blanket with him on the cold ground at Valley Forge;.... On account of the injury to the United States through him, the war of 1812 was begun, and his fertile brain suggested the defence of New Orleans....

No sneer of race, no assumption of superiority, no incrusted prejudice will ever obscure this record, much less obliterate it, and while it stands, it is the Negro's passport to every right and privilege of every other American (quoted in Sollors, Titcomb, and Underwood 1993, 44).

In both the United States and Brazil, wars fought in the same decade provided opportunities for freedom and citizenship to enslaved Black people–general emancipation in the US and individual manumission in Brazil. The US Civil War, which began in 1861 and ended in 1865, was the bloodiest conflict fought on American soil. It generated traumas and ideologies that persist to this day, mainly in the form of the Confederate flag, considered a racist and even separatist symbol, but still raised by White supremacists–even during the Capitol attack on January 6, 2021.

For many Black people who were formerly enslaved or born free, the battlefront offered a chance to prove not only their worth as upstanding citizens but their courage–giving the lie to racist stereotypes spread by the likes of Gobineau and Lapouge who, as we have seen, claimed that physical courage on the battlefield was an exclusive virtue of "Aryans," whose warlike temperament was seen as evidence of racial superiority. Over 180,000 Black men, including two sons of the abolitionist writer and statesman Frederick Douglass–formerly enslaved himself–enlisted in the 54th Regiment of the State of Massachusetts. It was made up of Black soldiers led by a White officer, Colonel Robert Gould Shaw, who died alongside them and was buried with them in a common grave.[51] The courage shown by that first Black regiment when fighting in the US Civil War led President Lincoln to order the recruitment of another 180,000 Black American soldiers.[52] Massive Black recruitment guaranteed the victory of the North, and as a result, the emancipation of enslaved Black people in the South (Hubbell, 1980). As we will see in Chapter 4, Booker T. Washington recalled the exploits of this regiment in one of the most important speeches of his career, given in 1897 on the occasion of the unveiling of the monument that portrays the colonel and his soldiers in bas relief, now one of the key exhibits in the National Gallery of Art in Washington, DC.[53]

The writer and leader Martin Robison Delany (1812-1885) helped mobilise the 54th Regiment and those in other states, becoming the first Black American to win an enlistment contract. Delany came up with the idea of forming a *corps d'Afrique* like the Zouaves, the fearsome French forces who fought against the Algerians in North Africa and wore Arab jackets, waistcoats, sashes, baggy trousers and fezzes, suggesting that from the beginning, he was thinking of ways to make Black people play a leading role in the Civil War. His idea did not come to fruition, but a similar project was successfully carried out in the northeast of Brazil, in the form of the Zuavos Baianos, who fought in the Triple Alliance War.

The need to send more soldiers to the front when volunteers were scarce led to the recruitment of Manuel Querino himself,

---

[51] The history of this regiment entered popular culture through the film *Glory* (1989), starring Matthew Broderick, Morgan Freeman and Denzel Washington. Frederick Douglass only appears in two scenes in the film, portrayed by the actor Raymond St. Jacques, but the story omits his sons' enlistment. The film is considered a pioneer in the positive portrayal of Black history in US films.

[52] Massachusetts National Guard. 54th Massachusetts Volunteer Regiment. Selected Honor Guard. https://www.massnationalguard.org/index.php/history/54th-regiment.html.

[53] The French journalist known as Th. Bentzon witnessed that speech and later wrote a lengthy review of *Up from Slavery* which was translated into Portuguese and published in a newspaper in Bahia in 1902 (see Appendix III).

probably by force. For enslaved Black people, the war was an opportunity for manumission, at the cost of enormous risk to life and limb, since—as Querino (1922, 165) observes in *A Bahia de outrora* (The Bahia of Yore)—many never returned, or came back from the front with life-changing injuries.[54] According to Kátia Mattoso (2003, 178), "numerous enslaved persons used this recourse to obtain freedom during the Paraguayan War...."

This conflict also gave them a chance to prove their courage on the battlefield and is part of the oral and sung history of the Afro-Brazilian martial art/dance capoeira. Among the capoeira songs collected by Waldeloir Rego (1968, 117), we find a reference to this conflict in song number 103: *"Eu tava na minha casa/ Sem pensá, sem maginá/ Mandaro me chamá/ Pra ajudá a vencê/ A guerra no Paraguai"* ("I was in my house/Not thinkin', not dreamin'/They had me called up/ To help win/ The war in Paraguay"). There is also a reference to "Maitá" in another song (number 37), which Rego believes to be a "corruption" of Humaitá, the Paraguayan army's main stronghold: "In view of the episodes of the war between Brazil and Paraguay, precisely at the time when capoeiras began to arrive at the height of activities, the songs always refer to *Humaitá*" (Rego 1968, 185).

In *A Bahia de outrora*, Manuel Querino observes, "During the War with Paraguay, the government of what was then the Province [of Bahia] sent a good number of capoeiras; many of their own free will and very many voluntarily conscripted. And the efforts of these defenders of the Fatherland were not in vain in the theatre of war, especially in bayonet assaults" (1922, 65). He then mentions the action of the Zuavos Baianos in the attack on Fort Curuzu and highlights the courage of two capoeiras: Cesário Álvaro da Costa, decorated with the habit of the Order of the Cross by the Emperor's

---

[54] Manuela Carneiro da Cunha (2012, 68) observes: "Manumission was a private matter in which neither the State nor the Church intervened. When the government promised to emancipate enslaved persons who fought in the Triple Alliance War, the enslavers protested vehemently."

son-in-law, the Count d'Eu, and Antonio Francisco de Mello, who was decorated and promoted from Cadet First Sergeant Assistant of the 9th Army Hunters Battalion to Adjutant of the 5th Battalion in Rio de Janeiro and later to Captain. Before noting that capoeira had been declared a crime subject to "corporal punishment and other measures related to the case" by the ordinance of October 31, 1821, Querino (1922, 65-67) observes: "I am giving these two examples to justify that capoeira has its uses on certain occasions."

Albuquerque and Fraga Filho (2006, 224) confirm that the cases Querino mentioned were not just anecdotal:

> Forced recruitment into the Army and National Guard was a way of punishing them. However, when they were introduced into the military ranks, capoeiras gained a following among the free population and created the possibility of prestige and social advancement for the Blacks who practised it. So it was not uncommon for soldiers and even senior officers in the Army and the Police itself to practise it.

As for the Zuavos Baianos, according to Hendrik Kraay (2012, 140), "Military and police authorities apparently went out of their way to maintain its racial profile...." One of the Black men who enlisted was Dom Obá II (Cândido da Fonseca Galvão). A declared monarchist, Dom Obá "stressed his service to the emperor as evidence of his belonging to the Brazilian nation" (Ibid., 122). According to Silva (1997, 38), Dom Obá "actively participated in the recruitment of volunteers for the Paraguayan War" in 1865, in his hometown of Lençóis. However, these Black companies were not formed exclusively by volunteers. For example, Kraay cites the case of an enslaved man who drowned when Zuavo soldiers tried to recruit him by force. Even so, the author found cases that "suggest a certain solidarity between Zuavos and the enslaved" (Kraay 2012, 141).

Black Vindicationism

Directly contradicting the racialist pessimism of Nina Rodrigues and most Brazilian intellectuals of his day, Manuel Querino was part of the illustrious tradition of Black Vindicationism—Black and White authors who defended Black people at the time when racialism predominated in the worlds of science, academia and politics. It began as a tactic used by supporters of the abolition of slavery–for example, in 1848, the Quaker abolitionist Wilson Armistead published *A Tribute for the Negro: Being a Vindication of the Moral, Intellectual, and Religious Capabilities of the Colored Portion of Mankind; With Particular Reference to the African Race* (1848). In addition to underscoring the virtues and skills of Black people, the book is illustrated with respectable and dignified portrayals of Africans and their descendants.

An African nationalist writer and physician of Igbo heritage, **James Africanus Beale Horton (1835-1883)**, better known as Africanus Horton, was born in Sierra Leone and attended King's College, London, and Edinburgh University, where he trained to become an army medical officer. He wrote two books refuting derogatory racialist theories about Africa and Africans. First published in 1868, his best-known work is *West African Countries and Peoples, British and Native: And a Vindication of the African Race*. Originally published in 1868, Horton's book confronted the pseudoscientific notions set forth by racialist anthropologists and other thinkers of his time, such as the German/Swiss scientist August Christoph Carl Vogt (1817-1895) and the British speech therapist James Hunt (1833-1869) (Horton 2011, 44-45).[55]

Africanus Horton criticized the French anatomist and zoologist Louis Pierre Gratiolet (1815-1865), who along with Vogt,

---

[55] Published in the *Journal of the Anthropological Society of London* in 1864. Hunt and Captain Burton, whom Horton calls the "*noli me tangere* of the African race...who, from his writings, has led everyone to believe that he has a fiendish hatred against the negro [sic]" (2011, iii), co-founded the Anthropological Society of London in 1863.

"unhesitatingly propagated the most absurd and erroneous doctrine—that of the closing of the sutures in the negro [sic] follows the simious or animal arrangement, differing from that already given as the governing condition in man" (Ibid., 44). In his article, later a brochure, entitled "On the Negro's Place in Nature, Hunt repeated and propagated the notion that "analogies are far more numerous between the Negro and apes than between the European and apes," concluding that "the Negro is inferior, intellectually, to the European" (Hunt 1864, xvi). Nevertheless, as Horton observes in his preface, despite his avowed hatred of Black people, Captain Richard F. Burton had "forgotten himself" and proclaimed their intellectual superiority in one of his works (2011, iii).

Horton supports his defence of Africans and their descendants by citing the Quaker abolitionist: "Is it not the fact, then, as remarked by Mr. Armistead, that it is only when the negroes [sic] are in possession of privileges and advantages equivalent to the rest of mankind, that a fair comparison can be drawn between one and the other" (2011, 50). Making a point that would be taken up and reiterated by Booker T. Washington and Manuel Querino, Horton also quoted the "great Clarkson" (the abolitionist leader Thomas Clarkson, 1760-1846):

> Men have presumptuously dared to wrest from their fellows the most previous of their rights, to intercept, as far as they can, the bounty and grace of the Almighty, to close the door to their intellectual progress, to shut every avenue to their moral and religious improvement... (in Horton 2011, 50-51).

A leading Black vindicationist of African descent who confronted and refuted Gobineau's theories in the homeland of the "father of scientific racism," was the Haitian intellectual **Anténor Firmin (1850-1911).** The author of *De l'egalité des races humaines* (2002)–published in Paris in 1885 as a direct challenge to *Essai sur l'inegalité des races humaines*—Firmin (2002, 450) observes that "All men are gifted with the same qualities and the same defects, without distinction of colour or anatomical shape. The races are equal." A response to pseudoscientific racism, his work uses what he called "positivist anthropology," and even suggests that miscegenation, or *métissage*, would lead to the "positive eugenics" of the human race.

Firmin cites the example of Alexandre Dumas, and rejects suggestions that being of mixed race (or mulatto) could explain the neuroses of a French author whose genius is undeniable, comparing him with Byron. Firmin also compares Dumas with the French poet and novelist Alfred de Musset who, according to the Haitian intellectual, manifested much more extreme neuroses (Firmin 2002, 205). Anténor Firmin and his work were once forgotten outside their homeland, but thanks to the efforts of American professor Carolyn Fluehr-Lobban, *De l'egalité des races humaines* has been translated into English as *The Equality of the Human Races*, first published in New York in 2000, and then in 2002 by the University of Illinois Press.

As for Brazil, the ground-breaking work of the White physician and sociologist **Manoel José Bomfim (1868-1932)**, long overlooked in his home country, recognised the contribution of Black people to the construction of Brazilian society in *A América Latina: males de origem* (Latin America: Original Ills; 2005), first published in 1903. In his lifetime, his views made an enemy of Sílvio Romero, a prominent intellectual from Bomfim's home state of Sergipe who was a fervent White supremacist and eugenicist (Gledhill 1986). Bomfim's memory has been retrieved by Ronaldo Conde Aguiar in *O rebelde esquecido* (The Forgotten Rebel), who asks:

> Why, after all, is this Manoel Bomfim not mentioned? The question comes from Vamireh Chacon, who attributed the silence that befell the Sergipe sociologist to "reactionary philistinism, and its brother, pseudo-revolutionary philistinism." Aluizio Alves Filho admitted that Manoel Bomfim's own discourse caused him to be forgotten. "Let us not fool ourselves," he observed. "Manoel Bonfim is not just a forgotten essayist; more than that: *he is part of a narrative which they seek to silence*" (2000, 509).

Silencing inconvenient narratives is one of the strategies used to maintain the hegemonic discourse—in this case, the supposed inferiority and even invisibility of Africans and their descendants in the construction of Western civilisation. In the cases of Bomfim and Firmin, this strategy was highly effective until the end of the twentieth century. When it fails, another strategy is to discredit the author of the narrative with accusations of lack of education, intellectual inferiority, poor scholarship, and even plagiarism. This was the case with Manuel Querino. As for Booker T. Washington, the trajectory of his posthumous reputation would be even worse—he went from the "most famous Black man in the world" and leader of the "Black nation" to a "Judas" and "Uncle Tom."

CHAPTER 2
SELF PORTRAITS AND "THE EYES OF OTHERS"

In this chapter, I use the autobiographies Washington commissioned from ghost writers and the biographical and autobiographical data Querino and his biographers supplied to show how the two men forged their self-images as Black role models, and how these writings formed part of their Anti-Racist strategies— demonstrating through their own life stories how Black people could "rise up" from humble beginnings through hard work and education.

This chapter also highlights another tactic Querino and Washington shared: forming alliances, partnerships, and "mentee-mentor" relationships with Whites from the intellectual and political elites.

Regarding relations with the Black community, I analyse Manuel Querino's works defending Africans and people of African descent and his (often turbulent) relationship with the Sociedade Protetora dos Desvalidos. As for Booker T. Washington, we will see how he played a double game to make it seem that he supported the "Jim Crow" system while using stratagems to defend Black people's rights, and even their lives.

When comparing the lives of Booker Taliaferro Washington and Manuel Raymundo Querino, I have sought both the similarities and differences between their life stories, realities, and trajectories. These two figures are the protagonists and subjects of this study for several reasons, including their origins and skin-colour, as well as the fact that they were contemporaries. They were both Black or mixed race, of uncertain parentage, had White mentors and allies since their youth, used similar tactics to fight similar (often identical) racialist ideologies, and were passionate advocates of education, particularly for formerly enslaved people who had been denied schooling as an instrument of seigneurial control.

However, as we saw in Chapter 1, their situations were very different. Washington was born enslaved in the US South, and emancipated as a child, in 1865, after the US Civil War. Querino was born free in northeastern Brazil, but orphaned as a child due to a cholera epidemic. He was a militant abolitionist until his country finally abolished slavery in 1888—the last in the Americas to do so.

Although Washington became the "most famous Negro in the world" (Fisher 1985 [1915], 13; Harlan 1986, 107), founded the Tuskegee Normal and Industrial Institute—now an historically Black university–and was the de facto president or "virtual monarch" of the Black nation in the United States, according to Harlan (1975b, 304). Querino was a labour leader, politician, civil servant, journalist, artist, art historian, teacher, and scholar who achieved national fame in Brazil during his lifetime. Although they followed different trajectories, both experienced a decisive time in their lives that led to an "inflection point." Querino is best known for what he did afterwards; Washington, for what he did before.

There are also strong similarities in their ways of thinking. Both men believed that education was the path to a good individual and collective future. They also valued vocational training and strove to reverse measures taken after abolition in their respective countries to deny emancipated people their rights as citizens. In short, each defended Black people and combated racism in his own way.

There is one other point in which the two men's lives converged: Querino was aware of Washington's work as an educator, and Washington was keenly aware of Brazilian politics.[56] He knew that Bahia, in particular, had a large Black population, as he attempted to find another Black American consul to represent the United States in that state as the successor to Dr Henry W. Furniss (Losch 2009). Finally, Washington and Querino were both Black thinkers in the diaspora who believed in the need to confront negative stereotypes while providing positive role models for their brothers and sisters of colour, including their own life stories as self-made men.

Booker T. Washington

The son of an enslaved Black mother named Jane[57] and a White man, Washington was born into bondage in Hales Ford, in Franklin County, Virginia. He, his mother, and his half-siblings were the chattel of the Burroughs family, who owned a farm in that county. In his autobiography *Up from Slavery*, he says he believes he was born in 1858 or 1859 but had no idea of the month or day (Washington 2000, 1). Usually, anyone researching the biography of a Black person born in the United States in the nineteenth century—particularly if they were enslaved—faces an insurmountable obstacle: the lack of baptismal, marriage, and burial records throughout most of the country. Only regions previously colonized by the French and Spanish, whose tradition of maintaining "obsessive records" was continued by their American successors, do we find such data–like

---

[56] According to Tiéde, an American magazine, *The Brazilian Review*, which was published in English in Rio de Janeiro, published a report that Booker T. Washington had endorsed a Black Brazilian congressman, although his backing was "effectively ignored" (2022, 72).

[57] Washington's autobiographies and all his biographers describe Jane as his birth mother, but his death certificate states that his biological parents were unknown. The *New York Times* obituary refers to Jane as his "stepmother." There is no doubt, however, that Washington always considered her to be his mother and loved her as a son, describing her as one of his greatest influences and role models.

the information the biographer of the *"voudou* priestess" Marie Laveau has found in New Orleans (Long 2006, xviii-xix). Unfortunately, the case of Booker T. Washington—initially given just one name, "Booker"—falls into the general rule, although thanks to probate records for the Burroughs farm, we do know his monetary value as an enslaved child—$400 (Harlan 1975b, 8). The Black educator's obituary in the *New York Times*, published on November 15, 1915, blames his mother, Jane, for this omission, observing that, during slavery, Black mothers did not have the habit of recording their children's birth dates or recalling those details for very long. Considering that it was illegal for enslaved people to learn to read and write, it would been nearly impossible for Booker T. Washington's mother to have recorded any event, no matter how important. He never knew the exact date on which he was born. He was actually two or three years older than he had thought. The date which the Tuskegee Institute adopted to mark its founder's birthday is April 5, 1856. His half-brother John found it in the Burroughs family Bible shortly after Booker's death. The book was taken to Tuskegee, where it was later destroyed in a fire (Mathews 1948, 6).

As for Booker's father, it was not uncommon in any slavocracy for White men to impregnate enslaved Black women. The child of an enslaved woman was born enslaved as well, and in the US, White fathers rarely manumitted their mixed-race children. According to his biographers Harlan and Norrell, Washington's daughter always said that her paternal grandfather was Ben Hatcher, a "drunken blacksmith" (Norrell 2009, 18). However, several other possibilities have been raised. The fact is that, if Washington knew his biological father's name, he never chose to reveal it.

Another biographer, Basil Mathews, posits that Washington's first name was derived from the Hausa word *bukar*, based on information supplied by his brother Hubert Mathews, who spent nearly twenty years in Nigeria among the Hausas. According to Hubert, Hausa mothers called their young sons "bukar," which was the equivalent of "sonny." The Hausa name was derived from the

Arab name of the first Caliph of Islam and successor of Mohammed, known as Abu-Bakr (Mathews 1948, 8).

It was a cruel irony for young Booker to be nicknamed "Book," as he was only allowed to carry books as a child:

> I had no schooling whatever while I was a slave, though I remember on several occasions I went as far as the schoolhouse door with one of my young mistresses to carry her books. The picture of several dozen boys and girls in a schoolroom engaged in study made a deep impression upon me, and I had the feeling that to get into a schoolhouse and study in this way would be about the same as getting into paradise (Washington 1986 [1901], 6-7).

His autobiographies contain examples of humiliations and privations experienced as an enslaved child, some of them "borrowed" from the experiences of his older brother, John. According to Harlan (1975b, 15): "Booker's later autobiographical writings had elements of myth and fiction that enlivened the narrative but created problems for anyone searching for the truth." Although Harlan might seek to minimize Washington's traumatic childhood, when we read the accounts of other formerly enslaved individuals, we can see that the psychological pressure on a young man like Booker must have been severe. According to Frederick Douglass, it did not matter whether he was treated well or badly when he was in bondage. The mere fact of being enslaved took any satisfaction out of life (1845, 349).[58]

The prints illustrating Washington's first autobiography, *The Story of My Life and Work* (1900) portray the Burroughs farm as if it

---

[58] Douglass managed to "self-emancipate," but after he published his first autobiography, he had to travel to England to avoid re-enslavement, as American law provided that an escaped captive could be arrested in any part of the country and returned to their enslaver. British abolitionists negotiated and paid compensation to his former master to obtain his definitive manumission.

were a plantation, where the owner was dressed like a Southern aristocrat. There was nothing aristocratic about the Burroughs family. In terms of their standard of living, education, and customs, they were more like their bondspeople. When Washington revisited the farm as an adult, he noted that even the "big house" was much smaller than he had remembered (Harlan 1978, 6).

While they were enslaved, Booker's home was a rough cabin with a dirt floor—it was also the farm's kitchen. Jane worked as a cook day and night, producing meals for the Burroughs family and their captives. According to Washington, "While the poorly built cabin caused us to suffer with cold in the winter, the heat from the open fireplace in summer was equally trying" (1986, 4). Young Booker and his siblings "slept in and on a bundle of filthy rags laid upon the dirt floor" (Ibid., 5).

In *My Larger Education*, Washington (2008, 7-8) recounts, apparently without a trace of irony, that he formed a strong relationship with the cattle and pigs on the farm when he had his breakfast–the same boiled corn that the animals ate. He says that he found it delicious. Reading between the lines of his autobiographies, which often mention food, assuaging hunger must have been a constant part of his childhood. In *Up from Slavery*, he recalls his mother, Jane, waking the children to feed them a chicken she had "found" and cooked–probably one of their few sources of protein (1986, 4-5).

One childhood memory that surely belonged to Booker himself was the sacrifice John made for him, breaking in his flax shirt until it was soft enough for his younger brother to wear. According to Washington, "I can scarcely imagine any torture, except, perhaps, the pulling of a tooth, that is equal to that caused by putting on a new flax shirt for the first time" (1986, 11). He never forgot this kindness. He and John maintained a close bond until the end of Booker's life.

Perhaps the worst trauma, which Washington did not include in *Up from Slavery* (meant for White readers),[59] but did reveal in *The Story of My Life and Work* (written for a Black readership), was the punishment suffered by his Uncle Monroe, who was tied to a tree and whipped until he begged for mercy (Washington 1900; Harlan 1975b, 16). That terrible scene "made an impression upon my boyish heart that I shall carry with me to my grave" (Washington 1900). Punishing an enslaved person in front of their family to increase their humiliation was also practised in Brazil, as the historian João José Reis describes the same policy in his biography of the African priest Domingos Sodré (2015, 59).

Washington also told stories of bondspeople who outwitted their enslavers, giving one example (possibly apocryphal, as he liked to recount such edifying tales) in a speech in Boston in 1903: a captive named Jerome S. McWade appeared one day in the red velvet waistcoat his enslaver had worn at his own wedding. McWade explained that he hadn't stolen it himself, but had bought it from the thief. His enslaver said that buying stolen goods was also a crime, but McWade retorted, "Why sir, you bought and paid for me the same as I bought and paid for that red velvet waistcoat. Well, wasn't I stolen, same as the waistcoat was? Wasn't I stolen out of Africa?" (Harlan 1975b, 16-17).

Washington's ability to wield wit and dissimulation proved valuable in his interactions with both Black and White opponents and rivals throughout his life. Today, we know that he used subterfuge and even "frontmen" and spies to promote his agenda. One of his foremost aims was achieving full freedom for Black Americans when a system of racial segregation was being

---

[59] Heather Cox Richardson (2004, 225-226) believes that it was primarily directed at Northern White readers (Washington wrote *Up from Slavery* in collaboration with the White ghost writer *Max* Bennett Thrasher. It was translated into Portuguese by Graciliano Ramos in 1940 as *Memórias de um negro* (Memories of a Black Man). *The Story of My Life and Work* was produced by a Black ghost writer, Edgar Webber.

established after the US Civil War during the period known as the "nadir," gradually revoking rights acquired at the time of Emancipation, including the right to vote and own land.

After they were emancipated in 1865, Jane took Booker and two other children, John and Amanda, on a long journey to West Virginia, where she would be reunited with Booker's and John's stepfather and Amanda's father, Washington "Wash" Ferguson. The children walked hundreds of miles, while their mother rode in a cart because her health had been damaged by life in bondage. When they arrived, Ferguson put Booker and John to work in a salt factory and a coal mine to help support the family.

Like many people recently freed from bondage, Washington was hungry to learn. In *Up from Slavery*, he stressed that

> From the time that I can remember having any thoughts about anything, I recall that I had an intense longing to learn to read. I determined, when quite a small child, that, if I accomplished nothing else in life, I would in some way get enough education to enable me to read common books and newspapers (1986, 27).

With his mother's support, Booker overcame his stepfather's opposition and went to school. There, he found that his classmates all had a first and last name. Instead of adopting Wash Ferguson's surname, he took his first name instead, which, of course was also the surname of the "founding father" of the United States. In *Up from Slavery*, however, he merely says the idea came to him during roll call (1986, 34). He later discovered that his mother considered their surname to be Taliaferro, so he took it as his middle name. According to Washington:

> In some way a feeling got among the colored people that it was far from proper for them to bear the surname of their former owners, and a great many of them took other surnames. This was one of the first signs of freedom....so in many cases "John

Hatcher" was changed to "John S. Lincoln" or "John S. Sherman," the initial "S" standing for no name... (1986, 23-24).

It is interesting—perhaps a Freudian slip—that Washington used the example of "Hatcher" as the discarded surname of a former enslaver because, according to his daughter, Portia, that was the name of his mutually disowned biological father.

In any case, without a birth certificate, bearing names he had chosen himself, he was "rising up" from slavery and building his own identity. He had taken the first step on the path towards becoming a self-made man. The historian Heather Cox Richardson observes:

> Using his own extraordinary journey from slavery to international prominence as a symbol for Black Americans in general, the erudite and crafty "Wizard of Tuskegee" appropriated the Northern worker myth and made it central again to the Black American experience. He painted his own life as the ideal of what Northerners had hoped would happen to freedpeople after the war. In a sense, *Up from Slavery* was a black person's version of Horatio Alger's *Ragged Dick* (2004, 225).

In the words of one of his most sympathetic biographers, "Washington personified the power of a man to educate himself" (Norrell 2009, 3), but that does not mean he did it alone. Thanks, once again, to his mother, Jane, he found a job as a domestic servant in the home of Viola Ruffner, a former governess. The Yankee wife of a Southern general, she had never abandoned the Calvinist values of her Northern culture.

Chapter three of *Up from Slavery* is entitled "The Struggle for an Education." In the course of that struggle, two women were his greatest influences: first Jane, then Viola. According to Norrell, "Jane was the figure most responsible for shaping her son's character" (2009, 21). While enslaved, she had stolen food for her children, "But once freed, she enforced a strict code of honesty in all things. She instilled the virtues of hard work and thrift...." (Ibid.). Washington told this story in *Up from Slavery* and *The Story of My Life and Work*, in which he declares,

> ...the lessons in virtue and thrift which she instilled into me during the short period of my life that she lived will never leave me. Some people blame the Negro for not being more honest, as judged by the Anglo-Saxon's standard of honesty; but I can recall many times when, after all was dark and still, in the late hours of the night, when her children had been without sufficient food during the day, my mother would awaken us, and we would find that she had gotten from somewhere something in the way of eggs or chickens and had cooked them during the night for us. These eggs and chickens were gotten without my master's permission or knowledge. Perhaps, by some code of ethics, this would be classed as stealing, but deep down in my heart I can never decide that my mother, under such circumstances, was guilty of theft. Had she acted thus as a free woman she would have been a thief, but not so, in my opinion, as a slave. After our freedom no one was stricter than my mother in teaching and observing the highest rules of integrity (Washington 1900).

This justification was very important to Washington, because one of the racist stereotypes he most vehemently rejected and fought was dishonesty.

As for his first employer, "Viola Ruffner instilled in Booker the essence of...the Protestant ethic, which taught that the values of industry, sobriety, thrift, self-reliance, and piety accounted for success in modern capitalist societies" (Norrell 2009, 26-27). According to a short story by Dorothy Canfield Fisher entitled "The Washed Window," which gives a detailed description of her teaching methods–apparently following Washington's own account–Viola Ruffner, née Knapp, was the daughter of a carpenter from Arlington, Vermont. The short story claims that she was ostracized by Whites for teaching Black students in the South (Fisher 1955). However, other biographies of Viola Ruffner give an entirely different version of her life, and make no mention of her specifically teaching Black students. Nevertheless, there is no doubt that Booker T. Washington felt that he had learned valuable lessons from her, and considered her a friend.[60]

Washington's autobiographies and biographies also describe his struggle to reach the Hamilton Institute in Virginia in 1872, after a long trek by boat, train, cart and on foot, going hungry and sleeping under an elevated plank sidewalk in Richmond (Harlan 1975b, 53-54). He was accepted and hired as a janitor at the institute to pay for his studies because he impressed another Yankee woman, Mary F. Mackie, with the meticulous cleaning methods he learned from Viola Ruffner (Mathews 1948, 45). In Washington's words, "The sweeping of that room was my college examination, and never did any youth pass an examination for entrance into Harvard or Yale that gave him more genuine satisfaction" (Washington 1986, 53). He graduated in 1875 and spent a year at the Weyland Seminary in Washington, DC (from 1878 to 1879). After leaving that institution, Washington returned to Hampton, where he spent two years as a teacher and as a "house father" for Native American students.

General Armstrong

One of Booker T. Washington's greatest influences was General Samuel Chapman Armstrong (1839-1893), the founder and principal of the Hamilton Institute. He was also Washington's mentor, teacher, and "great white father" (Harlan 1975b, 58). According to Harlan:

> Not only in a Freudian but in a literal sense, General Armstrong became the illegitimate mulatto boy's father, the "most significant other," his paternal protector, fosterer, and guide not only during

---

[60] For example, see a letter from Washington to Ruffner. Washington, Booker T., "Correspondence from Booker T. Washington to Viola Ruffner - September 18, 1901." Ruffner Family History Records. 71. https://digitalcommons.longwood.edu/ruffnerfamily_records/71

his school days but for the rest of his life. And when Washington later became Hampton's most distinguished graduate, the bond strengthened between the younger man and his teacher. Washington came to model his career, his school, his social outlook, and the very cut of his clothes on Armstrong's example (Ibid.).

Samuel Chapman Armstrong was born in Hawaii in 1839. His father was a Presbyterian missionary who was also the Hawaiian minister of education, and his mother, a former schoolteacher who had taught at a Pestalozzian infant school in Brooklyn after graduating from the Westfield Normal School in Massachusetts.

Armstrong attended Williams College, which Harlan describes as putting greater emphasis on character building than academic achievement (Ibid., 59). During the US Civil War, Armstrong rose to the rank of general at the head of the 9th United States Colored Troops (USCT), made up of formerly enslaved Black Americans (Ibid.; Engs 1999, 46; Mathews 1948, 46). Like the 54th Massachusetts Infantry Regiment led by Col. Robert Gould Shaw, in the USCT, White officers led Black soldiers. According to one of his biographers, Armstrong's decision to join a Black regiment was motivated more by missionary than military sentiments (Engs 1999, 46-48). They fought in the Peninsular Campaign of 1864 to 1865 and the Battle of Petersburg, where Confederate General Robert E. Lee was defeated (Harlan, 1975b, 59).

While he was in command of the USCT, Armstrong set up a school for the Black soldiers in his regiment, most of whom were formerly enslaved and had been barred from any kind of formal education. After the war, he worked at the Freedmen's Bureau and established the Hampton Normal and Agricultural Institute in Hampton, Virginia in 1868.

Armstrong had a relatively positive view of Black people for his time, believing that the "children of the tropics"—equating Africans with the Indigenous peoples of Hawaii—were more "backward" than "inferior" (Harlan 1975b, 60-61). For Harlan, the general was a

"Christian soldier"—"a convergence of several forces that had caused the Yankee spirit to prevail in nineteenth-century America: missionary parentage, the Williams College influence, the regimen of the soldier" (Ibid., 58). According to Booker T. Washington's biographer, "Armstrong would not discourage a bright young dark man from higher education and higher aspirations, but believed that the whole black race should abstain from politics and civil rights agitation until industrial education had done its work" (Ibid., 61).

At General Armstrong's recommendation, Washington was engaged to set up a normal and industrial school for Black people in Alabama in 1881. With the help of his students and wealthy donors, Washington built the Tuskegee Institute on a former plantation where they had to make their own bricks to build the walls. Aided by the students' hard work and donors' financial contributions, the institute grew until it comprised over eighty buildings.

Washington devoted nearly all his time to fundraising for Tuskegee. For many years, without these constant efforts, the institution could have failed at any moment. When its principal stopped travelling for three months to care for his dying wife, Olivia, he was obliged to ask General Armstrong for a loan (Harlan 1975b, 155-156).

In *Up from Slavery*, Washington expresses strong admiration for Armstrong—what the general's biographer describes as "fawning celebration" (Engs 1999, xi)—calling him "a great man, the noblest, rarest human being that it has ever been my privilege to meet" (Washington 1986, 54). Coming from someone who had met many distinguished figures in Europe and the United States, this is high praise indeed. The two men formed a strong bond that only ended with the death of the general who, according to Washington, spent two of the last six months of his life at his former student's home at the Tuskegee Institute (Washington 2000, 37-38).

Washington contributed a lengthy essay on his "great white father" to a biography of Armstrong by the general's daughter Edith Armstrong Talbot (1904, 206-210). Transcribed in full in Appendix V, it defends Armstrong (and Washington himself) against the charge of providing vocational training to Blacks with a view to relegating them to a "caste" of manual labourers. As Talbot observes:

> Many Southerners no doubt acquiesced in the idea of industrial education for Negroes, because they thought that to keep them artisans, mechanics and farmers was to keep them in a class by themselves, and a class separated from their own by a lack of culture and of common social meeting-ground. It was no wonder that the colored race distrusted Armstrong's scheme of combined labor and learning and that they sought the advantages of Hampton for many years more because of the intellectual than the manual training afforded there (1904, 210).

Andrew Carnegie

Tuskegee's many buildings included a library named after its patron, the Scottish-born industrialist and naturalized American, Andrew Carnegie. According to David Nasaw, "Carnegie, given to hero worship, spoke of Booker T. Washington with the same reverence he used when referring to William Gladstone, Matthew Arnold, Abraham Lincoln, and Herbert Spencer" (2006, 714). Despite having a relatively "advanced" view of Blacks, Carnegie preferred to invest in vocational and teacher training institutions like Tuskegee and Hampton instead of funding Black universities like Fisk or Atlanta (during the age of segregation, which only ended in the 1960s, these were the only universities which accepted Black students in the US South). In 1900, Carnegie donated $20,000 for the construction of the library that bears his name.[61] He visited the institute in 1906 to personally verify that the library had been built by the students

---

[61] In his autobiography, Carnegie also mentions a bequest of $600,000 to Tuskegee and Washington's request that instead of setting aside part of that fund for himself and his wife, the trustees should be responsible for disbursing "suitable provision" for their needs. For Carnegie, "This is an indication of the character of the leader of his race. No truer, more self-sacrificing hero ever lived: a man compounded of all the virtues" (2022, 154).

themselves, brick by brick. He was so impressed that he called Washington "one of the geniuses of the century" (Ibid.). In his autobiography, Carnegie gave this description of his relationship with Tuskegee and its principal:

> My connection with Hampton and Tuskegee Institutes, which promote the elevation of the colored race we formerly kept in slavery, has been a source of satisfaction and pleasure, and to know Booker Washington is a rare privilege. We should all take our hats off to the man who not only raised himself from slavery, but helped raise millions of his race to a higher stage of civilization (2022, 154).

Southern White supremacists were enraged by Carnegie's faith in the ability of Black people to "lift themselves up" and evolve-the philanthropist even declared that the "lowest" Black person in the South was more advanced than his own Scottish ancestors 200 years earlier (Watson, 1916, 30; Nasaw, 2006, 715). However, Carnegie preferred to emphasize the progress and "fitness" of the "Negro," and his positive view of the situation of Black Americans in the South. In the early twentieth century, he overlooked lynchings, sharecropping, peonage, segregation, and the political sidelining of Blacks. For Carnegie, the "problem of the Negro in America" had been solved by the end of slavery, and the fact that the material resources of the South grew faster after emancipation was "empirical evidence" of this (Nasaw 2006, 274 and 715).

Carnegie saw Washington as the "combined Moses and Joshua of his people" and an "educational genius," as both men believed in the importance of vocational education—Carnegie perhaps more than Washington, as the educator also believed in the value of training teachers and multiplying the number of schools available to the Black community. Carnegie invited Washington to his home in New York City several times, introducing him to his friends and helping arrange his tour of Great Britain in 1910, including a stay in Skibo, Carnegie's castle in Scotland (Nasaw 2006, 714-715).

Washington's patrons also included many other famous names, Black and White. One of Tuskegee's most eminent Black donors was Sarah Breedlove, better known as the businesswoman Madam C. J. Walker, who funded scholarships for the institute (Bundles 2020). After a long and complex interaction with the "Wizard," Walker became his admirer towards the end of his life. When Washington died, she declared that he was "The greatest man America ever knew"—a statement which Norell considered "extravagant" (2009, 421).

Besides Carnegie, Washington's White patrons included George Eastman, the founder of Eastman Kodak, who donated $5,000 to Tuskegee after reading *Up from Slavery*, and even invited its principal to dine at his home, although "he never advocated racial integration" (Kramer 2012).[62] Other White donors, including John D. Rockefeller, Jr., stayed the night in Washington's home at Tuskegee in a region where the punishment for such temerity would inevitably be lynching–of the Black host, and possibly his White guest–were it not for the protection of the Tuskegee campus.

Julius Rosenwald

A less familiar name among the most important figures in Tuskegee's history is Julius Rosenwald, the head and co-owner of Sears, Roebuck. After reading *Up from Slavery* and a biography of William H. Baldwin, Jr., the president of the Southern Railway, Rosenwald began taking an interest in Black education—a good part of Baldwin's biography is devoted to his work as a Tuskegee board member and his relationship with Washington. Rosenwald's admiration for Baldwin was increased by the fact that he had

---

[62] According to a Black History Month essay by David Kramer (2012), "In 1892, along with President Benjamin Harrison and Frederick Douglass, Washington was invited to the dedication of Kodak Park." The fact that Washington dined at Eastman's home in the early twentieth century was kept secret by both men and only discovered sixty-five years later. Kramer viewed Washington's acceptance of Eastman's invitation to dine with him and a group of Britons as an act of courage.

convinced Andrew Carnegie to donate $600,000 to the institute (Ascoli 2006, 87; Deutsch 2011, 89). Rosenwald's first step was to sponsor Black YMCAs. The Jewish businessman met Washington face to face for the first time on May 18, 1911, at an event marking the YMCA's 53rd anniversary in Chicago, where the Black educator gave the opening address. Rosenwald accepted Washington's invitation to visit Tuskegee, where he spent four days in October of that year and was highly impressed, comparing it favourably to industrial schools for Whites. A month later, Washington wrote to former President Theodore Roosevelt, who was also on the institute's board, to inform him that Rosenwald, "the Jew who has recently given so much money for YMCA work among colored people in the cities," had agreed to become a trustee, observing that "I think he is one of the strongest men we have ever gotten on our Board" (Deutsch 2011, 107).

On at least one occasion, Rosenwald hosted Washington in his Chicago home for several days. In addition to serving on the board of trustees and supporting the institute with financial and material contributions, including large shipments of remaindered or damaged shoes, Rosenwald also helped support other Black schools in the US South. A demonstration of Rosenwald's trust in Washington was that any request for support that the businessman received from Black schools had to go through the educator first (Ascoli 2006, 87-92). The Booker T. Washington Papers collection in the Documents Division of the US Library of Congress contains several letters exchanged between Washington and Rosenwald regarding requests of this nature. It also contains letters confirming receipt of shipments of shoes from Sears, Roebuck, and explaining how the principal of Tuskegee intended to distribute them to students so they would be most appreciated: sold for a token price rather than simply given away.

Booker vs. the "Talented Tenth"

W. E. B. Du Bois and other Black intellectuals who considered themselves the "Talented Tenth," criticised Tuskegee's curriculum because it lacked the traditional disciplines of a liberal education, such as Greek and Latin. At the time, knowledge of those languages and classical literature were considered the hallmark of a truly cultured individual. According to Kenneth Goings and Eugene O'Connor:

> The study of Greek and Latin expressed the determination by Black Americans to pursue a liberal arts, classically oriented education, one to which they felt they had both an inherent and historic right. If classical civilization had "humanised" Europeans (as was claimed by the White majority), then it had certainly humanized Africans, and therefore they were entitled to the same rights and privileges as their White fellow citizens (2010, 523).

In *Up from Slavery*, Washington observes that after emancipation in the United States, most formerly enslaved persons saw education as a way of escaping manual labour and finding an easy way to make a living as teachers or preachers (Washington 1986, 81, 128).[63] In his view, freedpersons believed that learning Greek or Latin "would make one a very superior human being, something bordering almost on the supernatural" (Ibid., 81) that "entitled them to special distinction" (Ibid., 122). He observed that many of the teachers could barely sign their own names. In one case, he remembers a teacher who, when asked if the world was flat or round, replied that that depended on the preference of most of his students, whom he called his "patrons" (Ibid., 81).

Washington saw vocational education as a way of developing his students' character, observing in the chapter on the Reconstruction that, at a school he visited in Washington, DC, the students

> knew more about Latin and Greek when they left school, but they seemed to know less about life and its conditions as they would

---

[63] It should be noted that Washington briefly attended the Wayland Seminary in Washington, DC, before deciding his vocation lay in teaching.

meet it at their homes. Having lived for a number of years in the midst of comfortable surroundings, they were not as much inclined as the Hampton students to go into the country districts of the South, where there was little of comfort, to take up work for our people, and they were more inclined to yield to the temptation to become hotel waiters and Pullman-car porters as their life-work (Washington 1986, 88).

In another chapter, Washington notes that he found a young man studying French grammar amid squalid surroundings: he was wearing grease-stained clothes and lived in a filthy one-room cabin with a garden and yard full of weeds (Ibid., 122). Washington believed that leading a dignified, hard-working life was more important than learning subjects that had no immediate benefit for the student. In his view, Black freedpersons should first take care of their clothes, their homes, and their gardens, in short, their own dignity and quality of life.

Washington had always championed Black people's access to a liberal education, but the Tuskegee Institute emphasized theory and practice within a rural context. For example, when students studied mathematics, they based their calculations on the realities of the farm. They started out by learning to sleep in a bed with sheets, eat with a knife and fork, brush their teeth, in short, everything that the principal of Tuskegee himself had to learn when he entered the Hampton Institute. This approach can be compared with the educational model of Rural Family Houses, introduced in France in the 1930s and today reproduced in various parts of Brazil, including the lower south of the state of Bahia. It should be recalled that emancipation in the United States resulted in the sudden influx of more than four million freedpersons into the free labour market, almost all of whom were illiterate, and many without a trade. Not to mention the pressures of attempts at re-enslavement (through peonage), revocation of civil rights, segregation, and racist violence that they would face in the decades following Reconstruction. For

Washington, the approach he adopted was the best way to lay the foundations of a future Black middle class:

> Though I was but little more than a youth during the period of Reconstruction, I had the feeling that mistakes were being made, and that things could not remain in the condition that they were in then very long. I felt that the Reconstruction policy, so far as it related to my race, was in a large measure on a false foundation, was artificial and forced. In many cases, it seemed to me that the ignorance of my race was being used as a tool with which to help White men into office, and that there was an element in the North which wanted to punish the Southern White men by forcing the Negro into positions over the heads of the Southern Whites. I felt that the Negro would be the one to suffer for this in the end. Besides, the general political agitation drew the attention of our people away from the more fundamental matters of perfecting themselves in the industries at their doors and in securing property.
>
> The temptations to enter political life were so alluring that I came very near yielding to them at one time, but I was kept from doing so by the feeling that I would be helping in a more substantial way by assisting in laying the foundation of the race through a generous education of the hand, head, and heart (1986, 84).

Washington was not just training farmers and carpenters, but mainly teachers who would establish other vocational and normal schools—the "Little Tuskegees" that formed part of his sphere of influence, which his enemies and some biographers dubbed the "Tuskegee Machine." It also included several Black organizations and institutions, particularly the National Negro Business League. In addition to the Tuskegee Institute, which is now a historically Black university, the creation of the National Negro Business League in 1900 was one of Washington's greatest legacies. It provided Black businesspeople an alternative to chambers of commerce then restricted to Whites, enabling them to further commercial, agriculture, educational and economic development for Black people (Wormser 2002). It was reincorporated in Washington, DC, in 1966 with the racially neutral name of the "National Business League."

Washington preferred to employ tactics (as well as strategies, as his power and influence grew) that Smock compares to the tales of Uncle Remus and the "trickster" Bre'r Rabbit, who tricks his tormentor, Bre'r Fox by begging him do anything, even roast him alive, but not to throw him into the briar patch. In fact, the briar patch was Bre'r Rabbit's comfort zone and shelter. In a chapter entitled "Inside the Briar Patch," Smock cites a remarkable episode that occurred in 1895, when Washington apparently failed to help a Black man named Tom Harris, who had "crossed the colour line" by consorting with a White minister, and enraged a mob of Whites who were determined to murder him. His leg shattered by a bullet, Harris sought refuge at Tuskegee, but when the masked men with torches arrived at Washington's door, their quarry was gone. Washington "told just enough of the truth to quiet the passions of the mob," saying that he had sent Harris away (Smock, 2009, 142). This earned him praise for his "prudent and conservative" conduct from the *Tuskegee News*, but raised concerns in the Black community. Many years later, it was discovered that Washington later explained in a letter to the Black minister Francis Grimké that he had sent the wounded man off-campus to protect the Institute's students from "the fury of some drunken white men," but arranged for him to hide before sending him to Montgomery for medical treatment and paying for it himself (Smock 2009, 142-143). As Washington said and would repeat many times, he saw this strategy of dissimulation as the only way to confront the "special challenges" facing Black people in the South (Smock 2009, 143). Ida B. Wells "openly chastised Washington for his failure to publicly denounce lynching" in the 1880s and 1890s (Dagbovie 2007, 242).

Booker T. Washington gained nationwide fame in the US when he gave a speech at the Atlanta Exposition in 1895, in which he declared that Blacks and Whites would live separately, but work together: "In all things that are purely social we can be as separate as the fingers, yet one as the hand in all things essential to mutual progress" (Washington 1986, 221-222). This speech was later called the "Atlanta Compromise" by his detractors. While her father was speaking, Washington's daughter, Portia, saw "a mob of rednecks formed up beside the stage waiting to set upon my Pa if he had said but one word against the South" (quoted in Stewart 1977, 28). Instead, by the end, the White supremacists were "wildly applauding and slapping their thighs" (Stewart 1977, 28).

It was not just "redneck" violence that Washington had to face. The response from Black American colleagues would be harsh and unforgiving–and the tenor of that speech would be associated with Washington for the rest of his life, and posterity.[64] Nevertheless, he received a note from a future nemesis, W. E. B. Du Bois, dated September 24 of that year, written in Wilberforce, Ohio. It is worth quoting in full: "My Dear Mr Washington, Let me heartily congratulate you upon your phenomenal success in Atlanta–it was a word fitly spoken."[65]

Washington invited Du Bois to join the faculty at Tuskegee, but after some reflection, the younger man decided to go to Atlanta University instead. Later, Du Bois would criticize Washington because, for most of his life, he preferred to avoid confrontations with Whites and was accused of "accommodation."[66] According to Du

---

[64] As recently as the Netflix series "Self Made," inspired by the life of Madam C. J. Walker (2020), Washington is shown giving a similar speech to a profoundly sceptical Black audience.

[65] This note can be found among the *Booker T. Washington Papers*.

[66] Du Bois was one of the founders of the NAACP, and at first he was the only Black person on the board. All the other directors were White (that is, they self-identified as such). According to Norrell (2009, 390): "Through the [magazine] *Crisis*, Du Bois gained broad influence on the thinking of Black Americans. Otherwise, the NAACP was largely a White-run organization into the 1920s." Its founders included Blacks and Whites, Christians and Jews, men and women, among them Ida B. Wells, the Black activist and writer who led a campaign against lynching and harshly criticized Washington's "accommodation" strategy. However, the list of the first

Bois (2019, 56), "His programme of industrial education, conciliation of the South, and submission and silence as to civil and political rights, was not wholly original.... But Mr. Washington first indissolubly linked these things...."[67] David G. Du Bois (1999b, 317) wrote that his father believed Washington's philosophy of self-sufficiency removed the burden of responsibility from Whites regarding the future of Blacks they had enslaved, and placed it directly on the shoulders of the freedpersons. Du Bois argued that the "Talented Tenth," an elite group of Black intellectuals born in the North–of which he was a member–should lead the mass of people recently emerged from slavery.

Like Du Bois, most of the "Talented Tenth" were born free and descended from persons who had been emancipated from slavery two or three generations before. Many were mixed-race or "mulattos," and, like Washington, rejected the notion that their "White blood" made them in any way superior to Blacks with "pure African blood." In the chapter of *My Larger Education* entitled "What I Have Learned from Black Men" (Washington 2008), Booker T. Washington made a point of listing the names and brief biographies of men of "pure African extraction," including Major R. R. Moton,[68] George W. Clinton, Bishop of the African Methodist Episcopal Zion Church, and one of the most distinguished figures in the history of agricultural science, George Washington Carver (1864-1943), who

---

directors contains the name of just one Black person, Dr Du Bois, as director of publicity and research (NAACP 2009, 16).

[67] One of Du Bois's best-known works, *The Souls of Black Folk*, originally published 1903, contains a chapter entitled "Of Mr. Booker T. Washington and Others," one of his harshest critiques of his rival (Du Bois, 1999a).

[68] In the case of Robert Russa Moton, Washington's successor at the helm of the Tuskegee Institute, the "purity" of his African DNA was not based on his appearance alone. According to Washington, Moton traced his African ancestry through an unbroken lineage on both sides of his family, including a great-grandfather who was said to have been an African chief and trader who was tricked into boarding a slave ship by Whites, and enslaved along with the prisoners of war he had just sold them (Washington 2008).

lived and taught at Tuskegee from 1896 until the end of his life (Kremer 2011).

Dinner at the White House

Washington consolidated his fame among Blacks and Whites around the world with the publication of *Up from Slavery* in 1901. That same year, he was invited to dine at the White House with Theodore Roosevelt, then the President of the United States. Inspired by the White supremacist press in the South, many denounced this "audacity," and as a result, both Washington and Roosevelt received death threats. News of this episode went around the world and inspired both an infamous anonymous poem entitled "N*****s in the White House," published in American newspapers between 1901 and 1903, and the opera *A Guest of Honor*, by the Black composer Scott Joplin (he registered the copyright in 1903, but did not include a copy of the score, which has since been lost).

In the chapter of *My Larger Education* entitled "Colonel Roosevelt and What I have Learned from Him," Washington discussed "a matter which I have hitherto constantly refused to discuss in print or in public, though I have had a great many requests to do so" (2008, 73-74). In that book, originally published in 1911, he observes that "it seems to me that an explanation will show the incident in its true light and in its proper proportions" (Ibid, 74). When visiting a friend in Washington DC, he

> ...found an invitation from President Roosevelt asking me to dine with him at the White House that evening at eight o'clock. At the hour appointed I went to the White House and dined with the President and members of his family and a gentleman from Colorado. After dinner, we talked at considerable length concerning plans about the South which the President had in mind. I left the White House almost immediately and took a train the same night for New York. When I reached New York the next morning I noticed that the *New York Tribune* had about two lines stating that I had dined with the President the previous night....

Within a few hours the whole incident completely passed from my mind....

My surprise can be imagined when, two or three days afterward, the whole press, North and South, was filled with dispatches and editorials relating to my dinner with the President....

Some newspapers attempted to weave into this incident a deliberate and well planned scheme on the part of President Roosevelt to lead the way in bringing about the social intermingling of the two races. I am sure that nothing was farther from the President's mind than this; certainly it was not in my mind. Mr. Roosevelt simply found that he could spare the time best during and after the dinner hour for the discussion of the matters which both of us were interested in (Washington 2008, 74).

In this account, Washington omits one aspect of the dinner that most incensed Southern White supremacists–the presence of Roosevelt's wife and one of his daughters at the table[69]–and stressed his culinary encounters with other eminent White people:

The public interest aroused by this Dinner seemed all the more extraordinary and uncalled for because, on previous occasions, I had taken tea with Queen Victoria at Windsor Castle; I had dined with the governors of nearly every state in the North; I had dined in the same room with President McKinley at Chicago at the Peace Jubilee Dinner; and I had dined with ex-President Harrison in Paris, and with many other prominent public men (Washington 2008, 74).

In Harlan's analysis (1975b, 324) dining at the White House was "the culmination of his [Washington's] struggle 'up from slavery'...."

---

[69] A member of the War Department later claimed that it was just an informal lunch with "a sandwich balanced on the knee" (Harlan 1975b, 322).

It silenced his main Black critics. "The college-bred professional men...who had always looked down a little on Washington's humbler manner and course, found it hard now to argue with success (Harlan 1975b, 305). For a long time, the mere fact of sharing a meal at the White House "was the final crown of success that secured his position as virtual monarch of the black people in the United States" (Ibid, 304). Once again according to Harlan, whose objectivity will be analysed in the next chapter,

> Washington's rise was spurred by his own intense, faustian [sic] ambition, but equally important at every juncture of his career was the help of a succession of fatherly white men, General Ruffner, General Armstrong, William H. Baldwin, Jr., Theodore Roosevelt. To these men, White racists all, though relatively mild and benevolent in their racism, Washington became inordinately attached. They strongly influenced his life and also to some extent his thought and attitudes (Ibid., 324).

Now on the lookout for any further behaviour of this kind, White supremacists would again be scandalized by the alleged proximity between Washington and the daughter of White businessman Sam Wanamaker at a dinner in 1905—a false rumour spread by William Randolph Hearst's newspapers which we would now call "disinformation." However, Washington was more concerned by reports in William Monroe Trotter's *Guardian* newspaper "condemning him for associating with wealthy Whites" (Norrell 2009, 326-328).

From another perspective, when Washington followed his strategy of forming partnerships with White allies—wealthy patrons and powerful politicians—he could only choose between "relatively mild and benevolent" racists and those who believed in lynching as an instrument of control, rejected Black education as a useless effort, and would not even allow Washington to enter through the back door.

Theodore Roosevelt

We know from his biographies and analyses of his racial thinking that Theodore Roosevelt was a "neo-Lamarckian" when it came to race—believing in the theory of evolution through the inheritance of acquired characteristics—but his reading included the works of the most radical racial determinists, from Madison Grant and Houston Stewart Chamberlain to the French theorist Jean Finot, whose unusual approach to the subject argued that "the concept of race really had little meaning, that racial terminology often proved empty and vague, and that much of race theory was little better than myth" (Dyer 1980, 13-14). Over time, his greatest intellectual guides were the Lamarckian sociologist Edward Alsworth Ross and the palaeontologist Henry Fairfield Osborn, director of the Museum of Natural History in New York (Ibid., 14).

Based on his own experience with the "Rough Riders" in Cuba during the 1898 war with Spain, Roosevelt had developed a less than favourable opinion of Black people's military abilities shortly before becoming vice president of the United States in 1901 (he became president after the assassination of his predecessor, William McKinley, in September of that year). Even so, before he became president, Roosevelt had apparently renewed his belief in "gradual black improvability" (Dyer 1980, 101). While convinced that, in general, Blacks were inferior to Whites, he allowed that there were some exceptions, such as Booker T. Washington, and thought that those exceptional men were the only ones to merit full citizenship (Ibid., 109).

Largely, the development of Roosevelt's racialist thinking and practice was influenced by politics. During his second term, especially after that dinner with Washington undermined his political backing among White supremacists (particularly in the South), Roosevelt was much less supportive of the Black community's interests. He believed in the need for social controls over Blacks, and his position came to the fore in Texas during the "Brownsville Affray" in 1906, when he took a stance that would trigger a crisis in his relationship with Washington and the beginning of the end of the

Black leader's prestige. The soldiers of the town's Black regiment were falsely accused of taking part in a riot, killing a bartender, and injuring a policeman (charges that were quashed many years later, when it was proved that they did not even leave the barracks). When Roosevelt decided to punish them with a dishonourable discharge, without the right to a pension, Washington suffered the public humiliation of unsuccessfully trying to convince him to back down (Harlan 1983, 309-311).

Tuskegee in Africa

The influence of Washington and the Tuskegee Institute reached as far as Africa. In 1900, following an agreement with a delegation of Germans who had visited the institute the previous year, three graduates and a teacher from that institution travelled to Togo, then a German colony, to oversee the development of cotton growing in that country. Others followed later, making a total of nine Tuskegee representatives in Africa. They faced numerous difficulties, such as a lack of draft animals, which had to be replaced by human labour, and four of them died of tropical diseases. One of the travellers, John Winfrey Robinson, remained in Togo and established an agricultural school in Notsé which trained 200 Togolese. However, he, too, died in 1909 and the enterprise perished soon after (Norrell, 2009, 201-201; Zimmerman, 2010, 7-8).[70]

---

[70] Robinson learned the Ewe language and was assimilated into the local culture to the point of marrying two Togolese women in a polygamous union, one in Tove, the site of the experimental farm, and the other in Notsé. He also had an American wife, who presumably met her African co-wives (Zimmerman 2010, 146). The Germans' aim was to introduce cotton growing, which would be a profitable business for the colonists while subordinating Indigenous Africans in the same way that Black people were subjugated in the cotton fields of the US South. Robinson asserted that he stood for more than cotton, and that that crop should only be introduced when it served to enrich the people. If yams and maize brought them more profits, those crops should not be replaced. He also wanted to maintain and improve trade on the coast, but the colonists prevailed. The experimental

Although he agreed to work with the German colonizers in Togo, Washington rejected an invitation to visit Leopold II of Belgium due to the brutal regime established in the Belgian Congo, and protested its inhumanity when reports of forced labour and police violence reached the United States in 1904 (Norrell 2009, 203).

In 1907, the Americans living in Liberia asked Washington to negotiate an intervention from the US government to relieve the tensions that were threatening to explode into civil war between the Americo-Liberian settlers and Indigenous peoples. Washington placed his secretary, Emmett J. Scott, at the head of a commission to investigate the situation, which recommended making Libera a US protectorate, like Puerto Rico. The American government did exactly that. Washington advised the Americo-Liberians to treat Indigenous Africans more sensitively and build a more productive and self-sufficient economy. He also got a sponsor to fund scholarships for "tribal" and American-born Liberians to study at Tuskegee (Norrell 2009, 375; Rosenberg, 1985). The Booker Washington Agronomic and Industrial Institute (now the Booker Washington Institute) was established in Liberia in 1929.

His larger influence

At least two US presidents consulted Washington, who advised them on several matters regarding the Black community in the United States. This included recommending Black men for important roles. Sometimes, his own prestige made him less effective. For example, correspondence found in the Booker T. Washington Papers shows that he made a major effort to replace the US consul in the Brazilian state of Bahia, the Black physician Henry Watson Furniss, who had held that post from 1898 to 1905, with another diplomat of the same race (Losch 2009, 239). One of the candidates was the son of an enslaved woman from Bahia who had been kidnapped and taken to the United States. However, Washington was unsuccessful, because

---

cotton farm was established in an area destroyed by the German military, in the ruins of the region's traditional pottery industry (Ibid., 135-136).

the Black candidates believed he had the power to get them a better posting. In the end, Furniss was replaced by a White career diplomat, Albert Morawetz (Ibid., 239 note 64).

Although he only had a secondary education, Washington received honorary degrees from two eminent US universities: a master's from Harvard in 1896 (Norrell 2009, 148) and a doctorate from Dartmouth in 1901 (Rauner Library 2022). Washington gives considerable emphasis to his honorary master's degree in *Up from Slavery*. According to him, when he received the letter informing that he would receive the degree from Harvard:

> This was a recognition that had never in the slightest manner entered into my mind, and it was hard for me to realize that I was to be honoured by a degree from the oldest and most renowned university in America. As I sat upon my veranda, with this letter in my hand, tears came into my eyes. My whole former life–my life as a slave on the plantation, my work in the coal-mine, the times when I was without food and clothing, when I made my bed under a sidewalk, my struggles for an education, the trying days I had had at Tuskegee, days when I did not know where to turn for a dollar to continue the work there, the ostracism and sometimes oppression of my race–all this passed before me and nearly overcame me (Washington 1986, 296).

He came to be considered the "Black president" and successor of Frederick Douglass, which generated resentments and rivalries within his own "nation." For example, there were attempts to sabotage his lectures, mainly the Boston "Riot" of 1903, orchestrated by a Black intellectual, William Monroe Trotter, the founder of the Boston *Guardian* to disrupt one of Washington's speeches (Rudwick 1963, 16).[71] The "Wizard of Tuskegee"[72] responded aggressively to

---

[71] Born in the North, from a wealthy family (Du Bois 1995, 135), Trotter had been a colleague and friend of W. E. B. Du Bois since their student days at Harvard. Trotter joined forces with Du Bois in 1905 to organize the Niagara Movement, the

Trotter's declaration of total war. According to his biographer and defender Robert J. Norrell, Washington dealt with his Black enemies "with fierce cunning. Both sides got down into the mire, and all would inevitably get up bruised and dirty, with Booker's reputation damaged once and for all" (2009, 284). He used every possible means—including manipulation of the press, spies, and bribes—to sabotage his adversaries, White and Black.

In *My Larger Education* (1911), Washington devotes a chapter to this episode, entitled "The Intellectuals and the Boston Mob," in which he gives his opinion on the Black elite (who, according to him, had fallen out with each other to the point of not speaking): "They know books but they do not know men. They know a great deal the slavery controversy, for example, but they know almost nothing about the Negro. Especially are they ignorant in regard to the actual needs of the masses of the colored people in the South today" (Washington, 2008). He expresses confidence in his fellow Black people, due to "their willingness (and even eagerness) to learn and their disposition to help themselves and depend upon themselves as soon as they have learned how to do so" (Ibid.).

Washington hired a White Harvard graduate, **Robert Ezra Park (1864-1944)** as his publicist, ghost writer, and later director of public relations for Tuskegee, between 1905 and 1914 (American Sociology Association). Park would go on to found the Chicago School of Sociology and became the mentor and supervisor of the

---

forerunner of the NAACP, to combat segregation, the disenfranchisement of Black people, and Booker T. Washington's "policy of compromise and conciliation" (Lewis 1993, 97).

[72] Washington's opponents called him "the Wizard of Tuskegee," or simply "the Wizard," in a reference to the Wizard of Oz— the terrifying, all-powerful figure who, in the end of Frank L. Baum's novel, published in 1900, is revealed to be a fraud, a despicable little man hiding behind a curtain. The subtitle of the second volume of Harlan's biography is *The Wizard of Tuskegee*. In his biography of Du Bois, David Levering Lewis frequently refers to Washington as "the Wizard" (Lewis 1993, 265, 306, 309), including the title of chapter 15, "Rise of *The Crisis*, Decline of the Wizard."

anthropologist Donald Pierson, the author of *Negroes in Brazil* (1942). Park also had an interest in Brazil, having visited Bahia in 1937 (Valladares 2010).

During his seven-year collaboration with Washington, Park produced three of his employer's most important titles: *The Story of the Negro* (1909), *My Larger Education* (1911) and *The Man Farthest Down: A Record of Observation and Study in Europe* (1912). He also ghost-wrote Washington's article "Cruelty in the Congo Country," published in *The Outlook* on October 8, 1904 (Harlan and Smock 1979, 85-90) and his biography of Frederick Douglass published in 1907 (Washington 2009), among others.

While Tuskegee was a haven for eminent Black Americans like George Washington Carver, Washington maintained a policy of never allowing White staff and teachers to live full-time at Tuskegee, so Park lived and worked off campus. According to the editors of the *Booker T. Washington Papers*, Washington did not want the institute's success to be attributed to Whites. He wanted to make it a model of self-help for Blacks (Harlan and Smock 1979, 454, note 1).

The power of the "Wizard" was severely weakened when the riots that erupted in the cities of Atlanta and Brownsville, in August and September of 1906, showed that his strategy of combating racism by producing a dignified, sober, hard-working Black middle class, in short, people who embodied all the values of the Protestant ethic, had failed. It did not staunch the hysteria incited by Atlanta newspapers, which stirred up a wave of violence with sensationalist headlines reporting crimes, alleged and true, committed by Blacks against Whites (mainly allegations of rape and assaults on White women). The violence in Atlanta did not spare the businesses of wealthy Blacks, who were forced to close their doors and leave the city (Harlan 1983, 295-296).

The Brownsville Affray arose from a misunderstanding. Shocked by the tragic events in Atlanta, residents of that Black township mistook a group of White police officers for a lynch mob and fired at them, setting off a wave of violence that resulted in the deaths of Blacks and Whites. As we have seen, members of a Black regiment were unjustly accused of taking part in the "riot," and President Teddy Roosevelt dishonourably discharged the soldiers despite Washington's best efforts (Harlan 1986, 309-311) According to Luker (1998, 256):

> Reports of lynchings, peonage, and disenfranchisement, coinciding with the Atlanta and Brownsville riots in August and September 1906, threatened Booker T. Washington's powerful hold on black allies and his influence with white racial liberals. Brownsville strained his close alliance with AME Bishop Abraham Grant and destroyed his friendship with T. Thomas Fortune... Washington lost control of the Afro-American Council in 1907, but black radicals were unable to capitalize on his weakened position..... There was no comparable revolt among white radical activists, but the events raised doubt about Washington's wisdom in race relations.

To make matters worse, in 1911, Washington suffered a very personal humiliation–he was nearly lynched in New York City. He needed sixteen stitches for the wound on his head, but was arrested and denied medical attention until he could prove that he really was the famous Dr Washington. The leader of the mob that attacked him, the White janitor Albert Ulrich, was tried and acquitted of assault, having claimed that Washington addressed his "wife" as "sweetheart."[73] The Black leader vehemently denied this, and considered it the worst accusation of all (the others included attempted burglary and voyeurism). In fact, the woman in question was Ulrich's mistress–he had a wife and children in New Jersey. At least, Washington had the meagre satisfaction of seeing him convicted of abandoning his family. But the humiliations continued after the verdict, exacerbated by the press and his enemies, White and Black. They questioned his explanation for being in a White

---

[73] As in the case of Emmett Till, the "justification" for lynching could be based on a far lesser "offense," such as allegedly whistling at a White woman.

residential area on a Sunday, not far from New York's notorious Tenderloin district. Washington claimed that he had received a letter from his secretary and future biographer, Emmett J. Scott, asking him to see his accountant at that address. Scott confirmed his story, but the letter was never found (strange for a person who even filed notes on scraps of paper, forming the vast collection that would become the *Booker T. Washington Papers*) and the accountant said that he knew nothing of an appointment scheduled at that address. Washington's enemies speculated that he was looking for a White prostitute. His biographers postulate the possibility of a lover, also White, due to the address. We will never know for sure, but the "Ulrich Affair" dealt a heavy blow to Washington's once-pristine moral reputation. Even the hotel which had been his "home from home" in New York declared him persona non grata.

Relations between Washington and the NAACP had already deteriorated to a level that included harsh criticism by two directors of that association, John E. Milholland and Du Bois, of Washington's optimistic lecture on the situation of Black people in the South, given in London in 1910.[74] These attacks were followed by allegations of racial fraternization in the mainstream press, and a lawsuit filed against an NAACP founder, all instigated by Washington and the "Tuskegee Machine."

After his rival was assaulted in New York City, Oswald Garrison Villard issued an official statement from the NAACP regretting this clear evidence of racial discrimination while rejecting Washington's version of events (Norrell 2008, 400).[75] According to Harlan, Villard

---

[74] Black activist and writer William Pickens, a member and future director of the NAACP, also appears to have signed a protest against the London lecture, since the Booker T. Washington Papers contains a personal letter from Washington addressed to Pickens requesting a list of items from the lecture which he opposed (Harlan and Smock, 1981a, 471).

[75] Villard was a grandson of the White abolitionist William Lloyd Garrison. Born in Germany to Helen Frances ("Fanny") Garrison and a German father, Henry Villard, he became a director of the NAACP and tried to replace Washington and Du Bois as leader of the Black race.

saw this egregious episode and its negative impact on Washington's power as an opportunity to overcome the differences between the "Wizard" and his Black opponents, and induce Washington to join the NAACP (1983, 391-392). That hope was never fulfilled.

Towards the end of his life, Booker T. Washington dropped the "mask" and took an open and aggressive stance against Black disenfranchisement, lynching, and "Jim Crow" segregation. He never explained this change in strategy. In August 1908, he wrote a letter "as a protest against the 'lynch law' in the South" that was published nationwide (Drinker 1915, 141-144). Three years later, not even his status as the famous Dr Washington–could spare him from the violence which all members of his race might suffer at any time at the hands of Whites in the United States, under the flimsiest pretexts, with near impunity.

In a posthumous article entitled "My View of Segregation Laws," Washington summed up his position on "Jim Crow" as follows:

...segregation is ill-advised because 1. It is unjust; 2. It invites other unjust measures; 3. It will not be productive of good, because practically every thoughtful negro resents its injustice and doubts its sincerity. Any race adjustment based on injustice finally defeats itself. The Civil War is the best illustration of what results where it is attempted to make wrong right or seem to be right. 4. It is unnecessary; 5. It is inconsistent. The negro is segregated from his neighbor, but White business men are not prevented doing business in negro neighborhoods; 6. There has been no case of segregation of negroes in the United States that has not widened the breach between the two races. Wherever a form of segregation exists it will be found that it has been administered in such a way as to embitter the negro and harm more or less the moral fiber of the White man. That the negro does not express this constant sense of wrong is no proof that be does not feel it (Washington 1915, 114).

Booker T. Washington was married three times. He had a daughter, best known as Portia Pittman, with his first wife, Fannie Smith Washington, and two sons, Booker T. Washington Jr. (known as "Baker") and Ernest Davidson Washington, with his second wife, Olivia Davidson Washington. He and his third wife, Margaret Murray Washington, also adopted Margaret's orphaned niece, Laura. All his wives were closely linked with Tuskegee. Washington always tried to shield his family life from the scrutiny of the media. His biographers have been unable to find personal letters he exchanged with any of his spouses, which must have existed because he was constantly travelling throughout the country to raise money for Tuskegee and spread his vision of race relations in the United States. Although he was accused of wanting to keep Blacks from getting a higher education, he sent his children to top universities. They did not achieve the academic success he must have hoped for, although Portia became an accomplished pianist. The press revelled in their failures, as did Washington's old enemy William Trotter.[76]

When Portia dropped out of Wellesley, Washington sent her to Germany, where she studied piano with a private tutor, Martin Krause, a former pupil of Franz Liszt (Stewart 1977, 62). On her way to Berlin, Portia met the Black British composer Samuel Coleridge-Taylor, who had come to admire her father, although he had initially taken against him after reading Du Bois's scathing critique of the "Wizard" in *The Souls of Black Folk* (Ibid., 57-60).

According to Norrell (2009, 417), "there was something compulsive about Booker Washington's lifestyle, especially his need to travel across the United States to preach his gospel of racial progress and to raise money for the Tuskegee Institute." Washington's health could not withstand the stress of incessant

---

[76] According to her biography by Ruth Ann Stewart, "Portia had a particular reason to dislike Trotter as he had published the fact that she had flunked out of Wellesley.... [She] sought any ammunition available to counteract adverse publicity against her father and to settle the score with Trotter for herself" (1977, 49).

travel and worry. When he came down with his final illness, and doctors in New York had given up hope of curing him, he insisted on being transferred to Tuskegee. Two days later, on November 14, 1915, he died of kidney failure due to diabetes.[77] When one of his New York doctors, Dr Bastedo, announced to the press that "Racial characteristics are, I think, in part responsible for Dr Washington's breakdown," this was interpreted to mean that his patient had syphilis (Ibid., 418-419; Harlan 1983, 451-452).[78]

The funeral, held three days later, brought thousands of people to the chapel at the Tuskegee Institute, where Washington's body lay in state. At the time of his death, he owned at least two houses, one on Long Island, in New York State, and the other on the Tuskegee campus, designed by the Black architect Robert Taylor in the "Queen Anne" style and built in 1889.[79] Despite being worthy of a statesman, the funeral rites were kept simple, without long-winded eulogies—just a long queue of teachers, graduates, students, and visitors passing by the coffin to pay their last respects (Norrell 2009, 420).

In accordance with his wishes, Washington was buried in the small cemetery on the institute's campus, next to the chapel. He had wanted a modest tombstone that only showed his name and the

---

[77] Norell attributes his kidney failure to high blood pressure (2009, 418).

[78] A report to Julius Rosenwald states that Washington's personal physician, Dr George C. Hall, who was in Chicago when his patient fell ill, "was much put out because of the 'racial characteristics' statement as applied to the case mentioned and credited to Dr Bastedo.... That expression, Dr Hall says, means a 'syphilitic history' when referring to Colored people and he declares a doctor making such a diagnosis in this case isn't the right kind to treat this patient" (Harlan 1983, 452).

[79] The first Black person to graduate from the Massachusetts Institute of Technology (MIT) and the first university-educated Black American architect in his country, Robert R. Taylor (1868-1942) designed several buildings at Tuskegee, where he also was also on the faculty, and oversaw the institute's facilities, property and infrastructure (Weiss, 2012, xv). He joined the Executive Council as early as 1906 (Williams 1998). The university campus, including the homes of Booker T. Washington – known as "The Oaks" – and George Washington Carver, was listed by the US Congress in 1965, and the homes were renovated by the US National Park Service in that same year (National Park Service,1966).

years of his birth and death, but instead, his resting place was marked with a "granite boulder as big as the rock of ages." According to his unfailingly caustic biographer Louis R. Harlan, it dominates the cemetery "as [Washington] had dominated the others buried there during their lives." And Harlan cannot resist some final jibes: he observes that, "ironically," pickpockets appeared among the crowd at the railway station, and that after the funeral, a teacher at the institute who had previously suffered a nervous breakdown "jumped to her death from a high window on the campus" (Harlan 1983, 456-457). Nevertheless, Harlan–much less Norell–could not fail to mention the profound emotions of the elderly Black men and women who went on foot to Booker T. Washington's funeral, coming from afar to see him one last time (Harlan 1983, 456; Norrell 2009, 420).

Manuel Querino

Born in the town of Santo Amaro da Purificação in the Recôncavo region of Bahia, most likely on July 28, 1851, Manuel Raymundo Querino was believed to be the son of a carpenter, José Joaquim dos Santos Querino, and his wife, Luzia da Rocha Pita. However, a handwritten note on his death certificate states that he was the "illegitimate son of Maria Adalgisa," which raises questions about the identity of his biological father. Based on physical similarities in their portraits, it is possible that his father was in fact his White guardian, Manuel Correia Garcia (1815-1890), who is known to have been married twice, and to have had seven children, of whom five survived (Querino 2001, 34).

The biographical essay by José Teixeira Barros (1922, iv-v), published in all editions of one of Querino's best-known works, *A Bahia de outrora* (Bahia of Yore), simply states that he was born "in a humble, but hard-working, and honourable home" and that "while still a child and an orphan," he was handed over to his guardian by the Orphans' Court in the provincial capital, Salvador. Teixeira Barros does not specify the date. All we know about José Joaquim dos Santos Querino and Luzia da Rocha Pita is that they were free

Blacks–their status was crucially important, as slavery would only be abolished in Brazil decades later–who may have died during the cholera epidemic that scourged the region in 1855 and 1856 (Calmon 1980; Cooper, 1986). The Black population–most of which was enslaved–was inordinately affected by the disease. According to Donald B. Cooper:

> No class or race escaped the ravages of cholera completely, but black people paid by far the highest tribute to the disease. It seems that no less than two-thirds of the victims of cholera in Brazil were black. It was a nineteenth-century, South American holocaust, a new 'black death' that ranks as Brazil's greatest and most dramatic demographic disaster(1986, 486).

All told, approximately 25,000 people lost their lives in the entire province of Bahia (Tavares 2001, 273). A relatively large town and the biggest sugar production hub in the province, Santo Amaro was one of the hardest hit. Querino was lucky to survive. It was his first brush with death.

Manuel Correia Garcia

Querino's guardian, Manuel Correia Garcia, had a profound influence on his ward's life and interests. According to J. Teixeira Barros (1922, v):

> A man educated in Europe and dedicated to teaching, he sought to awaken the love of work and study in his ward's spirit, and Manuel Querino began devoting to the cultivation of his intelligence the moments of leisure afforded by his efforts to learn the art that later would later ensure him the means of subsistence.

In a speech he gave when a portrait of Querino was unveiled in the gallery of honour of the Instituto Geográfica e Histórico da Bahia (IGHB) in 1928, Antonio Vianna described Correia Garcia as "an enlightened spirit, educated in Europe, cultivator of letters and lover of teaching things." A retired teacher, politician, journalist, and lawyer, he was provincial deputy for the Liberal Party, practiced Spiritism,[80] and held a PhD from the University of Tübingen in Germany. Sent by the provincial government to study at the Normal School in Paris, along with the future director of the Normal School of Bahia, João Alves Portela, he returned to the city of Salvador to organize a teacher training school and the entire primary education system in the province in 1842. He was also the main founder of the Instituto Histórico da Bahia (Historical Institute of Bahia), in 1855 or 1856 (Calmon 1980).

According to a biographical essay penned by Manuel Querino himself in 1896 (see Appendix V), Manuel Correia Garcia was born in Salvador on August 15, 1815, the legitimate son of a "Portuguese merchant of the same name" and Leonor Joaquina de Abreu. Garcia's father died when he was three (Querino 2001, 33). An interesting point in the narrative, which occupies an entire paragraph, is Querino's observation that "[Garcia's] mastery of the language that Racine had so enriched" was so great that the "three wise men" in the committee of the French institute where he and a colleague were due to take an entrance exam not only exempted him from taking the test but his colleague as well—he had not appeared before the committee because he had been ill—and both were enrolled in the Normal School in Paris (Querino 2001, 33). It is therefore probably no coincidence that Querino also learned French and used that language in his scholarly works.[81]

According to Vianna, Correia Garcia "Sought to guide his ward into intellectual work and managed to instil in him a passion for

---

[80] Correia Garcia was a "disciple" of the Spiritist leader Luís Olímpio Teles de Menezes (Wantuil 2002). Kardecist Spiritism is still widely followed in Brazil.

[81] Another figure who may have been a role model and influence, in this and other senses, was João da Veiga Murici. A nineteenth-century Black intellectual and activist, he taught Greek, Latin, Portuguese, and French. One of Querino's last publications was an essay on Veiga Murici's life (Querino 2009, 220).

Self Portraits and "The Eyes of Others"

study, the love of books that would accompany him to the grave" (1928, 306). Even so, the only future he foresaw for the young man was as a craftsman—specifically a painter and decorator—so "He also gave him a practical way of making a living, sending him to learn the art of painting" (Ibid.). However, the aspirations nurtured in the environment of culture and study he experienced in his guardian's home drove Querino much further: he would follow Correia Garcia's example, not only in teaching but in politics and historical and anthropological research. In an unsigned manuscript intended as a eulogy after Querino's death, the writer emphasizes that Querino was mainly responsible for pursuing secondary and higher education: "It was an illustrious and patriotic man, Dr Correa Garcia, who guided the first steps of his education, which was rudimentary. The rest, he did by himself."[82]

What was Querino's experience like during his training as a painter and decorator? In his autobiographical entry in *Artistas baianos* (Bahian Artists), he merely states that he studied at the Liceu de Artes e Ofícios (School of Arts and Crafts) where he learned the "basics," and at Vinte e Cinco de Março College (Querino, 1911, 146). But the Liceu was established in 1872, and he was already a professional painter and decorator before he became a founding student of that institution, so his apprenticeship must have started much earlier. We know that, in nineteenth-century Bahia, the training of artisans, including those whom Querino called artists, still followed the lines practiced in Portugal since the Middle Ages. Apprentices learned their trades in the workshops of master craftsmen. The usual limit was two apprentices per teacher, "aimed at learning efficiency," but "there was non-compliance with the regulations or ordinances regarding the number of apprentices in the workshops of the masters. It was common to have apprentices in the workshops of artisans who were not master craftsmen, so there

---

[82] "Mensagem sobre falecimento." Archives of the Instituto Geográfico e Histórico da Bahia. BHA04D.053. Quoted in full in Chapter 3.

was a break in the hierarchy, which in Bahia must not have been very strict" (Freire 2006, 70-71).

In 1868, by then a "grown man" of about seventeen, Querino decided to seek his fortune in the neighbouring province of Pernambuco and travelled there in the company of a nephew of Manuel Correia Garcia. The Triple Alliance formed by Brazil, Argentina, and Uruguay had declared war on Paraguay in 1865. It may be that the young men left Bahia to avoid the press gangs that Querino (1955, 195) describes in the chapter of *A Bahia de outrora* entitled "Recruitment" as the reason why "the streets were deserted, and the troubadours fell silent." Later, Querino went on to another neighbouring province, Piauí, but the winds of war took him South. He was "recruited" in the backlands, possibly by force, and sent to Rio de Janeiro for military training. According to Vianna (1928, 306), "For the young artist from Bahia, the first phase of his public life began." Afterwards, he would have been sent to the front, like thousands of other conscripts and volunteers, many of whom died or returned in the sad levies of "maimed invalids, recounting the incidents, exhaustion, and deprivations they had experienced" (Querino 1955, 193). Fortunately, his intelligence and education, particularly his ability to read and write—rare skills at a time when about 85 percent of the free population was illiterate—and possibly his frail physique, spared him from certain death. Instead of going on to the front, he remained in Rio to work in his battalion's clerical division, and was promoted to corporal in March 1870. When the war ended that same year, he was demobilized in October through the influence of his chief political patron, Sousa Dantas (Vianna 1928, 306), a political ally of Correia Garcia in the Liberal Party.

Manuel Pinto de Sousa Dantas

In the chapter on "Political Workers" in *As artes na Bahia* (The Arts in Bahia), Querino (1913, 159) describes Dantas as "a spirit destined for politics; gentle and happy, he knew perfectly well how to stir up opinions in struggles at the podium and in the press; he possessed the dizzying intoxication of the noisy and brilliant fame of agitators."

Dantas was born on a plantation in Inhambupe, in the semi-arid Agreste region of Bahia, on February 29, 1831. He was the first cousin of Cícero Dantas Martins, the Baron of Jeremoabo, a member of the Conservative Party, who would later become his political enemy (Sampaio 2001, 93). Sousa Dantas graduated from the Olinda Law School in 1851. He was the municipal Orphans' Court judge in Santo Amaro, from 1853 to 1856, and held the positions of interim attorney of the treasury, Orphans' Court judge and public prosecutor in Salvador between 1857 and 1858.[83]

Although he belonged to the Liberal Party, Dantas's own political patron was the leader of the Conservative Party, the Baron of Cotegipe, João Maurício Wanderley. In Salvador, Dantas acquired the *Diário da Bahia* newspaper in 1868. In 1876, at a time when his party was struggling against the hegemonic grip of the Conservative Party, he founded the Sociedade Liga Operária Baiana (Bahian Workers' League Society) in the *Diário da Bahia*'s main meeting room, and became the first president of that association (Leal 2009, 228). According to Leal (2009, 231), the league "would play the role of educating through work, with a view to promoting the enlightenment of the working class involved, associated with collective efforts, intelligent and enduring, to achieve the common good, 'characteristic of free peoples.'" As we will see, Manuel Querino also played an important role in the Liga Operária Baiana.

In *As artes na Bahia*, Querino (1913, 160) stresses the part which Dantas played "in introducing workers to politics as an element of power, fighting for an ideal with a view to making the vote of that category count." And he goes on to say:

> We owe him the founding of the Liceu, the School of Fine Arts, and subsidies and protection given to the Liga Operária. Not the Liberals; they were against the founding of the school of arts and crafts in 1864; [and] strongly opposed the first subsidy of the

---

[83] The main source for these biographical details on Dantas is Grinberg (2002).

School of Fine Arts, except for the president of the provincial assembly, Dr Cesar Zama, who favoured the concession (Querino 1913, 160-161).

After a political career as a deputy in the General Assembly, Dantas held various positions in the Executive branch. In 1883, he was summoned by Emperor Pedro II to chair his cabinet of ministers, equivalent to being appointed prime minister,[84] and seek a solution to the problem of slavery. That quest resulted in several proposals produced by the abolitionist Ruy Barbosa. Known as the Dantas Bill (1884), it would gradually free the enslaved population in five ways: "the age of the slave; due to failure to register; through the emancipation fund; for violation of the slave's legal domicile" (Menezes 2009, 92). The bill, which also called for the emancipation of enslaved people over the age of 60, was harshly criticised because it did not include compensation for the enslavers (Cruz 2022, 79; Mendonça 2008, 30). This controversy led to the downfall of the Dantas cabinet and the dissolution of the legislature (a bad omen for the emperor). When Dantas died in Rio de Janeiro nearly a decade later, on January 29, 1894, Querino lost his most powerful patron.

Leal observes that the time Querino spent in Rio, then the Imperial capital of Brazil, may have influenced him politically, as "he certainly had access to liberal ideas imported from Europe, to the experience of the Americas and to the troubled clashes in the parliament of the Brazilian Empire" (2009, 213). Querino was still in the capital in 1870, the year the Republican Party was founded.

Having returned to Bahia in 1871, Querino resumed working as a painter and decorator while studying at night. He learned French and polished his native Portuguese at Colégio 25 de Março. Later, at the Liceu, he studied the humanities. There, he took French and Portuguese exams, passing "with distinction" in the language of

---

[84] As chairman of the council of ministers, Sousa Dantas became known as "Conselheiro Dantas," which is still the name of streets in Brazil to this day, including Salvador.

Racine and receiving "full marks" in Portuguese (Vianna 1928, 307). When his teacher and mentor, the Spanish artist Miguel Navarro y Cañizares–also a friend of Manuel Correia Garcia–left the Liceu and founded the Academy (later School) of Fine Art, Querino followed him. He was hired as a painter while the future art school was being built, and also went on to become a founding student of that institution (Silva 2005, 233).

Miguel Navarro y Cañizares

Born in Valencia, Spain on September 29, 1832, Cañizares married Geltrudes Guidi, and had two daughters, named Emília and Matilde (Silva 2008, 251). He began his artistic training at the Real Academia de Bellas Artes de San Carlos in Valencia between the ages of 11 and 24 (1845-1858). He also attended the Real Academia de Bellas Artes de San Fernando in Madrid, where his teacher was the Spanish painter Federico de Madrazo y Küntz (1815-1894). In 1864, Cañizares won a prize that enabled him to study in Rome. He was awarded the Cross of the Order of Isabella the Catholic on December 2, 1867. While in Rome, he was commissioned by the Archbishop of Caracas, Silvestre Guevara y Lira, to paint the cathedral of the Venezuelan capital, but by the time he arrived there in early 1872, the cleric had been exiled by General Antonio Guzmán Blanco. Despite that setback, Cañizares remained in Caracas, where he painted a portrait of the general on horseback. He even "sent guidelines for the founding of a School of Fine Arts in that country" to the Minister for Development. He probably decided to leave Venezuela due to political upheavals during Guzmán Blanco's dictatorship (Silva 2008, 272).

After his experience in that turbulent part of South America, Cañizares spent nearly two years in New York City. It was from there that he set off for Brazil, arriving in Salvador aboard the steamer *John Bramall* on April 4, 1876. He originally intended to settle down in Rio de Janeiro, "where he believed excellent opportunities awaited for him to demonstrate his talent as a portraitist, painter of allegories, and religious subjects for the good local clientele," but he stayed in Salvador because Rio was beset by an epidemic of yellow fever (Silva 2008, 277).[85]

According to Viviane Rummler da Silva (2008, 251-273), we do not know if Cañizares's connection with the Imperial Liceu de Artes e Ofícios arose through his own initiative or whether he was invited to teach there. In addition to Querino, his students included Manuel Silvestre Lopes Rodrigues (1859-1917), Carlos da Costa Carvalho, Enedino de Santana, Tito Weindinger Batista and Vieira de Campos, "disciples who soon stood out in the local arts scene, achieving renown and acclaim in accordance with the credits given by the director of the Liceu" (Silva 2008, 277). Querino himself observes (1911, 119) that "In a session of the directorate of the Liceu de Artes...a letter from Professor Cañizares was read, offering to teach the higher education course in drawing at that establishment, whose classes began on the 28th of [that same] month."

In his first year at Liceu, Cañizares fell out with the directors and José Antonio da Cunha Couto, a Bahian painter. According to Querino (1911, 119): "Things were moving along as usual, when changes in a portrait of Emperor Pedro II ordered by the directors of the Liceu resulted in Professor Cañizares' departure in early December 1877." The Spanish artist founded the Academy of Fine Art that same year (Silva 2008, 279).

According to the Academy's Book of Minutes of 1881, Cañizares proposed that everyone who could prove they were impoverished should be admitted free of charge. Rummler da Silva observes: "Therefore, is believed that even amid [financial] difficulties, the Academy has always served the general community, especially the less privileged classes..." (2008, 226-227).

---

[85] In *Artistas baianos* Manuel Querino observes that: "In February 1876, Professor Cañizares, born in Valencia, Spain took shelter in this city, having received news that yellow fever was rampant in Rio de Janeiro, where he was bound. He settled on Estrada Nova, now Dr Seabra Street, and there he gave a small exhibition of his paintings that caught the attention of the public that appreciates artistic beauty" (1911, 118-119).

However, after just five years in Bahia, Cañizares quarrelled with the directors of what had become the School of Fine Art, and decided to leave the province altogether. Querino observed:

Bahia owes a debt to Professor Cañizares for the invaluable service of having advantageously revived the teaching of drawing. During his stay in this capital, he produced several works, mainly portraits.... Due to a lack of intelligence within the School's congregation, Professor Cañizares left for Rio de Janeiro, where he has resided since 1881 (1911, 123-124).

His successor as president was also well known to Querino—the historian Brás Hermenegildo do Amaral (Querino 1911, 125).[86] However, Querino quotes a conversation overheard in the Quinta dos Lázaros cemetery between two "prominent characters" from the School of Fine Arts, lamenting that after the death of Professor Lopes Rodrigues and in the absence of Cañizares, "the School [had fallen] into decline" (Ibid).

In Rio de Janeiro, where the Spanish artist settled in 1882 (not 1881, the year given by Querino), Cañizares sought the patronage of the emperor whose commissioned portrait had led to his departure from the Liceu (Silva 2008, 279). Cañizares received a gold medal for his participation in the 1st Centenary Exhibition marking the Opening of the Ports of Brazil to Friendly Nations, held in 1908. After a long and productive sojourn in that city, he died in the Imperial capital on October 24, 1913, and was buried in São João Batista Cemetery (Ibid., 257).

---

[86] Brás do Amaral was a fellow member of the Instituto Geográfico e Histórico da Bahia, and his name can be found on lists of books by Querino distributed free of charge—*Artistas baianos* and *O colono preto como fator da civilização brasileira* (IGHB Archives cx.023D.018 and cx.01D.011, respectively). [87] A scanned copy of that CV is available online at: http://www.scribd.com/doc/138235645/Curriculo-de-Manuel-Querino-em-seu-proprio-punho. It is no longer housed in the IGHB archives.

Manuel Querino stayed on at the School of Fine Art and graduated in 1882 with a teaching certificate in geometric drawing. That same year, he became a jury member for the academy's exhibition. He then enrolled in the architecture course. He passed the second year with distinction, but, according to Antonio Vianna (1928, 307), "he was not awarded a degree because one of the third-year subjects was not taught." In his third-person autobiographical entry in *Artistas baianos*, Querino gives a more detailed explanation: "...he did not take the third-year exam due to the lack of [lecturers] to teach the subject of resistance of materials and stability of constructions. Due to this circumstance, he did not receive a degree in architecture. He also attended classes in the anatomy of human body shapes, aesthetics and art history, plaster copying, and oil painting" (1911, 147).

On the title page of his textbook *Elementos de desenho geométrico* (Elements of Geometric Design, 1911), Querino is described as a "graduated artist, awarded two silver medals, honourable mention, approved with distinction in the course of architecture at the School of Fine Arts." In a curriculum vitae written in his own hand, Querino identifies himself once again as a "graduated artist, approved with distinction in Architecture."[87] Since the last title in the bibliography of that résumé is *O colono preto*, we can deduce that it was written after 1918. All indications are that, instead of highlighting the setback of missing out on a degree in architecture, he decided to emphasize his title of prize-winning artist (or designer) with an undergraduate degree. However, the following excerpt shows that Querino was aware of the status he had lost when he gave up on the dream of being a "doctor":

> Social customs, diverting the callings of youth with the blind pursuit of a diploma, stifled, in turn, the taste for art, making it

---

[87] A scanned copy of that CV is available online at: http://www.scribd.com/doc/138235645/Curriculo-de-Manuel-Querino-em-seu-proprio-punho. It is no longer housed in the IGHB archives.

increasingly incompatible with industry, which caused its decline, for which the artists themselves bear great responsibility, due to the vanity of only wanting to have children who are doctors, as if there were a privileged class to make the individual notable (Querino 1913, 23).

It may be a case of "sour grapes," but his stance may also explain why he was content with a teaching certificate. A qualified teacher, he taught at the Colégio de Órfãos de São Joaquim (São Joaquim Orphans' College) and the Liceu, where he was appointed a teacher of geometric drawing in 1885 and received his certificate as a founding member from the general assembly.

As a painter and decorator, designer, and artist, he produced works that received honourable mention and silver medals from the School of Fine Art and bronze, silver, gold medals from the Liceu (Vianna, 1928).

He was also a civil servant in Bahia, and held several posts in the Department of Public Works, and later in the Department of Agriculture, where he was "recognized as one of the most distinguished employees due to his technical skills and ethics" (Barros 1946, 9).

In his political life, he showed solidarity with his guardian and political patron, as well as his Black brethren, by embracing the Liberal Party's causes: republicanism and abolitionism. On August 1, 1878, he signed the Republican Manifesto. Although he did not reach the eminence of the leaders of the abolitionist campaign, such as Rui Barbosa and José do Patrocínio, Querino joined the Sociedade Libertadora Baiana and wrote articles published in *Gazeta da Tarde* (now *A Tarde*, one of the leading newspapers in the Brazilian Northeast), to raise public awareness about the injustices of slavery. A militant abolitionist, he worked side by side with Frederico Marinho de Araújo and Eduardo Carigé, among others (Querino 1955, 8-9). Unlike many of his colleagues, he believed that the only reason for racial inequality was the lack of opportunities for Blacks. Therefore, he defended abolition followed by the preparation of freedpersons for the world of paid work. Based on his own experience, he was convinced that human beings could not progress without a good education. Much to his dismay, this did not come about in Brazil in his lifetime, and affirmative action was long deferred.

In *As artes na Bahia* (The Arts in Bahia), Querino makes a comparison between Brazil and the United States in the chapter entitled "Aristocracy in Teaching" (1913, 38-42). With a scathing tone, he criticises the contempt for work in his country, and exaggerates the advantages of the US:

> Once the foundations of the Brazilian nation were laid, no one considered the formation of the artistic element.
>
> Worshipers of the progress made in the United States of North America have not known how to imitate the useful lessons of that country's greatness. There, the government disseminated education in such a way that the enslaved had an advantage, as they not only employed the professional skills of refugees but also, and at the same time, sent artists of merit to Europe to be educated in teaching centres, the result of which is that we know of wonderful artistic and industrial prosperity, in conditions rivalling the nations of the old world.
>
> Here, work was considered a secondary and contemptuous object, because it was exclusively for the enslaved.
>
> And so, the worker was left homeless, without education, without rights and without awareness of his personality, as a powerful instrument of progress and greatness for the country (Querino 1913, 38-39).[88]

Enslaved people in the United States learned trades on their enslavers' farms and plantations but were forbidden to learn to read

---

[88] Querino (1913, 46-47) also makes a similar observation in the chapter entitled "The Decline of the Arts": "... the well-oriented government spread instruction in such a way that even the enslaved had an advantage."

and write. It may be that Querino was referring to the efforts of Booker T. Washington and others to ensure the education of freedmen. We know from the fact that he serialised a Portuguese translation of an article by Harriet Beecher Stowe on that subject in one of his own newspapers (see Appendix II), that he was keenly aware of the contrast between efforts to educate emancipated persons in the US and Brazil.

According to Lopez and Mota (2008, 52), the "'pure' republicanists [sic] advocated a regime change which, like France, would result in greater public participation in the nation's political life." As we saw in the previous chapter, the outcome of the movement to replace the Imperial government with a Republic left Manuel Querino profoundly disillusioned.

A militant journalist before and after the proclamation of the Republic in 1889, in addition to being a frequent contributor to the *Gazeta da Tarde* and other publications (Querino 1955, 8-9), Querino founded and edited two short-lived newspapers of his own: *A Provincia* (The Province, 1887-1888) and *O Trabalho* (Labor, 1892). The first defended the causes of abolition and workers and the second continued his defence of free labour after Abolition.

The only known surviving issue of one of these newspapers, which is fortunately in digitized form, contains an editorial that expresses Querino's pessimism about the state of the working class as early as 1892, just four years after Abolition in Brazil:

O Trabalho–Bahia, 6 March 1892, no. 9, 1
Editor-in-Chief–Manuel R. Querino

Current Events[89]
The sensitive and difficult situation of public affairs invites all well-meaning citizens to cruel despair. The doubt that grips all spirits, even the most reflective ones; the real, positive and

---

[89] The editorial for this issue, most likely penned by Querino himself.

manifest disbelief that is observed in all faces, is a sure characteristic, regrettably, that very extraordinary and special circumstances loom on this nation's horizons, foreboding terrible and discouraging things. The disregard which all this has produced is an incalculable evil; nothing, even mere fiction, seems safe to us.

Faith and credit have given way to mistrust. Patriotism has evaporated, and the nation has fallen prey to the cleverest or the strongest.

Disorder is in full sway, directing the governmental oligarchy. A bloodthirsty and barbaric spirit is blatantly on the rise, in the havoc it creates.

The poor no longer know what to do or where to go. Work is increasingly scarce, the little there is, is poorly paid, the price of staple goods is rising, the collision in these circumstances is horrible.

Misfortune knocks at our door, and there are still those who boast about it, doing harm to others.

Amid the conflict, everyone will get involved, and its authors will hardly be protected; because misfortune, oblivious to all, strikes indiscriminately, throwing itself, oftentimes, against those who invited it for others.

And because things that are beyond our control also go against our expectations, it so happens that all the vengeance and disorientation that we witness, not having a pedestal to support them, can easily collapse, because ephemeral glory disperses like a cloud of dust.

Everyone knows the imminent danger that the collapse of a heavy atmosphere could bring us.

At the end of all this, the less well-off, the active and working classes, can no longer bear misfortunes, because they are enduring them due to circumstances in which they played no part.

They are on trial for other people's crimes.

The most difficult trials, want of all kinds, hunger with all its miseries, seem inclined to absorb us in their fearsome abyss.

Querino was clearly concerned about the rights of the working class before and after Abolition in 1888. According to his friend and biographer José Teixeira Barros (1946, 6):

> No one was more committed to raising up the arts in Bahia than Manuel Querino, and no other artist was such a vehement advocate of unifying the working class in such a way that it would constitute a force, a will, a powerful element of action, within the collective. His greatest ideal was to remove artists from the tutelage of politics, which overwhelms everything, to make them independent and autonomous.

At that time, the construction industry's job market was controlled by middlemen who monopolized building projects and dictated wages. The first attempt to rectify this situation was the establishment of the Sociedade Liga Operária Baiana (Bahian Workers' League Society) to guarantee decent wages for workers. Leal observes that this organization was

> ...the gateway to [Querino's] political activity, committed to the workers' causes. There, he became a representative of the working classes, one of the first leaders of the nascent Bahian working class and an interlocutor of Blacks with the established powers, militating in a broader socio-political movement under the "umbrella" of abolitionism (2009, 231).

The league was eliminated, and its aims distorted, through the interference of politicians who, "using the prestige of power and the promises of ephemeral advantages, had the sagacity to abolish the artist's noble ambition" (Barros 1946, 6). Fifteen years later, in 1890, the Workers' Party was organized under the leadership of a directorate chaired by Gonçalo José Pereira Espinheira, with the motto: "With order, firmness, and work, we will attain our aspirations." The party's board had nine members, among them Manuel Querino (Calmon, 1980).

He was a Workers' Party candidate for Federal Deputy (the Brazilian equivalent of congressman) in 1890, but although he was elected as a delegate in the Brazilian Workers' Congress in Rio de Janeiro, the party did not take part in the elections held on September 15 of that year (Leal 2004, 375). This organized, disciplined association composed entirely of workers struck fear in the elite, mainly the bosses and industrialists. Intimidated by the backlash, Gonçalo Espinheira announced that the movement "did not contemplate politics," and the party was renamed the Centro Operário da Bahia (Bahia Workers' Centre). "A supporter of bringing workers closer together and vocational education, Manuel Querino must have warmly approved this solution. It was the 'least worse' [option]" (Calmon 1980). According to Leal,

> With the dismantling of the Workers' Party, which led to the creation of the Centro Operário da Bahia by Domingos Silva and his allies in 1894, Manuel Querino, despite having become a member, was displaced and lacked the necessary influence to execute his plan to unite the working class, or to develop its political networking with the bases of workers and artists [including skilled artisans] (2004, 231).

Despite this setback, Querino's journalistic campaign and the leadership capacity shown at the head of the Worker' Party garnered him the appointment as an unelected member or "intendente" of the City Council, the city of Salvador's first municipal legislature, in 1890 or 1891 (Vianna, 1928; Calmon, 1980). According to Calmon, "he was appointed, between 1890 and 1891, to succeed one of the 'Intendentes' initially chosen by the State Governor" (1980).

Between 1893 and 1897, when Querino did not sit on the city council, that period was marked by three achievements and a major disappointment: he joined Salvador's National Guard as a first lieutenant, became an assistant draftsman in the Public Works

Department 1893, and began teaching industrial design at the Colégio dos Órfãos de São Joaquim in 1895. However, when he applied for the position of professor of linear drawing at the School of Fine Art, the chosen candidate was Agrippiano Barros (Leal 2004, 377).[90]

He returned to the City Council in 1897 as the first alternate called in to "replace Deocleciano Ramos, who resigned from his elected office" (Calmon, 1980). He held the post until December 26, 1899, but lost the election to fill Ramos's post. That same year, he left politics due to reprisals from the "powers that be" (Calmon, 1980).

Disillusioned by political life, Manuel Querino began devoting himself to the work for which he is most remembered: several studies that are of fundamental importance for the history of the visual arts in Brazil, Brazilian history in general, and the formation of Black identity in his country. One of the few intellectuals of his time, and probably the first Afro-Brazilian, to recognize and publicize the African contribution to Brazilian society,[91] he played a key role in retrieving and documenting the contributions of Africans and their descendants to Brazil's development. He also preserved a considerable amount of information about the arts, artists and artisans of Bahia and furnished abundant data on the customs,

---

[90] According to a list of the School of Fine Arts' faculty published in *Diário da Bahia* in 1909, Barros was still teaching linear and elementary drawing for descriptive geometry that year.
http://memoria.bn.br/DocReader/Hotpage/HotpageBN.aspx?bib=313394&pagfis=392
31&url=http://memoria.bn.br/docreader#

[91] Caio Prado Júnior, in his book *Formação do Brasil contemporâneo* (The formation of Contemporary Brazil), published in 1957, observes: "Beyond that driving force, the contribution of enslaved Blacks and Amerindians to Brazil's formation is almost nil." The author made it clear that he considered both "the Indigenous people of the Americas and Black Africans to be peoples of a very low cultural level compared to that of their rulers" (Prado Júnior 2000, 280). Even so, he recognized that: "...the role of Africans in the cultural formation of the colony would have been different if they had been allowed, if not full, at least a minimum opportunity to develop their natural aptitudes" (Ibid., 355).

culture, and religions of Africans and their descendants, as well as Bahia in general.

As an author and scholar, it would be difficult to overstate the importance of Manuel Querino's role as a Black Vindicationist, pointing out the contributions made by Africans and their descendants to Brazilian society. According to E. Bradford Burns, "His historical studies had a twofold purpose. On the one hand, he wanted to show his fellow Blacks the vital contribution they had made to Brazil, while, on the other, he hoped to remind the White Brazilians of the debt they owed Africa and the Black" (1974, 82).[92] Burns observes that the typical mentality of the time is reflected in the work of historians such as Rocha Pombo and João Ribeiro: "In a text of 493 pages, Rocha Pombo spoke directly about the Black in only seventeen, most of which concerned the slave trade and the abolition movement" (Ibid).

Referring to Manuel Querino and Nina Rodrigues in 1928, Bernardino J. de Souza, the permanent secretary of the IGHB, noted in a letter to Gonçalo de Athayde Pereira published as an appendix in Pereira's biography of Querino,[93] that: "[I]t was they, so far in Bahia who were the two greatest scholars of the African race." Souza also observed: "I constantly receive requests for information about their work from Rio, S. Paulo and other states in Brazil" (Pereira 1932, 34). One of Querino's greatest contributions was his insistence that

---

[92] E. Bradford Burns (1933-1995) was probably the first scholar outside Brazil to appreciate and publish about Querino's life and work in English, not only producing a bibliographical essay and partial translation of *O colono preto* (1974) but prominently featuring Querino in *A History of Brazil* (1993).

[93] A letter from Athayde Pereira to Bernardino de Souza dated June 27 1932 shows that the appendix was added because Souza himself suggested that the addition of Querino's portrait to the IGHB's gallery of illustrious men should have been mentioned in his biography. Pereira explains that he was out of town when the event occurred and fell ill afterwards, so this was the first he had heard of the tribute. Pereira explains that he and Querino had been colleagues at the Bahia Department of Agriculture for nearly 24 years and had become close friends. Archives of the Instituto Geográfico e Histórico da Bahia IGHB.CX23D.246.

studies of Brazilian history consider the country's African roots and the presence and influence of Africans. Brazil, he emphasized, was the result of a fusion of Portuguese, Indigenous people, and Africans, but the African contribution was being overlooked. According to Burns: "...his major contribution, in retrospect, appears to be his efforts to assess the role the Africans played in the formation of Brazil. He reflected, in part, greater self-awareness on the part of the Black community, as well as an effort of the nationalists to come to grips with Brazil's racial diversity and its implications. He was the first Black to write Brazilian history, a task to which he brought a much-needed perspective" (1974, 78). Querino underscored these contributions in his book *O colono preto como fator da civilização brasileira* (The Black Colonist as a Factor in Brazilian Civilization, 1918). For example, he asserted that Afro-Brazilians played a leading role in defending Brazil and maintaining national integrity (Burns 1993, 322). According to Vianna, *O colono preto* was written "specifically for the Conference of Scholars, which was the 5th Geography [Conference], held in this city on September 7, 1916" and "managed to interest that illustrious assembly, which gave him honourable approval, making him one of the notables of the event" (1928, 312).

As Burns observes in *A History of Brazil,* "As Querino turned his attention to history, he hoped to rebalance the traditional emphasis on the European experience in Brazil. No Black had ever given his perspective on Brazilian history before." Querino emerged as one of the first Brazilians–and the first Black scholar–to "detail, analyse, and do justice to the African contributions to Brazil" (Burns 1993, 320). He turned the tables and used Social Darwinism for his own ends: believing that the African race was "unevolved" because of slavery and the consequent lack of opportunities (Querino 1938, 22), he saw in his own example and those of other eminent Black men whose lives he documented, that when Black people are respected and receive a proper education, their social and economic "evolution" is guaranteed. He presented his conclusions at a time when scientists believed that the Black race would eventually die out, particularly when it came into contact with Whites, due to their pessimism about the results of miscegenation.[94] Querino rejected that pessimism and other beliefs associated with scientific racism spread in Brazil by Raimundo Nina Rodrigues, Sílvio Romero, and other White and "socially White" intellectuals.[95]

Querino took advantage of his high status in the Candomblé community to record African customs in Bahia firsthand. According to Vianna, "In the famous Candomblés of Gantois, which gained so much fame until just a few years ago... in that setting of African-style practices, for example, Querino found a resting place for many hours, quite a few hours, to record them in flagrante" (1928, 311). Querino was a high-ranking member of the Gantois religious community (Albuquerque 2002, 233 and 2009, 220-221 and Lima 2010, 94). He describes his role as an *ogã* (also spelled *ogan)* as follows:

> He is an honorary authority in candomblé .... Each saint is represented in various individuals who, while not taking part in the precepts of the sect, nevertheless have the right to certain privileges .... When [an ogan] enters the candomblé temple, the drums signal the beginning of the procession according to the

---

[94] In a speech given at the First Universal Races Congress, held in London in 1911, the physician João Batista de Lacerda (1846-1915) predicted that what he called the *métis* would disappear from Brazil by 2012, and that "This will coincide with the parallel extraction of the black race from our midst" (Skidmore 2003, 112-113). For a detailed analysis of the ideology of whitening in Brazil at the beginning of the First Republic (1889-1930), see Skidmore, *Black into White* (1974, 81-94).

[95] There have been numerous references to Nina Rodrigues's possible African ancestry (see, for example, de la Fuente and Andrews 2018, 196-197). Even if he were "Black" according to the rule of hypodescent that prevails in the US, he was not considered Black or "mulatto" in Brazil due to his class and appearance – much darker-complected Brazilians were considered "socially White," such as the statesman and newspaper-owner Severino Vieira (see chapter 4). If Nina Rodrigues did have African ancestry, he was certainly not an "Africanophile" (Calmon 1949, 154). In this case, he may have believed that mixed-race people were weak and doomed to die out because of his own frail health (he died in Paris at the age of 43).

saint to which he is consecrated.; the women pay obeisance, and he has the right to wear a hat indoors, go anywhere in the temple without special authorization. The women who have the same *saint* are called–*his daughters*, and when they see the ogan they kneel and ask his *blessing* wherever they might be.

He is obliged to reward such great veneration with money....

Some people, whose number here includes individuals of social status, have joined the ranks of the *ogans* in the candomblés. While the Africans ran things, they did not allow Brazilians to become ogans. Later, an influx of [Brazilian ogans] began and they were accepted in order to facilitate police permits (Querino 1955, 82-84).

In addition to his own observations as a participant, Querino is believed to have relied on the celebrated *babalawo* (Ifá priest) Martiniano Eliseu do Bonfim as an informant. Bonfim had also worked with Nina Rodrigues. The son of formerly enslaved Yoruba-speaking Africans from Oyo (now in Nigeria), Bonfim spent his youth in Lagos, where he learned Yoruba and English. Speaking in Yoruba, he recounted his autobiography in an interview with the Black American ethnomusicologist Lorenzo Dow Turner (Ayoh'Omidire and Amos, 2012; Capone 2016). Except for the photograph of Bonfim's mother published in *A raça africana e os seus costumes na Bahia* (The African Race and its Customs in Bahia, see Fig. 17, Chapter 5), the only direct evidence I have found of a personal connection between Querino and Bonfim is the fact that his name appears on two lists of books by Querino that were distributed free of charge.[96]

---

[96] According to the lists, Bonfim received free copies of the second edition of *Artistas baianos* and the first edition of *O colono preto como fator da civilização brasileira*. The lists can be found in the archives of the Instituto Geográfico e Histórico da Bahia (IGHB), cx.01D.011 (Colono Preto) and cx.03D.018 (Artistas baianos).

In addition to studying Candomblé communities, Querino also helped defend them. In his day, Afro-Brazilian religious expressions were officially illegal–they would only be legalized in the 1930s. Querino drew the attention of city officials to the persecution of practitioners of Afro-Bahian religions. Because society labeled these religions as "barbaric and pagan," the police frequently appeared at the terreiros during the ceremonies, destroying and confiscating property and injuring participants. Querino denounced these attacks in the newspapers (Burns 1974, 83). Lisa Earl Castillo has transcribed a manuscript in which Querino gives a detailed account of a violent raid of Procópio de Ogunjá's Candomblé by the infamous police chief known as Pedrito (Pedro de Azevedo Gordilho) (Castillo 2010, note 17). In *A raça Africana*, Querino declares:

> Unquestionably, African fetishism[97] exerted a well-known influence on our customs; and we will consider ourselves well paid if the limited material we have gathered can contribute to the study of national psychosis [sic] in the individual and in society. *And, taking this opportunity, I hereby register my protest against the disdainful and unfair way in which people try to disparage the Africans, constantly branding them crude and rough, as a congenital quality and not a simple circumstantial condition, common, moreover, to all the unevolved races* (1938, 22, emphasis added).

As Artur Ramos observed: "It is notable how, already in his time, Manuel Querino rebelled against the prejudice of anthropological inferiority of the Black, attributing his backwardness to sociocultural contingencies, and not racial inferiority" (Ramos 1938, 22)

He was a member of the Sociedade Protetora dos Desvalidos, an association created in 1832 by the African freedman Manoel Victor

---

[97] Querino spelled fetichism *"feiticismo,"* whose root is "magic," and also means "sorcery," instead of the usual Portuguese spelling *fetichismo*, derived from "fetish."

Serra to build up a fund aimed at protecting the disabled and the elderly–a pioneering version of modern-day private pension funds (Braga 1987, 23). Relations between Querino and this society were not always based on "fraternal kindness" (Butler 2000, 164). After leaving the society–we do not know in what year, and the sources disagree as to whether he resigned or was asked to leave–Querino requested his reinstatement in 1892. That request was rejected by a vote of five to one. Querino appealed the decision, but a second vote produced the same result. He was finally reinstated on August 22, 1894 (Braga 1987, 57) According to Julio Braga

> There seems to have been a reciprocal exchange of prestige. The Society, a few years after having denied him readmission, would receive him and, more than that, would make the concession of appointing him as a clerk at his own request, when the normal thing would be to hold an election. He was now a professor, the first [of that profession] to join the Society and who would later be revered with the enthronement of his portrait in the auditorium and with the installation of a literary-cultural-recreational guild that bears his name (1987, 58).

Then, in 1896, Querino requested a disability pension from the society, but the board of directors decided to suspend payments when it learned that the "invalid" had been seen in processions, weddings, and outings, demonstrating that he was in perfect health. However, one of the directors warned that Querino could use his influence in the government to withhold the society's subsidy. Whatever the reason, that subsidy actually was suspended. A few years later, when Querino applied for a retirement pension, the board denied his request because "by his nature [Querino] is no longer a member of this institution" (Butler 2000, 165).

Despite the ups and downs of Querino's relations with the Sociedade Protetora dos Desvalidos, reflected in the documentary sources, in 1951, the SPD took part in the celebrations of the 100th anniversary of Querino's birth. Until 2009, it maintained a room named after him. The Manuel Querino guild continues to exist, and his portrait can still be seen in that institution's auditorium, and the society actively celebrates his memory.

Because he was buried in the sacristy of the church of Nossa Senhora do Rosário dos Homens Pretos—the blue church built by and for Black people which is now a landmark in the Salvador's Historic District—we know that Querino was a member of the Confraternity of Our Lady of the Rosary of Black Men.[98] According to Mariana de Mesquita Santos, "The practice of joining Black confraternities and other mutual-aid associations was common among Africans and Afro-Brazilians in the nineteenth century" (Santos 2021, 222). She observes that, "monumentalized" by his burial in the confraternity's church, Querino's membership "symbolized the social, political, and cultural significance of the confraternity housed in that temple, inherited from colonization and slavery, which was reinvented during the Empire" (Ibid., 223).

Querino was a founding member of the Instituto Geográfico e Histórico da Bahia (IGHB) when it was established in a townhouse in Terreiro de Jesus plaza (in what is now Salvador's Historic District) on May 13, 1894–the date on which Brazil still celebrates the signing of the law that abolished slavery in 1888–and later became a "sócio benemerito" or charter member (Vianna 1928, 308). He launched at least two of his books there (the second edition of *Artistas baianos* and *O colono preto como fator da civilizão brasileira*–the distribution lists can still be found in the IGHB's archives), and published several articles in its journal (see Nascimento and Gama 2009). Although the institute has traditionally been considered the domain of the White elite in Bahia, in addition to having an illustrious Black founding member in Querino, it also had a famous Black president—the

---

[98] Originally the Irmandade de Nossa Senhora do Rosário da Baixa dos Sapateiros às Portas do Carmo, as of 1899, it was called the Venerável Ordem Terceira de Nossa Senhora às Portas do Carmo (Santos 2021, 224, note 2). It is also known as the Ordem Terceira do Rosário dos Homens Pretos (Third Order of the Rosary of Black Men).

engineer, author, and polymath **Teodoro Sampaio (1855-1937)** (see Fig. 2-1). Sampaio presided over the IGHB from 1922 to 1927 (Silva 2006, 192), taking office the year before the institute moved to its present-day headquarters near Praça da Piedade a few months after Querino's death in 1923. Querino may not have lived to see the official opening of the new building complex, but he must have accompanied its design and construction with great interest, given his background in architecture.

Fig. 2-1. Teodoro Sampaio

Querino was also a member of the Sociedade Montepio dos Artistas (Artists' Mutual Insurance Society), which is still active today and has a largely Black membership. Displaying Masonic symbols in its meeting room, Montepio's headquarters is located near the Sociedade Protetora dos Desvalidos and the original site of the IGHB, and a short walk from the church of Nossa Senhora do Rosário dos Homens Pretos, the Liceu de Artes e Ofícios, and the original home of the School of Fine Art (previously the mansion of British-born physician and patron of the arts, Jonathas Abbott, whose collection formed the basis of what is now the Bahia Museum of Art).

Combining his keen interest in his African roots and a true Bahian's love of the revelries held between Fat Tuesday (even before) and Ash Wednesday, Querino was also the director of an African-inspired Carnaval group, "Pândegos da África" ("Revellers from Africa") in 1900. According to Albuquerque and Fraga Filho (2006, 232):

> For him, the club's parade reproduced celebrations that still took place in Africa. It is not up to us here to assess the veracity of the information given by such an illustrious reveller; it is more important to point out the club's predisposition to reaffirm the cultural ties between Bahia and Africa, despite the dissemination of racist theories that ranked the African continent as the lowest on the scale of evolution.

The club was founded by Bibiano Cupim, a master builder, butcher, carpenter, and "banker" for the Jogo do Bicho.[99] Among his many activities and interests, Cupim had several other opportunities to interact with Querino: at the Centro Operário (Workers' Center), the Sociedade Protetora dos Desvalidos, the Third Order of the Rosary of Black Men, and the Gantois candomblé community, where both men were *ogãs* (Albuquerque 2002, 233 and 2009, 220-221 and Lima 2010, 94).[100] Cupim's name is on the list of recipients of free copies of *Artistas baianos* handed out in 1916, but not for *O colono preto como fator da civilização brasileira*, which was distributed in 1918.[101]

---

[99] An illegal lottery that is still popular in Brazil today. Its "bankers" have traditionally been associated with Rio's Carnaval.

[100] I would like to thank Lisa Earl Castillo for pointing out the connection between Bibiano Cupim and Querino.

[101] Archives of the Instituto Geográfico e Histórico da Bahia. CX.03D.018 and CX.01D.011.

We can follow Querino's rise to fame through the bios in some editions of his books. In 1903, in the first edition of his textbook *Desenho linear das classes elementares* (Elementary Linear Drawing), Querino is described as "an artist graduated from the School of Fine Art of Bahia and teacher of Industrial Drawing at Colégio dos Órfãos de S. Joaquim, Escola Bahiana, etc." In 1911, in his other textbook, *Elementos de desenho geométrico* (Elements of Geometric Drawing), we read that Querino was a "Graduated artist, awarded two silver medals, honorable mention, approved with distinction in the architecture course at the School of Fine Art, with bronze, silver and gold medals from the Liceu de Artes e Ofícios; teacher at the Colégio dos Órfãos de S. Joaquim, the Liceu de Artes e Ofícios and other schools." That edition is dedicated "To His Excellency. Sr. Coronel José Alves Ferreira for the benefits lavished on behalf of the working class and those disinherited from fortune, [this] meagre but sincere homage from the author." In the second edition of *Artistas baianos* (Bahian Artists), published in 1911, the author is simply identified as a "member of the Geographical and Historical Institute of Bahia," and the dedication is addressed to a much more eminent figure: "To His Excellency Mr. Miguel Calmon du Pin e Almeida. An example and stimulus for studious youth."[102] *As Artes na Bahia* (The Arts in Bahia, 1913) identifies the author as "From the Geographical and Historical Institute of Bahia, and Teacher of Industrial Drawing" and *O colono preto como fator da civilização brasileira* (1918), as a "member of the Geographical and Historical Institute of Bahia and the Ceará Institute." The second edition of *A Bahia de outrora* (1922) merely gives the author's name, with no description at all. Presumably, by that time, he needed no introduction.

Manuel Querino was married twice. He and his first wife, Ceciliana do Espírito Santo Quirino, were wed sometime between

---

[102] Miguel Calmon du Pin e Almeida (1879-1935) was an engineer and abolitionist, and a nephew of the Marquess of Abrantes, whose name he shared. He was the Brazilian Transport Minister from 1906 to 1909 and Minister of Agriculture from 1922 to 1926.

1878 and 1883. They had four children, Maria Anatildes, Manoel Querino Filho, Paulo and Alzira. Ceciliana died between 1894 and 1897, possibly in childbirth in 1894, the year Alzira was born. Querino married his second wife, Laura Barbosa Pimentel, who was also widowed, on July 23, 1897, in São Pedro Parish in a civil ceremony conducted by the Justice of the Peace Arthur Rodrigues de Macedo. According to the marriage certificate, Querino was 45 and his wife was 36. Querino's new father-in-law was Colonel Feliciano Pimentel, whose Paraguayan War medals Captain Querino donated to the IGHB in 1901. The witnesses were Dr Arthur Ferreira de Barros and Hermelino Estevão de Sant'Anna.

Querino died unexpectedly of malaria on February 14, 1923, Ash Wednesday, at his small estate in Matatu Grande, now in the Brotas district of Salvador, leaving Laura Pimentel Querino and only two children: the musician and craftsman Paulo Querino, and Maria Anatildes Querino.[103] His son Manuel Querino Filho had been a painter, and his daughter Alzira had shown an "appreciable penchant for music, having maestro Guilherme Mello as a teacher" (Pereira, 1932, 20). Manuel Filho died in 1908, and Alzira in 1921 (Leal 2004, 302, 678). According to Pereira: "These two blows devastated that spirit, strong and hardened by the toil of life" (1932, 20).

Manuel Querino's funeral was held in the Quinta dos Lázaros cemetery, which was the last resort for those who could not afford to be buried in a church or the city's elite Campo Santo burial ground. As we will see in the next chapter, several newspapers published his

---

[103] The fact that Querino died unexpectedly is made clear by an unsigned memorial eulogy housed in the IGHB archives. He had been working on a study of Bahia's Independence for the centenary celebrations to be held in July 1923 (Mensagem sobre Falecimento BHA04D.053). Published in *Revista do IGHB*, no. 48, 1923, with the title *Notícia histórica sobre o 2 de Julho de 1823 e sua comemoração na Bahia*, this article concludes with the following note: "Professor Manuel Querino, a diligent researcher of traditional things in Bahia, did not manage to finish this work. Death surprised him, merciless and treacherous" (Nascimento; Gama 2009, 81).

obituaries, many on the front page. This was the case with *A Tarde*'s February 14 issue, in which Querino was described as a "useful life" and "frequent contributor." On the front page of its February 15, 1923 issue, the *Diário da Bahia* reported: "The funeral of the greatly mourned Bahian took place yesterday, with large attendance, his widow and children receiving countless testimonies of regret. The last farewells were said to him at the graveside by Major Cosme de Farias, Dr Martinho Braga, Professor Ozeas Santos, and Antonio Vianna." According to the obituary published in *O Democrata* the following day (translated in full in the next chapter), Cosme de Farias represented the Centro Operário, Ozeas Santos, the School of Fine Art, and Antonio Vianna, the "Geographic and Historical Institute." Also taking part in "the funeral procession were the Municipal Superintendent, the Secretary of Agriculture, and a representative of the Secretary of Police and Public Security" (Leal 2004, 376-377, n. 862).

As we have seen, his remains now lie in the sacristy of the church of Nossa Senhora do Rosário dos Homens Pretos, in Salvador. We do not know when they were translated there, nor the names of those responsible for doing so. All we have are their initials on the marble plaque set into the sacristy floor. The inscription reads: "Here lie the remains of Professor Manoel R. Querino *28.7.1851 +14.2.1923 [With] gratitude from [his] friends J.M.C.E.G.L.G.C."[104]

According to his colleague and friend Antonio Vianna (1928, 309), "The Centro Operário celebrated public funeral rites on the 30th day of the passing of the lamented artist, leaving me with the task of speaking, at the time, about his life and his desire, a task that I had also been given by the Geographical and Historical Institute...." [105]

---

[104] As the plural "friends" is used, the "E" may have meant "and," so the two friends' initials would have been J.M.C. and G.L.G.C.

[105] José Teixeira Barros also recalled that Vianna had spoken at the memorial at the Centro Operário when he suggested that Vianna speak in his place at the unveiling of Querino's portrait at the IGHB on May 13, 1928. Carta para Bernardino de Souza

Despite his prestige and influence, Querino died relatively poor, although, according to his post-mortem inventory, he owned the small estate in the district of Matatú, where he died, as well as a bungalow in Ondina (at the time, it would have been considered a country retreat—today it would be one of the most prestigious addresses in the city).

Thanks to the inventory of his estate, we also know that he was an art collector. It shows that, in addition to "ornaments, works and objects of art, crockery and glass," his home contained "eleven paintings [framed] with glass, and clay figures inside representing the Steps of the Sacred Passion" —all these objects were valued "by common accord" at 55$000 (fifty-five thousand réis). There were also "twenty-four clay figures of regular size," valued at 72$000 (seventy-two thousand réis), "a Christ Crucified," valued at 15$000 (fifteen thousand réis), "a plaster figure" valued at 16$000 (sixteen thousand réis), "eleven ordinary paintings" valued at 22$000 (twenty-two thousand réis), and "sixteen paintings with a crayon drawing" (48$000). The inventory also included a guitar (50$000), and a gramophone (80$000).[106]

In the words of Antonio Vianna, Manuel Querino "[D]evoted himself body and soul to traditionalist studies, reviving with an unsurpassed and irrefutable accuracy, types, and habits, things and ideas that were condemned to perpetual oblivion" (1928, 308). As we have seen, Querino published several titles, including *Artistas baianos* (1909); *As artes na Bahia* (1909) and *Bailes pastoris* (Shepherds' Dances, 1914). His best-known works are *A raça africana e os seus costumes na Bahia* (1916), on the customs of Africans and their descendants in Bahia, *A Bahia de outrora* (1916), on Bahian folklore, and *O colono preto como fator da civilização brasileira*

---

sobre o tributo à memória de Manoel Quirino (Archives of the Instituto Geográfico e Histórico da Bahia, IGHB.Cx23D.071).

[106] APEBa. Tribunal Superior de Justiça, 06/2697/17. I would like to thank Lisa Earl Castillo and Urano Andrade for their help in finding the inventory of Querino's estate.

(1918). He also wrote *Modelos das casas escolares adaptadas ao clima do Brasil* (Models of Schoolhouses Adapted to the Brazilian Climate, 1883) and two textbooks: *Desenho linear das classes elementares* and *Elementos de desenho geométrico*, about "understanding notions of linear perspective, theory of shadow and light, projections, and architecture" (Querino 1911, 147-148; Trinchão and Souza 2021), in addition several articles published in the journal of the Geographical and Historical Institute of Bahia (Nascimento; Gama 2009a). He produced revised and expanded second editions of two books—*Artistas baianos* (in 1911) and *A Bahia de outrora* (in 1922). Published months before he died, this title announces that further books were due for publication: *Um século de artes na Bahia* (A Century of the Arts in Bahia), *As modinhas bahianas* (Bahian Modinhas), *Bailes pastoris—com música* (Shepherds' Dances—With Songs), and "O Dia 2 de Julho de 1823" (July 2, 1823). Only the last work, on Bahia's Independence Day, was published unfinished in the IGHB's journal to commemorate the centennial of Independence, celebrated a few months after his death (in Nascimento and Gama 2009b, 81).

In a letter dated March 2, 1928, José Teixeira Barros informed Bernardino de Souza that *Modinhas e toadas da Bahia* (Modinhas and Tunes of Bahia), "illustrated with musical examples," was in the possession of Querino's daughter, Maria Anatildes, but he did not know her address (unfortunately, the manuscript was not published).[107] By this time, Laura Querino had passed away.[108] The work for which Querino is best known in Brazil, *A arte culinária na Bahia* (Culinary Art in Bahia), his pioneering study of Bahian cuisine,

---

[107] Carta para Bernardino de Souza sobre o tributo à memória de Manoel Quirino (Archives of the Instituto Geográfico e Histórico da Bahia, IGHB.CX23D.071). I would like to thank Laiala de Araújo Félix dos Santos for her help with obtaining access to this document.

[108] In his letter to Bernardino de Souza, Teixeira Barros refers to Laura Pimentel Querino as the "finada viúva" or "deceased widow." He also states that he was helping arrange the publication of Manuel Querino's posthumous works at her request (Archives of the Instituto Geográfico e Histórico da Bahia, IGHB.CX23D.071).

was first published in 1928, thanks to his friend Teixeira Barros and his son, Paulo Querino (Vianna 1928, 309).[109]

In 1938, the psychiatrist and anthropologist Artur Ramos edited and annotated *Costumes africanos no Brasil* (African Customs in Brazil), an illustrated compendium of several of Querino's works. As we will see in the following chapter, Ramos's disparaging comments about Querino's scholarship contributed to his negative posthumous image. There have been many editions since–most published without the illustrations.

Referring to the poet Cruz e Souza and the novelist and journalist Lima Barreto, both of whom were Black, Bosi observes, "the grandchildren of enslaved people and the children of freedmen, they had patrons and received a refined education of a European nature, which gave them hope of professional achievement and acceptance in the liberal circles of the newly created Republic. But the barriers were already starting to rise: with the loss of their protectors, both fell into limited situations, without prospects" (2002, 186-187). This led Cruz e Souza to write poems such as "Dor negra" (Black Pain) and "Emparedado" (Walled In). Lima Barreto exposed his "naked and raw" feelings in his fiction.[110] Like them, Querino was a Black man who received a "refined education of a European nature" and eventually lost his "protectors" (Querino 1938, 11). Querino's response was to study and assert the positive contributions of Africans and their descendants in Brazil. According to the folklorist Frederico Edelweiss, his efforts brought him "both sympathy and animosity–mostly animosity" (1946, 2).

---

[109] José Teixeira Barros's letter to Bernardino de Souza casts doubt on the extent of Paulo Querino's involvement. Teixeira Barros observes: "I have not heard from Paulo Querino for some time, possibly out of embarrassment due to the failure to observe the contract (Archives of the Instituto Geográfico e Histórico da Bahia, IGHB.CX23D.071).

[110] In the novel *Recordações do escrivão Isaías Caminha* (Memories of the Clerk Isaías Caminha), the title character is an intelligent and ambitious young man who only discovers that he is Black—and its limiting consequences in a structurally racist society—when he leaves the countryside to seek his fortune in the big city.

CHAPTER 3
REVISION AND RECLAMATION:
The Posthumous Trajectories of Washington and Querino

In this chapter, I use obituaries as the basis for following and analysing the high and low points in the remembrance and reputations of Washington and Querino. The negative view of Washington put about by the "Talented Tenth" during his lifetime persisted due to the writings of Du Bois and other Black activists in the United States during the Civil Rights struggles of the 1960s. However, thanks to Ishmael Reed (2000) and, more recently, Robert Norell (2009), among others, the Black American educator's life and work are being reinterpreted in the context of his time.

Despite the prestige that Manuel Querino clearly enjoyed in life, he also suffered unjust treatment before and after his death. Querino and Nina Rodrigues's contemporaries considered them the greatest authorities on Afro-Bahian culture (Souza 1932, 34). However, the validity of Querino's work as a credible source began to be questioned in the 1930s, culminating in a charge of plagiarism (Ott 1947). Nevertheless, today Querino is increasingly valued in Brazil and beginning to attract interest abroad.

The obituaries and death notices that followed and reported upon the passing of Washington and Querino provide valuable information about how the two Black leaders were seen at the end of their days, before paternalistic, White supremacist, or ideological narratives arose to distort those views. Over time, the negative image of the former became fixed, and the memory of the latter was erased—with occasional flashes of remembrance—for several decades.

Booker T. Washington

As we have seen, Washington's leadership was severely weakened by the aftermath of the "Brownsville Affray" in 1906, when he failed to influence the US President—his former ally Teddy Roosevelt—on a matter of the greatest importance to the Black nation (Harlan 1986, 309-311). Despite his denunciation of segregation towards the end of his life, Washington's philosophy always associated with the approach of "accommodation" seen in his speech dubbed the "Atlanta Compromise," given in 1895, and *Up from Slavery*, published in 1901 (Dagbovie 2007, 256). Even so, Washington never lost the support of ordinary Black folk, who saw him as an example of faith, good humor, courage, and endurance. According to R. S. Baker, in *Following the Color Line*:

> Wherever I found a prosperous Negro enterprise, a thriving business place, a good home, there I was almost sure to find Booker T. Washington's picture over the fireplace or a little framed motto expressing his gospel of work and service. I have heard bitter things said about Mr. Washington by both coloured people and white. I have waited and investigated many of these stories, and I am telling here what I have seen and known of his influence among thousands of common, struggling human beings. Many highly educated Negroes, especially, in the North, dislike him and oppose him, but he has brought new hope and given new courage to the masses of his race. He has given them a working plan of life. And is there a higher test of usefulness?

Revision and Reclamation

Measured by any standard, white or black, Washington must be regarded to-day as one of the great men of this country: and in the future he will be so honoured (1908, 222).

A White journalist who worked with Washington and Du Bois in the course of his research—but, according to Harlan (1983, 305-306), was more influenced by the former—Baker described Washington as an opportunist and an optimist, but above all a realist who saw and dealt with the world as it was, while Du Bois was an idealist, agitator, and pessimist, who saw the world as it should be and called for immediate change (Norell 2009, 383):

> Where Washington reaches the hearts of his people, Du Bois appeals to their heads. Du Bois is not a leader of men, as Washington is: he is rather a promulgator of ideas. While Washington is building a great educational institution and organizing the practical activities of the race, Du Bois is the lonely critic holding up distant ideals. Where Washington cultivates friendly human relationships with the white people among whom the lot of the Negro is cast, Du Bois, sensitive to rebuffs, draws more and more away from white people (Baker 1908, 223).[111]

However, the factor that did the greatest damage to Washington's posthumous reputation was the longevity of his arch-rival Du Bois, who died in 1963. Du Bois's best-known book, *The Souls of Black Folk*, contains the philippic "Of Mr. Booker T. Washington and Others." Translated into Portuguese in 1999, it consolidated Du Bois's view of Washington among academics in Brazil (see Chapter 4).

---

[111] Baker also placed Washington in the centre of the continuum of the movement toward racial reform, with Du Bois at one extreme and Senator Ben Tillman (who advocated lynching Blacks to "keep them in their place") at the other. Many saw this as an exaggeration, including Washington's friend and successor as principal of the Tuskegee Institute, Robert Moton. (Harlan 1986, 307; Baker 1908).

Obituaries and death notices of Booker T. Washington

As we saw in the previous chapter, Booker T. Washington's death was reported on the first page of *The New York Times*. Published on November 15, 1915 issue, the article includes, on page 8, the reactions of Teddy Roosevelt and Julius Rosenwald:

> OYSTER BAY, N.Y. Nov. 14—Colonel Theodore Roosevelt, when told of the death of Booker T. Washington, said:
> "I am deeply shocked and grieved at the death of Dr Washington. He was one of the distinguished citizens of the United States, a man who rendered greater service to his race than had ever been rendered by any one [sic] else, and who, in so doing, also rendered great service to the whole country. I mourn his loss, and feel that one of the most useful citizens of our land has gone."
>
> ****
>
> Julius Rosenwald, of Chicago, an admirer of Booker T. Washington, who aided him in his work by contributions to Tuskegee Institute, who has just returned from Tuskegee and is at the Hotel St. Regis, commenting on the educator's death last night, said:
> "In the death of Booker T. Washington this country has lost one of its foremost educators. By emphasizing the dignity of labor he has rendered a great service not only to his own race but to the white race as well. I know no nobler character than he possessed. The injustices he was made to suffer never embittered him. Those who knew him best were proudest of his friendship. His life enriched not only this country but the entire world."

The Booker T. Washington Papers housed in the US Library of Congress include several folders on Washington's death, containing visiting cards, documents on funeral arrangements, guest lists, the order of service (in two folders), obituaries, and poems *in memoriam*. There are dozens of clippings from US newspapers, many representing the Black press, the vast majority praising "Dr Washington" and lamenting his sudden passing. These include the

Boston Globe, the *Constitution*, the *Montgomery Advertiser*, the *Baltimore Sun*, the *New York Call*, the *New York American*, the *Washington Post*, the *Brooklyn Standard Union*, the *Chicago Post*, the *Afro American*, the *Amsterdam News* (from New York), and *New Republic*.[112]

Outlook, the magazine that serialised *Up from Slavery*, published his obituary in issue no. 111, on November 24, 1915. Entitled "Booker T. Washington's Death is a National Calamity," it concludes as follows:

> There will not soon be likely to arise a Negro leader whom the white people of the South and of the North will so readily heed. It is not probable that such a man will appear twice in a generation. The Negroes' chief spokesman before their white fellow-men is gone. And this is the white people's loss. It is a greater injury to misunderstand than to be misunderstood, and without this spokesman the white people will be more in danger of misunderstanding their black fellow-countrymen. To this degree at least, the burden which this one black man has been bearing will now fall largely on white shoulders (Harlan and Smock 1984, 470).

The Black New York newspaper *Amsterdam News* carried an article on December 17, 1915 about a lecture given by Rabbi Stephen B. Wise at Carnegie Hall, illustrated with a photo of the religious leader, entitled: "Rabbi Wise Flays Those Who Raise the Color Line—Eulogizing Life of Dr Washington in Carnegie Hall—Great Hebrew Flays the Unjust—Wants Everyone Given a Chance—Head of City's Free Synagogue Pays Wonderful Tribute and Urges That Three Monuments Stand for Dead Educator." Wise said he wanted three monuments to Washington—Hampton Institute, which educated

---

[112] Unless other sources are cited, these clippings can be found in the *Booker T. Washington Papers* collection at the US Library of Congress, where they are available on microfiche, box 566, reel 422.

him, Tuskegee, which he created, and a better attitude from White Americans regarding "their" Americans of color.

The article reports that:

> Dr Wise showed conclusively that this was one of the things Dr Washington strove to bring about, and sharp at times was his criticism of those who attempted to deny opportunities to colored men and women because they were colored, for he said with much force and emphasis: "In the face of Booker Washington's noble character and greatness those who sneered at him because he was a Negro are unworthy to fasten the latches of his shoes." The noted Hebrew then mentioned the meeting held in Carnegie Hall ten years ago in memory of Carl Schurz philanthropist and friend of the colored people, who was Secretary of the Interior in President Hayes cabinet. Speaking from this platform with ex-President Grover Cleveland, Col Theodore *Roosevelt and Hon Joseph H. Choate, Dr Washington said among other things: "If I had to be born again and the good Lord would ask me in my unborn state what I wanted to be, I would say please, Lord make me an American Negro."* Dr Wise cited this to show the late leader's love for his race, but added: "It may be that the newly freed race leaned too heavily upon Booker Washington but now the race must take the place left by its leader or that place will remain vacant. *The world does not adjudge the colored race by Booker T. Washington, but the whole race may be misjudged by its wretches.*"[113]

The tone of most of the clippings in the collection is positive and complimentary. However, a front-page obituary in a newspaper obtained from a different source, *The Bennington Evening Banner*, published on November 15, 1915, manages to tarnish Washington's character, praise his intelligence, and belittle his race in the same

---

[113] The part in italics was outlined and the words in bold face underlined in the clipping.

paragraph. Entitled "Leader of Negro Race is Dead at Tuskegee," it observes: "While opinions may have been at variance at times as regards Mr. Washington's private character, no variance was possible when his intellectual merits were considered. He was an organizer for good among his people. He constantly preached common sense to a race as impulsive as children."[114]

However, the harshest criticism came from Washington's old foe Du Bois, in an editorial on page 82 of the December 1915 issue of *The Crisis*, the outlet of the NAACP:

> [Booker T. Washington] was the greatest Negro leader since Frederick Douglass, and the most distinguished man, white or black, who has come out of the South since the Civil War.... On the other hand, in stern justice, we must lay on the soul of this man, a heavy responsibility for the consummation of Negro disfranchisement, the decline of the Negro college and public school and the firmer establishment of color caste in this land (1915, 82).

This obituary and Du Bois's subsequent comments were widely reported and sparked retorts and rebuttals. For example, in a letter to the editor of the Black newspaper *New York Age*[115] published on January 13, 1916, a reader who signed him or herself L. E. Fisher wrote that *The Crisis* (that is, Du Bois) seemed intent on destroying the impact of a great man's life. Fisher also accuses Du Bois of reinforcing racial segregation in the United States for suggesting in a section of his editorial in the January 1916 issue that a memorial to

---

[114] US Library of Congress, Chronicling Humanities. Historic American Newspapers https://chroniclingamerica.loc.gov/data/batches/vtu_canaan_ver02/data/sn95066012/00202196676/1915111501/0224.pdf

[115] The November 18, 1915 issue of *The New York Age* dedicated its entire front page to the news of Washington's death, with the headline "Booker Taliaferro Washington Dies within Tuskegee's Walls – The Entire Country Mourns and All Pay Tribute to a Great Man." https://www.flickr.com/photos/vieilles_annonces/8498443761

Booker T. Washington should be contributed "by the colored people alone," more specifically "his colored friends."[116] Fisher observes that Du Bois uses the "Jim Crow" language of "colored people alone," and questions whether the editor of *The Crisis* had any interest in a memorial to Washington that was actually intended to honour him. As we will see below and in the next chapter, if Du Bois wanted to create an "anti-memorial" to Washington, particularly among Black Americans, his aim was largely fulfilled.

Booker T. Washington's biographies and biographers

Several biographies of Booker T. Washington were written by or co-authored with ghostwriters he employed during his lifetime, and by friends and admirers after his death. Far from being an admirer, his chief biographer, Louis R. Harlan, expressed deep contempt for the subject of his biographies (1975b; 1986) and other essays (1988). However, other authors, particularly Robert J. Norell (2009), have emerged to rectify previous narratives and help raise Washington "up from history." When analysing these works, one experiences what the anthropologist Karl Heider calls the "*Rashomon* effect," a reference to the Kurosawa film which delves into the nature of truth by giving multiple perspectives on a samurai's murder. Heider demonstrates that ethnographers like Margaret Mead and Derek Freeman could disagree profoundly in their observations and interpretations of the same subject (1988, 73).

---

[116] Entitled "A Suggestion," this section of the editorial reads: "A simple and feasible memorial to Booker T. Washington may be contributed by the colored people alone. As we said in our last number the mortgage on the Frederick Douglass Home, near Washington, D.C., must be raised. Mr. Washington was interested in this project and helped raise part of the mortgage. Could not his colored friends and admirers raise the rest and present it to the Douglass Home as a Booker Washington Memorial Fund?" (1916, 135). https://modjourn.org/issue/bdr508419/

THE CRISIS

BOOKER T. WASHINGTON

HE death of Mr. Washington marks an epoch in the history of America. He was the greatest Negro leader since Frederick Douglass, and the most distinguished man, white or black, who has come out of the South since the Civil War. His fame was international and his influence far-reaching. Of the good that he accomplished there can be no doubt: he directed the attention of the Negro race in America to the pressing necessity of economic development; he emphasized technical education and he did much to pave the way for an understanding between the white and darker races.

On the other hand there can be no doubt of Mr. Washington's mistakes and short comings: he never adequately grasped the growing bond of politics and industry; he did not understand the deeper foundations of human training and his basis of better understanding between white and black was founded on caste.

We may then generously and with deep earnestness lay on the grave of Booker T. Washington testimony of our thankfulness for his undoubted help in the accumulation of Negro land and property, his establishment of Tuskegee and spreading of industrial education and his compelling of the white south to at least think of the Negro as a possible man.

On the other hand, in stern justice, we must lay on the soul of this man, a heavy responsibility for the consummation of Negro disfranchisement, the decline of the Negro college and public school and the firmer establishment of color caste in this land.

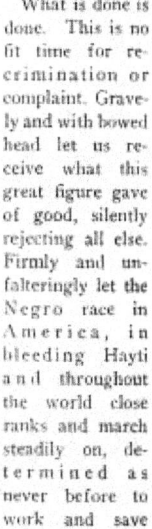

What is done is done. This is no fit time for recrimination or complaint. Gravely and with bowed head let us receive what this great figure gave of good, silently rejecting all else. Firmly and unfalteringly let the Negro race in America, in bleeding Hayti and throughout the world close ranks and march steadily on, determined as never before to work and save and endure, but never to swerve from their great goal: the right to vote, the right to know, and the right to stand as men among men throughout the world.

It is rumored that Mr. Washington's successor at Tuskegee will be Robert Russa Moton, Commandant of Cadets at Hampton. If this proves true Major Moton will enter on his new duties with the sympathy and good will of his many friends both black and white.

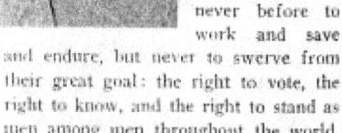

Fig. 3-1. W. E. B. Du Bois's unsigned obituary of Booker T. Washington

The same can be said of Washington's biographers. Following their employer's guidelines, his ghostwriters helped create the legend of a self-made man, someone who embodied all the values of the Protestant ethic—hard work, thrift, piety, sobriety, independence, and delayed gratification—and overcame numerous obstacles to become the leader of his "nation." Heather Cox Richardson places this effort in the context of White supremacist efforts to roll back and eliminate the rights Black Americans had obtained after Emancipation—particularly in the South, describing *Up from Slavery* as "a clever political and fund-raising tract... meticulously crafted both to attract mainstream Americans and to swing them toward Washington's way of thinking" (2004, 225-226).

After Washington's death,[117] his private secretary, Emmett Jay Scott, demonstrated that his loyalty went beyond the grave by joining forces with Lyman Beecher Stowe, the grandson of the author of *Uncle Tom's Cabin*, to complete a biography begun while Washington was still living. According to Scott, the principal of Tuskegee had not read the book, which bolsters his legend and extends the narrative to include its protagonist's funeral rites. Theodore Roosevelt penned the foreword.

Other authors wrote biographies of Washington soon after his passing, including Frederick E. Drinker and, Benjamin Franklin Riley. Published in 1915, Drinker's *Booker T. Washington: The Master Mind of a Child of Slavery* is well-documented, but little known (Dagbovie 2007, 241). In his introduction to Riley's biography, E. Y. Mullins, of the Southern Baptist Theological Seminary of Louisville, Kentucky, praises Washington as being "remarkably sane and balanced as to the place and future of the Negro," never confronting the system of segregation because "there were other matters of far greater moment," such as economic independence (1916). Although the facts were far more nuanced, this image of Washington—

---

[117] For a comprehensive overview and analysis of views of Washington in the US during the hundred years following his death, see Pero Gaglo Dagbovie, "Exploring a Century of Historical Scholarship on Booker T. Washington" (2007).

considered praiseworthy by Southern White supremacists—was firmly established by another White biographer from the South, Louis Harlan (1975b; 1986), an ally of the Civil Rights movement. Written over the course of three decades, and based on primary sources, Harlan's biographies of Washington were strongly influenced by an anachronistic view that emerged during the Black activism of the 1960s and even before, following the line of thinking of W. E. B. Du Bois.

Fortunately for this analysis of the biographer and his subject, Harlan provides a memoir of his work in an essay entitled "Sympathy and Detachment: Dilemmas of a Biographer" (1988). **Louis Rudolph Harlan (1922-2010)** was born in Mississippi, but grew up in the suburbs of Atlanta, Georgia. He considered his Southern origins an advantage for understanding Booker T. Washington, although he also expressed the awareness that, being White, he would never fully comprehend Black people, as he could not experience life as they did.

Harlan first became interested in Washington when he was a graduate student at Johns Hopkins University, where his advisor was the White historian C. Vann Woodward. According to Norrell, Woodward influenced Harlan's view of Washington, as his mentor took an ironic and disdainful stance towards the "Wizard of Tuskegee" in *Origins of the New South*, published in 1951. It was Woodward who dubbed Washington's famous oration at the Atlanta Exposition the "Atlanta Compromise" (1951, chapter 13). In his turn, Woodward was influenced by Du Bois, and accepted the Black American intellectual's verdict that Washington had abased himself before Whites, collaborating with the oppressor, aligning himself with "carpetbagging" capitalists like Andrew Carnegie who "colonized" the South, and selling out his race in exchange for power (Norrell 2009, 434-435). By the 1960s, members of the Civil Rights movement in the United States saw Washington as an "Uncle Tom" and an enemy of Black activism. Woodward and Harlan were also part of that movement.

Returning to Harlan's autobiographical essay (1988), he confesses that, when he thought of researching Washington's life, his intention was to produce an ironic or satirical biography. Then, he discovered the collection now known as the Booker T. Washington Papers in the US Library of Congress, acquired from Tuskegee in 1943. For Harlan, they opened up a new and unique world, hidden from the eyes of Whites and protected by Blacks. Washington and Emmett J. Scott had kept all of their correspondence over a period of more than fifteen years, providing the biographer with a treasure trove. Harlan edited these documents and organized them in an eleven-volume work entitled *The Booker T. Washington Papers*, published by the University of Chicago Press.

Harlan observes that, at first, he thought of Washington as the stereotypical "Uncle Tom," and adds that, in his view, that image still contained a great deal of truth. He believed that Washington had betrayed his race and the cause of justice and equality for all when he accepted segregation and money from the robber barons who ruled the United States. Behind this public character, however, Harlan admits that he found a much more complex, more humane, and more "manly" man, with a secret life known only to his closest confidantes.[118]

Harlan suggests a psychoanalytic approach, peeling away layers of Washington's personality like an onion. To reveal what at its core? A power-crazed man? A Minotaur? A lion? A fox? Br'er Rabbit?[119] Or, like the Wizard of Oz, was he just a frightened little man hiding behind a curtain? But perhaps there was nothing there at all—just a personality that had disintegrated in the frantic effort of trying to be everything to everyone in a multifaceted society (Harlan 1988). We

---

[118] Doubts about the "masculinity" of Black leaders who opted for non-violent tactics (or strategies) also arose later, when Malcolm X made similar comments about Martin Luther King, Jr. (Branch 1998, 13).

[119] A trickster-hero from the tales of Uncle Remus, a fictional character created by a White author, Joel Chandler Harris, who based his fables on the oral traditions of Black people in the United States.

perceive in this series of options that, although in his preface, Raymond Smock (1988) stresses the sensitivity and compassion with which Harlan supposedly treated Washington, strong traces of irony and scepticism still persist—an attitude that was hard to overcome for a biographer whose main goal should have been objectivity.[120]

A review in the *New York Times* of Robert Norrell's *Up from History* aptly summarizes the challenge faced by any biographer of Booker T. Washington in our time (Steele 2009). Starting from the paradox that "masking is an inevitable coping mechanism for the oppressed, but it is always oppressive in itself. It sacrifices great ideas and good people for the look of unity," the reviewer, Shelby Steele, who is Black, observes:

> No black man in American history has been more a victim of this paradox than Washington. And it is hard to think of a historical figure more in need of biographical rescue. Yet Washington is an awkward challenge for the contemporary scholar. He is so thoroughly stigmatized as politically incorrect that rescuing him could seem a political act in itself, and even a balanced book could be dismissed as a polemic. But Robert J. Norrell, in his remarkable new biography, "Up From History," gets around this problem the old-fashioned way: by scrupulously excavating the facts of his subject's life and then carefully situating him in his own era (Steele 2009).

In the prologue to his book, entitled "The Meaning of the Veil" (a reference to *Lifting the Veil of Ignorance*, a statue of Washington erected on the Tuskegee campus), Norell uses a literary device very common in popular biographies: he begins with a dramatic episode in his subject's experience to pique the reader's interest while

---

[120] Harlan also makes ironic references to the story of Moses in the chapter titles of his biography of Washington, an allusion made without any irony at all in the titles of Taylor Branch's classic trilogy on Martin Luther King, Jr. and the struggle for Civil Rights in the United States (see, for example, Branch 1998).

illustrating the book's purpose—retelling Washington's life in context. The event chosen—a visit by President Theodore Roosevelt to the Tuskegee Institute on October 24, 1905—is not one of the episodes commonly associated with Washington's life story. Norell sets the scene in a tense, dramatic moment: armed detectives from the Pinkerton agency are on the lookout for "other white men who had sworn violence against his [President Roosevelt's] friend. Threats against the life of Booker Washington had been pouring into Tuskegee for weeks" (Norell 2009, 1-2).

Norell goes on to give a detailed portrait of Washington that day:

A stocky, light brown man of forty-nine years, about five feet nine inches tall, Washington had grown a little heavy over the past decade, years that coincided with constant work, much travel, and incessant worry. His gray eyes, now a little cloudy and marked beneath with dark circles, looked out from a usually placid face with a penetrating intelligence at odds with his genial, slow speech. Perhaps no other man in the United States had a better command of contemporary events and issues—certainly those that pertained to the South—than Washington (Norell 2009, 3).

Washington was considered old, if not elderly. As Norell observes further on in his prologue, in 1905, the average life expectancy for a Black man in the United States was thirty-five (2009, 12).

While we await the details of the festivities organised to welcome the President of the United States—who would not stay to eat or sleep over—we discover that one of the causes of tensions and threats that day was the famous dinner at the White House in 1901, an act of audacity so "obnoxious" that, according to a South Carolina Democratic Senator "Pitchfork Ben" Tillman, it would require "lynching a thousand n******s in the South before they will learn their place again" (Norell 2009, 4; Bennett 2008, 58).

Viewed and celebrated by many as a great achievement, being the first Black American to dine at the White House was, in fact, a pyrrhic victory for Black civil rights. According to Norell, to appease

White Southern voters, Roosevelt had emphasised his Southern roots and never again invited Washington (or any other Black person) to the White House for dinner. Much worse, he had quietly stopped appointing Black men to government posts. Therefore, on the day in question, Washington did not know where things stood with his powerful friend.

Furthermore, Washington counted three White men, all named "Tom," among his bitterest foes. A local congressman, Tom Heflin, had threatened to lynch the founder of the Tuskegee Institute. Another congressman, Tom Watson of Georgia, had accused Washington of teaching Blacks that they were superior to Whites, insisting that "whites needed to put the arrogant Negro in his place." Finally, there was the North Carolina novelist Thomas Dixon Jr.,[121] who "portrayed Booker as a wolf in sheep's clothing, a sneaky conspirator to create racial equality, a Negro who tried to raise his race's economic status over whites." Dixon predicted that southern Whites would start killing Blacks, and Booker T. Washington would be solely to blame (Norell 2009, 5).

At the same time, the educator—who received honorary degrees from prestigious universities, but had not completed secondary school—was being attacked by the "Talented Tenth." Norell reminds his readers that when Washington delivered his famous speech at the Atlanta Exposition of 1895, an epidemic of lynchings was raging in the South, and White hatred of Blacks was intensifying. At the same time, the "Black nation" was looking for a leader to replace Frederick Douglass, who had died that year. The rights achieved by Black Americans after Emancipation in 1865 were being gradually eroded. "Between 1895 and 1905, most southern states had

---

[121] Considered the antithesis of Harriet Beecher Stowe, Thomas Dixon Jr. was the author of books such as *The Leopard's Spots* (1902) and *The Clansman* (1905). The latter inspired the film *Birth of a Nation* (1915), which praised the role of Ku Klux Klan in defence of southern Whites—especially White maidens—against the alleged violence and immorality of Blacks freed by Emancipation in the United States.

disfranchised Black voters, instituted segregation in most public places, and tolerated White terrorism against Blacks" (Norell 2009, 6). Even so, some northern Blacks saw Washington's attempts to reach a compromise with White southerners and ease these racial tensions as cowardice. They wanted him to be a "protest lion" like Douglass (Ibid.). Chief among those critics were William Monroe Trotter, who was involved in the "Boston Affray," and W. E. Burghard Du Bois, as he was known at the time, who joined forces to form two organizations to oppose what they called the "Tuskegee Machine"—the Niagara Movement and the NAACP.

Despite opposition from Whites and Blacks, Washington still maintained a positive (not to say positivist) view of the world—according to Norell, in 1905 "His instinct was to believe that the future would be better than the present.... He assumed that history was the story of progress—for Americans, for Black people, and for Booker Washington" (2009, 12). Nevertheless, Norell concludes his prologue with an account of the image of Tuskegee's founder and president after his death, when Washington would increasingly be characterized as a weakling and even a traitor, demonising him to the point where, referring to the statue "Lifting the Veil," which shows Washington removing the "veil of ignorance" from the head of a Black man, the author Ralph Ellison, a former Tuskegee student, has the protagonist of his novel *Invisible Man* question whether this veil is being removed to enlighten the Black man or lowered to blind him (Ellison 1995, 36; Norell 2009, 14). As he looks at the statue, the narrator sees a flock of starlings "flighting" before him and, suddenly, the bronze face of the "Founder, the cold Father symbol" is covered in "liquefied chalk—creating another ambiguity to puzzle my groping mind: Why is a bird-soiled statue more commanding than one that is clean?" (Ellison 1995, 36).

Booker T. Washington's posthumous image as a "bird-soiled statue" is haunting—not least because the metaphor is the work of a great writer, and an important figure in the Civil Rights movement. One could say that Washington's image was "soiled" by his Black rivals and White detractors—whether White supremacists or Civil

Rights activists like Harlan. However, a metaphor more powerful than "lifting the veil" comes from Washington himself, in *Up from Slavery*—"throwing off the mask":

> As the great day [of Emancipation] grew nearer, there was more singing in the slave quarters than usual. It was bolder, had more ring, and lasted later into the night. Most of the verses of the plantation songs had some reference to freedom. True, they had sung those same verses before, but they had been careful to explain that the "freedom" in these songs referred to the next world, and had no connection with life in this world. Now they gradually threw off the mask, and were not afraid to let it be known that the "freedom" in their songs meant freedom of the body in this world (1986, 19-20).

Racial violence and the overturning of freedoms given and won in the US South forced the "Wizard" to re-don the mask he had learned to wear as an enslaved child, to protect himself, his family, and the students and faculty of Tuskegee.[122] Viewing his actions out of context is a grave injustice. What should be appraised, and appreciated, is Booker T. Washington's legacy—chiefly, the historically Black university that Tuskegee has become. In Brazil, there were many who wished—and still wish—that someone like Washington had appeared in their country to ensure that Africans and their descendants emancipated in and before 1888 had access to even the most basic education and vocational training. One of those Brazilians was Manuel Querino.

---

[122] Paul Laurence Dunbar's poem "We Wear the Mask" movingly articulates this dilemma. https://www.poetryfoundation.org/poems/44203/we-wear-the-mask

Manuel Raymundo Querino[123]

When following Querino's posthumous reputation, we find that he was overlooked or belittled during the Second Afro-Brazilian Congress held in Bahia in 1937[124]; treated paternalistically by the psychiatrist and anthropologist Artur Ramos, who edited a collection of Querino's works first published in 1938,[125] and accused of plagiarism by the German-Brazilian friar and art historian Carlos Ott in 1947. For decades, Querino was virtually erased from Brazilian history, chiefly remembered for his posthumous work on Bahian cuisine. However, his obituaries and biographies clearly show the prestige he enjoyed in life.

Obituaries, biographies, introductions, and portrayals of Manuel Querino

Possibly the most moving eulogy for Querino is a manuscript message housed in the archives of the Instituto Geográfico e Histórico da Bahia (IGHB). Unsigned and undated, it is a powerful

---

[123] Over the years, there have been different spellings of Querino's names, including Manoel, Manuel, Raimundo, Raymundo, Quirino, and Querino. The editions of his works published in his lifetime show his first name as Manoel and Manuel. Therefore, for the sake of consistency, I have adopted the spelling used by his biographer Gonçalo de Athayde Pereira in 1932.

[124] Referring to *A raça africana e os seus costumes*, Renato Mendonça (1940, 104) observes: "Without much learning or capacity for interpretation, Querino limited himself to collecting the material, a fact that makes it more valuable for the demanding ethnographer." Mendonça was a diplomat who wrote history books and made "incursions" into anthropology and linguistics https://diplomatizzando.blogspot.com/2012/12/renato-mendonca-um-intelectual-na.html

[125] In his foreword, Ramos (1938, 5) describes Querino as follows: "Despite lacking the methodological rigour and scientific erudition of Nina Rodrigues, Manuel Querino was an honest researcher, a tireless worker, driven by that unsuspected interest that came from his own African origins." However, Ramos's criticisms of the ethnic identification of Africans in Querino's work in that edition were largely unfounded (see Gledhill 2010 and 2023).

expression of how greatly Querino's passing—which appears to have taken everyone by surprise—was mourned:

> The death of Manuel Querino opened a void among us that is unlikely to be filled. The companion we lost was a conscientious and robust worker, which explains and justifies the hurt we all feel. In him, the class of artists saw the disappearance of one of its most distinguished and prominent figures, adding to the circumstance that no one can currently find a good replacement.
>
> Manuel Querino was born in Santo Amaro in 1851, so he lived [for] about seventy-two years, occupying this existence usefully and nobly.
>
> It was an illustrious and patriotic man, Dr Correa Garcia, who directed the first steps of his education, which was rudimentary. *The rest he achieved by himself.*
>
> He cultivated and adorned his intelligence, slowly, with the resources he obtained, as the miser does with the pennies he acquires, to build up capital.
>
> He started working as a painter and decorator.
>
> As the Liceu de Artes e Ofícios [School of Arts and Crafts] was established here, he began to study some languages and the elements of the positive sciences there.
>
> The bent of his genius, however, led him to the arts, so when the painter Miguel Cañizares, along with some men of taste, founded the Academy of Fine Arts, Querino followed him and set to work in the drawing course, where he distinguished himself, and where he obtained the respective diploma.
>
> After the Academy was transformed into a School of Fine Arts, he enrolled in the architecture course, completing the 2nd year, but did not finish the course due to a lack of subjects that the School did not have the resources to maintain.
>
> During that time, he produced several works, especially decorative [designs], and tried to improve himself in geometric drawing.

Always unpretentious and devoid of feelings of spite and ill will, he joined the Department of Agriculture, where he served in various positions, rising to that of official.

He was passionate about the abolitionist issue, like many men of colour, and rightly so, and it consumed all his attention and efforts.

Educating his spirit, he began to write for the public, devoting his attention to both the aspects that refer to the arts and those which understood the earliest customs of Bahia.

He researched traditions and studied the works of architects, painters, and sculptors who flourished here, and left us a precious work on this subject, in his book *Artistas baianos*, followed by another that completes it, *As artes na Bahia.*

He also wrote a work demanding recognition of the African race for the powerful effort with which it contributed to clearing the lands of Brazil [for farming], *O colono preto.*

His monograph on *A Bahia de outrora* [the folklore of Bahia] also provides a great deal to savor for those who are interested in the [traditions] of our country.

He had a special predilection for things connected with Africans, which is why he closely studied the few who are still living, and he even wrote another work on African customs that he never published.

He also leaves unpublished a memorial he had written for the book celebrating the centenary of the Independence of Bahia.

In addition to these larger works, he wrote a compendium on linear drawing of the elementary classes, as well as another on the elements of geometric drawing.

At an age which, in our climate, is already considered advanced, he still possessed the surest vigour of spirit, as his final works attest (emphasis added).[126]

---

[126] Archives of the Instituto Geográfico e Histórico da Bahia (BHA04D.053).

At least six newspapers in the states of Bahia and Rio de Janeiro published obituaries or death notices of Querino. Two Bahian publications based in Salvador, *A Tarde* and *Diário de Notícias*, put his obituaries on their front pages on the day of his death, February 14, 1923. As it was also Ash Wednesday, *Diário de Notícias* placed his photograph below pictures of Carnaval:

THE DEATH OF PROF. MANUEL QUIRINO
At 5:30 this morning, on his country estate in Matatú Grande, the victim of a persistent illness that, about twenty days ago, had confined him to his bed, surrounded by the love of his family, Professor Manuel Quirino passed away. With the modesty followed as a standard of life, the deceased was not only a passionate scholar of the men and events of Bahia of yore, but a perfect connoisseur of this branch of history, a paragon of the Black race. On this subject, he leaves a copious output, shedding light on points that he could only clarify through his special studies, having presented interesting and highly original memoirs on the occasion of the 5th Congress of Geography and History, held in this city.

A member of the Historic Institute, he made himself heard there, at several gatherings, in his specialty. It so happens that we remembered one of those topics that he favoured, a subject set down in curious chapters in our [newspaper] columns—Culinary art in Bahia. What an admirable depth of knowledge, on a little-versed subject, on the origins of the tastiest dishes of our land's inviting cuisine, from the adaptation here of delicacies of African origin to the creation of others inspired by them!

In his field, Manuel Quirino was unique. He was one of those necessary people, because they are irreplaceable. Who else would be capable of writing sheets and sheets of paper, about, for example, artists of colour, from Bahia, exquisite, albeit obscure?...

In losing him, Bahia has lost *one of those rare artists with the singular advantage of working with letters (Diário de Notícias* 1923, emphasis added).

A Tarde published the following notice, also illustrated with a photo of Querino:

A USEFUL LIFE HAS BEEN EXTINGUISHED
PROFESSOR MANUEL QUERINO IS DEAD
A civil servant, teacher at the school of arts and crafts, and passionate chronicler of the men and things of Bahia, Manuel Querino was a tireless researcher of our age-old traditions. From him, we could glean information about the past of the province with the longest [history] in Brazil, as from the best living source. That is why, when we learned of his death today, it was with the painful impression that the disappearance of a useful life always leaves us, replete with healthy examples of love of work, dedication to good literature, and devotion to the nation, for the cultivation of its history, in addition to the esteem we had for him as an excellent collaborator of *A TARDE*.[127]

Three days later, on February 17, the same newspaper published the following note on page one, entitled "Manuel Quirino Street": "A proposal was presented yesterday at the City Council calling for Matatú Grande Street, in Brotas, where the Bahian artist and writer died, to be renamed Professor Manuel Quirino Street. In a posthumous homage, approving this proposal, the Council adjourned its session." There is still a Manuel Querino Street in Matatú de Brotas.

As we saw in the previous chapter, the *Diário da Bahia* also featured his obituary on page one of its February 15, 1923 issue. Here it is in its entirety:

---

[127] I would like to thank the Black Brazilian journalist and scholar, Dr Cleidiana Ramos, for transcribing this nearly illegible obituary, which she found in *A Tarde*'s digital archives.

THE DEATH OF PROF. MANUEL QUERINO

Professor Manuel Querino's death had a profound impact on his circles of friends, as well as those who considered him the recorder of the past, of the men and customs of yesteryear in our land, in excellent books.

He was 72 years old, and the activity he carried out, as a teacher at the Orphãos de São Joaquim and at the Liceu de Artes e Ofícios, gave the impression of the robustness of a young man, because, in the leisure activities of the teacher and civil servant of Agriculture, he was incessantly productive.

Lately, he was completing an exhaustive monograph on the 2nd of July festivities [of Bahia's Independence], from their origins, having managed to obtain the drawings of the first daises erected for these civic celebrations.

A man of colour, he wrote a remarkable book, *O colono preto*, describing and emphasizing the values of the Black race in the exploration and culture of Brazilian territory.

[In] sugarcane farming and industry, the basis of economic progress in nascent Brazil, it was the Black arm that began them and made them prosper.

O colono preto was, perhaps, the best work of the Geography Congress held in Bahia.

Before this invaluable contribution to our history, Manuel Quirino wrote and published *A Bahia de outrora, homens e coisas do passado*, and *Artistas baianos*, the renowned [artists of Bahia], from the founding of Bahia to the present day.

The City Council would pay a well-deserved tribute to the illustrious historiographer of our land if it named the street of the Liceu de Artes e Ofícios or the street of the Colégio dos Orphãos de S. Joaquim after Manuel Quirino.[128]

The funeral of the late lamented man from Bahia took place yesterday, with a large gathering in attendance, his most excellent widow and children receiving countless expressions of condolence.

---

[128] This recommendation was not followed.

The final farewells were said to him at the graveside by Major Cosme de Farias,[129] Dr Martinho Braga, Professor Ozeas Santos, and Antonio Vianna.

O Imparcial published a notice—also on page one—entitled "An Illustrious Bahian Who Is No Longer Among Us—The Death of Prof. Manuel Querino" on February 15, 1923:

> With the death of Professor Manuel Querino, in addition to a brilliant, overly modest spirit, Bahia yesterday lost one of the most fervent cultivators of our country's traditions.
>
> Beginning his life as a craftsman and later teaching the specialty in which he was a master of undeniable value, Prof. Manuel Querino, through his work, his honesty and enlightenment, achieved the prominent place in society to which he was entitled, having been elected city councillor more than once.
>
> As a civil servant and even as a teacher, Manuel Querino enjoyed a wide circle of admirers, helping with his interesting and curious historical research to enrich the country's literature with the publication of several highly appreciated works such as 'Bahia de outrora', 'O Colono Preto' and 'Artistas baianos.'
>
> In Manuel Querino we all had the most authoritative source on the subjects that were dealt with in his books [illegible] due to his determination to render services to the history of this country.
>
> In the working-class milieu from which he came and in whose midst he was always the most illustrious representative,

---

[129] Cosme de Farias (1875-1972) was a "rábula" or self-taught lawyer who championed the poor, combated illiteracy, and became a legendary figure in Bahia. A district of Salvador is named after him. Between 1914 and 1921, his People's Committee Against the High Cost of Living met periodically at the headquarters of the Centro Operário da Bahia and the Sociedade Montepio dos Artistas (Castellucci 2005), two entities with which Manuel Querino had close ties. Like Querino, Cosme de Farias inspired a character in Jorge Amado's novel *Tent of Miracles*.

he enjoyed unlimited prestige and consideration, being a member of various associations of this nature and also of the Historical Institute where he made himself heard so many times with great respect and admiration.

Note here that the adjective "modest" is used to suggest that perhaps he suffered from false modesty.

The following obituary stresses the "large gathering" in attendance when he was laid to rest:

His funeral took place yesterday afternoon at the Quinta dos Lázaros cemetery, with a large gathering in attendance, including the City Intendent [Mayor]. the Secretary of Agriculture and a representative of the Secretary of Police and Public Security.

At his graveside, Major Cosme de Farias uttered words in his memory on behalf of the Centro Operário; Antonio Vianna, on behalf of the Instituto Geográfico e Histórico; Prof. Oséas Santos, on behalf of the School of Fine Art.

Many wreaths and chaplets were placed on his tomb, along with heartfelt messages *(O Democrata,* February 15,1923, p. 2).

I have not been able to find any obituaries for Querino in newspapers from his hometown, Santo Amaro, but *A Ordem,* from nearby Cachoeira (published on Thursdays and Saturdays) reported the news of his death on page one on February 21, 1923. The focus here was clearly on his work as a labour leader:

PROFESSOR MANUEL QUERINO IS DEAD
Bahia has just lost one of its most amiable figures and one of its most distinguished personages.

Born a worker, he became a worker, and as a worker he died.

In the last years of his life, it didn't matter that he set aside his professional equipment and tools, because he continued to be a worker, always surrounded by the best esteem and consideration of the people.

This was Professor Manuel Querino, one of the most beloved figures in Bahia.

A devoted researcher of things from the country's past, Manuel Querino had become the purest source of information for everyone.

He was about 72 years old and his burial was the ultimate proof of public sympathies towards the lamented deceased.

Manuel Querino's death occurred on the 14th of this month.

For this deeply felt loss, our condolences to Bahia.

The only death notice published in Brazilian newspapers outside Bahia that is available in the Brazilian National Library's digital newspaper collection,[130] appeared on page two of *A Noite*, from Rio de Janeiro, on February 17, 1923. Here, Querino is remembered more prominently than Professor of Medicine Oscar Freire de Carvalho, a follower of Nina Rodrigues, who died in São Paulo on January 11:

TWO GREAT LOSSES FOR BAHIAN EDUCATION
Honouring the memory of professors Oscar Freire and Manuel Querino

BAHIA, 15 (Delayed) (A NOITE special service)—With a large gathering [of mourners], the funeral of Professor Manuel Querino took place yesterday afternoon at the Quintas cemetery. Major Cosme Farias, Lawyer Martinho de Souza, Professor Oscar Santos and Mr. Antonio Viana spoke at the graveside.

The "Diario da Bahia" recalls, as a tribute to the deceased, that the street by the Liceu [should] be named Manuel Querino Street.

The Polytechnic School will hold a solemn ceremony this evening in Professor Oscar Freire's memory.

Unlike Booker T. Washington, Manuel Querino was fortunate in his biographers, who were also close friends. However, he was not so lucky when it came to the authors of forewords to posthumous

---

[130] <http://hemerotecadigital.bn.br/>.

editions of his works. The first known biography of Querino was the introduction to *A Bahia de outrora*, by **José Teixeira Barros (1863-1933)**, dated May 1916. A journalist and author (Vianna 1928, 305), Teixeira Barros wrote a seminal article on whale fishing in Bahia, published in the inaugural issue of *Revista do Norte* (Castellucci Junior 2008, 188). According to Teixeira Barros himself, he was also a militant abolitionist. In his biographical essay, he tells us "I first met Manuel Querino in 1887, when the abolitionist campaign was most persevering, and in one of the sessions of the Sociedade Libertadora Baiana [Bahia Freedom Society], held in the newsroom of *Gazeta da Tarde*" (Barros 1922, iii). Teixeira Barros published essays in the journal of the Instituto Histórico da Bahia (Calmon 1949, 134) and was a member of both that institution and the IGHB. Bernardino de Souza invited Teixeira Barros to give a speech when Querino's portrait was unveiled in the IGHB's gallery of honour, but he declined, supposedly due to "his excessive reticence,"[131] suggesting that another friend of Querino, the journalist and poet Antônio Vianna, speak in his place (Vianna 1928, 305). As we saw in the previous chapter, Teixeira Barros played a key role in the posthumous publication of *A arte culinaria na Bahia*.

We can consider Teixeira Barros's essay an authorised biography, as it was published in a book by Querino during the author's lifetime. It is also a vital source for future biographers. Barros stresses his subject's origins: "Manuel Raymundo Querino was born into a humble, but hard-working and honourable home on July 28, 1851, in the neighbouring town of Santo Amaro, in this state" (Barros 1922, iv). He also makes a point of mentioning the factors and aspects of Querino's rise from painter and decorator to teacher and writer, as well as his studies, awards, and professional, educational, and

---

[131] In a letter from Teixeira Barros to Bernardino de Souza dated March 2, 1928, Barros explains that he had not been able to speak in public for many years, on account of a severe stutter (Carta para Bernardino de Souza sobre o tributo à memória de Manoel Querino. Archives of the Instituto Geográfico e Histórico da Bahia, IGHB.CX23D.071).

political activities. The biographical essay concludes with a list of works Querino had published thence far, noting that another book, *Costumes africanos*, was awaiting publication, and that "this work is of a certain magnitude and will highly recommend the author to public appreciation and to the applause of the cognoscenti" (Barros 1922, vii).

Another invaluable biographical essay is the speech which Vianna gave in Teixeira Barros's stead at the ceremony held at the Instituto Geográfico e Histórico da Bahia on the fortieth anniversary of Abolition, May 13, 1928, when "the portrait of the renowned seeker of traditions was hung in the gallery of honour" (Vianna 1928, 305).[132] After recounting Querino's life story, Vianna expressed his profound admiration for his late friend:

> Manuel Raymundo Querino is studied as an artist, as a public man, as a patriot, as a friend of his race, as a brother of the humble and a revealer of oddities.
>
> This multiplicity of aspects does not fit the same critical concept of those who come to deal with the individuality of so many facets....
>
> If he did not appear in the immortal galleries of painters or in the favourite archives of classical artists, he nevertheless revealed those qualities which raised him in the discerning esteem of his contemporaries (Vianna 1928, 310).

Vianna also stressed the privileged access Querino enjoyed as a participant and observer of Candomblé terreiros:

> From his humble birth, he brought simplicity of manners and contact with common things from which he was able to draw

---

[132] As we will see in Chapter 5, this portrait is no longer part of the IGHB's collection, and its whereabouts are unknown. Pedro Calmon (1995, 20) and E. Bradford Burns (1974) both mention it in their articles on Querino (See Gledhill 2011a and 2020, Chapter 9).

surprising things of interest. His work of observation, carried out day by day in the heart of the community, reveals this to us. Where would anyone, other than Querino, find the free entry, the cordial welcome, in the refuges of exotic religions whose followers, wary of the insincerity of the elites, live enclosed in the secrecy of their belief and their rites? These precious repositories were not closed to him. They welcomed him as a friend who would never betray their trust (1928, 310).

At another point, he observes: "How many times have I heard him make extensive considerations, in a private lecture, about the moral greatness of the Black, the African, who, enslaved, molested and without rights, fanatically faced the fulfilment of duty" (Vianna 1928, 311).

Finally, he describes Querino as a "Man of action, a man of vigour, a man of initiative" who "single-handedly would have come to comprise an interesting library, where scholars would come to imbibe knowledge that is perhaps unknown to those who rightly consider themselves to be scholars in other branches of knowledge." And he concludes: "He will always be admired by posterity, upright for the honesty with which he conducted his research, exemplary in the exact fulfilment of duty, unsurpassed in modesty, which enhanced his value, of which this tribute, today, is a serene judgment" (Vianna 1928, 316).

Published that same year (1928), Querino's study of Bahian cuisine, *A arte culinária na Bahia*, is one of the works for which he would become best known, with a preface by Bernardino de Souza. Entitled "By Way of a Foreword—About the Geography of Food," it contains "considerations" presented at a session of the IGHB by its permanent secretary. Souza begins by describing the author as "my old friend Professor Manuel Querino, steadfast investigator of our past," but the essay itself deals with culinary studies in general and goes far beyond the researcher's life.

In 1932, Manuel Querino was still viewed positively – although he seemed to be considered an "unclassifiable" enigma. Published in *A*

Tarde, a leading Bahian newspaper, a review of a book by the engineer, playwright and journalist Sílio Boccanera Júnior (1863-1928) compares Boccanera with Querino, who was his contemporary, and another Brazilian intellectual of African descent:

> Sílio Boccanera Júnior and Manuel Querino were intellectual creatures who were misunderstood in their time. No activity, however, is more praiseworthy than that which they pursued, toiling with archives, lengthy quotations from old books, tombstones, buildings, and facts and figures from our remote, or recent, historical past. Manuel Querino has a body of work which still requires classification, in the field of informative production, the pursuit of things from yesteryear, so much to the taste of those who are curious about the life of our ancestors. Sílio Boccanera did the same. He was devoted to chronicling times gone by. His gaze was lost in the receding horizons of the past, eager to make enlightening contributions regarding the types, customs, and events of the evolutionary life of the province, of which he became an indefatigable commentator, in study after study, generally received with coldness, if not antipathy. Why, if not because of a regrettable defect of culture, do we attach so little importance to works that resemble what we once were, in the escalation of time? Why, if not out of disaffection for native things, do we relegate to oblivion the rebellious voices evoking the traditions and legends and feats of our lands and our people? Manuel Querino, Sílio Boccanera Júnior, and, more recently, Silva Campos (so different, by the way, in terms of style) are the best raconteurs of our past. A posthumous work by Sílio Boccanera Júnior, one of those collections of things gone by, has just been published. It is his *Bahia epigráfica e econográfica* (Epigraphic and Iconographic Bahia), containing valuable documents collected

from all angles of our old and traditional city (Chiacchio, 1932).[133]

The first posthumous biography of Querino, *Prof. Manuel Querino, sua vida e suas obras* (Prof. Manuel Querino, His Life and Works), is a thirty-four-page booklet published in the same year as the book review. The author, Gonçalo de Athayde Pereira, had been a friend and colleague of Querino for many years, having worked alongside him at the Bahia Department of Agriculture.[134] Pereira also published works on diamond mining in the Lençóis region of Bahia, and the town of Rio das Contas. The "epistolary foreword" dated May 24, 1932, was penned by José Teixeira Barros, who observes:

> Singular and, for that very reason, deserving of high praise, is the friend's spontaneous and unremitting initiative, when he exalts, in these pages, so full of sincerity, the profile of a man of the moral worth of Manuel Raymundo Querino, who did not bend to irreconcilable whims.
>
> The noble writer did not want the dense penumbra of unjust oblivion to envelop, at all, the memory of the modest worker who so greatly advocated the distinction of the working class, at the same time that he urged it to take an interest in the momentous ideals of social and political scope, conducive to public happiness.
>
> His thoughtful and plain words were always heard in workers' societies and associations, outlining itineraries and guidelines with which they should head towards their ambitious destinations.

---

[133] I would like to thank Dr Cleidiana Ramos for finding this article in *A Tarde's* digital archives and sharing it with me. It is interesting to note that the historian João da Silva Campos (1880-1940) was Black. A photograph of Sílio Boccanera indicates that he was mixed race—Brown but "socially White." This may have been a reason for the comparison of these three scholars.

[134] Pereira explains his relationship to Querino in a letter to Bernardino de Souza which is housed in the archives of the Instituto Geográfico e Histórico da Bahia (IGHB.CX23D.246).

On opportune occasions, he resorted to the press, sometimes covertly, sometimes with individual responsibility. For this reason, he was surrounded by a broad aura of popularity (Pereira 1932, i).

Here, Barros discusses the meaning of popularity, comparing Querino with "the famous tribune César Zama" (Pereira 1932, ii).[135] Towards the end of his "letter-foreword," Barros describes Querino's life as "active and febrile, punctuated with bitter hardships and harsh disappointments," and concludes (Pereira 1932, ii):

> The esteemed friend can repeat to himself this expressive phrase by Montalembert: "Amidst the discouragement, hesitation, and apostasies that besiege us, may at least our voices and our lives remain in harmony with our past."
> Faith remains unshakable.

Gonçalo de Athayde Pereira's biography of Querino also contains an important appendix—a letter from Bernardino de Souza recalling that Querino's portrait was "unveiled together with that of the Brazilian scholar Nina Rodrigues, in the gallery of our illustrious men" on May 13, 1928. Making clear that Querino was held in great esteem by his contemporaries and colleagues, Bernardino observes: "It is well known that they were, until now in Bahia, the two greatest scholars of the African race. I constantly receive requests for information about their work from Rio, S[ão] Paulo and other Brazilian states" (Pereira 1932, 34).[136]

---

[135] Aristides César Spínola Zama (1837-1906) was a politician, physician and author. His home in Caetité, Bahia Brazil, is now an historic monument. http://cpdoc.fgv.br/sites/default/files/verbetes/primeira-republica/ZAMA,%20C%C3%A9sar.pdf .

[136] In a letter from Pereira to Bernardino de Souza, found in the archives of the IGHB, Pereira explains that he had not mentioned the unveiling of the portrait in the biography because he had not heard the news – he had been away in Juazeiro, in the northern part of Bahia, and fallen ill upon his return (IGHB.CX23S.246).

On the first page of his biography, Pereira describes Querino as "an artist, civil servant, modest, hardworking, always cheerful, dignified and, above all, fulfilled his functional duties," and states that "He lived in honourable poverty, taking care to raise his four children with the desire to provide each of them with an art or craft to guarantee their future" (Pereira, 1932, 3). Further on, he explains that he had mentioned the life of Manuel Querino and his "functional activities, without dealing with his biography" because his life story was probably well known, as "it has already been published so many times in newspapers and magazines that travel the world in memoirs and leaflets, as a posthumous tribute from his friends and admirers, in which renowned publicists here and outside the State have studied and appreciated him from various perspectives, each more interesting and sincere [than the last]" (Pereira 1932, 21). He adds a list of the personages who had written and spoken about Querino, including Miguel Calmon, Braz do Amaral, Torquato Bahia,[137] Gonçalo de Athayde Pereira himself, Cosme de Farias, João de Barros, Teodoro Sampaio, and Bernardino de Souza. Pereira extends an invitation to future biographers, insisting that his "rough lines" did not amount to a "work that substantiates the important events in the simple life of Manuel Querino and the important role he played in the course of his existence, often full of obstacles, whose resulting evils he endured with the evangelical patience and resignation of a true believer like himself" (Ibid., 25). And the biographer recounts an event that occurred after Querino's death, which aptly illustrates the "obstacles" and "evils" he endured in life:

---

[137] Francisco Torquato Bahia da Silva Araújo (1850-1919) wrote the foreword to the first edition of *Artistas baianos (1909)*, and Querino dedicated the second edition of *As artes na Bahia* (1913) to him, describing him as a "distinguished man of letters." Torquato Bahia was the founder of chair no. 28 of the Bahia Academy of Letters, of which he was also the first treasurer when it was established in 1917 (https://academiadeletrasdabahia.org.br/).

...Prof. Manuel Querino applied for one of the Caminhoá awards, and that year, there were four applicants, so the amount to be distributed was divided among the four candidates: Dr Bernardino de Souza, Dr Borges de Barros, Eng. Silio Boccanera Filho and Prof. Manuel Querino. The opinion on Manuel Querino's essays was given by Eng. Teodoro Sampaio. All the others received the amount that fell to them, except Querino, because his essays, with a favourable opinion, were destroyed and did not reach the Treasury. Neither his widow nor her children received the amount pertaining to the applicant Manuel Querino. The State was governed by Dr J. J. Seabra. Secretary of the Interior Dr Landulpho Medrado. Judging committee: Teodoro Sampaio who was the rapporteur for Querino's essays. Junqueira Ayres, president, and Braz do Amaral. It was yet another disappointment for the artist and writer to add to his other sufferings, and also worthy of mention (Pereira 1932, 25-26).

Other posthumous affronts would follow, both subtle and overt. An editorial published on the front page of *A Tarde* on December 6, 1932,[138] entitled "Black Fronts: A new problem—Why?—Men of colour and Brazil—Bahia and artificial problems—Direction of a development—Anachronistic impertinence," lists Manuel Querino among the illustrious Black men who (in the editorialist's view) were proof that a Black movement was unnecessary in Bahia, let alone Brazil:

> We must forget the past and rip up the nation's history to believe it indispensable to improvise "black fronts" to appreciate men of colour. The presumptuousness of questions of race and the spectre of "ethnic minorities" which horrify and unsettle Europe

---

[138] Most of the first page is devoted to reports on political exiles, including former president Artur Bernardes, a reminder that it was published after Getúlio Vargas's 1930 coup. I would like to thank Dr Cleidiana Ramos for obtaining it from the Cedoc *A Tarde* archives.

have never perturbed Brazilian statesmen. And the foreign writers who believed, a century ago, that diversity in populations made national disintegration possible, soon saw their prophecy unfulfilled and their premonition unavailing with the progressive and rapid Aryanization—the Brazilian "melting pot" [in English]—of the elements that make up our people. We are, in the world, a people born and developed outside the odious framework of racial preventions—in this respect superior to all other peoples. The Bahia of Luiz Gama, Montezuma, Rebouças, Manoel Querino, Elias Nazareth, [and] Teodoro Sampaio, does not need "black fronts" copied from other climes to present the perfect fraternization of its children to Brazil. The most regrettable problems are the artificial problems.

The list includes other Black men who are still well-known names in Brazil today. Luiz Gama (1830-1882) was an abolitionist, writer, and *rábula* (self-taught lawyer), born free but enslaved by his White father at the age of ten; "Montezuma" was Francisco Jê Acaiaba de Montezuma, Viscount of Jequitinhonha (1794-1870), a jurist, diplomat and politician; André Rebouças (1838-1898) was a military engineer and abolitionist, and Elias de Figueiredo Nazareth (1870-1922) was a teacher and director of the Normal School of Bahia, whom Manuel Querino mentioned in "Os homens de cor preta na história" (Nascimento and Gama 2009, 193; Santos 2020, 95).[139] As we have seen, Teodoro Sampaio (1855-1937) was a polymath who became president of the Instituto Geográfico e Histórico da Bahia. His mother was an enslaved Black woman and his father, a White priest who gave him his surname and ensured that he received an education. Although the editorial placed Querino in good company, by using him as evidence of "racial democracy" in Brazil, let alone

---

[139] Nazareth and Querino had much in common. Nazareth published a compendium on linear design, and was a member of the Instituto Geográfico e Histórico da Bahia, which he represented at a Geography conference in São Paulo (in Nascimento and Gama 2009, 193).

"Aryanization" (meaning "whitening" in this context), it went against everything he championed. It is also ironic, because in the years and decades that followed, Querino's race and class were (subtly and overtly) used to denigrate his scholarship.

Among the first to do so was the editor of the anthology of Querino's work entitled *Costumes africanos no Brasil* (African Customs in Brazil), published in 1938.[140] A White psychiatrist and ethnologist from Alagoas, Artur Ramos (1938, 5) observes: "Within the long period of silence that fell on the work of Nina Rodrigues—almost two decades!—the only voice that was raised, full of enthusiasm and emotion, in defence of the Brazilian Black, was that of Manuel Querino, in Bahia, speaking of the African contribution to Brazilian civilization." But then, Ramos goes on to belittle Querino in the second paragraph: "While lacking the methodological rigor and scientific erudition of Nina Rodrigues, Manuel Querino was, nevertheless, an honest researcher, a tireless worker, driven by selfless interest which stemmed from his own African origins." Ramos agrees with João Ribeiro that *A raça africana e os seus costumes na Bahia* was "one of the most important [works] we have about the African race in Brazil"—"Because, despite its flaws, some quite serious, which remove from this work the imprint of being rigorously scientific, it is still one of the most solid landmarks of honest documentation about Black people in Brazil" (Ramos 1938, 56).

Even so, Ramos recognises that Querino had access to information which had escaped Nina Rodrigues's notice, because the "humble Black teacher" was surrounded by "old Africans, *pais* and *mães de santo* (high priests and priestesses)," both at the Gantois Candomblé community, in the Federação district of Salvador (now Alto do Gantois), and at his home in Matatu Grande. Ramos tells the

---

[140] The first edition of the anthology is illustrated, and brings together *A raça africana e os seus costumes, O colono preto como fator da civilização brasileira, A arte culinária na Bahia,* and several chapters from *A Bahia de outrora.* As we will see, several editions have been published since then.

story of Querino's life and quotes Gonçalo de Athayde Pereira when recounting an episode in which Querino followed his conscience, defied the "powers that be," and failed to be re-appointed as city councillor as a result.[141] Ramos observes, "And thus it was all his life. In his modest position as third official of the Department of Agriculture, he suffered the most incredible humiliations." Ramos concludes: "Manuel Querino symbolized this type of average civil servant, hardworking and conscientious in his work, but without the advantages of that incredible thing which in Brazil is called a *pistolão* (patron or godfather). Simply put, Manuel Querino was a civil servant without a pistolão" (Ramos 1938, 11).

To conclude his critique of Querino's "scientific" credibility with a coup de grace, Ramos explains:

> There would be much to discuss and improve in these essays by Manuel Querino. Studies in Africanology have taken a vertiginous turn in our days. Methods have improved, and there is a concern among the heirs of the School of Nina Rodrigues with maintaining the strict traditions of the school, in the sector of Black-Brazilian studies. *Self-taught*, working with methodological independence, without direct connections with the traditions of the Bahian School, Manuel Querino allowed himself to slip into flaws and shortcomings which, in a way, rob some of his works of precise scientific flavour (1938, 15, emphasis added).

Even so, Ramos does not deny that the author of the collection he edited had some value:

---

[141] "...he opposed authoritarian laws, unjust reforms, displeasing the powers that be while winning the support of those who would be harmed by those reforms, which were only intended to benefit friends and cronies of the system. On that occasion, he formed a bloc with others and had several civil servants restored to their posts after they were fired by an unjust reform: and this cost him the re-election, retiring happily to his obscurity, knowing that he had done his duty, at ease with his conscience as a civil servant" (Ramos 1938, 10).

These failures become merits, however, if we look at the deficient conditions in which he worked and researched, without any means of aid, without stimuli from the environment, isolated with his secrets and disappointments. He fled to the study of people of his race as an escape. In the seclusion of Candomblé, listening to the elders of the Gantois terreiro, he turned his back on a world that had been almost hostile to him (Ramos 1938, 15).[142]

Ramos's words recall those of the Black American historian John Hope Franklin, from "The Dilemma of the Negro Scholar," quoted in relation to Querino by E. Bradford Burns: "The world of the Negro scholar is indescribably lonely; and he must, somehow, pursue truth down that lonely path while, at the same time, making certain that his conclusions are sanctioned by universal standards developed and maintained by those who frequently do not even recognize him" (Franklin 1969; Burns 1974, 81, note 16).

The foreword to the third edition of *A Bahia de outrora*,[143] by the folklorist, linguist, bibliophile, and ethnologist Frederico Edelweiss (1892-1976), expresses greater solidarity with the author.[144] Writing in 1946, the year before Querino would be accused of plagiarism by Carlos Ott, Edelweiss observed:

---

[142] This is not the place for a detailed analysis of the "flaws" that Ramos found in Querino's work, but I have analysed his criticism of the Bahian scholar's ethnic identifications of Africans in Bahia, and found that far from being incorrect, as Ramos claims, they are sometimes based on the Africans' self-identification (Gledhill 2010 and 2023).

[143] There are two "third editions" of *A Bahia de outrora*: one published in 1946, with forewords by Edelweiss and Barros, annotated by Edelweiss; the second, with the same forewords, illustrated by Carybé and Ligia, was published in 1955 by Editora Progresso as part of a series of works by Querino that also included *A arte culinária na Bahia* (1951) and *Bailes pastoris* (1957).

[144] Edelweiss was also a member and president of the Instituto Geográfico e Histórico da Bahia (Sena 1977). Like Querino, Martiniano Eliseu do Bonfim, and Cosme de Farias, he inspired a character in Jorge Amado's *Tent of Miracles* (2003).

Manuel Querino was the strange result of his reactionary social aspirations and his penchant for traditionalist studies. In the former, he was doomed to failure. How many times must he have heard that trite and still common phrase: "That Black doesn't know his place!"? His defence of his racial brethren brought him both sympathy and antipathy; mostly antipathy (Edelweiss 1946, 1-2).

Three years later, Pedro Calmon published the second edition of his *História da literatura baiana* (History of Bahian Literature),[145] in which he draws a striking comparison between Nina Rodrigues and Manuel Querino:

It is curious to note that, as an Africanist, [Nina Rodrigues] was not an Africanophile. On the contrary, he sprinkled his essays with pessimism, marginalizing them with sober comments, not wanting to perpetuate the policy of flattering the ethnic element he studied, nor having the originality to superimpose it on other social influences. It would be up to Manuel Querino to insist, not only on defending, but on the spiritual vindication of the Blacks as a factor of progress; *himself one of those splendid Black artists who, with their personal case, dispel common prejudices about the inferiority of the race* (Calmon 1949, 154, emphasis added).

Published in 1955, *A raça africana* is part of the series of works by Querino published by Editora Progresso, and features a new foreword by the owner of that publishing house, the "businessman, publisher, university professor, administrator, and bibliophile" Pinto de Aguiar (Tavares 2011, 9). Aguiar bases his foreword primarily on the one Artur Ramos included in *Costumes africanos no Brasil* (1938), while bringing his own perspective. Aguiar begins with the following statement—"The contribution of Manuel Querino to the study of the position of the African group in our culture is one that cannot be

---

[145] The first edition was published in 1902.

forgotten or underestimated." However, he then goes on to underestimate Querino himself in the following paragraph (1955, 5):

Even though his conclusions, derived from a self-taught curious spirit, without scientific training, and without methodological intuition, have been surpassed, his observations have the inestimable value of being collected at a time when the phenomenon of racial miscegenation and acculturation had not yet, in a way, robbed their customs, rites, and human types of the purity, or at least a great proximity, to the original standards and sources (1955, 5).

Like Vianna and Ramos, Pinto de Aguiar stresses Querino's privileged access to the most restricted spaces of Afro-Bahian culture, due to his respectful attitude towards his brothers and sisters of colour:

His African descent, and attitude of deep sympathy and understanding of the beliefs, habits, and destinies of his blood brothers, gave him access to the most esoteric areas of cults and Black families, allowing him to collect at the source this immense wealth of information that he passed on to us, in the simplicity of his relaxed and picturesque prose (Aguiar 1955, 5).

Aguiar agrees with Ramos's observation that, in this regard, the work of the "great Black man from Bahia" was "more valuable, as a set of observations, than that of the sage from Maranhão [Nina Rodrigues]" (Ibid., 6). And he concludes by reinforcing the image of the "humble Black teacher, the artist devoted to his work, the exemplary head of his family and devoted friend, the defender of the causes of workers of his level, of the scholar of Black issues in Brazil" (Ibid., 11).

In 1969, Jorge Amado published *Tenda dos milagres (Tent of Miracles)*, which, among many other subjects, recounts the clash between the beadle and mixed-race researcher Pedro Archanjo and his archenemy, Nilo Argolo, a lecturer at the Bahia School of

Medicine, a bastion of scientific racism (2008). Despite some differences of opinion in academic circles regarding the basis for the latter character, João Reis correctly asserts that it was inspired by Nina Rodrigues (Reis 2008b, 295).[146] As for the inspiration for Pedro Archanjo, Amado himself explains: "...he is the sum of many people combined: the writer Manuel Querino, the Babalaô Martiniano Eliseu do Bonfim, Miguel Santana Obá Aré, the poet Artur Sales, the songwriter Dorival Caymmi, and the alufá Licutã [from the 1835 Revolt of the Malês]—and myself, of course" (Amado 1992, 139).[147] According to Reis, "the 'intellectual' and militant side" of Pedro Archanjo "was inspired by the mestiço Manuel Querino..." (2008b, 295).

In 1973, the Universidade Federal da Bahia Centre for Afro-Asian Studies (CEAO) offered an extension course called "The Life and Work of Manuel Querino," during which the historian and journalist Jorge Calmon—entitled "Manuel Querino, the Journalist and the Politician." Later, his lecture would be published as an article by CEAO, in May 1984, and a booklet entitled *O vereador Manuel Querino* (The City Councillor Manuel Querino), published by the Salvador City Council in 1995 (Calmon 1984, 1995).[148] This essay

---

[146] It should be noted that, although their views on Africans and their descendants differed dramatically – putting Querino at one end of the spectrum and Nina Rodrigues at the other – there is no indication of any animosity between them in real life. When Querino refers to Nina as "malogrado" – which some have interpreted as pejorative – it simply means "ill fated," as he died relatively young. He also states that he was taking up where Nina left off (1938, 19). The fact that their portraits were unveiled in the IGHB's gallery at the same ceremony in 1928, is a strong indication of the prestige both scholars enjoyed at that time.

[147] Jorge Amado personally confirmed this to me at an event at the Jorge Amado House Foundation in Salvador's historic district in the 1990s. Fortunately, he also stated it categorically in his "non-memoir" *Navegação de cabotagem* (1992), as some Brazilian academics refused to believe that Pedro Archanjo was inspired by Querino, despite the clear similarities between the fictional character's bibliography and that of the Black Bahian scholar.

[148] An English translation can be found in the anthology *Manuel Querino (1851-1923): An Afro-Brazilian Pioneer in the Age of Scientific Racism* (Gledhill 2021).

provides data previously omitted from Querino's biographies, such as the names of his (presumably) foster-parents José Joaquim dos Santos Querino, who gave him his surname, and Luzia da Rocha Pita. Calmon also notes that Querino went to Piauí "with a nephew of his guardian" (Calmon 1995, 16-17).

Calmon highlights Querino's activism as an abolitionist, noting that he stayed "in the background," not going so far as to "stand shoulder to shoulder...with the great leaders of opinion in this campaign" (Calmon 1995, 17-18). However, Calmon explains that "Manuel Querino certainly did not figure among the Blacks and men of colour who, freed from the shackles of slavery, fought, in the Bahia of his time, against the campaign for Emancipation, forming what Luís Anselmo described as 'a veritable force against freedom'" (Ibid., 18). Calmon mentions Querino's "poised and assertive" appearance and the portrait of Black intellectual which could still be found in the gallery of honour of the IGHB when he was writing (Ibid., 20). He also draws attention to the active and militant role Querino played in journalism and the labour movement, and concludes by quoting from *O colono preto*, observing that the following phrase "fits Manuel Raymundo Querino like a glove":

> Whoever compels our history will certify the value and contribution of the Black in the defence of national territory, in agriculture, in mining, as an explorer, in the independence movement, with weapons in hand, as an appreciable element in the family, and as the hero of labour in all useful and profitable applications (Querino 1918, in Calmon 1995, 32).

Returning to the introductions and forewords to Querino's works, the more recent editions present a much more positive and less paternalistic image of the author. In his introduction to the second edition of *Costumes africanos no Brasil*, published in 1988 to commemorate the centenary of abolition in Brazil, the Brazilian historian and anthropologist Thales de Azevedo[149] describes Querino as follows:

> The unpretentious author, who does not take on the false airs of a theorist, but adheres to what has been seen and verified and opines with the experience of a direct observer, registers essential aspects of the phenomena he followed.... Not using terminology only later developed with the interpretation of certain data, he already demonstrates his perception—sometimes under the French designation of acclimatization, with a possibly positivist influence—the acculturation and reinterpretation that would become the target, many years later, of elaborations by theorists which Herskovits condemned. Even when he is wrong, for example, when associating certain beliefs with spiritism or Islam, he reveals that he glimpses phenomena that were taking shape and would take on vital significance over the years for our understanding of the Afro-Brazilian world (Azevedo 1988, 8).

Azevedo states that Querino's observations anticipated the field of Anthropology developed by Tylor, Boaz, and Kroeber, and explains that Nina Rodrigues was influenced by exponents of racial prejudice such as Topinard, Haeckel, and Lombroso (Ibid.). It seemed that Querino was finally regaining his place among the founders of Brazilian anthropology. In his foreword, the editor, anthropologist Raul Lody, stresses Querino's intellectual background—"in accordance with European standards, particularly French"—which did not prevent him from addressing "the daily life of Afro-Brazilian Salvador, a world marked and indivisible by African and Portuguese roots." Lody describes Querino as a "practical ethnologist" who observed and took notes "with sensitivity and humanist detail," and declares that the Bahian scholar's work was fundamental—"the basis

---

[149] The author of numerous works, Thales de Azevedo is best known worldwide for his seminal study of "the elites of color" in Salvador, originally published by UNESCO in 1953 as *Les élites de couleur dans une ville brésilienne.*

for many, many other works grounded on the 'discoveries' and 'revelations' of the author of *Costumes africanos no Brasil*" (Lody 1988, 11).

In the third edition of *Costumes africanos no Brasil*, published in 2010 with a new foreword by the Afro-Brazilian historians Wilson Mattos and Marluce de Lima Macêdo, Querino is described as a "Black Bahian intellectual," and this new edition of his work as:

> A significant and necessary initiative in the current Brazilian context, when subjects related to Black populations, their histories, experiences, and knowledge, are becoming a more substantive part of the concerns that involve, on the one hand, *the process of building public policies for affirmative action*, and on the other hand, the necessary reconfiguration of the assumptions that underlie academic practice, particularly with regard to teacher training (Mattos and Macedo, 2010, emphasis added).

The editors of this edition consider this work to be "important 'classic' in the field of the so-called 'Studies of Black Populations in Brazil,' given its pioneering spirit and its singularity in relation to the treatment (or lack thereof) that was devoted to this subject at the time of the first edition of the work, in 1938, edited by Artur Ramos" (Mattos and Macedo, 2010). We could extend this pioneering spirit even further back, to the time when Querino first published the works collected in this anthology, beginning in 1916.

One of the more recent biographies of Querino was *Manuel Querino: um herói da raça e classe* (Manuel Querino: a hero of race and class), published in a bilingual edition (Portuguese/English) by the historian Jaime Sodré in 2001. Sodré underscores the controversy that arose in 1947, when Carlos Ott[150] accused Querino of plagiarism

---

[150] Karl Borromaeus Ott (1908-1997), known in Brazil as Carlos Ott, was born in Bieringen, Germany. A Franciscan friar with a degree in Philosophy from the Antonianum of Urbee, Germany in 1937, he left the order when he arrived in Bahia in the late 1930s (Freire 2013; Gilfrancisco 2009). There, he devoted himself

because he had included data in *Artistas baianos* (Bahian Artists) that he had obtained from an anonymous sixteen-page manuscript (34.5 x 33 cm) without citing the source (Ott 1947, 197-198). Found by Ott in Brazil's National Library, the manuscript lists twenty-three painters and fifteen sculptors, while *Artistas baianos* contains 216 "biographical indications." In her article "Manuel Raymundo Querino: The First Historian of Bahian Art," Eliane Nunes also addressed this issue and stressed the prejudiced and inaccurate way in which Ott characterized Querino as a "mere artisan (a painter of walls; later a teacher of drawing)" (Nunes 2007, 244; Gledhill 2021, 72; Ott 1947, 201), without considering that, in addition to starting his professional life as a painter and decorator (very different from a "painter of walls"),[151] Querino was trained by a Spanish artist with a European background and studied design and architecture at the School of Fine Art.

The art historian Luiz Alberto Ribeiro Freire (2005) has also come to Querino's defence, quoting these words from Clarival do Prado Valladares:

> Before C. Ott's accusation continues to degrade Querino's memory, it is fair to ask whether the use of an "anonymous text," limited and incomplete, used by an author in the late 1800s and early 1900s as a subsidy for a work that extends far beyond that document was, in fact, a wilful act [of plagiarism]. Querino

---

to Archeology, Ethnology, and Art History, and was a founding professor at the UFBA School of Philosophy (Monteiro, 2007) and a researcher at the Historical and Artistic Heritage Department (DPHAN) (Ott 1947, 197).

[151] According to Luiz Freire, a painter and decorator could paint walls, but they also produced designs before the advent of patterned wallpaper, and painted decorative scenes, following an ancient tradition exemplified by the murals of Pompeii. We see examples of this type of decorative painting on the walls of Bahian mansions, such as the current headquarters of Casa de Angola, and in the Salvador City Council building (personal communication, Feb. 2014). According to Querino himself, he also helped Miguel Navarro y Cañizares to paint a curtain for the São João Theater and was solely responsible for painting "the curtain of a small theater, measuring 20 spans by 16" (Querino 1911, 148).

understood it as a document of a local traditions, which he sought to organize and publish, allowing posterity better to study the past, even at the price of correcting the mistakes of those who made the first paths, the first bridges, the first light of the knowledge.

In his introduction to *A mão afro-brasileira* (later translated as *The Afro-Brazilian Hand)*, Emanuel Araújo observes that Querino was a rare example of "researchers of the past who paid attention to the artist's ethnicity" (1988, 9; 2010, 15). According to Araújo:

> The Bahian Manuel Querino—writer, scholar, and Black journalist—was, in a way, the pioneer of these studies, obviously limited to Bahia. Many critics question Querino's work due to the inaccuracy of data and historically unproven attributions, but the truth is that he preserved important names and references that would certainly have fallen into oblivion, had it not been for his initiative (Ibid.).

It should be noted that Querino did not actually specify the artists' ethnicity—not even his own—although he did suggest it by illustrating the first edition of *Artistas baianos* (1909) with photographs of several, some of whom were clearly Black or Brown. As we will see in Chapter 5, he included his own portrait in the second edition (1911).

In his book *A talha neoclássica na Bahia (Neoclassical Carvings in Bahia)*, a study of church architecture, Luiz Alberto Ribeiro Freire hails Manuel Querino as one of the three pioneers of Bahia's art history, along with his nemesis, Carlos Ott, and Marieta Alves (Freire 2006, 85).

Maria das Graças de Andrade Leal's biographical research, which resulted in her PhD dissertation "Manuel Querino: Entre letras e lutas (1851-1923)" (Manuel Querino: Between Writings and Struggles [1851-1923]") defended in 2004, and the book with the same title published in 2009, provides the broadest and most detailed view of Querino's life and work produced to date. The result of a meticulous study which the author herself describes as a "work of mining, interpretation, narration, based on his own testimony set down in his writings," this biography focuses primarily on aspects of Querino's life and work as a journalist, labour leader, and politician. According to Leal, "Manuel Querino remains vital. The contents of his 71 years of existence will continue to be questioned and explored..." (2009, 419).

Also notable is the work of the historian Jaime Nascimento, who has helped keep the memory of Manuel Querino alive through the re-publication of his articles, accompanied by critical essays (Nascimento and Gama 2009). Nascimento also organized several editions of the "Manuel Querino—Black Personalities" seminar, beginning in 2009, which resulted in a book on several Black Brazilian personages that brings together papers presented during the first seminar (Nascimento and Gama 2012).

The centenary of Querino's birth was celebrated in Rio de Janeiro and Bahia in 1951. The main Bahian entities which took part in the celebrations were the Instituto Geográfico e Histórico da Bahia, the Sociedade Protetora dos Desvalidos, the Bahia Academy of Letters, the Bahia Folklore Commission, and the Centro Operário da Bahia. Querino has also received several tributes in the twenty-first century. In 2002, the scholar and playwright Aninha Franco began publishing new editions of Querino's works, beginning with *A arte culinária na Bahia*. The newspaper *Correio da Bahia* dedicated the special section of its Sunday issue to Querino, entitled *Sábio do Povo* (Sage of the People), on February 16, 2003 (republished with the same title in 2004, in the form of a magazine in the series "Memories of Bahia II"). In 2005, a portrait of Querino was placed in the gallery of the UFBA School of Fine Art. According to Freire

On December 12, 2005, the EBA Congregation officially unveiled his portrait painted by the teacher and painter Maria das Graças Moreira Ramos (Graça Ramos), sponsored by Professor José Dirson Argolo, with a plaque hailing him as a founder of the History of Bahian Art. On that occasion, two of his biographers, Professor Jaime Sodré and Professor Maria das Graças Leal, gave lectures (2010, 526).

To commemorate this posthumous tribute, the Cultural Section of the newspaper *A Tarde* used the portrait by Graça Ramos to illustrate the cover of its December 17, 2005 issue, entitled "Perfil retocado" (Retouched Profile). However, by 2023, the portrait was no longer to be seen in the School of Fine Art.

Reopened in 2008 and renamed the Manuel Querino Library at the suggestion of Vivaldo da Costa Lima, the library of the Institute of Artistic and Cultural Heritage of Bahia (IPAC) held a seminar on Querino in 2009. On September 23, 2013, the Regional Electoral Court (TRE) paid tribute to Querino at its headquarters, in the Administrative Center of Bahia. In 2014, Luiz Alberto Ribeiro Freire and Maria Hermínia Oliveira Hernandez organized and edited the *Dicionário Manuel Querino de Arte na Bahia* (Manuel Querino Dictionary of Art in Bahia).[152] In their introduction, the editors observe:

> The *Dicionário Manuel Querino de Arte na Bahia* honours the founder of the History of Bahian Art, Manuel Querino...who in 1909 published the books: *Artistas Bahianos: indicações biográficas* and *As Artes na Bahia*, with the 2nd edition of the first title published in 1911. Between the 1940s and 1970s, Brazilian and foreign researchers continued this research. The Bahia-born Maria Amália de Carvalho Santos Alves (Marieta Alves, 1892-1981) and the German based in Bahia, Karl Borromaeus Ott (Carlos Ott, 1908-1997) carried forward the biographical method based on documentary research and the observation of artistic production.[153]

Also in 2014, the Black American historian Henry Louis Gates, Jr., included Querino in his book *Black in Latin America* and compared him to Booker T. Washington, W. E. B. Du Bois, and Carter G. Woodson (Gates, Jr. 2014). (Querino could also be compared with the

---

[152] http://www.dicionario.belasartes.ufba.br/wp/.
[153] http://www.dicionario.belasartes.ufba.br/wp/apresentacao/.

Afro-Puerto Rican bibliophile Arthur [Arturo] Alfonso Schomburg, who "dedicated his life to gathering evidence of 'Negro' contributions to world civilization" [Hoffnung-Garskof 2001, 4]). As mentioned in the foreword to this edition, the early 2020s have witnessed an upsurge in publications and events honouring Querino,[154] particularly in 2023, the centenary of his death. The Projeto Querino podcast launched in 2022 by the journalist Tiago Rogero and the historian Ynaê Lopes dos Santos, which focusses on retrieving Black history in Brazil, has gained widespread recognition within and outside the academic community. Inspired by the *New York Times'* 1619 Project, it contains a segment on Manuel Querino and was named in his honour.[155] That same year, the *Atlanta Black Star* included him in an online series about the erasure of Black people from the history of Latin America.[156] Thanks to these and other recent efforts to reclaim and rehabilitate the memory of Manuel Querino, a Black Bahian intellectual who was born nearly four decades before the abolition of slavery in his country is beginning to regain the prestige he enjoyed in life. However, these efforts must persevere, as Querino has been remembered and erased before.

---

[154] See, for example, https://www.correio24horas.com.br/salvador/escrevendo-a-propria-historia-as-estrategias-de-manuel-querino-na-bahia-pos-escravidao--0321

[155] See the article in *The Guardian* by Tom Phillips: "A story Brazil never wanted to tell': the podcasts reclaiming the country's Black history" https://www.theguardian.com/world/2022/oct/06/brazil-history-african-brazilians-tiago-rogero-querino-project.

[156] "*Atlanta Black Star* is the largest Black-owned digital publication in the United States. The publication is based in Atlanta, Georgia but covers stories throughout the United States and the world focusing on issues impacting the Black community including politics, culture, social justice, education, health, entertainment and more. The site has over 14 million monthly unique visitors" (information provided by the *Atlanta Black Star*).

CHAPTER 4
BRAZILIAN READINGS OF BOOKER T. WASHINGTON

This chapter follows shifting perceptions of Booker T. Washington in Brazil since the early twentieth century, and the process of reintroducing his life and work in that country's newspapers. After the publication of Up from Slavery *in the United States in 1901, a seven-chapter review by a French journalist was translated into Portuguese and published in numerous instalments in the Brazilian newspaper* Diário da Bahia, *in 1902. Subsequent reports published in other Brazilian newspapers and magazines—including Black publications like* Quilombo *in 1950—kept Washington in the public eye for decades. Today, however, few Brazilians are aware of Washington's story, and the scholars and Black activists who do know about him have largely based their impressions on Du Bois's* Souls of Black Folk.

Booker T. Washington achieved national renown in the United States for his speech at the Atlanta Exposition in 1895, and was thenceforth anointed Frederick Douglass's successor as the leader of the "Black nation."[157] However, it was the publication of *Up from Slavery* in book form in 1901 that made Washington "the most famous Negro in the world" (Fisher 1915, 16). That same year, Washington's worldwide fame—for some, notoriety—was bolstered when he dined at the White House with Theodore Roosevelt and members of his family. Such a seemingly harmless invitation from the President of the United States enraged Southern White supremacists, who felt that a Black man sitting at the same table as a White man, especially the President, along with the First Lady and their children, set a bad precedent for social relations between the races. For them, it also posed the immediate danger of miscegenation, due to Washington's proximity to White women, as there were rumours—debunked by Deborah Davis (2012)—that Alice, Roosevelt's teenage daughter by his first marriage, was also present.

The uproar triggered by that dinner dealt a major setback to Washington's attempts to maintain a peaceful coexistence with White supremacists, who reacted violently to the slightest sign of rebellion against strict "Jim Crow" segregation. However, the hardest and most enduring blow to Washington's prestige came two years later, delivered by a member of his own "nation," albeit with a very different background: in W. E. B. Du Bois's best-known work, *The Souls of Black Folk*, first published in Chicago in 1903, his philippic "Of Mr. Booker T. Washington and others" censured Washington's approach to race relations and Black education. As we will see, all these milestones in his life were well known in Brazil at the time, as they were widely reported in the national press.

The main aim of this chapter is to show how Brazilian readers, particularly Black leaders and intellectuals like Manuel Querino,

---

[157] A version of this chapter was published in Brazil with the title "Expandindo as margens do Atlântico Negro: leituras sobre Booker T. Washington no Brazil" (Gledhill 2013a).

became familiar with *Up from Slavery*—a detailed account of Washington's life and work from his own perspective—long before its first full translation into Brazilian Portuguese in 1940. It will also follow changing views of Washington throughout the twentieth century and the beginning of the twenty-first. In the Black Atlantic, there were several ways to disseminate knowledge—from the more traditional ones, such as word of mouth, translations and newspapers, to technological innovations like the telephone and telegraph. Learning to read in Portuguese, even more so in foreign languages, was a rare privilege in early twentieth-century Brazil, but in his introduction to *A raça Africana e os seus costumes na Bahia*, first published in 1916, Manuel Querino made it clear that he was familiar with Washington's oratorial skills, and expressed his admiration for the Black American educator in unequivocal terms (1988, 23). Did he read *Up from Slavery* in French or Spanish, or did he have access to a translation?

Reading about *Up from Slavery* in Brazil

Co-written with a ghostwriter, the White speechwriter and publicist Max Bennett Thrasher, and intended primarily for White readers, *Up from Slavery* presents a Horatio Alger story that is all the more moving for also being a "slave narrative."[158] In addition to consolidating his position as a leader in the Black community, Washington used it to boost fundraising for the Tuskegee Institute. It was also responsible for his fame around the world, and would soon

---

[158] Washington's first autobiography, *The Story of My Life and Work*, was written by a Black ghostwriter, the journalist Edgar Webber. Meant for a Black readership, the book sold well, but Washington felt it left a great deal to be desired (Harlan 1975, 243-245). According to Harlan, "If Washington sometimes seemed to lack sensitivity to his authorship and its responsibilities, it was partly because he was a public man whose time was not entirely his own. And he kept an unusually tight rein on [Thrasher], remembering perhaps the misjudgements of Edgar Webber" (1975, 247). Horatio Alger Jr. (1832-1899) was an American author who wrote novels about men who were born poor but managed to succeed in life, achieving the "American dream" through perseverance, hard work, courage, and loyalty.

be translated into several languages. The French edition of *Up from Slavery* was published in 1904, translated as *L'autobiographie d'un nègre* by Othon Guerlac (1870-1933), a Franco-American born in Alsace and educated in France (Cook 1955, 319-320).

In 1916, writing in the city of Salvador, Bahia, Manuel Querino posed the following question: "Who could be unaware of the prestige of the great American citizen Booker Washington, the emeritus educator, the consummate orator, the sage, the most genuine representative of the Negro race in the American Union?" (1988, 23). How did he arrive at that assessment? By that time, Washington was already well known in Brazil,[159] but it is very likely that Querino had read the lengthy review of the autobiography serialized in the *Diário da Bahia* in 1902.[160] He certainly had access to it, as the library of the Instituto Histórico e Geográfico da Bahia still contains copies of that newspaper from that time.[161] French journalists and Brazilian translators helped expand the shores of the Black Atlantic, making it multilingual and global, and ensuring that news about Washington and his activities in the United States and Europe reached Brazilians in general, and particularly a Black scholar in the Northeast.

Washington was apparently best known in Brazil because of the White House dinner and *Up from Slavery*, but he was also renowned for his work as an educator. An article entitled "O negro da cara branca" ("The Black Man with the White Face") (see Appendix IV), appeared on the first page of the *Diário da Bahia* on Thursday, March 20, 1902. This unsigned piece, also published as "O preto no branco" (Black on White) in *O Paiz* in Rio de Janeiro on May 3 of that year, mentions a favorable review by the French scholar and writer

---

[159] Lívia Tiéde observes that she has found over a hundred reports on Booker T. Washington in the Brazilian press, starting in 1899 (2023, 129).

[160] At least two Brazilian newspapers translated and published French reviews of the English edition of *Up from Slavery*.

[161] Unfortunately, many issues are now missing, and had to be supplemented with copies found in the archives of the Central Library of Bahia and a translation of the original French review published in the *Revue des Deux Mondes*.

Augustin Léger.[162] In addition to providing a summary of *Up from Slavery*, the writer twice mentions the (in)famous dinner at the White House, noting that the *Diário da Bahia* had already reported it. The unknown author concludes:

> And amid all the indignation and all the revolt that arose in the United States when they learned that he was sitting at the president's table, there is something admirable and truly astonishing: it is to see the passion and ardor this man expends and uses to get them to forgive their fellow men for that dreadful *crime* of possessing, under the epidermis, a regrettable pigment that blackens them, against their will, by force.[163]

The original version of Léger's enthusiastic review of *Up from Slavery* was published in France in *Le Correspondant* on February 10, 1902. According to Cook, "It began with a reference to the dinner at the White House, which the Frenchman did not consider particularly newsworthy" (1955, 321). Léger recommended Washington's autobiography as "the perfect companion volume" to *Uncle Tom's Cabin*, and noted Washington's success as "an orator, educator, and friend of presidents," praising his "fusion of manly qualities, endurance, tenacity, positive turn of mind, and strong determination which... today characterize American citizens to a great degree" (Léger 1902, 475 in Cook 1955, 321). However, two pages later, Léger also expressed his fear that Washington's prestige could lead to "a fresh outbreak of the fiercest kind of prejudice" and observed that, as a "mulatto," he "seems to testify to the excellence of mixed bloods who, even in the most favorable instances, are subject to terrible atavistic tendencies and most often lead to disastrous degeneration." Nevertheless, in the Frenchman's view, Washington was "in all

---

[162] Augustin Léger was the author of *La jeunesse de Wesley*, Paris: Librairie Hachette & Cie, 1910, and *Journal d'um anarchiste*, 2nd ed. Paris: A. Savine, 1895, among other works. See Cook 1955.
[163] *Diário da Bahia*, March 20, 1902, 1. Emphasis in the original.

probability, only an unusually fortunate exception" (Léger 1902, 474-476, in Cook 1955, 321).

Apparently published in response to the anonymous piece, "O negro da cara branca," although the first instalment came out just two days later, a review of *Up from Slavery* by "Th Bentzon" was serialised in the *Diário da Bahia* between March and April 1902. Here, too, we see that Washington was already well known to readers in Bahia.[164] This is clear in the introduction to the first instalment, which is also unsigned:

> Dear Editor of the *Diário da Bahia*—Based on the report, possibly a transcription, published in this newspaper, entitled "The Black Man with the White Face," it can be inferred that Booker Washington has only received hostility from Whites in the northern United States.
>
> That is not precisely true: nor was his only honour from the Presidency of the Republic that of Mr. Roosevelt seating him at his table, which, as a matter of fact, did not scandalise all white Americans, just several, albeit never the majority.
>
> With this in mind, and on account of your news of Augustin Léger's critique of Booker Washington's autobiography, I have decided to submit some pages by Th. Bentzon, also reviewing the same work of this illustrious black man, whose biography is a focus of brilliant examples for the edification of all races.
>
> I would be glad to see them published, so interesting and useful is the story of this superior black man."[165]

"Th Bentzon" was the pen name of the French journalist, writer, translator, and aristocrat **Marie-Thérèse de Solms Blanc (1840-1907),** using her mother's surname. Influenced by the French novelist George Sand (Amandine Aurore Lucile Dupin, Baroness de Dudevant), whom she had met through her stepfather, Bentzon

---

[164] See the annotated English translation in Appendix III.
[165] *Diario da Bahia*, March 22, 1902, p. 2.

began producing translations, book reviews, travelogues, and fiction. Her works were published by major literary magazines in France. She also wrote several novels. Bentzon traveled to the United States in 1895 and 1897, and wrote reports on her experiences there. She also visited Canada, Britain, Germany, and Russia. As a translator and literary critic, Bentzon helped French readers become better acquainted with the works of many English-speaking authors, such as Henry James, Mark Twain, and Walt Whitman, as well as Booker T. Washington (Gale 1999, 28). The *nom de plume* Th Bentzon was "well known wherever French is habitually read,"[166] according to an obituary prominently featured on page 8 of the São Paulo newspaper *Correio Paulistano* on February 15, 1907, which mentions her review of *Up from Slavery* as one of the highlights of her career: "Translating long extracts of the work by Mr. Booker Washington, *Up from Slavery*, and drawing a sympathetic portrayal of the distinguished Black educator, Mrs. Bentzon continued her meritorious work of popularizing and internationalizing the most generous Anglo-Saxon ideas."[167]

Bentzon's review of Washington's best-known autobiography was first published in France in October 1901, in the monthly *Revue des Deux-Mondes* (Cook 1955, 319-320; Bentzon 1901).[168] The long excerpts from the book included in the review, published in several issues of *Diário da Bahia*, always on the second page, may have been the only translation into Portuguese of *Up from Slavery* to which

---

[166] "Having written for many years in the *Revue Bleue politique et literaire* and the *Revue des Deux-Monde*, her audience is the general public, and her writings are read with pleasure wherever a current of ideas and feelings has been established from Paris" (*Correio Paulistano*, Feb. 15, 1907, 8).

[167] The obituary also praises Bentzon's review of the novel *Canaã*, by Graça Aranha. (*Correio Paulistano*, Feb, 15, 1907, p. 8).

[168] Bentzon's review was not the first article originally published in French in the *Revue des Deux-Mondes* that appeared in Portuguese in the *Diário da Bahia*. I have found another, entitled "An Unpublished Correspondence by Father Didon," about the French-Dominican cleric, writer, and educator who was also a staunch opponent of divorce. The first instalment of this article came out on March 8, 1902.

Brazilians had access in their own language until 1940, when Graciliano Ramos translated it with the title of *Memórias de um negro* (Memoir of a Black Man).[169]

According to Mercer Cook, Bentzon may have been responsible for the first mention of Washington in the French press (1955, 319). In 1897, she attended an important speech he gave when a monument to Colonel Robert Gould Shaw and the 54th Massachusetts Regiment was unveiled on Boston Common. Robert Gould Shaw (1837-1863) was a White officer who led a Black infantry regiment during the US Civil War. He died during the second Battle of Fort Wagner, near Charleston, South Carolina, and was buried along with his soldiers in a common grave—the ultimate humiliation, for the White supremacists who buried him. Today, a plaster cast of the "Shaw Memorial," a bas relief by Augustus Saint-Gaudens, is one of the key exhibits in the National Gallery of Art in Washington, DC.

In 1898, Bentzon wrote that Washington's gift for oratory had overshadowed the other speakers, including the eminent philosopher and Harvard professor William James:

> However brilliant the orators, the great success seems to be that of Boker [sic] Washington, professor in a Negro university, who speaks as a representative of the coloured people; and it must be admitted that he looks like any other Negro. Nevertheless, under that dark skin and those flat features, there is a fine intelligence. In a brief speech, with each word striking home and with an abundance of general ideas, he proves that the abolition of slavery has freed not only the Blacks, but that it has above all liberated the Whites, whose moral development was impossible under that iniquitous regime. He does not exaggerate the progress already achieved by his race; he firmly enumerates all

---

[169] In contrast, the Spanish translation, *De esclavo a catedrático*, was published in 1902 (Washington 1902), and widely read in Latin America (Alberto et al. 2022, 358).

the qualities it still lacks, but he has faith in a future aided by the college, the industrial school, by habitually sustained effort. To do one's duty on the battlefield is not the most difficult task. A day will come when nothing that is permitted the white man will be denied or refused the Negro. His tone is proud, without boasting. Boker [sic] Washington will remain in the memory of Bostonians as the principal figure, the headliner of the day, above all else, as a living argument in favour of his cause.[170]

Fig. 4-1. Detail of the "Shaw Memorial"

---

[170] Originally published in the *Revue des Deux-Mondes* on December 1, 1898 and translated by Cook (1955, 319).

Bentzon also describes Washington's oratory and appearance—quite common, in her opinion—in her review of *Up from Slavery*. However, her main focus there is on the autobiography itself, which she describes as "work of reconciliation, a book of advice on how to solve the most difficult social problem," which "promises to become the Bible of a race, the star that, in fact, will guide it forward, always prudently and safely" *(Diário da Bahia,* March 28, 1902, 2).

The review begins by addressing one of the most remarkable achievements of young Booker's life—the 500-mile journey from his home in Malden, West Virginia, to the Hampton Institute, in Virginia, in 1872. Ragged and hungry, he was forced to sleep under a sidewalk because the inns did not accept Black people.[171] Bentzon notes the similarity between this episode and the narrative of Benjamin Franklin's journey from New York to Philadelphia, although Franklin was not born into slavery, and was never denied accommodation due to the colour if his skin. However, this experience was not the only similarity between Franklin and Washington, as the Black educator's homilies came to be compared with Franklin's proverbs in *Poor Richard's Almanack*, which preached humility and frugality.

After describing his odyssey, in which Bentzon directly compares Washington with Homer's Ulysses, the French writer returns to the beginning of Washington's story—the point where *Up from Slavery* begins: Booker's birth as an enslaved child without a surname, and childhood. The French journalist quotes a long excerpt from the first chapter, "A Slave Among Slaves," which begins: "I was born a slave on a plantation in Franklin County, Virginia: I am not quite sure of the exact place or exact date of my birth, but at any rate I suspect I must have been born somewhere and at some time....The earliest impressions I can now recall are of the plantation and the slave quarters..." (Washington 1986, 1). Regarding his life in bondage,

---

[171] One of Washington's many biographers, Arna Bontemps (1972), also begins with that episode. A Black American poet, novelist, and librarian, Bontemps' numerous works also include biographies of George Washington Carver and Frederick Douglass.

Washington adds: "I had no schooling whatever while I was a slave, though I remember on several occasions I went as far as the schoolhouse door with one of my young mistresses to carry her books. The picture of several dozen boys and girls in a schoolroom engaged in study made a deep impression on me, and I had the feeling that to get into a schoolhouse and study in this way would be about the same as getting into paradise" (Washington 1986, 7). Thus ends the first instalment.

The remainder of this lengthy review continues in the same fashion: interpretations and analyses of the autobiography, interspersed with long extracts from the book, originally translated into French by Bentzon, and then into Portuguese by an unknown translator.[172] The main focus is on Booker's youth and education, particularly his experiences as a student and teacher at the Hampton Institute and the founder of the Tuskegee Institute in 1881.

In the instalment published in the *Diário da Bahia* on March 25, 1902, Bentzon underscores the stance Washington would take later in life regarding the "problem of slavery," which she considers to be "broader" and "more precise." Then she goes on to quote this extract, in a translation that is somewhat different from the original:

There is no reason to censure Southern white people [the original English text begins: '*I have long since ceased to cherish any spirit of bitterness against the Southern White people on account of the enslavement of my race.*]; *no one section of the country was wholly responsible for its introduction, and, besides, it was recognized and protected for years by the General Government.*

Having got its tentacles fastened on to the economic and social life of the Republic, it was no easy matter for the country to relieve

---

[172] Unless indicated otherwise, the extracts quoted here come from the original English edition (the one used here is Washington 1986). At times, the extracts in the appendix have been translated from the Portuguese while checking them against the French and English originals, and annotated to show how and when the translations differ significantly from Washington's book.

itself of the institution. Then, when we rid ourselves of prejudice, or racial feeling, and look facts in the face, we must acknowledge that, notwithstanding the cruelty and moral wrong of slavery, the ten million Negroes inhabiting his country, who themselves or whose ancestors went through the school of American slavery, are in a stronger and more hopeful condition, materially, intellectually, morally, and religiously, than is true of an equal number of black people in any other portion of the globe.

This is so to such an extent that Negroes in this country, who themselves or whose forefathers went through the school of slavery, are constantly returning to Africa as missionaries to enlighten those who remained in the fatherland.

This I say, not to justify slavery—on the other hand, I condemn it as an institution, as we all know that in America it was established for selfish and financial reasons…– but to call attention to a fact, and to show how Providence so often uses men and institutions to accomplish a purpose

When persons ask me in these days how, in the midst of what sometimes seem hopelessly discouraging conditions, I can have such faith in the future of my race in this country, I remind them of the wilderness through which and out of which, a good Providence has already led us.

Ever since I have been old enough to think for myself, I have always told myself that the Black man got the same amount of good and evil from slavery that the White man did"[173] (Bentzon, *Diário da Bahia,* March 25, 1902, 2).

The instalment published on March 28 begins by praising the zealous work of men and women who worked for "the regeneration of the freedman," people who could be compared to the "great missionaries," because "there is more than one kind of apostolate and martyrdom. Washington painted an admirable picture of this

---

[173] Here, the original reads "the black man got nearly as much out of slavery as the white man did" (1986, 17).

compact body of apostles who, inspired by Jesus Christ, participated in a work of redemption, teaching [people] by the hundreds in schools for Blacks founded as if by magic" (Bentzon, *Diário da Bahia*, March 28, 1902, 2). Bentzon also notes that Washington does not dwell on the difficulties he faced in 1876 and 1877, after graduating from the Hampton Institute and returning to the town of Malden as a teacher. Expressing herself in terms that seem sympathetic towards a group that did its worst to terrorize Black people, she clearly states a fact that Washington glossed over:

> It was a time of heightened activity for the Ku-Klux-Klan, a quasi-fantastic movement [formed] after the Civil War, extending it beyond the illusory declaration of peace. To resist the unbearable abuses of politicians, who were punished with the epithet of carpetbaggers, a White league was formed: sometimes murderous battles were fought between them and the metropolitan police. Unfortunately, the numerous secret societies involved in this hidden war went too far with the terror that was supposed to prevent Blacks from assembling, to increase scrutiny. Among the individuals disguised for this type of policing, there were real bandits: the Ku-Klux mask sheltered many passions, so innocent people were martyred to death and schools were set ablaze because the teachers who put an end to Black people's long years of ignorance were more than suspect. Booker Washington avoids dwelling on this dark period of the Reconstruction (Bentzon, *Diário da Bahia*, March 28, 1902, 2).

It is in this context which Bentzon describes *Up from Slavery* as a "work of reconciliation" and "the Bible of a race" (Bentzon, *Diário da Bahia*, March 28, 1902, 2).

In the next instalment, published on April 1, 1902, Bentzon begins by praising Washington's oratory and goes on to recount instances in which he and Frederick Douglass were discriminated against on account of their race. For example, a Native American student, whom Booker accompanied, was served at an establishment that refused to serve his Black teacher. According to Bentzon:

The Redskin [sic] was welcomed warmly, but the Black man was absolutely rejected. Such incidents are not rare! Frederick Douglass, the man of color most distinguished for his superior talents, traveled to Pennsylvania in a baggage car despite having purchased a ticket.

When some Whites expressed regret that such humiliation had been inflicted on him, Douglass got up from the suitcase on which he was sitting and declared: "They cannot degrade Frederick Douglass. This insolence only degrades those who practice it"[174] (*Diário da Bahia*, April 1, 1902, 2).

Here, Bentzon makes a direct comparison between Douglass and Washington, stating that Booker avoided making "scathing retorts," simply observing that "train conductors often find themselves greatly perplexed when deciding who is more or less colored" (*Diário da Bahia*, April 1, 1902, 2).

In the following instalment, Bentzon analyses Washington's teaching philosophy: "I visited our Southern cities," says Washington, "and asked who the most honest and influential coloured men were in that place. You will know that fifty-percent of cases were Blacks who learned a trade during the days of slavery" (*Diário da Bahia*, April 3, 1902, 2).

Bentzon observes that Washington believed any plan for Black education should take the knowledge they had already acquired into consideration:

> In a way, every large southern plantation was a kind of practical school for farmers, masons, carpenters, cooks, weavers,

---

[174] Washington recounts the incident as follows: "When some of the white passengers went into the baggage-car to console Mr. Douglass, and one of them said to him: 'I am sorry, Mr. Douglass, that you have been degraded in this manner,' Mr. Douglass straightened himself up on the box upon which he was sitting, and replied: 'They cannot degrade Frederick Douglass. The soul that is within me no man can degrade. I am not the one that is being degraded on account of this treatment, but those who are inflicting it upon me'" (1986, 100).

seamstresses, etc. Their training had a self-serving nature, and intelligence did not develop along with the hand, yet this fragmented education allowed the freedman to earn a living. Therefore, he [Washington] had to improve it, develop it, all the more so because the prosperity of the South depended on the work of Black people, which had been forced labor shortly before. It was a mistake to attempt to build on the bedrock of slavery that which in New England had been built on the foundations of freedom *(Diário da Bahia,* April 3, 1902, 2).[175]

However, twenty years after Emancipation, the Black people who had learned trades on the plantations while enslaved began to pass away, and there was no one with the necessary skills to replace them. Instead of arts and crafts, Black people were acquiring a superficial knowledge of science and letters, which, according to Bentzon, "only served to irritate Whites and aggravate prejudice" (Ibid.). For Washington, writes Bentzon, it would be absurd to say that there was no difference between Blacks and Whites and that everyone should receive the same type of education, without taking their past circumstances into account.

In this and the following instalment, which was probably published on Saturday, April 5,[176] Bentzon mentions Olivia Davidson and her efforts to raise funds for Tuskegee when its construction first began. The French reviewer refers to Miss Davidson (as she was at the time) as though she were already Washington's spouse. In fact, Booker was married to his first wife, Fanny, at the time. Bentzon

---

[175] Washington declared: "Of one thing I felt more strongly convinced than ever, after spending [a] month in seeing the actual life of the colored people, and that was that, in order to lift them up, something must be done more than merely to imitate New England education as it then existed. I saw then more clearly than ever the wisdom of the system which General Armstrong had inaugurated at Hampton" (1986, 118).

[176] This issue of the *Diário da Bahia* is missing from the collections of the Biblioteca Pública do Estado da Bahia and the IGHB. I have translated it from the original French (Bentzon 1901, 782-784).

accurately describes Olivia's educational background—she, too, was a Hampton graduate, after which she studied at the Framingham Normal School in Massachusetts. The future Mrs. Olivia Washington is praised for refusing to "pass for white," despite the urgings of people at Framingham. Bentzon notes that she used the knowledge she acquired at the normal school to introduce new teaching methods at Tuskegee. The entry on "Olivia Davidson Washington" in *Notable Black American Women* credits her with co-founding Tuskegee along with Booker: "For not only did [Olivia] Washington learn sophisticated pedagogical techniques, but she established important contacts which proved invaluable during fundraising for the future Tuskegee Institute" (Dorsey 1992, 1222). According to Harlan, as Lady Principal, Olivia's "special forte was in persuading the girl students, fresh from the tenant shacks of the Black Belt, to emulate her genteel sensibility, New England self-restraint [although born in Virginia and raised in Ohio], and feminine modesty. For Washington she was obviously a good influence" (1975b, 149).

**Fig. 4-2. Olivia Davidson Washington
(1854-1889)**

Bentzon also observes that even "the most obstinate old Southerners esteem and support" the fact that Tuskegee students acquired a range of skills, from carpentry to tailoring. Not only was Washington deferentially called "professor" (but never "mister") but the "aristocrats who call themselves Southern Democrats" were not at all perturbed by seeing the principal of Tuskegee share a car with President McKinley and the governor of Alabama. "This is progress," notes Bentzon, "the importance of which is beyond the ken of us Europeans (1901, 784).

In the instalment dated April 6, the reviewer returns to the subject of Washington's oratorical skills (chapters XIII through XV of the autobiography are devoted to his success in this area) and notes that he surprised his Southern White audiences when he praised the South for the good it could do, and they waited in vain to hear that Black man insult the former slaveholding states.[177] According to Bentzon, "His line of action has not varied since he settled in Tuskegee and pledged to do justice to Blacks and Whites alike. However, this policy does not prevent him from sincerely denouncing the injuries suffered by people of colour" (*Diário da Bahia*, Apr. 6, 1902, 2). She also emphasizes one of Washington's most controversial stances: "As for the vote, the Blacks should increasingly consider the interests of the community in which they live, whose future largely depends on them" (Ibid.). As always, Washington conveyed one message to Whites and another to Blacks:

His robust faith is contagious: in the North, he receives invitations from Whites and Blacks: from the former, he obtains funds to expand his school; and to the others he vehemently preaches the need for industrial and technical education and the

---

[177] Washington writes: "Without my knowing it, there were a large number of people present from Alabama, and some from the town of Tuskegee. These white people afterward frankly told me that they went to this meeting expecting to hear the South roundly abused, but were pleasantly surprised to find that there was no word of abuse in my address. On the contrary, the south was given credit for all the praiseworthy things that it had done" (1986, 200).

futility of political agitation that will only harm their voting rights. Education and property together are the only elements that give the right to vote (Ibid.).

One of the most serious charges levelled against Washington was his "accommodationist" approach to civil rights. Bentzon quotes a "former confederate" who describes him in terms that recall the non-violence of Martin Luther King, Jr., whom Malcom X derided as a "modern house Negro" (Marable 2011, 264-265):

> He never made a specialty of waving a red flag in front of every bull he encountered; in return, however, he achieved what all the books, speeches, incendiary prospectuses, martial law, decrees and amendments to the Constitution could not do… By peaceful methods inspired by Jesus Christ, Booker Washington conquered where Caesar would have been vanquished (Bentzon, *Diário da Bahia*, April 6, 1902, 2).

Bentzon notes that Washington always wanted to be heard by an audience "of former Confederate slaveholders," and his dream came true when "that occasion arose in 1893, at the international meeting of Christian workers, held in Atlanta, Georgia" (Ibid.). Two years later, he gave his famous speech at the Atlanta Exposition in 1895. Bentzon concludes this instalment by observing that it was the first time a Black man had shared the same podium with Whites at a national event in the United States.

The instalment published on April 9th describes the impact of Washington's most famous speech, and the recognition he received from major figures of the time, such as US President Grover Cleveland. The biggest complaints came from fellow Blacks, who wanted Washington to demand more rights for their people. However, he had stated: "It is important and right that all privileges of the law be ours, but it is vastly more important that we be prepared for the exercises of these privileges. The opportunity to earn a dollar in a factory just now is worth infinitely more than the opportunity to spend a dollar in an opera-house," and *"In all things purely mundane, Whites and Blacks can be as separate as the fingers, yet we form a whole in all things essential to mutual progress"* (Washington 1986, 223-224; Bentzon, *Diário da Bahia*, April 9, 1902, 2). As a result of that address, Booker T. Washington was widely acclaimed as the leader of his race in the United States, despite the objections of his opponents and rivals.

In this instalment, Bentzon gives an account of Washington's oratorical skills, which she witnessed firsthand, while revealing her own prejudices:

I had the opportunity to see him in 1897, among the notables who had gone to Boston to unveil the monument to Colonel Shaw, the young [White] officer who died heroically at the head of a black regiment.

After the monument was unveiled, speeches were given in the Music Hall which, despite its size, did not have enough room for the large, hand-picked audience.

The most influential and distinguished people approached the Governor of Massachusetts, and at first glance, the principal of Tuskegee cut an extremely modest figure. The white blood that must flow in his veins had not erased any of the characteristic traits of the race. He is a black like all the others: prominent lips, flat nose, heavy jaw, yet with an expression of intelligent kindness in his eyes, and his voice was sonorous and confident. The oratorical success of the day fell to him. In Boston, the black man had been preceded by the legitimate reputation that made him the first of his race to be distinguished with the diploma of an honorary member of Harvard University. When he rose to his full height, everyone felt they were in the presence of a powerful force. He spoke of the great military feats of the Civil War, then, turning to the black soldiers present there, he said: *"To you, to the scarred and scattered remnants of the Fifty-fourth, who, with empty sleeve and wanting leg, have honoured this occasion with your presence, to you, your commander is not dead. Though Boston erected no monument and history recorded no story, in you and in the loyal race which you represent, Robert Gould Shaw would have a monument which time could not wear away."*[178]

Governor Wolcou [Roger Wolcott] enthusiastically raised "Three cheers to Booker Washington!" No one else was applauded with such great enthusiasm. Overcome by the general feeling, the black sergeant who was the standard-bearer made an overwhelming gesture: it was he who, after the battle where [a large] part of the regiment had fallen, exclaimed "No matter! The old flag never touched the ground."

I repeat, Washington's speech eclipsed all the others who spoke that day.

In part VI, published on April 13th, Bentzon observes that the Tuskegee Institute ran smoothly, even when Washington was away, because it did not depend on just one man. Its faculty and staff included eighty-six people, and it functioned like clockwork. Bentzon observes that Tuskegee graduates returned to their hometowns gladly in order to establish schools, organize clubs, and engage in other activities aimed at raising up their local Black community, since most lived in poverty, ridden with debts.

However, the revolution took place thanks to the influence of one man. The Tuskegee Institute has produced great benefits: there, *literary, industrial, and religious* education unfold in harmony, with a normal school for teachers, a school of arts and crafts, a Bible school to train good preachers, who, in Washington's mind, can play other roles when needed *(Diário da Bahia,* April 13, 1902, p. 2, emphasis added).

Bentzon is full of praise for Washington's family life, but mixes up his wives (he was widowed twice; by the time he published *Up from Slavery*, he was married to his third wife, Margaret Murray Washington). Then, probably offended by Washington's analysis of her fellow countrymen, Bentzon describes Washington's remarks

---

[178] The words in italics are from a newspaper article on the ceremony quoted in *Up from Slavery* (1986, 252).

about his travels in Europe in 1898 as "the most unfair and least interesting part of *Up from Slavery*," (Ibid.) while omitting his observation about the French:

> The love of pleasure and excitement which seems in a large measure to possess the French people impressed itself upon me. I think they are more noted in this respect than is true of the people of my own race. In point of morality and moral earnestness I do not believe that the French are ahead of my own race in America.... In the matter of truth and high honour I do not believe that the average Frenchman is ahead of the American Negro; while so far as mercy and kindness to dumb animals go, I believe that my race is far ahead. In fact, when I left France, I had more faith in the future of the black man in America than I had ever possessed (Washington 1986, 282).

The final instalment of the review, published on April 15th, puts *Up from Slavery* in context and analyses its influence. Bentzon draws attention to the fact that the autobiography had a powerful impact when it was serialized in *The Outlook*. In her view, "The miraculous rise of a slave, the son of a despised race, takes him to a sphere in which the superior characters of a country of high civilization hover." But the French author also reminds her readers that Washington was not the only Black person to achieve that feat in the United States, and mentions Frederick Douglass, as well as other names that are not as well known today: Senator Blanche Kelso Bruce (1841-1898); Hiram Rhoades Revels (ca. 1827-1901), the first Black US senator; Bishop Daniel Alexander Paine (1811-1893), who in addition to being a cleric was an educator and writer; and educator, historian, and biographer William J. Simmons (1849-1890).

Bentzon compares Washington's book with the work of another Black author published at the same time—*The American Negro: What He Was, What He Is, and What He May Become* by William Hannibal Thomas (1901), whom she describes as:

...a man of colour who betrayed his race, which he exposes in a dire situation. In his view, Blacks are intelligent but prone to theft, and as for morals, none aged fifteen, lads or lasses, have maintained their innocence. He states that ninety percent of Blacks lead a licentious life in America, and seeks to demonstrate that, until now, the freedman has produced nothing good (*Diário da Bahia*, April 15, 1902, p. 2).

It is in this context that Bentzon turns her focus on W. E. B. du Bois, having mentioned him in passing in part VI. She describes him as an "eminent man of colour" and "graduate of Harvard University, now professor of history and political economy at the University of Atlanta." She mentions his study *The Philadelphia Negro* to demonstrate that Northerners were also biased against Blacks, noting that prejudice in that city was "extraordinarily violent." Although Washington advised Black people to stay in the South, Bentzon asserts that, in that region, "when racial hatred erupts, it is appalling. The summary justice applied to Blacks accused of an unpardonable crime—the rape or attempted rape of a woman—is notorious." And in addition to lynchings in Georgia and Louisiana, she reports several which occurred outside the South, in Kansas, Colorado, and Ohio.

Finally, Bentzon observes that, after emancipation, the position of Black people became even more difficult: "Once, to be treated humanely, it was enough for [a Black person] to be an honest and faithful servant; today, if he wants to maintain the role of a free man, he must have excessive prudence, subtle politics, and the virtues of a saint" (*Diário da Bahia*, April 15, 1902, 2). While conceding that "the Booker Washingtons will always be rare," she believes that "the development of the race needs thousands of them," and quotes the words of a Black minister: "Yes, thousands of Washington—one at every bend in the road, one on every mountain." And Bentzon concludes: "Similarly, we would need them for the crusade of 'deploying industry under conditions of morality' and transforming our mediocre graduates into good farmers" (Ibid.).

In her conclusion, Bentzon advocated precisely what Washington was accused of doing, namely training Black people to work the land instead of pursuing higher education. Clearly, in her view, they would be at best "mediocre" if they followed the latter course. In fact, and as we have seen, Washington took a more nuanced approach.

Booker T. Washington in the Brazilian press

Black-owned publications and the Black press in Brazil

Manuel Querino was a militant journalist who not only published numerous articles in major Bahia newspapers but founded two publications of his own. However, the publications Querino edited are not considered part of the Black press because they were intended for a general readership. As the editors of *Voices of the Race: Black Newspapers in Latin America, 1870-1960* observe in their introduction:

The case is somewhat more complex in the region's many cities and towns with Afrodescendant majorities or significant minorities..... Afrodescendant intellectuals took part in the broader development of publishing in Santo Domingo, Rio de Janeiro, and Salvador da Bahia as well [here, Querino is mentioned in a footnote]. But writers in these contexts did not typically create explicitly Black publications.... Yet the absence of an avowedly Black press is not necessarily a mark of the absence of Black racial identifications (Alberto et al. 2022, 15).

Even in the one issue of *O Trabalho* that has survived, Querino's Afro-Brazilian identity is clear.

Another example of a newspaper whose owner could be considered "Black," but is not considered part of the "Black press" is the *Diário da Bahia*. Established in 1856, it was one of the most important newspapers in Salvador in Querino's day. At the time Bentzon's review was published, its owner and editor-in-chief was the Governor of Bahia, Severino dos Santos Vieira (Quadros n.d.).[179] Vieira acquired the *Diário da Bahia* in 1900, the same year he became governor (Ibid.). His portrait clearly shows that he would have been considered Black in the United States, according to the "one-drop rule" (see Fig. 4-2). However, due to the complex system of ethnic/racial identification in Brazil, which is based on variations in facial features, hair type, skin color, social class, and power, it is unlikely that Vieira was viewed (or self-identified) as "Black," due to the phenomenon Carl Degler calls the "mulatto escape hatch" (Degler 1971). Wealth and class were also considerable factors—to this day, "money whitens" in Brazil. Therefore, the *Diário da Bahia* also would not be considered a "Black" newspaper, although it published articles of interest to Afro-Brazilian readers like Querino (see appendices III and IV).

Fig. 4-3. Portrait of Severino Vieira

---

[179] One of the previous editors of the *Diário da Bahia* was Querino's chief political patron, Manuel Pinto de Souza Dantas.

There were numerous outlets for the Black press in Brazil. The University of São Paulo has digitized issues of twenty-four titles published in São Paulo alone. A prominent example was the São Paulo newspaper *O Clarim d'Alvorada* (The Clarion of the Dawn). One of its writers was Theophilo Booker Washington, who signed himself "Boocker" [sic] or "Booker." In one of his columns, which were entitled "Negro" (Black)—sometimes with an exclamation mark—he listed the names of Black artists and writers. In an article reminiscent of Manuel Querino's essay "Homens de cor preta na história" (1923; Black Men in History), he mentions the sculptor Edmonia Lewis, born in New York, and the "poet Jaun [sic] Latino," the author of a prefatory poem to *Don Quixote*. According to "Booker," Juan Latino was born in North Africa and taken to Seville, where he was sold to the family of the "famous Gonzalo de Cordova." He showed great ability to learn and, once emancipated, taught grammar, Latin and Greek at the University of Granada.[180] "Booker" also mentions Alexander Sergeyevich [Pushkin], Russia's greatest poet, observing that he "inherited his African blood from his maternal line" *(Clarim d'Alvorada,* November 15, 1925, no. 16, 2). Theophilo Booker Washington had a law degree and began writing for *O Clarim d'Alvorada* in 1925, while still a young student. This "Booker" was clearly proud that his father, Theophilo Dias de Castro—the editor and publisher of another Black São Paulo newspaper, *O Progresso* (Santos 2021, 83)—had named him after the principal of Tuskegee. I have not found any mention of the eponymous Booker T. Washington in the digitized issues of *O Clarim d'Alvorada* that are available online.[181] However, according to Tiéde, *O Clarim* had an intense relationship with the *Chicago Defender*

---

[180] According to Henry Louis Gates, Jr., "el negro Juan Latino" was the first known Black poet. Gates first learned about Latino from an essay by Arthur (Arturo) Schomburg in *Ebony and Topaz: A Collectanea,* edited by Charles S. Johnson (c. 1927), which is unfortunately out of print. https://www.theroot.com/who-was-the-1st-black-poet-1790898218

[181] USP Imprensa Negra Paulista http://biton.uspnet.usp.br/imprensanegra/

(2023, 131), a Black American newspaper founded in 1905, whose editor and publisher Robert S. Abbott was, like Washington, an alumnus of the Hampton Institute (Ellis 1994, 43).[182]

Tiédé has found an article about Washington in the Black newspaper *Alvorada*, based in São Paulo, which came out in 1947. Published on the second and third pages, it includes a photograph of the "Wizard of Tuskegee" with the caption "He Lifted the Veil of Ignorance." Mirroring a report from Marcus Garvey's *Negro World*[183] on the official unveiling of the controversial monument to Washington in Tuskegee, it takes a different perspective, explaining that the article is intended to inspire Black Brazilians with "the actions of the American leader who was a *'crusader' for the education of Black people around the world*" (Tiédé 2022, 75, emphasis added).

Abdias do Nascimento and *Quilombo*

One of Brazil's best-known Black activists and intellectuals, whose life spanned most of the twentieth century and part of the twenty-first, Abdias do Nascimento had a good opinion of Booker T. Washington—at least when he was the editor of *Quilombo*, the outlet of the Teatro Teatro Experimental do Negro (Black Experimental Theatre, TEN) published between December 1948 and July 1950.[184] I

---

[182] The *Chicago Defender* was the first to publish the "scoop" on Washington's death on November 14, 1915 (Ellis 1994, 122).

[183] *Negro World* was the outlet for Marcus Garvey's Universal Negro Improvement Association (Tiédé 2022, 75). As we saw in the Introduction, Garvey admired Washington and had wanted to meet him in person. He was also inspired by Washington's writings https://www.americanyawp.com/reader/22-the-new-era/marcus-garvey-explanation-of-the-objects-of-the-universal-negro-improvement-association-1921/

[184] Abdias do Nascimento (1914-2011) founded the TEN in 1944, with the aim of "retrieving, in Brazil, the values of the human person and Black-African culture, which has been degraded and negated by a dominant society that, since colonial times, carried the mental baggage of its European metropolitan background, imbued with pseudo-scientific concepts about the inferiority of the Black race. The TEN proposed to work for the social valorisation of Black people in Brazil through education, culture, and the arts" (Nascimento 2004, 210). The TEN carried out its

have found two mentions of the Black American educator, both positive, in the same issue, in two articles on very different subjects: Joe Louis, and Black film actors.

When Nascimento passed away in 2011, his obituary in *The New York Times* quoted Edward Telles, a professor of sociology at Princeton, who praised Nascimento's frank and courageous criticism of race relations in Brazil: "He was a legend.... From the 1930s through the 1990s, Brazil was considered a racial democracy, but nobody talked about race, and there was a clear racial hierarchy. Poor people were predominantly black, and the elites were almost all white. He wasn't afraid to tell people that racial democracy was a myth. And he said it for 60 years" (Weber 2011). According to Ollie A. Johnson, a professor of Africana studies at Wayne State University in Detroit, Michigan: "No other Brazilian fought harder and longer against white supremacy and racism in Brazil in the post-slavery era. For Americans to understand him and his contribution, you'd have to say he was a little bit of Marcus Garvey, a little of W. E. B. Du Bois, a little bit of Langston Hughes and a little bit of Adam Clayton Powell" (Weber 2011)—the absence of Booker T. Washington from that list is telling. The similarities between Abdias and Du Bois include both their pan-Africanism and their longevity—both lived more than ninety years, and their lives and works overlapped.

According to the Black Brazilian historians Petrônio Domingues and Flávio dos Santos Gomes, *Quilombo*

> ...became the main outlet for a democratic political movement with an anti-racist orientation, especially led by Black intellectuals and with the support of other sectors of Brazilian

---

dramaturgical and political activities in support of Black causes until they were restricted by the military dictatorship installed in Brazil in 1964. In 1968, Nascimento was forced to go into exile in the USA, where he continued to carry out the TEN's activities. For more information, see: Teatro Experimental do Negro (TEN), Enciclopédia Itaú Cultural. http://enciclopedia.itaucultural.org.br/grupo399330/teatro-experimental-do-negro.

society. It is a fact that such a political movement—with an emphasis on its press outlet—formed an ideological hub that sought to forge a new hegemony in the racial discourse of the time, but it is also true that it did not bring out just one, but several voices, multiple discourses and diverse ideas (2013, 116).

Funding for this publication came from some TEN members, such as Guerreiro Ramos, as well as White allies. It conveyed "a polyphony of voices," including an essay entitled "Orpheu Negro" ("Black Orpheus"), written by Jean Paul Sartre and translated by Ironides Rodrigues (Nascimento 2003, 64-65), in which the French philosopher "conferred a philosophical status on the theory of Negritude, with revolutionary political dimensions; a weapon in the fight against colonial domination" (Domingues and Gomes 2013). *Quilombo* featured a brief article on the first anniversary of the death of the White businessman Roberto Simonsen, backed the candidacy for federal deputy (congressman) of another White businessman, Eurico de Oliveira, and, in its January 1950 issue, reported the passing of the White psychiatrist and ethnologist Artur Ramos,[185] in a notice entitled "The Death of a Great Friend," stating: "With the death of Artur Ramos, Black Brazilians lose one of their best friends and one of their most lucid advocates" (Domingues and Gomes 2013; Nascimento 2003, 61). *Quilombo* also had White collaborators, including Péricles Leal. As Domingues and Gomes observe: "In fact, in all issues, the newspaper made room for (and gave 'voice' to) White people" (2013, 121).

As for Booker T. Washington, the March-April 1950 issue of *Quilombo* ranks the educator among the most distinguished Black Americans. Both he and W. E. B. Du Bois are included in the list of the main role models for their race in an article about a Black American boxing champion's visit to Brazil:

---

[185] As already noted, Ramos edited an anthology of Querino's works in which he disparaged their author (Ramos 1938)

Joe Louis, with his spectacular victories in boxing, and the correctness of his attitudes as a citizen and patriot, has placed himself among the Blacks who have done the most for the projection of their race, alongside, for example, Boocker [sic] T. Washington, Paul Robeson, [George] Washington Carver, Marion [sic] Anderson, Dubois [sic] and other great names (Nascimento 2003, 86).

In the same issue, an article entitled "Cinema and Black Artists" reviews *The Birth of a Nation* (1915), directed by D.W. Griffith, describing it as "the first major film in which Black people participate in dramatic action" (Nascimento 2003, 88).[186] However, it goes on to observe:

> The film was viciously attacked by several liberals such as [Charles W.] Eliot[187] and Booker T. Washington, the celebrated Black leader. They accused Griffith of attempting to diminish the ideal and principles in whose name [the US Civil War] was fought. They also disapproved of the director having shown proof of racial partiality, denouncing the excesses committed by Blacks after the abolition of slavery and having his Black characters played by White actors "daubed with black paint" (Nascimento 2003, 88).

The Birth of a Nation was based on *The Clansman*, a novel by Thomas Dixon. An old enemy of Washington, Dixon began to view the "Great Conciliator" with suspicion after the famous White House

---

[186] The source is an article entitled "David Wark Griffiht" [sic], by Jacques Manuel, published in *Revue du Cinema* n° 2. An analysis of all nine issues of *Quilombo* makes it clear that it was a very sophisticated and cosmopolitan publication, which also reprinted articles published in the NAACP magazine *The Crisis*. However, it is interesting to note that the source of the review was originally published in France. Decades after *Diário da Bahia* published Bentzon's review of *Up from Slavery*, the French connection continued.

[187] Charles William Eliot (1834-1926), then president of Harvard University.

dinner. A Black man dining with the US President and his family, and the subject of the film reflected one of the White Southerners' greatest fears: contact between White women and Black men, which for White supremacists and racialists could only end in miscegenation. In the novel and the film, a White woman jumps to her death to escape the "lust" of a Black soldier—played by a White actor in "blackface."

Washington tried to stop the film from being released, fearing that it would incite racial conflict. His fears were realized. White horsemen decked out in Ku Klux Klan robes appeared near the movie theatre when the film opened in Atlanta. Even the President of the United States, Woodrow Wilson, reportedly said after a special viewing at the White House: "It's like writing history with lightning. My only regret is that it is all so terribly true" (Norell 2009, 413).[188] The film caused riots in several cities and was the subject of lawsuits and protests for years. Like many crises, it had the advantage of bringing together two great institutions that were generally at odds: the "Tuskegee Machine," and the NAACP.

Although Abdias do Nascimento's publication had a largely positive view of Washington, Tiéde observes that Black activists in Brazil came to a different assessment of the "Wizard of Tuskegee," particularly when he was being held up as a paragon by the White Brazilian press. According to Tiéde,

Dismantling Washington's image was not a viable alternative, as this would "confirm" the racist assumption that Black Brazilians were unable or unwilling to succeed in a free society. Instead, the Black press supported two representations of Washington that leveraged his impeccable image for their own ends. First, to counter the trope that his success dwarfed those—and thus exposed the inadequacies—of his Brazilian contemporaries, they drew parallels between Washington and successful [Black Brazilian] men.... Second, these journalists understood that Washington's abstract example of

---

[188] According to Benbow (2010), this quotation may be apocryphal.

liberal success alone was not enough for African Brazilians to rise socially..... Diverging from representations of Washington in the mainstream press, Black writers focused on Washington's role as an educator. They argued that the foundation of an educational institution designed for Black people...would be a critical step towards lifting their race out of poverty through mass education (2022, 66).

As we know, Manuel Querino was one of the first Black journalists and intellectuals to view and describe Washington as a "prestigious educator" (1938, 22).

Washington in the eyes of the "White" (and White supremacist) Brazilian press

Booker T. Washington's name appeared in the mainstream Brazilian newspapers as early as 1899—*República,* from the northern city of Belém do Pará, published an article on Washington entitled "Um grande negro" ("A Great Black Man"). In addition to that report, Sílvia Tiéde found over 100 other articles on Booker T. Washington in the Brazilian press while researching her PhD dissertation on Frederico Baptista de Souza, a Black activist and publisher based in São Paulo (Tiéde 2023, 129). The searchable digital library published online by Brazil's National Library[189] provides several examples of such mentions. On October 24, 1901, the column "À Toa" (a title that can be translated as "At a Loose End"), on page 2 of the *Cidade do Rio* newspaper, ironically observes: "the famous dinner at the White House caused an uproar in the United States, but Americans in Santos were outraged when a Brazilian barber refused to serve their Black consul five or six years earlier."[190]

---

[189] The National Library's "Hemeroteca Digital" can be found at https://bndigital.bn.gov.br/hemeroteca-digital/.

[190] According to Losch (2009, p. 239): "In 1893, Henry Clay Smith was appointed by President Grover Cleveland as consul in Santos, in an attempt to please the small black block within the Democratic Party. In 1896, there was a scandal when it

On May 3, 1902, the Rio newspaper *O Paiz* published the same article on Léger's review of *Up from Slavery* which appeared in *Diário da Bahia*, this time in a column entitled *Lá para fora* ("In Foreign Parts"), with the subtitle *O preto no branco* ("Black on White"). On October 26 of the following year, another Rio newspaper, *Correio da Manhã*, published this report in its "Carta parisiense" ("Parisian Letter") section:

Paris, October 2
There is now in Paris the most intelligent Black in America, the only Black whom President Roosevelt admits into his palace. He is the famous Booker Washington, the new Black Messiah.

This extraordinary man, who at his earliest age was poor, living the most miserable life, is today a very rich capitalist and a great philanthropist. Thanks to Booker, Blacks in North America will have the freedoms and considerations they never had.

It was he who founded the University for Blacks, where the professors are also men of colour.

Newspapers had announced that Booker left for Europe to organize a trial colony in Soldão [Sudan] for Blacks from North and South America. And that this colony on the banks of the Nile was protected with the great fortune of the arch-millionaire Leigh Hunt. In this way, 8 to 10 million Blacks from the two Americas would civilize Africa, far from the hatred of the Whites.

Could it be true? Will this gigantic project go ahead? Interrogated by the editor of a Parisian newspaper, Booker said nothing positive. Neither yes nor no. But he said the mission was mainly in America. It is there that he works with sublime will to morally and materially uplift the Black man whom Americans so despise.

---

emerged in the papers that Smith had left his wife and five children destitute in Washington, and he resigned shortly before being fired."

Thanks to Booker, the Black University of Tuskegee already exists in free America, where 1,400 Blacks receive solid instruction administered by 100 professors who are also Black.

Black people, says Booker, must be a major factor in American life. The Union needs Blacks. They must be excellent manual workers, rivalling Whites in their love of work.

When will another Booker appear in Brazil to raise the level of the Blacks and save those whom the abolition of slavery has thrown into a vacuum, into uncertainty... (Correio da Manhã, Oct. 26, 1903, 3, emphasis added)

This report was reprinted in the 1905 edition of the *Almanaque Brasileiro Garnier,* on page 393, without the paragraph shown here in italics. There is no indication that Washington intended to establish a colony for Blacks in the Sudan—but he had sent students to African countries to establish schools and agricultural projects there, particularly in Togo (Zimmerman, 2010). In 1903, the principal of the Tuskegee Institute travelled to Europe to spend one of the few vacations he enjoyed in his life, at the age of 47, following medical advice. He received so many invitations to speak at events and dinners during his time in Paris that he began using the pseudonym "Homer P. Jones" (Harlan 1986, 282).

On August 26, 1903, *Gazeta de Notícias,* another Rio de Janeiro newspaper, announced on its front page that Washington, "a black philosopher, moral director of Afro-Americans in the United States" intended to "establish a new university for *coloured men* [italicized in English in the original]" noting: "Booker is going to found a university. For what? The United States needs to solve the crisis with the disappearance of the Blacks." The writer cites efforts to transport "Afro-Americans" to Liberia, Cuba, and the Philippines and notes that Stanley, the British explorer, advised "exporting them to the Free Congo. That is the only way for this not to end in total extermination." The article concludes by opining that the establishment of yet another university for Blacks could undermine this "peaceful solution."[191]

The obituary of Th Benzton published in *Correio Paulistano* on February 15, 1907, not only praises her review of *Up from Slavery* but comments favorably about Washington and his work:

> At the beginning of President Theodore Roosevelt's administration, Mrs. Th. Bentzon drew the attention of French readers to one of America's most distinctive figures, Mr. Booker Washington, whose moral energy and lucid intelligence had won formal support from the current President of the United States for his well-guided initiatives in favour of the education of the Black element in the United States.

On October 29, 1911, the *Gazeta de Notícias* published a short article on page 7 entitled "O ódio de raça" ("Race Hatred"), noting that a book which "the famous Black professor and writer Booker Washington" had recently published tells an anecdote about a Black friend who, being late and fearing he would miss his train, had to deal with a hackney cab driver who "with a tone of contempt, said that he did not transport Blacks in his carriage." But the Black man managed to get around this by offering to drive the carriage and pay for the ride: "Both satisfied their whims and needs, and the law of the races was left untouched."[192]

---

[191] Directed by two of Brazil's leading Black actors, Lázaro Ramos and Taís Araújo, the film *Medida Provisória* (Executive Order) deals with this very subject: in a dystopian future, the Brazilian government orders Black people to emigrate to Africa. Based on the play "Namíbia não!" by Aldri Anunciação, the film was released in 2020.

[192] I could not find this anecdote in Washington's autobiographies, but it is recounted in the biography by Scott and Stowe: "In making the point that, in spite of race prejudice, the handicaps to which his people were subjected in the South were after all superficial and did not interfere with their chance to work and earn a living, he told the experience of an old Negro who was accompanying him on one of his Southern educational tours" (1916, 30-31).

On January 3, 1912, *Correio Paulistano* published a front-page article entitled "A Questão das Raças" ("The Race Question") which reports on of the First Universal Races Congress, held in London, and mentions "...Mr. Burchharot [*sic*] du Bois, the undisputed head of the Black intelligentsia in that country. A Doctor of Philosophy from Harsard's College [*sic*], he is a Professor of History at the University of Atlanta and President of the 'National Association for the Advancement of Colored People.'" However, the writer reserves the most space and the highest praise for "Booker E. [*sic*] Washington," described as "one of the personalities to whom the education of Blacks owes the greatest debt," and who:

With tireless ardour, lectured everywhere on behalf of his blood brothers and founded numerous schools. But his most notable creation, which will make him famous, is the vast Institute which he organized in 1881 at Euskegee [*sic*], Alabama, for the professional education of Blacks. This establishment is in admirable condition to carry out the mission it has in mind. Numerous pupils of both sexes and of all ages receive practical instruction adaptable to their social condition from every point of view. A pedagogical section trains teachers of both genders who, in turn, will spread the Institute's beneficial activities in other regions.

It is by processes of this nature that the rise of a people is hastened. It is true that the work carried out by Mr. Booker E. [*sic*] Washington and the enthusiasm with which he works for the development of the Black race and his approach to the White race is worth more than many speeches and literary publications.

However, the brilliant results achieved, of which he can be rightly proud, are not enough for this philanthropist. His ambition is to make others profit from his experience; his desire is to carry out the advice of those who are moving towards the same end as he is and probably have some good teachings to impart. He has conceived a plan to hold a conference at Euskegee in 1912 to which he will invite missionaries, lawmakers, and all who are interested in or at the head of enterprises like his own.

People who attend this conference will have the opportunity to study the methods followed in the United States and to verify their results and see to what extent these methods can be applied in other parts of the globe.

Soon, at this meeting, the best systems for educating Blacks will be discussed. Each one will present their views, sharing their observations and what they have personally achieved (*Correio Paulistano*, January 3, 1912, 1).

On September 30, 1912, the *Correio da Manhã* published an article about normal schools in which it cites Booker T. Washington and the Tuskegee Institute as an example of the advances achieved by teacher training institutions in the United States.

On September 17, 1912, Miguel Calmon,[193] then a congressman for Bahia, gave a speech on the "problem of education" before the Chamber of Deputies that was published in full by the Rio newspaper, *Jornal do Commercio* (Sept. 20, 1912, p. 11).

> I could, for now, restrict myself to asking that the Tuskegee Normal Institute [sic], in the United States, founded by the incomparable educator that is Booker Washington, be taken as a model, but, so they will not call me a pessimist, for asking a school for Blacks for standards, since perhaps such a happy partnership of education for the countryside and the city is not to be found elsewhere, I will content myself with advocating the

---

[193] Miguel Calmon du Pin e Almeida was born in Salvador, Bahia, in 1879 and died in Rio de Janeiro in 1935. He served as a federal congressman in 1906 and from 1912-1913, as well as being Minister of Highways and Public Works (1906-1909) and Agriculture, Industry and Commerce (1922-1926) and senator for Bahia from 1927 until Vargas's coup in 1930. https://cpdoc.fgv.br/sites/default/files/verbetes/primeira-republica/CALMON,%20Miguel.pdf Manuel Querino dedicated the first edition of *Artistas baianos* to Miguel Calmon in 1909.

ideas already victorious in that country regarding secondary education for both sexes.

On September 17, 1913, an article entitled "Miguel Calmon," published in the Rio de Janeiro newspaper *O Imparcial* (p. 4), analyses the statesman's call for universal education in Brazil:

Widespread education everywhere; education propagated by the railroads, putting the most cultured centres in contact with the remotest parts of the interior; education received from the example of colonists imported from advanced nations, who brought us habits of rational work; professional education, not in words but in deeds, of which Booker Washington has given us an imperishable model.

I could not find any obituaries for Washington published in Brazil immediately after his death on November 14, 1915, although, as we saw in Chapter 3, it was widely reported in the United States and around the world.

In 1915 (no. 14, 9-10), *A.B.C.: Política, Actualidades, Questões Sociais, Lettras e Artes* of Rio de Janeiro published a sarcastic article on the Black Brazilian educator Hemetério dos Santos[194] entitled "The Booker Washington of South America: *Adelante com juicio* ["Go Ahead Prudently," in Spanish], Mr. Heméterio dos Santos!" The anonymous author both denies the presence of "racial hatred" in Brazil while using pseudoscientific racialist language (such as "macrocephali of post-Aryan ethnography"), suggesting that Santos— who, according to the author, calls himself a Messiah, intends to turn

---

[194] Hemetério José dos Santos (1858-1939) was a teacher, grammarian, philologist, and writer. Born in Maranhão, he taught in Rio de Janeiro for 20 years, at the Colégio Pedro II, Colégio Militar and Escola Normal. He was also in the military, reaching the rank of honorary lieutenant colonel. He became known for criticizing the work of Machado de Assis, whom he accused of being ashamed of his color (Muller 2008; Rodrigues 2013).

Brazil into a "Haiti" or "Liberia," and believes that anyone who is not "of color" is a parasite—poses a threat

> ...because the worthy educator does not spare his fellow man (fellow, so to speak, since the Messiah makes no distinction between men of colour and men without colour) the opportunity to hear from his lips the most vehement insults against the race that he did not deserve the supreme happiness of having, in its blood, a few drops of kaffir liquid...

On January 15, 1916, *Gazeta de Notícias* published a note on the second page, also unsigned and in this case untitled, which makes an unflattering comparison between Hemetério dos Santos and Booker T. Washington. The tone is ironic, and the racist language is not always veiled. It concludes:

> *Like the United States, we have our "Booker Washington." But unfortunately for Heméterio, there has yet to be a Roosevelt who, going against public opinion, would raise him to a prominent position.*
>
> We might as well send the obscured [sic] teacher to Abyssinia, to teach the descendants of Menelick [sic] *(Gazeta de Notícias, 1916, emphasis added).*

On September 22, 1921, *Correio da Manhã* published an article entitled "The Black Problem" on page 2, which presents Washington as a spokesman and defender of Black people:

> The Blacks already said philosophically through the lips of that great apostle who was Booker Washington, that they did not come spontaneously from Africa to America.... It was the Whites who went there to get them. Now, they feel perfectly comfortable in the new *"heimat"* [German for homeland], and have no interest in changing it.

On October 6 of the same year, in São Paulo, the *Correio Paulistano* published an article on page 3 signed by "João do Norte" (John of the North, the pseudonym of the fascist leader and intellectual from Ceará, Gustavo Barroso) (Oliveira 2003, 17), entitled "The Black University," in which the author praises Washington's work and makes the following rather optimistic observation, affirming the ideology of racial democracy:

> We do not have in Brazil, where the African race has produced astonishingly intelligent minds, a Tuskegee College, a Black university, nor types who have carried out a great and noble program like this extraordinary Booker Taliaferro Washington. *And this should only make us proud, because it is proof that in our country those who want to study are not divided by color and everyone is, not of this or that race, but Brazilians and brothers* (*Correio Paulistano*, 1921, emphasis added).

On October 15, 1922, *O Pharol* of Juiz de Fora published an article on miscegenation by Mário de Lima, a poet, polemicist, and educator from Minas Gerais, according to whom: "The theories of Wachez [sic] Lapouge and Gobineau are demoralised prejudices that the case of Japan, the political progress of China and the pedagogical work of Booker Washington, in the United States, completely devastated," and concludes: "The doctrine of living peoples is built on the ruins of the doctrine of dead races" (*O Pharol*, 1922, 2).

Page 4 of the issue of *Correio da Manhã* published on October 11, 1923 features an article entitled "Expansion of a prejudice... or outline of a protectorate," which discusses racism in the United States and describes dining with the "mixed-race genius" at the White House as a singular gesture by President Roosevelt.

Entitled "The D. João Nery 'orphanage,'" an article in the *Diário Nacional* (São Paulo), which appeared on page 7, on February 3, 1928, announces that "the foundations have just been laid for the important initiative of the Palmares Centre" and begins by praising Booker T. Washington as a model in the field of Black education, although his work

...still has no following in other countries, where the education of black men is one of the national problems. Among these countries, we are in first place, with a very large percentage in some parts of our territory. However, the consequences of indigenous negligence of the education of black men who were born here are approaching.

On June 21, 1928, page 6, the second instalment of a "patriotic lecture" by Baptista Pereira entitled "O Brasil e a raça" ("Brazil and Race"), serialized in the *Correio Paulistano*, cites Washington as a paragon of the Back race, along with José do Patrocínio.[195]

As early as 1934, a front-page note published in *A Noite* (Rio de Janeiro) on November 1, entitled "O voo negro" ("The Black Flight") announces that "the Booker T. Washington will land in Brazil," reporting that two Black American aviators were preparing a *raid*—a Pan-American goodwill flight organized by the Tuskegee Institute, "a university centre dedicated exclusively to the education of young people of colour," in a plane named after the institution's founder.

On November 7, 1937, the *Correio da Manhã* published an article covering most of a page (p. 12, Supplement), entitled "The Black Man who Dined with Roosevelt." Written by Luciano Lopes, a Baptist minister, history teacher, and member of the Rio de Janeiro Academy of Letters (Villaça 2006, 87), it compares Washington and the great boxing champion of the time—also mentioned in *Quilombo:*

The entire world today has its eyes on Joe Louis, who was able to knock down his contender with a powerful punch; but no one now remembers that other black man named Washington, who, having been a slave, practiced the miracle of obtaining, through his own efforts, a notable education and became the apostle of good among his companions in misfortune.

---

[195] Baptista Pereira also published a 153-page book with the same title (1928). José do Patrocínio (1853-1905) was a leader of the abolitionist movement, as well as a journalist, writer, and pharmacist.

The piece is illustrated with two scenes of (possibly enslaved) Black people in tropical settings and a portrait, supposedly of Washington, which only bears a vague resemblance to the educator but faithfully reflects his serious and decisive countenance.

On October 21, 1939, *Correio da Manhã* published an article about Booker T. Washington and George Washington Carver, the renowned Black American botanist who spent many years of his life living, teaching, and doing scientific research at the Tuskegee Institute.

The "Books" section, on page 5 of *A Noite*, announced on August 18, 1940 the launch of the translation of *Up from Slavery* by Graciliano Ramos:

> The Brazilian public is presented with the famous work of by a black man who sacrificed his entire life in a holocaust to his race in the United States. We know that President Mc. Kinley [sic], despite the rigor of racial prejudice in his homeland, personally visited the black man who, from a captive, rose to the most glorious social prestige, managing to organize an entire immense work in favour of the despised race.

On February 12, 1951, the Rio de Janeiro newspaper *Imprensa Popular* published a report on the front page entitled "Murdered by American Racism" and illustrated with photos of several Black Americans, stating that "Seven North Americans, belonging to the race that gave the United States a great scientist [sic] like Booker Washington, a great writer like Langston Hughes, and great artists like Paul Robeson and Marian Anderson, died this week in the electric chair." In this case, the author may have made the not uncommon mistake of confusing Booker T. Washington with George Washington Carver, two distinguished Black Americans, who shared the name Washington and a strong connection with the Tuskegee Institute.[196]

---

[196] This publication's anti-American position is evident in several articles on the same page, including a reference to "Yankee Imperialism" and titles such as "The

The Brazilian edition of *Reader's Digest* published an advertisement in *A Noite* on March 1, 1956, that one of the works in its upcoming issue was "A Janela Lavada" ("The Washed Window"):[197]

Around 1858, Booker T. Washington was born into slavery on a Virginia plantation. Until he was well grown, already a young man, he only wore one piece of clothing, a shirt made of burlap. But he would go on to become one of America's most distinguished educators. And he himself tells the story of how, in a single day, a White woman taught him a lesson that would open the doors to a civilized life for him (*Seleções* 1956, 6).

Fig. 4-4. Centennial postage stamp, issued in 1956

Yankees Trust Vargas", "American Bandits Attack a Brazilian" and "Another Gangster in Uniform Comes to Organize Yankee Blood Hospitals in Brazil."

[197] A short story by Dorothy Canfield Fisher originally published in 1955. It provides interesting but possibly fictitious background information on Viola Ruffner, née Knapp, who is said to have taught at a school for Blacks before marrying then-Lieutenant Ruffner. https://www.americanheritage.com/washed-window

An article by Cândido Mendes on a three-cent stamp issued in the United States to commemorate the centenary of Booker T. Washington's birth appeared in *Correio da Manhã*, on September 2, 1956 (p. 13). It reports that 120 million copies of the stamp were produced, with a picture of a cabin similar to the hovel in which Washington was born, and sums up his life like this:

> Born on a plantation south of Franklin, Virginia, in April 1856, Booker Washington worked in coal mines as a child. He later enrolled at the Hampton Normal and Agricultural Institute, where he worked to pay his way through school. He was a bricklayer, and later a teacher.
>
> In the difficult days after the Civil War and the emancipation of the slaves, Washington became famous for the message he addressed to the Whites and Blacks of the South to work together to develop friendship between the two races...
>
> A graduate [*sic*] of Harvard and Dartmouth Universities, Washington has written over 10 books on improving interracial relations and educating his people. One of these books, his autobiography, *Up from Slavery*, has become a classic and has been translated into over 20 languages.

It is hard to determine whether the author researched or translated this information. The word "bricklayer" *(pedreiro)* may have been confused with *porteiro* ("doorman"), which we saw in the translation of Th Bentzon's review in *Diário da Bahia*. There is no specific reference to the Graciliano Ramos translation, which was published in 1940. It may be that, by 1956, that work had been forgotten, as it only went beyond its first edition in 2020. As we will see in the following section, despite being one of Brazil's most renowned and beloved authors, the quality of the translation of *Up from Slavery* into Portuguese may have been compromised by Ramos's contempt for its author (Ramos 1979, 211-217).

The last mention of Booker T. Washington found in the National Library's digital newspaper collection is an article by the socialist, journalist, and social historian Raymond Postgate entitled "New

Views on the Soviet System." It was published in *Correio da Manhã* on May 31, 1957, page 7. Postgate observes: "Few people have written as sympathetically as [Padmore] about Marcus Garvey, who elected himself the 'black emperor' in the 1920s, or about Booker Washington, the standard bearer of the group they called Uncle Toms in the previous generation."

After that date, the only mention of the name "Booker" that I found in the online newspaper library in relation to Washington refers to his grandson, the saxophonist Booker Pittman (1909-1969), son of Portia Pittman, and stepfather and musical partner of the Brazilian jazz singer Eliana Pittman. His famous grandfather is now frequently mentioned in articles about Eliana Pittman.[198]

"Traduttore–traditore"

Othon Guerlac was the first to request permission to translate *Up from Slavery*, and his French translation was published eighteen months later. Before it came out, however, Washington's autobiography had already been published in Spanish in 1902 as *De esclavo a catedrático*, translated by Alfredo Elías y Pujol. Originally intended for Cuban readers, it was eventually read throughout Latin America.[199] It has also been translated into German, Norwegian, Swedish, Danish, Dutch, Finnish, Spanish and Russian, and reportedly into Arabic, Zulu, Hindi, Malay, Chinese, and Japanese. The first Braille edition came out in 1903 (Harlan 1975, 252).

---

[198] See, for example, Eliana Pittman homenageia ao pai, Booker Pittman, no Rio https://www.gentedesucessovip.com.br/entretenimento/musica/shows-performances/2814-eliana-pittman-homenageia-ao-pai-booker-pittman-no-rio and Eliana Pittman: Brazilian Treasure https://www.jazzwax.com/2021/05/eliana-pittman.html

[199] The translator's introduction includes a note from Booker T. Washington, expressing his hope that the Spanish translation of his book will be of use to "coloured youths" in Cuba who are preparing to embark on the "great enterprises of life." Washington stresses that his sole aim in writing the book was to teach young people the value of hard work and that "idleness debases and degrades" (1902, vi).

Graciliano Ramos is best known in Brazil as the author of *Vidas secas* (translated into English as *Barren Lives*). Despite being an acclaimed writer, his approach to the art of translation was more mercenary than literary (Silva 2006, 37). According to his biographer Denis de Moraes, he sometimes ceded "to the temptation of straightening out other people's prose."[200]

When translating *Up from Slavery* in 1940, he decimated two chapters of Booker Washington and mercilessly eliminated entire sentences. And he boasted of the feat: "The man was going well, some great observations, [then] suddenly he was all over the place. Time after time, he repeated ideas, used unnecessary words, ran around in circles. I cut out an infinity of idiocies, and many remain. *Negro burro* (stupid Negro)" (Moraes 1996, 266).

Ramos's approach to translating *Up from Slavery* is clear when we compare *Memórias de um negro* with the original. To begin with, Ramos deleted the preface that acknowledges the contribution of the White co-author/ghostwriter Max Bennett Thrasher, which explains that Washington hired him to write the book. In Ramos's hands, some chapter titles were stripped of their homely, parabolic style— "A Harder Task than Making Bricks without Straw" (chapter X) becomes "A Difficult Task"; "Making their Beds before they could Lie on Them" (chapter XI) is whittled down to "Furniture Manufacturing," and "Two Thousand Miles for a Five-Minute Speech" (chapter XIII) is just "A Five-Minute Speech." Possibly the biggest translation error could reflect Ramos's lack of knowledge of US history when he translates "The Reconstruction Period" as "The Awakening." The text makes it clear that Ramos interpreted the term—which, of course, refers to the reconstruction of the South after the US Civil War—as the "awakening" of the Black people.

Ramos truncates the famous opening lines into a terse, erroneous, and humourless statement about Washington's birthplace: "I was born a slave on a plantation in Franklin, Virginia. I do not know the

---

[200] According to Pereira (2010, 8), "As a translator, Ramos mistakenly acted as an editor. This was repeated when he translated *The Plague* by Albert Camus."

exact place and date of my birth; I believe, however, that I came into this world in 1858 or 1859, near Hale Fort [sic], a crossroads where there was a post office. I do not know the month and day" (Washington 1940, 1).[201]

In a posthumously published article, Ramos (1979, 211-217) excoriated Washington. Regarding his admission to the Hampton Institute and appointment to direct the Tuskegee Institute "three years later," the Brazilian author contemptuously observes that

> We cannot say that this was a flight of intelligence superior to ordinary intelligence. No. Booker Washington differed little from ordinary men. In the art of writing, he admired newspapers and biography. He mocked Greek and Latin, with gross irony, and was indignant to see a young man delving into the mysteries of French grammar. He spent three months in Europe, regularly sleeping fifteen hours a day. And the remarks he made there, in the moments stolen from sleep, were brief and yawning.... Despite this inner poverty, Booker Washington left us firm outlines of rural life in his country. In the pages in which he exempted himself from the obligation to present ideas, he was simple, true and human. Perhaps he owed his prosperity to that paucity of ideas. Booker Washington was thinking of a small number of things, but he was thinking hard. He had limited and concrete desires, and resourcefully fulfilled them (Ibid., 211-212).

According to Ramos (Ibid., 212), anticipating the title of Carl Degler's *Neither Black nor White* (1976):

---

[201] The original reads: "I was born a slave on a plantation in Franklin County, Virginia. I am not quite sure of the exact place or exact date of my birth, but at any rate I suspect I must have been born somewhere and at some time. As nearly as I have been able to learn, I was born near a crossroads post office called Hale's Ford, and the year was 1858 or 1859. I do not know the month or the day" (Washington 1986, 1).

He wasn't exactly black: he had fifty percent white blood. He made an effort to bring the two opposing ethnic groups together, he presented himself as a great friend to them; but he was cold, calculating, and seems to have secretly despised them. He did not belong to either race and made contributions to both: from the whites he took capital, from the blacks he demanded work. And he was insatiable.

These remarks may also reflect the fact that Ramos was a Communist. Many of his views on Washington parallel those of W. E. B. Du Bois, who joined the Communist Party late in life. For example: "Booker Washington was untroubled by literary education, but he was demanding in the workshop. And he did not dispense with religious ceremonies in the chapel. He also wanted blacks to be loyal, well behaved and, in elections, to vote for their former masters" (Ramos 1979, 212). It is important to note that, in a book co-authored with Alfred A. Moss, Jr., John Hope Franklin—another critic of the "Wizard"—observes that Du Bois's objections to Washington included his embrace of private enterprise:

> It was a doctrine of triumphant capitalism, which was strengthened by his contacts with ... wealthy American businesspeople. The Negro Business League, which Washington organized in 1900 to foster business and industry, was based on the philosophy that if one could make a better article and sell it cheaper, one could command the markets of the world.... [T]his philosophy was an adaptation of the theories of free competition and political individualism that had been taught by the school of classical political economy and was becoming more fictitious than ever by 1900.... Washington showed little understanding of these realities as he developed a program for the economic salvation of Black Americans (Franklin and Moss, Jr., 1994, 275).

In addition to his political objections, Ramos made it personal: he criticized Washington's "lachrymose" style on one page, noting that he "regretted having to leave his family... But these things were said with the same sentiment he expressed when singing the praises of Americans' intense philanthropy" (1979, 213). He concluded with this positive, albeit ironic, observation:

However, we do not see Booker Washington as an egotist. He was a man of action, very capable. In the United States he naturally took his place among the Blacks. And he forced them to work desperately hard while he fleeced the Whites. He wanted to give the Blacks financial independence. Greek, Latin, the arts, the sciences, all the inner trappings of which he himself was dimly aware, would come later (Ibid., 214).

The writer's grandson Ricardo Ramos defends him against accusations of racism, observing that: "Something displeased him about Booker Washington. Could it have been [his] subservience to Whites, which was invariably self-serving? It is not by chance that the Black movements in the United States, of the most diverse tendencies, now call him an Uncle Tom" (Ramos 2011, 139). Ironically, *Uncle Tom's Cabin* was censored in Brazil prior to Abolition, due to fears that it would inspire abolitionist sentiments, "self-emancipation," and even rebellions among the enslaved population, but today "Uncle Tom" (Pai Tomás in Portuguese) is synonymous with Black subservience to Whites.

W. E. B. Du Bois and *The Souls of Black Folk*

Booker T. Washington gained nationwide recognition in the United States when he delivered his famous address at the Atlanta Exposition in 1895. As we saw in Chapter 2, Washington received a note from W. E. B. Du Bois, hailing his speech and declaring that it was "a word fitly spoken." At the same time, Washington was harshly criticized for the same address by eminent Black intellectuals, whose ranks Du Bois would later join. Nevertheless, Washington never lost the support of the common folk of the Black nation whom Du Bois considered "the masses." According to the White journalist Ray Stannard Baker, who uses the same term:

I have heard bitter things said about Mr. Washington by coloured people and white. I have waited and investigated many of these stories, and I am telling here what I have seen and known of his influence among thousands of common, struggling human beings. Many highly educated Negroes, especially, in the North, dislike him and oppose him, but he has brought new hope and given new courage to the masses of his race. He has given them a working plan of life. And is there a higher test of usefulness? Measured by any standard, white or black, Washington must be regarded today as one of the great men of this country: and in the future he will be so honoured (1908, loc. 3830).

It is important to note that Washington dropped his conciliatory tone towards the end of his life. It may be that the "Ulrich Affair," which made it clear that not even the "most famous Negro in the world" was safe from episodes of sudden violence on the slightest pretext, was a factor which led Booker T. Washington to adopt a more open and aggressive posture regarding Black civil rights and the fight against "Jim Crow" in the years before his death in 1915. In the posthumous article entitled "My View of Segregation Laws," he took a clear and forceful stand against segregation, stating that it was not only unfair but served to widen the gap between the races, embittering Black people and doing nothing to improve the moral fibre of Whites (Washington 1915, 114).

However, the image of Washington as an "accommodationist" and subservient "Uncle Tom" persists in Brazil and the United States today, largely tarnished, propagated, and perpetuated by W. E. B. Du Bois. In his devastating essay on Washington in *The Souls of Black Folk*, Du Bois (2019, 73) concludes:

So far as Mr. Washington preaches Thrift, Patience, and Industrial Training for the masses, we must hold up his hands and strive with him, rejoicing in his honours and glorying in the strength of this Joshua called of God and of man to lead the headless host. But so far as Mr. Washington apologizes for injustice, North or South, does not rightly value the privilege and duty of voting, belittles the emasculating effects of caste distinctions, and opposes the higher training and ambition of our brighter minds,—so far as he, the South, or the Nation, does his,—we must unceasingly and firmly oppose them.

In his unsigned obituary of Washington, Du Bois spoke ill of the dead, charging him with responsibility for Black disenfranchisement, the decline of Black universities and public schools, and the consolidation of a racial caste system in the United States (*The Crisis* 1915, 82). The Black polymath Ishmael Reed questioned and refuted these arguments in his introduction to *Up from Slavery* entitled "Booker vs. the Negro Saxons" (2000), and the White historians Heather Cox Richardson (2004, 225-245) and Robert J. Norrell have reappraised Washington's life and work in the context of his time. According to Norell:

Booker Washington's response to his circumstances reflected a sophisticated mind that had contrived a complex means for achieving what, by any standard, were high-minded goals. But his was an awful time that set narrow and unjust limits on what he could do to pursue his ends. In Washington's view, his life was not just a struggle up from slavery but also a great effort to rise above history. Given the fate of his historical reputation, that remains the great challenge of his life, now almost a century after it ended (2009, 16).

Unfortunately, Norrell's book has not yet been translated into Portuguese, and the main Portuguese-language printed sources available to Brazilian intellectuals on Washington are Ramos's bowdlerized translation of *Up from Slavery* and Du Bois's brutal essay. Brazilians have access to an excellent translation of *The Souls of Black Folk*, entitled *Almas da Gente Negra* (1999b), thanks to the painstaking work of Heloísa Toller Gomes, who was also responsible for the annotations and introduction. It contains an afterword by Du Bois's stepson, David G. Du Bois, who observes that his stepfather believed Washington's philosophy of self-reliance "placed the burden of the entire task at hand primarily on the shoulders of black citizens fresh out of slavery, living under the devastation that followed the collapse of Reconstruction and suffering its terrible consequences" (1999b, 317).

David Du Bois also quotes one of his stepfather's last interviews, given in 1963 to Ralph Mcgill in Ghana:

> "I never thought Washington was a bad man," he said. "I believed him to be sincere, though wrong. He and I came from different backgrounds. I was born free. Washington was born slave. He felt the lash of an overseer across his back. I was born in Massachusetts, he on a slave plantation in the South. My great-grandfather fought with the Colonial Army in New England in the American Revolution." (This earned the grandfather his freedom.) "I had a happy childhood and acceptance in the community. Washington's childhood was hard. I had many more advantages: Fisk University, Harvard, graduate years in Europe. Washington had little formal schooling. I admired much about him. Washington," he said, a smile softening the severe, gaunt lines of his face, "died in 1915. A lot of people think I died at the same time" (McGill 1965).

More recent mentions

Over the years, Washington's image in the Brazilian press deteriorated from an illustrious Black educator and orator to an "Uncle Tom." At least one Black Brazilian intellectual, Wilson Roberto de Mattos, first learned about Washington through Du Bois's essay in *Souls of Black Folk*, which had a powerful influence on his opinion of the "Wizard of Tuskegee."[202] When I was researching my

---

[202] Personal communication during the VII Brazilian Congress of Black Researchers in Florianópolis, in July 2012. At the time, Wilson Roberto de Mattos was director of the Center for the Study of Afro-Indian-American Peoples - CEPAIA, at the State University of Bahia (UNEB). He also co-edited the EdUNEB edition of *Costumes Africanos no Brasil*, by Manuel Querino (2010).

PhD dissertation, defended in 2014, I found very few references to Booker T. Washington in Brazilian scholarly publications available online. However, Antonio Sergio Alfredo Guimarães (2004) draws a clear parallel between Querino and Washington, as well as W. E. B. Du Bois, in "Manoel Querino e a formação do 'pensamento negro' no Brasil, entre 1890 e 1920" ("Manoel Querino and the formation of 'black thought' in Brazil, between 1890 and 1920"), and suggested a comparative study. The PhD dissertation by Sérgio Antônio Silva (2006), entitled "Papel, penas e tinta: a memória da escrita em Graciliano Ramos" ("Paper, Pens and Ink: The Memory of Writing in Graciliano Ramos") mentions Washington in the context of the Brazilian author's translation of *Up from Slavery*.

The chapter entitled "Aurora negra: afro-paulistas e afro-americanos na modernidade" ("Black Dawn: Afro-Paulistas and Afro-Americans in Modernity") by Flávio Thales Ribeiro Francisco, provides information on Washington's life and work, but presents the same image disseminated by Du Bois and others, that the founder of Tuskegee advocated "strictly professional education, without the practice of any intellectual exercise." Francis also defines the "philosophy of accommodation" as the conviction that Black Americans should "develop their institutions without getting involved in the struggles for the conquest of full citizenship, that is, against racial segregation" (Ribeiro Francisco 2009, 64).

Nevertheless, in his Atlanta Exposition address, while calling for the peaceful coexistence of the races, Booker T. Washington was careful to assert that Blacks should have the right to education at all levels: "There is no defence or security for any of us, except in the highest intelligence and development of all. If anywhere there are efforts tending to curtail the fullest growth of the Negro, let these efforts be transformed into stimulating, encouraging and making him the most useful and intelligent citizen" (Washington 1986, 222). Washington also recognised that slavery had destroyed the work ethic among formerly enslaved people and their descendants, and that in the generation after slavery, many lacked job skills and qualifications. As we have seen, enslavers needed skilled labour to maintain their plantations—their bondspeople had to know how to farm the land and tend horses and livestock, as well as being Blacksmiths, carpenters, weavers, cooks, and so on—but after Emancipation, the children of freed bondspeople did not have access to such training. However, the predominant image among most Brazilian scholars—heavily influenced by Du Bois—is that Washington was collaborating with the efforts of White supremacists to keep Black people "in their place."

CHAPTER 5
PORTRAYALS AND PUSHBACK: Deploying Images as an Anti-Racist Tactic

To different degrees, portraits of free and enslaved Black people that emphasized their "personhood" contradicted images which accompanied discourses about race and national identity constructed by racialist ideologies based on pseudoscientific racism. In some cases, such as those of Washington and Querino, Black intellectuals and leaders produced and disseminated portraits of themselves in which they are well-dressed and strike assertive poses. They stand in stark contrast with anthropometric photographs such as those commissioned by Louis Agassiz in the US and Brazil.

Prologue

The marginalisation of Black people, which renders them invisible (Pereira and Gomes 2001, 133-134), is reflected in images employed in the US and Brazil. Today, Black activists in both countries are keenly aware of how people of colour are portrayed (or absent) in the media, advertising, cinema, television, and the visual arts, as they know that such images tend to reinforce stereotypes and perpetuate negative concepts about Blacks. In Brazil, in particular, the biggest problem is the "intentional erasure of the image of Black people in Brazilian society" (Ibid., 134).

At the turn of the twentieth century, Afro-descendants in both countries responded to derogatory portrayals and attempts to use anthropometric photographs to prove or justify the pseudoscientific ideology of White supremacy, by pushing back with a different kind of image: Black people who were well dressed or in uniform, on their own or with their family; cultured, intelligent, and taking part in educational, civic, and even nationalist activities to demonstrate their patriotism. In common with other eminent Black people, Booker T. Washington and Manuel R. Querino produced and published portraits of themselves, striking poses that reflected assurance and authority (see Figs. 5-1 and 5-2). Some of these images bore their signatures, following the style in fashion, to emphasize that they were literate at a time when few Blacks could sign their own name.

Since the days of the first daguerreotypes, photographers and their subjects established an aesthetic and a code which imbued each portrait with symbolism and meaning. According to Alan Trachtenberg:

> The look was all-important, and what to do with the eyes, the key problem... The term "expression" came to represent the chief goal of the portrait: a look of animation, intelligence, inner character. The true art of portrait making lay in the capture of an inner essence, and "expression" of "character" (1989, 26-27).

Portrayals and Pushback

Fig. 5-1. Booker T. Washington, ca.1903.
Photograph by C. E. Cheyne[203]

Turazzi notes that the way the "model" was dressed and the objects that accompanied them in the photo "could define, or at least momentarily produce, the illusion of an adventurous spirit, an intellectual or philosophical calling, glories and power." She also observes that "At the Paris World's Fair [*Exposition Universelle*] of

---

[203] Christopher Ethelbert Cheyne (1867-1943) was a White photographer who was born in Canada and died in Hampton, Virginia. http://hampton.pastperfectonline.com/byperson?keyword=Cheyne%2C+Christopher+Ethelbert

1878...Aymar-Bression praised the photographer who could get the most advantageous pose from his models—a 'true talent,' in his opinion" (1995, 14).

According to Trachtenberg, photographers adopted the concept that an individual's appearance reflected their character, and established a "sentimental repertoire of expressive poses." For example, there was a specific pose for lawyers, as well as others for preachers and orators. Poets should be seated at their desk. "In fact, the conventional poses addressed social more than moral categories, identifying character with role" (Trachtenberg 1989, 28).

Fig. 5-2. The frontispiece for the 2nd edition of *Artistas baianos*

Portraits of Washington, Querino, and other Black leaders can be compared with the photographs Mathew Brady took of former US presidents, military personnel, and intellectuals—images of White men which were "implicitly racialized" in a period of "exacerbated racial tensions, continuation of the debate on the supposed black issue, Jim Crow segregation, denial of African American citizenship and the increase of lynchings" (Smith 1999, 64-65). Black subjects faced the dilemma famously expressed by W. E. B. Du Bois: *"It is a peculiar sensation, this double-consciousness, this sense of always looking at one's self through the eyes of others,* of measuring one's soul by the tape of a world that looks on in amused contempt and pity" (2003, 9, emphasis added).

The few photographs we have of Manuel Querino always show him with a serious expression and a self-assured pose. Unlike other Brazilians of colour—notably, Machado de Assis, Brazil's greatest author—Querino did not attempt to "whiten" his image. On the contrary, through photographs and in his essay "Os homens de cor preta na história" (Black Men in History, Querino 1923; Nascimento and Gama 2009, 187-199), he made a point of showing that he and many illustrious Brazilians were Black.

The first edition of *Artistas baianos* (1909) contains several portraits of artists of African and European descent (including Querino's mentor, the Spanish artist, Miguel Navarro y Cañizares). The Afro-descendants are the painter Júlio de Magalhães Macedo and the musicians Adelelmo Nascimento Miguel dos Anjos Torres and Cornélio Vidal da Cunha. However, the plates that illustrate the second edition of *Artistas baianos* (1911) only include two artists—an engraving of the author as the frontispiece, clearly showing his African ancestry (Fig. 5-2), and a sketched portrait of the poet, historian, and soldier Ladislau da Silva Titára (1801-1861). A veteran of Independence who wrote the lyrics of the "2nd of July Anthem" celebrating Bahia's independence day when he was a lieutenant in the Army General Staff Corps (Querino 1911, 166, Note 1), Titára is shown in uniform, wearing four medals on his chest, along with the medallion of the Order of the Rose. He was an officer of that order, as well as a knight of the Order of the Cross. His African ancestry is also clear (see Fig. 5-3). Querino devotes just one footnote of *Artistas baianos* to the poet Titára (Ibid.), which makes it even more intriguing that he added his portrait to the illustrations for the second edition.[204]

Fig. 5-3. Ladislau dos Santos Titára

Another Afro-Brazilian who made tactical use of portraits was Francisco Dias Coelho, the "Black colonel of Chapada Diamantina." According to Moiseis de Oliveira Sampaio:

---

[204] Posters of Titára's portrait were exhibited at the Instituto Geográfico e Histórico da Bahia (IGHB) to mark the 200th anniversary of Bahia's Independence in 2023.

In his photographs, the images presented differed according to the social class to which they were directed. For the poorest, photographs were distributed [showing Dias Coelho] in the uniform of the National Guard, seated in a chair that resembled a throne, with a poised and imposing expression.... For the elite, the photograph was different. He appears in a suit, apparently well-tailored, with a neat necktie, also demonstrating poise, with a more serious and solemn countenance, but which in no way resembles the photograph [of Dias Coelho] in uniform, except for the subject. To the recipient of the second photo, the image conveyed that the subject was one of them, equally cultured and rich, although the photograph did not deny his colour (2009, 78).

In that respect, Colonel Dias Coelho could be compared with Booker T. Washington, who produced countless portraits of himself (studio, photojournalistic, prints, etc.) for the consumption of two audiences—White and Black. Washington was keenly aware of the Victorian tastes of White philanthropists. For them, he sought to project the image of a "man of taste and intellect." For his Black audience, he projected an air of power and "the authority upon which that power was based" (Bieze 2008, 51-52).[205]

Querino used his own portrait and images of other Black people to illustrate his work, with the aim of showing a positive image of Africans and their descendants and countering negative stereotypes, while demonstrating the contributions that "Black colonists" had made to Brazilian society (Vasconcellos 2009; Gledhill 2011). Furthermore, Querino's image has also been used in different ways by others. As we saw in Chapter 3, his portrait was placed in the IGHB's gallery of honour in 1928, along with that of Nina Rodrigues (Pereira 1932, 34). E. Bradford Burns mentions it in his essay on Querino, citing it as one of the few ways the Afro-Brazilian scholar's

---

[205] As he was "the most famous Black man in the world" (Bieze 2008, 6), there were also images Washington could not control, such as caricatures and cartoons published in newspapers and magazines.

"prominent place in Brazilian historiography" was recognized (1974, 84). In his foreword to *Costumes africanos no Brasil*, Artur Ramos states that "by unveiling his portrait together with that of the great master Nina Rodrigues, the House of Bahia [IGHB] paid him a tribute worthy of his merits" (1938, 12). Jorge Calmon uses the same portrait to give his readers an idea of its subject's character in an essay entitled "Manuel Querino, O Jornalista e o Político" (The Journalist and Politician):

> Now, let us briefly look at the kind of man he was: his appearance, his way of being. His portrait hangs in the [IGHB]. In fact, it was placed there, in its gallery of honour, five years after his death, in recognition of his contributions to the arts and culture and to that institution. This portrait shows us a man with a poised and confident mien, his face slender and well composed, his firm, pensive gaze expressing intelligence and constant curiosity.
>
> The impression the portrait gives us matches the testimony of those who knew Manuel Querino best (Calmon 1980).[206]

The portrait of Querino which illustrates the commemorative edition of this essay,[207] *O Vereador Manuel Querino* (City Councilman Manuel Querino), published in 1995, fits Calmon's description perfectly—"a poised and confident mien," a "slender and well composed" face and a "firm, pensive gaze"—which suggests that this is the photograph in question (see Fig. 5-4).

Clearly, the man in the portrait that was placed in the IGHB's gallery bears no resemblance to Artur Ramos's and Pinto de Aguiar's

---

[206] The English translation is from Gledhill 2021, 43.
[207] It was published on the 446th anniversary of the founding of the city of Salvador, the tercentenary of the death of Zumbi dos Palmares and the 60th anniversary of Jorge Calmon's career in journalism (Calmon 1995, colophon).

description of the researcher, labour leader and militant journalist as a "humble Black teacher" (Querino 1938, 12; Querino 1955, 11).[208]

Fig. 5-4. Portrait of Manuel Querino
Unveiled in the IGHB Gallery in 1928

In a eulogy on Querino that focuses on his relationship with the Liceu de Artes e Ofícios, the author, Francisco Miguel Chaves,[209] calls

---

[208] Pinto de Aguiar's foreword to the 1955 edition is a summary of the foreword by Artur Ramos, originally published in the 1938 edition.

for the arts and crafts school to display a portrait of its founding student and life member:

> He must have had enemies, for his was a frank and proud temperament, but the will-o'-the-wisp of spite and ill-will cannot subsist before the splendours of justice, particularly as he is a figure worthy of admiration and all the tributes for his tenacity, for the boldness with which he overcame all the difficulties of his humble origins to become, as he was, a great fighter, a combative spirit, persevering and victorious in the type of research to which he devoted himself. With such titles, in addition to those already recognized by the assembly I mentioned above, Manuel Querino may well be entitled to have the Liceu place his portrait among those whom they have honoured (Chaves 1923).

Nevertheless, justice would only be done in 2000—the year the Liceu finally closed its doors. Catarina Argolo's portrayal of Querino was inspired by the photograph hung in the IGHB's gallery, but the subject's complexion is slightly darker, his hair, greyer, and his expression, even more assertive. Since Chaves described Querino as being "frank and proud," that portrayal is supremely appropriate.[210]

Another more recent portrait of Querino, painted by Graça Ramos in 2005 (Fig. 5-5), was based on the image that illustrates *Artistas baianos* (Fig. 5-2). The Ramos portrait is part of the collection of the School of Fine Art.[211] In both, the subject's pose and gaze are very different from those of the IGHB photograph and another which was taken around the same time, based on Querino's appearance. It

---

[209] Chaves joined one of the Liceu's workshops at the age of twelve, and later held several posts on its board of directors, including vice-chairman. He worked in the newspaper publishing business and died in around 1933 (Leal 1996, note 172).

[210] By January 2023, that portrait was no longer to be found in the building which the Liceu had occupied for 133 years.

[211] By January 2023, the painting was no longer displayed among the numerous paintings hanging on the walls of the School of Fine Art – including works by Miguel Navarro y Cañizares – and at the time of writing it was still "in storage."

is a portrait which was unveiled at the Centro Operário after Querino's death. A retouched version served as the cover illustration for a collection of his articles in 2009 (see Figs. 5-27 and 5-28).

Fig. 5-5. Portrait of Manuel Querino
by Graça Ramos (2005)

Taken almost a decade earlier, the photograph used to create the frontispiece of *Artistas baianos* shows a balding, grizzled Querino wearing a pinstripe suit, and looking to his left. In the age of daguerreotypes, photographers were advised to have their subjects look "vaguely" at a distant object to avoid a blank stare or frown (Trachtenberg 1989, 26). It may be that this aesthetic still prevailed when the first photograph of Querino was taken. This could have been due to the incipient state of the art of photography in the first decade of the twentieth century in Bahia. In any case, instead of facing the viewer, as he does in more recent portrayals, Querino focuses on a distant object—perhaps a horizon to be expanded—which robs his expression of the poise and authority of a direct, frontal gaze. His expression in the earlier portrait is more of a dreamer than that of a leader, activist, and intellectual.

In Bahia, nineteenth-century photographers produced numerous images of enslaved and freed Black people as anthropometric subjects, or engaged in menial work, which helped create a stereotype of Blacks as marginalized and impoverished. Their subjects' expressions are empty or anguished. Black people photographed as "exotica" in Brazil wear plain or African-style clothing. Some Whites saw this image of Bahia as an affront because, according to the author of an unsigned article entitled "Propaganda Indigna" (Unworthy Advertising), published in *Bahia Ilustrada* in 1921, it came from "those who are envious of Bahia's greatness who, seeking to belittle it, paint it with the blackest colours in the eyes of those who truly do not know it." The author concludes that the images of Blacks and *caboclos* (usually people of mixed Indigenous descent) produced by Rodolpho Lindemann's studio "are intended to show extreme backwardness in Bahia, when the truth is that this glorious State is today one of the most beautiful and populous in the entire country"—with "types who are well-built, light tan, beautiful, or White or even Brown" (1921, n.p.).

While photographers like Lindemann were producing "exotic" images, Black intellectuals and other prominent members of the Black community—and they were not a few, as Querino shows in "Os homens de cor preta na História" (1923)—went to photographers' studios to produce images which reflected their "personhood" (Wallis 1995, 55). These people included two *iyalorixás* or high priestesses from the Gantois *terreiro* (religious community), who posed for *carte cabinet* photos that Querino included among the plates which illustrate *A raça africana e os seus costumes na Bahia* (1955) (see Figs. 5-19 and 5-20).

As Lisa Earl Castillo observes, in the Afro-Brazilian religious communities, portraits are used to remember ancestors, who are an important part of their cosmology. "The strong appreciation of old portraits in Candomblé can be understood as a result of the physical link with the material presence of the deceased" (2009, 18). Through these images, we can look into the eyes of those who lived in other times.

For all these reasons—the small number of photographs of Manuel Querino, the overwhelming minority of images of Black intellectuals from the beginning of the twentieth century, and the value of these portraits as "icons of memory" of ancestors—it was disappointing to find that the famous portrait whose unveiling was accompanied by Vianna's lecture, described by Artur Ramos and Jorge Calmon and mentioned by E. Bradford Burns (1974, 84), no longer hangs on the walls on the IGHB. In fact, it was not included in the inventory of its collection conducted in the 1970s, and its whereabouts are unknown. Today, we must rely on reproductions in books to see for ourselves what Querino was like towards the end of his life, and how he was seen by the colleagues, co-workers, and confreres who honoured him after his death.

Black People Portrayed: "Seen" vs. "Making Themselves Seen"

Referring to how the images of photographed subjects are used, Roland Barthes complains that: "others—the Other—do not dispossess me of myself, they turn me, ferociously, into an object, they put me at their mercy, at their disposal, classified in a file, ready for the subtlest deceptions..." (2022, 16-17). The French literary critic, semiotician, and philosopher could have been describing the position of enslaved Black people who were subjected to anthropometric, somatological photographs, or "exoticizing" images. In an essay on photographs of enslaved people taken in Brazil by

Christiano Júnior. in the nineteenth century, Manuela Carneiro da Cunha observes:

In a portrait, one can be observed and one can pose, alternatives that are frankly linked to the relationship between the portrayed and the portrayer. Whoever commissions a photograph shows himself, makes himself known, spreads himself out on the paper, himself and his attributes and properties, as he would like to be seen, as he sees himself in the mirror. He is the subject of the portrait.... [T]he enslaved individual is seen, not making themselves seen. They are viewed in ways that depersonalize them in two ways: showing them either as a "type" or as a job or role (1988, xxiii).

This was not always the case with portrayals of Black people. For example, prior to the invention of photography, eighteenth-century British abolitionists used oil portraits, drawings, and engravings of free Black individuals like Ignatius Sancho (painted in 1768 by Thomas Gainsborough) and Olaudah Equiano, among others (King et al., 1977), to demonstrate their capacity for "Europeanization" and inclusion in British society. When the Quaker abolitionist Wilson Armistead published *A Tribute for the Negro: Being a Vindication of the Moral, Intellectual, and Religious Capabilities of the Colored Portion of Mankind; With Particular Reference to the African Race* in 1848, it was illustrated with portraits of illustrious figures such as Olaudah Equiano, Toussaint L'Ouverture, Cinque (the leader of the rebellion aboard the slave ship *Amistad)*, and Frederick Douglass, as well as others who are lesser known today, such as Jan Tzatzoe, a Christian leader from South Africa, and the formerly enslaved cleric James W. C. Pennington. Although they were being used as "poster children" by the movement that demanded the abolition of slavery, it is clear from the facial expressions, poses and sophisticated clothes of the men portrayed that they were "making themselves seen."[212]

---

[212] In stark contrast with the images of these men, most of whom are wearing clothes considered elegant by the European standards of the time (Equiano is also holding a book), the book contains two engravings of scenes of the slave trade in Africa and New Orleans, in which the captives are almost naked.

These images bear no resemblance to the haunted gazes of enslaved Black people who would later be photographed for "scientific" purposes.

"Persons" vs. "Types"

When photography gained popularity in the second half of the nineteenth century, two aspects of the representation of human beings appeared: private portraits and anthropometric photographs. The first represented "persons," and the second, "types," which could include the mentally ill, criminals, or enslaved people. The use of *cartes-de-visite*, followed by *cartes-cabinet*, in the nineteenth century popularized the custom of commissioning portraits of individuals and families, which could be used to mark rites of passage like births, graduations, and funerals. These images were produced by the millions in photographic studios around the world (Becker 2008, 233-234). According to art historian Brian Wallis:

Generally, the nineteenth-century photographic portrait was designed to affirm or underscore the white middle-class individual's right to personhood, a fact underlined by legal and social structures as well. Further, the portrait signalled an individual's place in society, which explains why so many daguerreotypes feature sitters posed with the tools of their trade or other attributes (1995, 55).

In contrast, anthropometric images of enslaved, formerly enslaved, and free-born Black people and photographs of "types" are generally anonymous. The subjects are naked or partially clothed, and portrayed with the express intention of proving "White supremacy" or even that Africans had evolved from different ancestors, according to polygenists like Louis Agassiz. Another way of transforming the subject into an object that "is seen," this method was the brainchild of the British anthropologist Francis Galton, the "father of eugenics" and a cousin of Charles Darwin. In the nineteenth century, anthropometric photographs were used to "map" the bodies of jailed convicts, as well as in scientific analyses of gender and race. Galton devised two ways of recording supposed physical indices of basic biological differences: composite portraits, and a standardized system of family photography (Smith 1999, 62). He tried to identify a correspondence between the physical features of the subject portrayed that could lead to a diagnosis of diseases and even criminal tendencies. At the end of his life, after numerous failed experiments, he had to admit the impossibility of obtaining such "types" in practice.

For American pseudoscientific racists, the concept of a "Black American" was an oxymoron, as in their view, American nationality was exclusively White and Anglo-Saxon. Like Count de Gobineau and Nina Rodrigues, who made the same assertions about mixed-race Brazilians, Galton believed that miscegenation in the United States would result in "tragically weakened" offspring and dilute and weaken the "national character." Galton's theory of eugenics provided the scientific basis for the racialized hierarchy of the "Other" displayed in world exhibitions at the turn of the century (Smith 1999, 60).

According to Nicholas Mirzoeff, "The perfect body in Western culture was sustained and made imaginable by the imperfect body of the racial Other" (1995, 135). In his analysis of photographs of Black Africans taken in the Belgian Congo by the German zoologist Herbert Lang in the early twentieth century, Mirzoeff observes that, for generations of racists,

> ...the divine drive towards perfection was as much marked by the inferiority of the African body as by the perfection of the white. This profound interior difference was necessary to mark the superiority of the white and to convince Europeans that the Other played no part in the Self, that the colonizer was radically different from, and superior to, the colonized (Ibid., 136).

Anthropometric photography portraying enslaved and formerly enslaved individuals who were considered "types" and "representatives" of African "tribes" was introduced and perfected in the United States and Brazil by Jean Louis Rodolphe Agassiz (see

Chapter 1). The Swiss-American biologist and his second wife, the American educator and naturalist Elizabeth Cabot Cary Agassiz,[213] led the Thayer expedition to Brazil between 1865 and 1866. They were accompanied by the photographers Georges Leuzinger and Théophile Auguste Stahl (known in Brazil as Augusto Stahl), whom they hired to illustrate the book they co-authored about their research in Brazil (Ermakoff 2004, 230-253).

Louis Agassiz's project of photographing African "types" had originated in the United States, some fifteen years earlier. He did not invent the portrayal of "human types," but he was one of the pioneers in that field, and commissioned photographs of enslaved people from a plantation in Columbia, South Carolina in 1850. The idea for this project may have arisen in 1846, when Agassiz met Samuel George Morton, one of the leaders of the American school of polygeny, who collected 600 skulls of Native Americans (Gould 2003, 40-41). On that occasion, he presented Agassiz with a daguerreotype of a young African which Morton had exhibited at the Academy of Natural Sciences in Philadelphia (Wallis 1995, 45).

Agassiz began his photographic project during a tour of the plantation near Columbia. The legal importation of enslaved Africans had been banned in the United States since 1808 (Horne, 2007). Nevertheless, according to the colleague who suggested this visit, Dr Robert W. Gibbes, Agassiz was "delighted with his examination of Ebo, Foulah, Gullah, Guinea, Coromantee, Mandrigo [sic] and Congo Negroes. He found enough to satisfy him that they have differences from the other races" (Wallis 1996, 45). At Agassiz's request, Gibbes sent several of the enslaved subjects to the studio of a local daguerreotypist, Joseph T. Zealy, to be photographed. These images were exhibited at the 1893 World's Columbian Exposition, held in Chicago to commemorate the "discovery" of America (Turazzi 1995,

---

[213] Elizabeth Agassiz (1822-1907) was the founder and first president of Radcliffe College. https://www.radcliffe.harvard.edu/people/elizabeth-cary-agassiz

241), an event that restricted Blacks' official participation to "Colored People's Day," August 25, 1893.[214]

Alan Trachtenberg believes that Zealy's images of enslaved Africans "are among the most extraordinary daguerreotype portraits made in America," and reflect "the absolute power of the masters over the bodies of their slaves." They may also have served to stir up abolitionist fervour (Trachtenberg 1990, 53-54).[215] Since the earliest days of the daguerreotype, "Sitters were encouraged and cajoled to *will* themselves...into a desired expression—in short, a role and a mask which accord with one's self-image" (Ibid., 26). Stripped of this mask, "the eyes of the enslaved Africans can only reveal the depths of their being—for, as naked slaves, they are permitted no social persona" (Ibid., 56).

According to Brian Wallis, the Zealy daguerreotypes:

> ...had two purposes, one nominally scientific, the other frankly political. They were designed to analyse the physical differences between European whites and African blacks, but at the same time they were meant to prove the superiority of the white race. Agassiz hoped to use the photographs as evidence to prove his

---

[214] On that date, Frederick Douglass confronted attempts to humiliate him while giving the last speech of his life (Westerbeck, 2000, 147).

[215] Housed in Harvard's Peabody Museum, the Zealy daguerreotypes are still controversial, and the focus of academics, activists, and descendants of the people portrayed (Barbash, Rogers, and Willis 2020). For copyright reasons, as well as the desire not to propagate such images, they are not reproduced here, but they can be seen in numerous publications. The Brazilian historian Maria Helena P. T. Machado and the Swiss-Haitian-Finnish artist Sasha Huber have published books and essays on Agassiz and the daguerreotypes (see Machado and Huber 2010 and Sealy and Verna 2022). Published by the Peabody Museum Press, the cover photo of the catalogue *From Site to Sight* is the daguerreotype of "Renty, an African-born slave." It is also reproduced on page 56, along with a portrait of his daughter Delia, who, like her father, is stripped to the waist (Banta and Hinsley 2017). Huber has also had herself photographed in several locations, in the same fashion that enslaved Black people were made to pose in Brazil – with front, side, and rear views of their naked body, all in the same frame (Sealy and Verna 2022, 101-107).

theory of "separate creation," the idea that the various races of mankind were in fact separate species (1995, 40).

George Ermakoff's comment on the photographs taken for the Thayer Expedition in Brazil reinforces this observation:

...anthropometric photographs were intended to support comparative scientific studies of the human race. It was believed, then, that the observation of possible physical differences between different races could scientifically prove theories about racial superiority—now considered prejudiced. It was later proven that anthropometric photographs taken with this intention had no relevant scientific value (2004, 251).

That expedition's photographic products, which are now housed in the Peabody Museum of Anthropology and Ethnology at Harvard University, also include anthropometric photographs of Africans and their descendants which reflect Agassiz's racialism and portray their subjects in a subhuman and degrading manner. Agassiz used somatological photography to reiterate a hypothesis—the supposed inferiority of Black people. The anthropometric images of completely or partially naked Black men and women which Stahl produced for the Thayer expedition aim to strip the subjects of their humanity (Ermakoff 2004, 240, 241, 250-253). In this case, they used one of the "scientific poses" also utilized in medical photographs produced for São Paulo journals—the "full representation of the body" of the subject with an "erect posture." According to James Silva, there was an explicit intent to de-eroticize these images:

...a significant part of the guidelines regarding the way of portraying the naked body was limited to moral concerns. Nancy Stepan underscores this aspect when recalling how the medical photographs of that period, showing undressed female patients, worried doctors, who feared that they would become the target of voyeurism, even if to do so, as we have already been warned, it was necessary "to have a very fiery spirit and quite inflammable senses." In view of this, certain devices were adopted with the aim of stripping the images of any erotic appeal, through the use of insipid scenarios, devoid of the meanings associated with domestic furniture, by putting a black bar over eyes of the female patients photographed, etc... (Silva 2009, 253-255).

Apparently, the same techniques were also used in the images which Agassiz commissioned in Brazil.

As for the Black subjects "seen" in these photos, in the words of a descendant of an enslaved African king: "humiliation is present as a scar, always opening into a wound" (Couve 1964). To varying degrees, the portraits of free and enslaved Black people which emphasized their "personhood" contradicted the visual records which accompanied discourses on race and national identity constructed by ideologies based on pseudoscientific racism.

Advertising, self-promotion, and brainwashing

Another function of images was advertising (including self-promotion). A nineteenth-century pioneer in this area in the United States was P. T. Barnum (1810-1891), the founder of the famous Ringling Brothers & Barnum & Bailey Circus. A history of the circus originally published on the Ringling Brothers website explains:

> There is no proof that Phineas Taylor Barnum ever said "there's a sucker born every minute." He did, however, say that "every crowd has a silver lining," and acknowledged that "the public is wiser than many imagine." In his 80 years, Barnum gave the wise public of the nineteenth century shameless hucksterism, peerless spectacle, and everything in between—enough entertainment to earn the title "master showman" a dozen times over. In choosing Barnum as one of the 100 most important people of the millennium, *Life* magazine recently dubbed him "the patron saint of promoters" (Ringlingdocents.org).

Other nineteenth-century figures who pioneered the "modern media identity" were Mark Twain and Sarah Bernhardt. Michael Bieze, the author of *Booker T. Washington and the Art of Self-*

Representation, observes that, in this sense, Washington resembles these personages more closely than the figures with whom he is usually compared, namely Frederick Douglass and W. E. B. Du Bois (Bieze 2008, 112-113).

According to Peter Burke, "A more common solution to the problem of making the abstract concrete is to show individuals as incarnations of ideas or values" (2011, 68). Washington understood this concept very well, and sought to publicize images of himself and his colleagues and collaborators that conveyed the values most dear to White Victorians in the United States—photographs of intelligent, cultured, sophisticated Blacks who, in the eyes of Southern White supremacists, "knew their place" and did not pose a threat to the "Jim Crow" segregation system which succeeded slavery in the United States. In his own photographs, Washington can be seen riding a horse (hand inside his jacket, like Napoleon), and seated at a desk.[216] In at least one image, the desk is equipped with a telephone—advanced technology in the early twentieth century.

One of the first to identify the effects of racist stereotypes on Black people's self-image was Frantz Fanon, in *Black Skin, White Masks*, first published in 1952 (Fanon 1971). Following this line, referring to Black people in the Brazilian "cultural imaginary," Maria Nazareth Soares Fonseca observes:

> ...the view of Black people, when internalized and verbalized, often reveals the heightening of tensions that are shown in the way in which the poorest population endorses derogatory images of itself, because it also adopts the general opinion that Black people are criminals, bad, thieves, drug addicts, dishonest, epithets that form a closed circuit, a chalk circle that imprisons the individual in the colour of their skin (2001, 21).

---

[216] This pose could also be called "Napoleonic," as Burke observes that "the painting of Napoleon in his study by Jacques-Louis David (1748-1825), presented a relatively new aspect of power, the ruler as bureaucrat, tied to his desk even in the small hours of the morning..." (Burke 2011, 73).

The Black American publicist Tom Burrell (2010) also points out that, since the beginning of the seventeenth century, when the first Africans landed in the future United States, a "propaganda campaign" and brainwashing has reinforced the stereotypes of Black inferiority and White superiority which, when assimilated and internalized, has disastrous results for Black people's self-esteem. For Manuel R. Querino and Booker T. Washington, it was essential to confront and overcome negative images of Black people—not only to boost their self-esteem but to combat the stereotypes of inferiority "of body and mind" disseminated in newspapers, magazines, postcards, and books.

In Brazil, nineteenth-century photographers such as Rodolpho Lindemann, Christiano Júnior, Marc Ferrez, Jean Victor Frond, Georges Leuzinger, Militão Augusto de Azevedo, Alberto Henschel, and others produced images of Black people that reinforced the stereotype of the Other—an exotic, different, inferior creature. According to Pereira and Gomes, "The difference of the Other, understood by the privileged observer as being a lack of civilization—and therefore, a threat—encouraged the fixation of its image as something exotic to be exhibited in a freak show" (2001, 141).

In some cases, such as the images produced by Henschel and Christiano Júnior—"risqué" portraits and postcards of nude or scantily clad Black women—have an undeniably erotic content, especially for the period in question (Ermakoff 2004, 22 and 127). As Robert Levine observes: "The English [sic] photographer William Gaensly created a series of portraits of Brazilian slaves, aiming to depict their exotic nature. In the portrait of a Black man, photographed in Gaensly's studio, the subject's tribal scars [sic], applied in Africa, show clearly" (1989, 48).

Photographers also portrayed Black people seen in working in the streets and "types," selling most of these images as curiosities and souvenirs. Many of the subjects were free poor people, but the scenes depicting their livelihoods are completely devoid of social commentary. Collectors prized images that stirred their imaginations—members of "exotic tribes," the wonders of nature in remote places, "lowly slaves," feisty, seductive women—all to be enjoyed in the morally safe environment of the home (Ibid.). Gaensly was born in Switzerland and raised in Brazil (Gledhill 2008, 565). Levine was mistaken not only about the photographer's nationality but also the author of the photograph—the image he describes was produced in Lindemann's studio (Ermakoff 2004, 218). Nevertheless, the author's observations are valid.

In the United States, a genre of explicitly racist images emerged in the same period. In some, the Black person was completely dehumanized. For example, in the 1885 edition of Mark Twain's *Huckleberry Finn*, in which Jim, the fugitive bondsman, is a heroic figure, the illustrations portray him as more animal than human.

Deborah Willis began researching the work of Black photographers in the United States since the nineteenth century in response to the

> ...proliferation of negative, derogatory images of black people. White perceptions of black inferiority were often reinforced by the same images of black men that I had seen, and my intention was to challenge those images and the history books by identifying the breadth and depth of experiences of black people as recorded in photographs (1994, 13).

Willis's collection of nineteenth-century images of Blacks includes a *carte cabinet* showing the judicial hanging in 1896 of a formerly enslaved man convicted of murder—the photograph was taken by the Black photographer and abolitionist J. P. Ball. Was it his way of recording a "legal lynching" to denounce the countless injustices that were part of the violent daily life of Black people in the US South? According to Willis, "He knew that black oppression was often violently manifested in the lynchings that Ida B. Wells and others protested against, but which continue to this day" (Ibid., 15).

Other images featured in Willis's introduction to her edited volume *Picturing Us* are part of a series of late nineteenth-century lantern slides entitled "Trouble Ahead, Trouble Behind" (c. 1880s):

"examples of a genre commonly known as 'Black Americana,' which includes a wide variety of popular artifacts depicting crude, degrading, racial caricatures of African Americans" (Ibid.). In the first slide, a Black woman is shown kneading dough in a kitchen where a male child is drawing a picture of a woman on the wallpaper along with the word "Mamy" [sic], while a younger child sleeps in a wooden cot. The woman's house and activity suggest that they are impoverished. In the second slide, the woman is spanking the young "artist," the white flour on the palm of her hand leaving a mark on the child's bottom, while the toddler in the cot looks on. Willis compares this photo of a young Black man being punished, produced for the enjoyment of a White audience, with other images, such as the postcard of naked Black children at the edge of a pond entitled "Alligator Bait."[217] Willis notes that such toxic images "[play] on stereotypes and [perpetuate] racial myths" (Ibid., 17). She concludes: "These images now exist as frozen racial metaphors from a time when images of African Americans were rarely produced by or for African Americans" (Ibid.).

Booker T. Washington: Creating a new Black American iconography

One of Washington's anti-racist tactics was producing positive images of himself and other Black Americans. To this end, he worked with several photographers, White and Black. They included at least two White women (Bieze 2008), one of whom deserves more detailed analysis, due to the rich and controversial collection of images she produced before and during her collaboration with Washington.

Considered "America's court photographer" for her portraits of powerful figures, including Theodore Roosevelt (Daniel and Smock 2000, 5), **Frances Benjamin Johnston (1864-1952)** led an unusual life

---

[217] A search on Google Images using the words "alligator bait" in 2023 came up with a number and variety of images (photographs, sketches, and cartoons) about the use of Black children and adults for that purpose.

for most women of her time. Born in New York and raised in Washington, DC, she studied at the Académie Julian, the main art school in France which admitted foreign students (Berch 2000, 12). She returned to the United States to pursue a career as an artist and professional photographer, setting up a studio where her subjects included Susan B. Anthony and Mark Twain. In 1899, she produced images of the Hampton Institute which were so successful that Booker T. Washington hired her to photograph the Tuskegee Institute on two occasions—in 1902, and then again during the 25th anniversary celebrations of that institution in April 1906 (Harlan and Smock 1977, 502).

Johnston was also commissioned to photograph Black schools in Alabama called "Little Tuskegees" in 1902, when she fell afoul of White supremacists. She was on her way to one of the schools she intended to photograph, accompanied by a Black teacher, Nelson E. Henry, when they were threatened by a White mob who were incensed at the sight of a White woman with a Black man. Henry managed to escape, but George Washington Carver, who witnessed the episode, was nearly lynched (Kremer 1987, 149-150). Carver was traumatized, but the greatest damage was done to the school, which had to be closed as a result of this incident.

According to Shawn Michelle Smith, the series of images Johnston produced, portraying students at the Hamilton Institute, represent new visual tactics which aimed to be explicitly racialized portrayals of an aspect of American nationality, and confronted the biological determinism which reinforced Francis Galton's pseudoscientific racism. Displayed at the Exposition Nègres d'Amerique or American Negro Exhibit, which was part of the Universal Exposition held in Paris in 1900, these images engage in dialogue with, and contradict, other photographs in a historical context characterized by its fluidity and mutability. Smith observes that "visual culture is not a mere reflection of an imagined community, but one of the sites in which narratives of belonging are produced and propelled," and suggests that, much more than just a referent for photographic images, the nation was a product of those images. According to Smith, the photographs marked the beginning of "new visual strategies for representing both race and national character at the turn of the century" (1999, 59). Johnston's photographs served to create a different image of "American character."

In Smith's analysis, the overarching aim of the American Negro Exhibit was to define the place of Black people in the United States (Ibid., 58). Held seven years after the 1893 World's Columbian Exposition in Chicago, the Exposition Nègres d'Amerique marked the beginning of a "new era in the history of race representation" (Ibid., 59). According to W. E. B. Du Bois, who also took part by contributing albums of colour photographs of Black people entitled "Negro Life in Georgia," the exhibit was "planned and executed by Negroes, and collected and installed under the direction of a Special Negro agent, Mr. Thomas J. Calloway" (Ibid.). By portraying Black Americans as full members of Western civilization, it differed from representations of Blacks seen in other events, before and since, which recreated African villages to reinforce the idea of European superiority over "Black savages." In addition to photographs, the American Negro Exhibit used maps, charts, models, detailed descriptions of the efforts made to educate Black Americans, and hundreds of literary works by Black authors to demonstrate the advances made by Black people, measured by the criteria of western and White culture. Installed in the Palace of Social Economy, the exhibit won a Grand Prize. However, according to Smith, it was presented in the context of "solutions to national problems" in the United States—in this case, as a supposed solution to the "negro [sic] problem" Therefore, it was "confined within a white-dominated system of social surveillance" (Ibid., 60).

The Tuskegee Institute was also represented in the American Negro Exhibit. According to a letter from Thomas Calloway to Booker T. Washington, dated April 18, 1900,[218] his contribution was the first

---

[218] Letter found in the Booker T. Washington Papers in the Library of Congress. Container 38, reels 34-35. Calloway was a former teacher at the Tuskegee Institute (Harlan and Smock 1976, 244).

to arrive at the Paris exposition—a panel entitled "Tuskegee Institute, and its Industries" containing fifteen photographs (18 x 22 inches or 45.72 x 55.88 cm) organized as a collage (Bieze 2008, 60).[219] The Tuskegee panel won a gold medal, and the institute received a total of fifteen awards, including a Grand Prize. Booker T. Washington himself was awarded a silver medal.[220] In one photograph on the panel, we can see the name "Shepherd," the logo and surname of R. H. (Harry) Shepherd, a Virginia-born Black photographer based in St. Paul, Minnesota, who achieved national renown in the United States and worked with Washington between 1896 and 1901 (Ibid., 58).

According to Maxell (2002, 331-339), Booker T. Washington commissioned the Hampton Institute photos shown at the same exhibition, but Smith states that Johnston produced those images at the invitation of Hampton's second principal, Hollis Gurke Frissel (1999, 65).[221] In any case, when Johnston photographed the Tuskegee Institute, the series produced in 1902, which includes portraits of Washington, the Executive Council and the facilities, portrays the students of that institution just as those of the Hampton Institute were depicted for the Paris exhibition of 1900—well dressed, poised, and looking away from the photographer (Fig. 5-6). They belong to another world, remote from the observer but reflecting European values of civilization. Most importantly, these photographs contradict portrayals of Black people as "lazy," "savage," "lustful," "unintelligent," and "dangerous" (a crucial point for Washington), especially to Whites. The danger for Black people, observes Smith, was that these images could also bolster the notion that the system of

---

[219] The image can be found on the Library of Congress website: http://www.loc.gov/pictures/collection/anedub/item/98504044/

[220] Letter from Thomas Junius Calloway to Booker T. Washington, August 23, 1900. Booker T. Washington Papers. Container 38, reels 34-35.

[221] Knowing the tremendous influence that Booker T. Washington exerted on his alma mater, it is very likely that he was the *"éminence grise"* behind the photographs of Hampton displayed at the 1900 exhibition.

"separate-but-equal" racial segregation was working satisfactorily in the United States (Ibid., 72).

Fig. 5-6. Reading Room at the Tuskegee Institute Library, ca. 1902. Frances Benjamin Johnston

Smith suggests that the students in the Hampton Institute photographs are averting their gaze from the camera because were not allowed to look directly at the White female photographer, as doing so was a lynchable offense (1999, 66-67). However, the Tuskegee Institute photographs follow the same line, which, far from being symptomatic of racial segregation in the US South, reflected the aesthetics of the Arts and Crafts movement that came about in response to the industrial revolution—valuing human labour, particularly handicrafts (Bieze 2008, 92-93). Furthermore, the Black photographer C. M. Battey portrayed a class at the Tuskegee Institute in the same manner in 1917 (Willis 2000, 51). Therefore, the subjects' pose does not appear to be due to the photographer's colour or gender. A portrait of the Institute's faculty, showing Booker T.

Washington seated beside his wife, Margaret, who is flanked by Andrew Carnegie (front row, seated, first from left), was also taken by Johnston (see Fig. 5-7). In this photograph, the subjects' poses are confident, and, in Washington's case, relaxed. No one appears to be averting their gaze.

Fig. 5-7. Faculty of the Tuskegee Institute with Andrew Carnegie, 1906. Frances Benjamin Johnston

Patron of Black photographers

In addition to hiring a White woman to work in Alabama in the age of "Jim Crow" segregation—with near-fatal consequences—Washington also patronised Black photographers and helped create markets for their work. On April 7, 1849, Frederick Douglass opined in his newspaper *The North Star* that White artists could not portray Black people without being blinded by prejudice:

> It seems to us next to impossible for white men to take likenesses of black men, without most grossly exaggerating their distinctive features. And the reason is obvious. Artists, like all other white

persons, have adopted a theory respecting the distinctive features of negro physiognomy. We have heard many white persons say that "negroes look all alike," and that they could not distinguish between the old and the young. They associate with the negro face, high cheek bones, distended nostril, depressed nose, thick lips, and retreating forehead. This theory, impressed strongly on the mind of an artist, exercises a powerful influence over his pencil, and very naturally leads him to distort and exaggerate those peculiarities, even when they scarcely exist in the original (quoted in Shaw 2006, 13).

Although the camera lens can be said to be more objective, issues surrounding portrayals of Black subjects persist to this day, usually to do with lighting. According to Kaitlyn McNab, it is a "bias that's existed since film was invented" (2021).

In addition to R. H. Shepherd, a considerable number of Black photographers were active in the United States in the early twentieth century. They included C. M. Battey, Arthur P. Bedou, Villard Paddio, Addison N. Scurlock, Florestine Perrault Collins, Herbert Collins, Perry A. Keith, James Van DerZee, King Daniel Ganaway, James Latimer Allen, Elise Forrest Harleston, Eddie Acha, Richard Aloysius Twine, Ellie Lee Weems, and "countless others" (Willis 2000, 37). According to Deborah Willis:

> ...[bell] hooks demonstrates that the black photographers' vision was a powerful tool used to challenge the blatantly commercialized stereotypical cultural products that portrayed black Americans. Their vision demonstrated that black Americans in the early twentieth century were as multidimensional as everyone else (Ibid., 38).

At the same time, Bieze observes that Black photographers also produced images that could be misinterpreted or even reinforce negative stereotypes, such as Robert E. Williams, who portrayed them as "cotton pickers" and "watermelon eaters" (2008, 104). As we

Portrayals and Pushback

will see, Booker T. Washington took care to avoid those pitfalls and produce a consistently positive image of Black Americans.

In addition to posing for several photographers, Washington was also the patron of at least five—all Black—including two who held the post of official photographer at the Tuskegee Institute. The first was Charles D. Robinson—more out of convenience than for the quality of his work. According to Bieze, "For the needs outside the campus, Washington hired the leading black photographers in America including C.M. Battey, A.P. Bedou, Peter Jones, and Addison Curlock, and helped to launch the careers of others such as G. Addison Turner" (2008, 69). Two major Black photographers who worked closely with Washington were A. P. Bedou and C. M Battey.

In 1908 and 1915, Washington undertook rail journeys accompanied by a large and distinguished cortege that included his private secretary, Emmett Jay Scott, and a photographer—in both cases, A. P. Bedou (Harlan and Smock, 1980, 674-681; 1984, 321-330). **Arthur Paul Bedou (1882-1966)** accepted an invitation to become the official and private photographer of Booker T. Washington at the end of 1913, and continued in that role until the end of his patron's life in 1915 (Bieze 2008, 69 and 75). Born in New Orleans, his name was listed in his hometown's directory of photographers for over fifty years (Willis 2000, 39). Known for his exquisite portraits, he worked as a photographer, artist, and journalist, struggling to be recognized as an artistic photographer. However, to make a living, he was forced to produce cheaper, more commercial images aimed at the mass market (Bieze 2008, 75).

He first met Washington during the Annual Negro Conference at Tuskegee on February 18, 1903, when he did his best to impress the principal of the Institute. According to Bieze, his "snapshot aesthetic" captured the dynamism of the moment and met Washington's goals in the last phase of his life and career (Bieze 2008, 76-77). Bedou produced striking images of the rallies commanded by the Black leader, showing a "fiery orator pacing the stage speaking to his people" (Ibid., 107). According to Willis, "A Bedou photograph of Washington speaking before a large crowd draws the viewer to

Washington's gesture and the audience's response" (2000, 39). Bieze notes that "Washington's embrace of Bedou's style apparently represents the final phase of his life in which he openly and actively positions himself engaging the black populace rather than appealing to white elites" (2008, 76). Bedou portrayed Washington as a man of action at the time when the Black leader was turning his activities towards a more open and public activism (Bieze, 106-107). At the same time, Bedou produced portraits of private moments—such as the famous image of Washington on horseback. Photo historians Girard Mouton and Alma Williams, have described Bidou's style as a touch of romanticism combined with classical composition (Willis 2000, 40).

Washington made a distinction between documentary photos and artistic images (Bieze 2008, 69). According to Bieze, "Washington's support of A. P. Bedou's work in 1908 signifies more than a shift in style; it demonstrates a shift in philosophy. As Washington's disillusionment with white leadership grew, so did his willingness to be outspoken in support of race issues" (Ibid., 106).

Cornelius Marion Battey (1873-1927) was also a southerner, from Augusta, Georgia, but he spent most of his life in the North. By 1900, he had established his reputation as a Portrait photographer in New York City and Cleveland. His first subjects were Black musicians, statesmen, and Freemasons (Willis 2000, 38-39). He exhibited his portraits and won prizes in the US and Europe. His portraits of *Five Negro Immortals* assembled in the same print—of Frederick Douglass, John Mercer Langston, Paul Laurence Dunbar, B. K. Bruce, and Booker T. Washington (in the centre)—were sold with the title *Our Heroes of Destiny* (1911), later *Our Master Minds* (Willis 2000, 39; Bieze 2008, 73-74). They later appeared on the frontispiece of *The New Progress of a Race*, by J. L Nichols and William Crogman (1920). Battey produced one of the best-known portraits of W. E. B. Du Bois, as well as photographing powerful White leaders such as Theodore Roosevelt, Grover Cleveland, and Andrew Carnegie (Bieze 2008, 71 and 178). His photographs appeared in several issues of *The Crisis*. According to a brief biography in the "Men of the Month" section of that publication, he also photographed Sir Thomas Lipton and Prince Henry of Prussia. The article notes that he was an instructor in photography at Tuskegee at the time, and "Many of his racial studies have appeared in the *Crisis* magazine" (*The Crisis* May 1917, 31).

Fig. 5-8. Portrait of Booker T. Washington, ca. 1917.
C. M. Battey

Like A. P. Bedou, Battey first met Booker T. Washington in 1903 and tried unsuccessfully to penetrate Washington's "inner circle."

However, he was eventually hired to take the photographs used to illustrate *Tuskegee and its People* (1906). The photographer's portrayals of Washington were aimed at an urban audience, depicting the principal of Tuskegee as a "dignified public leader." While Bedou accompanied Washington on his railway tours of the South, Battey photographed him in his New York studio, producing "elegant portraits, many of which were destined to be sent to white supporters" (Bieze, 2008, 71-72, 76).

Battey was also a recognised educator. In 1916, after Washington's death, he joined Tuskegee's faculty as the head of the Photography Division, and replaced Bedou as the institute's official photographer (Ibid., 75). When *The Crisis* included Battey in its "Men of the Month" section, it described him as "one of the few colored photographers who have gained real artistic success" (Willis 2000, 39; *The Crisis* 1917, 31).[222] He spent the rest of his life at Tuskegee, training a new generation of Black photographers and producing dignified portraits of workers in the US South (Bieze 2008, 75).

Controlling the use of photographic images

Washington's correspondence, housed in the US Library of Congress and edited by Harlan and Smock in *The Booker T. Washington Papers* show how the Black leader controlled the use of the images and ensured their production. A letter addressed to General James Fowle Baldwin Marshall, written in 1881, gives an example of the use of documentary photographs to raise donations. Washington observes, "You will see by the photograph that we must have more suitable buildings" (Harlan 1972b, 151).

A letter to his secretary, Emmett J. Scott, written in 1904, shows how Washington sought to control published images to avoid associations with negative stereotypes of Black people—in this case,

---

[222] Battey also produced at least one cover photograph and published several "racial studies" in the NAACP's magazine. *The Crisis,* vol. 14, no. 1, 1917. https://www.marxists.org/history/usa/workers/civil-rights/crisis/0500-crisis-v14n01-w079.pdf

a supposed taste for alcoholic beverages. He criticizes the initiative of C. M. Battey, who insisted that he had been authorized to photograph a bar owned by an eminent Black businessman for a book that Washington was producing. The "Wizard of Tuskegee" observed that they could not afford to publish images of a bar in a book of that kind, while also showing the tact required when dealing with a potential donor:

> Of course, we cannot afford to put pictures [of] bar room fixtures neither the outside view of a bar room in a book of this kind, and I fear we shall have to let Mr. Nail down very gradually. Some of these pictures might be used at the Business League. Mr. Nail is a good strong man and I do not want to offend him in this matter. Mr. Moore told me that Mr. Battey told him he had authority from some one [sic] to take the pictures (Harlan and Smock, 1979, 11).

His autobiography *Working with the Hands*, the sequel to *Up from Slavery*, is illustrated with prints made from photographs by Frances Benjamin Johnston. Washington observes in the same letter that he preferred to use images that "will illustrate in a better manner the higher forms of work being done at Tuskegee." He notes that, "In the other illustrations the academic work, electrical engineering, architectural drawing, etc., are very largely omitted," and orders his secretary to "See that they get illustrations very soon" (Harlan and Smock 1979, 10-11). This letter also indicates that Booker T. Washington was sensitive to the Talented Tenth's accusation that Tuskegee focused solely on teaching Black students the skills required for manual labour.

Manuel R. Querino: Confronting Negative Stereotypes

The use of images in *A raça africana*

Manuel Querino used photographs to confront the pseudoscientific image of Black inferiority in two ways: first, as we have seen, by publicizing his own image of a poised, well-dressed intellectual "of colour"; and second, by publishing respectful, dignified images of Africans and their descendants. In short, he aimed to portray everything that was "civilized" in the eyes of Whites, contradicting the image of "half naked figures, unintelligent faces" (Agassiz 2000, 66; 2017) promulgated by Louis Agassiz and his fellow pseudo-scientists. Querino selected photographs of Black people—some of them produced for other purposes—as ethnographic documents to illustrate *A raça africana e os seus costumes na Bahia* (The African Race and its Customs in Bahia), but with the same attitude he displays and demands in the text, when he describes his African informants as

> *Venerable elders* [who provided me with information on African customs] without reservations or subterfuge, because these people saw nothing more in me than a friend of their race, and who, with sincere sympathy, always respected and did justice to the people that bondage had degraded, insulted, and persecuted, but never managed to change their innate, affectional qualities (1955, 23, emphasis added).

Even with images produced in Lindemann's studio for the purpose of commercializing exotic images of Africans in Brazil, these portraits take on a different meaning in the context of *A raça africana e os seus costumes na Bahia*:

Here is an example of the different meanings given to a single image. In Lindemann's caption [we read] "ganhador africano" ["African for hire"], a reference to work and race, in general to "street types." In Querino it acquires the status of an ethnographic document and, as such, serves to explain differences between people from a particular African ethnic group (Vasconcellos 2009, 105).

A raça africana is illustrated with 25 plates—23 photographs and 2 prints (including Figs. 5-9 to 5-25). Nine of the photographs portray "types" and "representatives" of African "tribes," representing unnamed subjects or people identified only by their position, as in the case of the "former high priestess of the Gantois terreiro, Egbá Type" (Fig. 5-19); five are private photographs of individuals and groups of people. They also include a photograph of "Ganhadores no Canto" ("Slaves-for-Hire in a Work Group") in which all are barefoot, indicating their enslaved status, but wearing dark jackets and hats (Fig. 5-22).[223]

In some cases, it is possible to name the individuals in the photographs, such as the "Igê-chá [Ijesha] Type," who has been identified as Majéngbásán (Brazilian name, Felicidade Silva Paranhos) (Fig 5-17), the mother of Martiniano Eliseu do Bonfim. Lisa Earl Castillo observes that her ethnic group was actually Ìbàràpá, from what is now the Nigerian state of Oyó. According to Martiniano's autobiography, given in an interview to Lorenzo Dow Turner, his mother was taken from her family in a town called Sàganùn (which no longer existed at the time of the interview) and enslaved in Lagos, from where she was transported to Brazil (Ayoh'Omidire and Amos 2012, 238).[224]

---

[223] The translation of *ganhador* depends on the context, as not all *ganhadores* were enslaved. Vasconcellos observes: "...Querino used the famous postcard 'Grupo de Carregadores Africanos – Bahia – Brasil' [Group of African Porters – Bahia – Brazil] printed by J. Mello in the late nineteenth century" (2009, 103). The fact that all are barefoot, despite being relatively well dressed, indicates that they were probably enslaved.

[224] Personal communication in Salvador, Bahia, in July 2023. Castillo clarified Majéngbásán's ethnicity in her article on the "Ketu" nation in Candomblé (2021a, 305; see Earl Castillo 2021b for the English translation off this article). The photograph of Majéngbásán can also be found in the Lorenzo Dow Turner

There are also three sculptures among the prints illustrating *A raça africana*, identified as African "ganhadores" (Figs. 5-23 to 5-25). These pieces are very similar—including the clothes, cloth wrappers, and the items they carry on their heads—with a set of four sculptures that appears in the first edition of *Artistas baianos* (1909). The latter are identified as "Street types (street vendors)," made from hog plum tree *(Spondias mombin)* bark (Fig. 5-26), by Erotides Américo d'Araujo Lopes, whose photograph in the same book indicates that he was White.

Nearly all the women wear a *pano da costa* (African-style wrap or shawl) in the non-liturgical style—during Candomblé rituals, it would be worn around the waist by higher-ranking priestesses and around the chest by more recent initiates. This style of dress was described by the French author C. M. A. Dugrivel in the early 1830s: "All the Black women in general wear a *pano da costa*, a kind of Greek-style shawl, with which they cover themselves with divine grace. As I am fond of all that is ancient, you can imagine how much pleasure it gives me to observe these customs and recall the golden age of Themistocles, of Pericles" (Dugrivel 1843, 377).[225]

The pose and manner of wearing the pano da costa of the woman who represents the "Benin Type" in Plate VI (Fig. 5-12), probably photographed at the beginning of the twentieth century, are very similar to portraits of Mãe Aninha, the first iyalorixá (high priestess) and founder of Ilê Axé Opô Afonjá. According to Christianne Vasconcellos:

> In the collection formed by Querino, the photographs on the theme of Candomblé were taken by Photografia Diamantina, established on Dr Seabra Street, Baixa dos Sapateiros, a popular shopping area, whose location was far from the commercial

---

Collection at the Anacostia Community Museum, Smithsonian Institution, Washington, D.C. (Ayoh'Omidire and Amos 2012, 235).

[225] Querino would have liked this comparison with Ancient Greece, as he made a point of comparing enslaved Africans in Brazil with Greeks enslaved in Rome.

circuit of the other photographic studios in the city, located in the parishes of Sé and São Pedro.... It is interesting to note that the photographs of high priestesses, which appeared only in the first decades of the twentieth century, were produced by Photographia Diamantina. The studio's importance lies in the evidence of the self-representation of this part of the Black population that wanted and paid for their own portraits; simultaneous to the production and circulation of public photographs of Black people chosen by European photographers to compose the series on urban types in Bahia (Vasconcellos 2008).

Two of these photographs (Figs. 5-19 and 5-20) are in the style of *cartes-cabinet*—that of the "former high priestess of the terreiro," easily identified as Maria Júlia da Conceição Nazareth, the founder of Ilê Iyá Omin Axé Iyá Massé, better known as Gantois, and her biological daughter and successor, Maria Pulquéria da Conceição Nazareth (1840-1918), "a charismatic and respected iyalorixá who opened the doors of the terreiro to intellectuals for research" (Nobrega and Echevarria 2006, 16-17). The latter was also the iyalorixá of Manuel Querino, who, according to Vivaldo da Costa Lima, was an ogã at Gantois (Costa Lima 2011, 94). The two women are portrayed standing, shown head to foot in clothes and jewelry that, in the second portrait, Querino describes as "full gala" dress. Both mother and daughter possess a stately dignity.

The symbols of royalty and regal poses may be subjective interpretations in some of these images, but another photograph leaves no doubt—according to Querino, it shows a descendant of a royal Ijesha family (Fig. 5-11). In the introduction to *A raça africana*, the Afro-Brazilian scholar regrets that "the Africans have died out who, being enslaved here, *occupied, in their homeland, a high social position, as a guide of the destinies of the tribe, or as depositories of the secrets of the religious sect*" (Querino 2006, 11-12, emphasis added). In the mid-nineteenth century, the British consul James

Wetherell commented ironically on the existence of "Negro princes" in Salvador:

> There are some of the blacks who have been princes in their own land, and whenever any of the same nation meet such a one they kneel down. They are nearly always talking at the extent of their voices, and when they can hold the conversation in their own language they do so. When they meet they generally have something to say, and in passing, after asking a question, they seem to repeat the same word or words several times over alternatively. They frequently talk to themselves aloud, and in nearly every instance, the subject of their soliloquy is money (Wetherell 1860).

According to Alberto da Costa e Silva, the presence of people of high social rank among Africans enslaved in Brazil and descendants of African royalty is a proven fact: "As Verger demonstrated, Africans from the Bight of Benin came to Bahia to study, trade, or escape political persecution, and not just as captives destined for sugar and tobacco plantations in northeastern Brazil or the mines of Minas Gerais" (2000, 129).

There are countless examples of derogatory images of Black people which circulated in the United States, Europe, and Brazil at the turn of the century, as well as before and afterwards. The book *Eu tenho um sonho: de King a Obama—a saga negra do norte* (I Have a Dream: From King to Obama—The Black Saga of the North), edited by Emanoel Araújo and published by the Museu Afro Brasil (Araújo 2011), presents a sample of images that illustrate the true nature of the "dragon" which Black leaders and intellectuals have had to slay when combating prejudice and serving as positive role models for their community.

American collectors still gather and make these images available, some to preserve the memory of a time when racist photographs, drawings, and cartoons constituted a genre of photography since its inception in the nineteenth century, representing and perpetuating the worst stereotypes of Black people, and even celebrating and encouraging heinous acts of lynching. Stereotypical images also perpetuated the "invisible man." According to Pereira and Gomes, "...images of Blacks could take on a real visibility or a stereotypical visibility which tends to be interpreted as invisibility" (2001, 138).

Derogatory images of Black people are produced to this day. Today, the tools used to produce negative images of the "Other" are more sophisticated. Instead of daguerreotypes and cartoons, we have AI and deepfakes. Clearly, despite Washington's and Querino's efforts to combat them by appealing to reason, morality, and justice—the original meaning of "woke"—racial prejudice still persists. As long as racism continues to be a hegemonic and self-perpetuating discourse, the task of overcoming prejudice—in words and images—will be more than Herculean. It is a labour of Sisyphus.

Fig. 5-9. Representative of the Ijesha tribe [*sic*]

Fig. 5-10. Representative of the Yoruba tribe

Portrayals and Pushback

Fig. 5-11. Representative of the Ijesha tribe. Descendant of a royal family

Fig. 5-12. Benin type

Fig. 5-13. Ijesha type

Fig. 5-14. Yoruba type

Estampa IX — Oondó Igê-chá Igê-chá

Fig. 5-15. Ondo, Ijesha, Ijesha

Estampa X — Typo Gêge

Fig. 5-16. Jeje (Fon-speaking) type

Fig. 5-17. Ijesha [*sic*] type. Identified as Majéngbásán, the mother of Martiniano Eliseu do Bonfim, she was Yoruba, originally from Oyo.

Estampa XII — Representante da tribu **Igê-chá**

Fig. 5-18. Representative of the Ijesha tribe

Estampa XII-a — A antiga mãe de terreiro do Gantois. Typo **Egbá**

Fig. 5-19. The former high priestess of the Gantois terreiro. Egba type

Estampa XXIII — Creoula em grande gala. A mãe do terreiro do Gantois. Pulcheria Maria da Conceição

Fig. 5-20. Creole woman in full gala dress. The high priestess of Gantois. Pulchéria Maria da Conceição

Estampa XIX — Candomblezeiros em grande gala

Fig. 5-21. Candomblé priestess and priest in full gala dress

Estampa XVIII — Ganhadores no canto

Fig. 5-22. Ganhadores (slaves-for-hire) in a work group

Estampa XX — Ganhador africano

Fig. 5-23. African ganhador

Fig. 5-24. Female African ganhador

Fig. 5-25. Female African ganhador

Fig. 5-26. Street types (vendors). Carved from cajazeira wood by
Erotides Américo d'Araújo Lopes

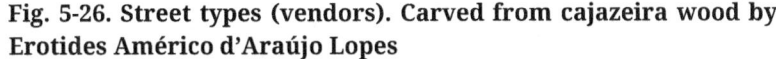

ig. 5-27. Portrait of Manuel Querino

Fig. 5-28. Book cover with retouched photo

BY WAY OF A CONCLUSION: Reflections on the Tactics and Trajectories of Querino and Washington

Manuel R. Querino and Booker T. Washington were multifaceted individuals who, when scrutinised deeply, are hard to pin down. Querino was a family man, abolitionist, labour leader, loyal student, educator, and respected researcher, but the Sociedade Protetora dos Desvalidos discovered that he was enjoying full health in 1896, after requesting a disability pension. We also know that he had a "frank and proud temperament" (Chaves, 1923), which always makes enemies, even more so in the case of a Black man in a society in which veiled racism reigned and is still widespread. He suffered bitter disappointments, as we can see in and between the lines of the biographies produced by his contemporaries, but he had admirers and loyal friends among his colleagues, co-workers, and confreres. He also had powerful White allies, chiefly Manuel Pinto de Sousa Dantas, who rose to Prime Minister of the Imperial government.

Like Querino, Washington was also a family man, educator, and leader—in his case, of a "nation" built by Black solidarity and consolidated by segregation enforced by the law and lynch mobs in an openly and violently racist society. He ran the Tuskegee Institute with an iron fist, established himself as a powerful leader of the "Black nation," and sometimes used unscrupulous tactics to maintain his power. Nevertheless, for most of his life, he preferred to avoid open confrontation with White supremacists. The contradictions that arose during the "Ulrich affair"—in which he was accused of flirting with a White woman, or worse, and nearly lynched in New York City—tarnished his reputation. He had bitter enemies in the Black community, notably Du Bois and Trotter, as well as White-supremacist foes like Senator Ben Tillman, congressmen Tom Heflin and Tom Watson, and the novelist Thomas Dixon, Jr., but he also had good friends, loyal followers, and wealthy, powerful allies, White and Black.

Querino and Washington both produced several books, some of which have been published in further editions (and in the case of Washington, numerous translations).[226] They also used their own biographies and positive images of Black people as tactics to combat racist stereotypes. Washington was a client and patron of several photographers, Black and White, male and female, who produced a vast collection of portraits and images. Washington's and Querino's obituaries demonstrate that, at the time of their deaths, they still enjoyed considerable prestige. Why, then, have their posthumous reputations suffered so many setbacks?

In addition to the charge of "accommodation," the accusation that weighed most heavily on Booker T. Washington's reputation was that he supposedly advocated strictly vocational education for Blacks. In *Schooling for the New Slavery: Black Industrial Education, 1868-1915*, first published in 1978, Donald Spivey criticizes Washington in terms similar to Du Bois's philippics, accusing him of following and

---

[226] By comparison, the works of the Black Haitian anthropologist Anténor Firmin and the White Brazilian sociologist Manoel Bomfim were once "shelved" and forgotten because they confronted the racialist ideologies of their time, only to be retrieved in the late twentieth century.

preserving the slavocratic values of the South: "His role was like that of the black overseer during slavery who, given the position of authority over his fellow slaves, worked diligently to keep intact the very system under which they both were enslaved" (2007, 62).

James Smoot Coleman uses the divergence between the views of Washington and Du Bois, perpetuated by Du Bois himself, in his analysis of the formal and agrarian/vocational education debate in Nigeria. For Western-trained Nigerian intellectuals, vocational and agrarian education served to keep Indigenous Africans in their colonized role as "hewers of wood and drawers of water," but for others, it perpetuated "tribal" agricultural and handicraft traditions and produced "the cult of the detribalized clerk"—Africans educated in accordance with the Christian-European curriculum. According to Coleman, this debate roughly followed the lines of "the well-known differences between the views of two American Negro leaders: Booker T. Washington, who advocated the agricultural and vocational training of the masses, and Dr W. E. B. Du Bois, who believed that education should first of all deal with the 'talented tenth'" (1971, 119-120).[227]

Thanks to constant repetition, this supposed dichotomy became set in stone, placing Washington at the extreme of strictly vocational training and Du Bois at the other end: elite higher education. However, as is the case with many Manichaean concepts, the reality was more nuanced. To begin with, in the analysis by Ellen Weiss, the biographer of the Black American architect Robert R. Taylor (2012, 58), calling the speech that Washington delivered in 1895 the "Atlanta Compromise" is a misnomer. Washington assured White southerners that they would find a productive work force in their own region if they sought to employ Black people rather than import foreign workers. But the educator and orator also wanted to help lift Black people out of poverty and the uncertainties of peonage

---

[227] Coleman observes that although "their protest was symbolic of a cultural awakening" the "westernized minority" of African intellectuals who opposed European education could also be called "accommodationists" (1971, 119).

(considered a different form of slavery), transforming them into farmers who used scientific methods, owned their own land, and could enjoy the fruits of prosperity.[228]

Finally, we must not forget that the primary objective of the educational establishment which Washington and his future wife, Olivia Davidson, cofounded, was teacher training. Today, the former Tuskegee Normal and Industrial Institute is an historically Black university (HBCU)—Washington's greatest legacy. According to Smock, in the "post-Civil Rights" era in the US, commentators increasingly compared President Barack Obama's leadership style to Washington's, particularly Obama's conciliatory approach and tendency to "play down the troubled past of the nation, look for compromise with whites, and promise a brighter future" (Smock 2009, 5). American conservatives also like to use Washington as a model for their mantra of self-help—that is, a Black leader who preferred that his community fend for itself instead of being assisted by the state. This is a rather anachronistic argument, given that, in Washington's time, the social security system introduced by President Franklin Delano Roosevelt in the 1930s did not yet exist. Tragically, Washington's tactics of promoting self-help and leading an orderly, successful life for Black people failed due to the climate of virulent racism which prevailed, particularly in the South, in the decades after the US Civil War. For example, the race riots in Atlanta in 1906 led to a massacre and razed the businesses of prosperous Blacks to the ground.

According to Ishmael Reed, in his introduction to the 2000 edition of *Up from Slavery*:

---

[228] This educational concept is being used today in the Southern Bahia Lowlands and other parts of Brazil. By combining technical education with the official secondary curriculum, the Family Houses aim to produce "rural entrepreneurs" and reduce the exodus of young people who leave the countryside for the big cities due to a lack of opportunities in their home regions (see Gimonet 2007).

So successful have Du Bois's followers and their intellectual descendants been in defining Booker T. Washington's reputation that he has been characterized by many as an accommodationist and worse. A more careful examination of the educator's career, however, reveals that Washington was more complicated than his critics would have us believe. As Louis R. Harlan says, "by private action [Booker T. Washington] fought lynching, disenfranchisement, peonage, educational discrimination, and segregation" (2000, xvi).

Clearly, Du Bois himself was chiefly responsible for the "accommodationist" label that still clings to Washington, but the biggest difference we perceive between the rival leaders is that Washington was a pragmatist, and Du Bois was an intellectual and idealist. The White journalist Ray Stannard Baker, who knew both men personally, observes that Washington appealed to his people's hearts, and Du Bois to their minds. Washington was "a leader of men"; Du Bois, "a promulgator of ideas" (Baker 1908). In a movement that aimed to confront racism against Blacks in the United States, an alliance between these talents, approaches, and visions would have been very fruitful. Instead of accepting Washington's invitation to teach at Tuskegee and influence the institute from within, Du Bois embarked on an open dispute for the leadership of the "Black nation," allying himself with other members of the "Talented Tenth" and the NAACP. Even so, far from escaping his rival's shadow, as Du Bois himself wryly observed: "Washington died in 1915. A lot of people think I died at the same time" (1999b, 317).

As for Manuel Querino, although he suffered setbacks during his lifetime, mainly as a politician and civil servant, the damage done to his posthumous reputation was also due to racial and class prejudice. The emphasis on his "humble" origins and the fact that he began his career as a painter and decorator is used by Ramos, Pinto de Aguiar, and Ott, among others, to disparage his academic and artistic qualifications. Normally, the modest origins of a self-made man— such as Andrew Carnegie, or, to give an example closer to Brazil and

Bahia, Jonathas Abbott—are celebrated to show how many obstacles he had to overcome and how high he had risen. The fact that Carnegie started out as a weaver or Abbott as a stable boy in no way detracted from their future accomplishments. Therefore, insistence on the alleged lack of intellectual sophistication of the "self-taught" Manuel Querino gives rise to serious concerns. It reminds us of the folklorist Frederico Edelweiss's observation: "How many times must he have heard that trite and still common phrase: 'That Black doesn't know his place!'?" (1946, 1).

Thanks to the successive efforts of Brazilian and foreign intellectuals over the course of several decades, Querino has been restored to his rightful place in the social and cultural history of Bahia, as a pioneer in the history of its cuisine, its arts, its popular culture and the appreciation of the contributions of African settlers to Bahian and Brazilian civilization. Despite the efforts of Norell and others, the rehabilitation of Booker T. Washington is yet to be achieved, as his portrayal as an accommodationist in Self Made, a recent series based on the life of Madam C. J. Walker, demonstrates.[229]

Final Reflections

A new look at Washington today could not only result in a reinterpretation of his tactics but would also be useful to remind us of the absolute absence of educational opportunities for emancipated people in Brazil after Abolition in 1888. Lack of education and job skills led to a condition which the Afro-Brazilian sociologist Jessé de Souza describes as the permanent declassification and marginalization of Whites and Blacks (Souza 2006, 61). Racial discrimination added to the burden of formerly enslaved Black people and their descendants.

At the turn of the century, the names of Black American leaders like Booker T. Washington, Frederick Douglass, and W. E. B. Du Bois

---

[229] It should be noted that *Self Made* is subtitled in Portuguese and available in Brazil on Netflix.

By Way of a Conclusion

were well known in Brazil. However, in *A raça africana e os seus costumes na Bahia*, originally published in 1916, Manuel Querino only mentioned Washington as a role model and representative of Blacks in the United States (1938, 22). It may be that Querino identified with Washington because they both came from humble beginnings and had struggled to get an education. Querino shared Washington's desire to ensure that Black people could at least learn a trade that would allow them to make a living and even prosper after Abolition. He made his long-standing interest in this issue clear when he serialised Harriet Beecher Stowe's essay on the education of freedmen in his newspaper *O Trabalho* (see Appendix II). However, no effort was made to educate emancipated Blacks in his country. In the early days of the First Republic (1889-1930), Querino took to the newspapers to denounce the lack of professional education opportunities, which were being progressively eliminated. Lack of funding may even have thwarted his ambition to become an architect, because the School of Fine Art could not afford to pay lecturers to teach the required courses.

Knowing that educational institutions for emancipated Blacks and their descendants existed in the United States, but not in Brazil, where race relations were less openly violent, segregation more subtle, and miscegenation a fait accompli, gave Querino good reason to value Washington's achievements. Like the author of the "Letter from Paris," published in a Bahia newspaper in 1903, Querino must have asked himself many times: "When will another Booker appear in Brazil to raise the level of the Blacks and save those whom the abolition of slavery has thrown into a vacuum, into uncertainty..."[230]

---

[230] *Correio da Manhã*, October 26, 1903, 3.

APPENDIX I
Timelines

Booker T. Washington

1856 Born into slavery on the Burroughs farm in Hales Ford, Virginia. He never knew his actual year of birth.

1861 The inventory of James Burroughs's estate includes "1 Negro Boy (Booker)" valued at $400. His mother, Jane, was valued at $250, his brother, John, at $530, and his sister, Amanda, at $200.

1861 April—the US Civil War begins.

1865 Emancipation. Jane and her children—John, Booker, and Amanda—travel 200 miles (the children on foot, their mother in a cart) to the town of Malden, West Virginia, to join Washington Ferguson, Jane's husband and Amanda's father.

Their stepfather puts John and Booker to work with him in a salt factory, and later in a coal mine.

1866 Booker begins his studies at the Tinkersville School.

1867 He starts working as a domestic in the home of General Lewis Ruffner and his Northern wife, Viola (General Ruffner owned the salt factory and mines).

1868 General Samuel Chapman Armstrong founds the Hampton Institute in Virginia.

1872 Booker travels over 500 miles to apply to study at the Hampton Institute, arriving on October 5.

1873 A depression begins in the United States.

1875 The Federal Government enacts the Civil Rights Law; Booker graduates from the Hampton Institute and begins teaching in Malden.

1878 He enrols in the Wayland Seminary in Washington, DC, intending to become a Baptist minister, but leaves after six to eight months;

He hears Frederick Douglass speak during his stay in Washington.

1879 He begins teaching night classes at the Hampton Institute and becomes the "house father" for a group of fifty Native American students.

1881 General Armstrong recommends Booker T. Washington as the principal of a new teacher training school being established in Tuskegee, Alabama; Washington opens the Tuskegee Normal and Industrial Institute, originally housed in a former church.

1882 August 2—Washington marries Fannie Norton Smith;

The Tuskegee Institute's first building is erected by the students, using bricks they made themselves.

1884 His eldest child, Portia Marshall Washington, is born.

1884 His first wife, Fannie, dies suddenly, of unknown causes.

1885 He marries his second wife, Olivia America Davidson.

1887 His second child, Booker T. Washington Junior, is born.

1889 February—His third child, Ernest Davidson Washington, is born.

1889 May 9—Olivia dies of tuberculosis.

1893 He marries Margaret James Murray. **May 11**—Samuel Chapman Armstrong dies at the Hampton Institute.

1895 September 18—Booker T. Washington gives a speech at the Atlanta Exposition.

1896 He receives an honorary master's degree from Harvard University.

1889 His first trip to Europe

1900 The National Negro Business League (NNBL) is founded;

publication of his first autobiography, *The Story of My Life and Work*.

1901 His best-known work, *Up from Slavery*, is published.

October 15 Theodore Roosevelt invites him to dine at the White House.

1903 W. E. B. Du Bois publishes *The Souls of Black Folk*, including an essay harshly criticizing Booker T. Washington and his philosophy.

1905 William Randolph Hearst's newspapers spread the rumour that Washington escorted the daughter of White businessman Sam Wanamaker to the table during a formal dinner, scandalising White supremacists.

1906 Atlanta race massacre and the "Brownsville Affray" severely weaken Washington's credibility and leadership.

1909 Creation of the National Association for the Advancement of Colored People (NAACP).

1910 Washington spends two months in Europe with his assistant, Robert E. Park, studying the less privileged classes there for *The Man Farthest Down*.

1911 March 19—Washington is nearly lynched in New York City.

1915 April—First National Negro Health Week.

November 15—Booker T. Washington dies at the Tuskegee Institute.

Manuel R. Querino

1850 Brazil definitively abolishes the slave trade *de jure* and *de facto* after decades of British pressure exerted through the Royal Navy.

1851 July 28—Manuel Raimundo Querino is born in Santo Amaro da Purificação, Bahia, in the Brazilian Northeast.

1855 A cholera epidemic kills Querino's foster parents; he is taken to the city of Salvador, where Manuel Correia Garcia—a White politician, educator and, historian—becomes his guardian.

1865 The Triple Alliance War against Paraguay begins; Manuel Correia Garcia founds the Instituto Histórico Provincial (Provincial Historical Institute).

1868 Querino leaves Bahia, possibly seeking to escape the draft, but is "recruited" in the province of Piauí. He becomes a clerk at his battalion's headquarters in Rio de Janeiro and is promoted to squadron corporal.

1870 Triple Alliance War ends; Querino signs the Republican Manifesto calling for the end of imperial rule in Brazil.

1871 Free Womb Law frees children born to enslaved women, with certain restrictions. Querino returns to Bahia, demobilized early through the influence of Manuel Pinto de Sousa Dantas, the leader of the Liberal Party in Bahia and later Prime Minister of Brazil. Querino begins working as a painter and decorator in Bahia and gets involved in local politics.

1872 Querino takes night classes at the Liceu de Artes e Ofícios, studying Humanities. He received a distinction in French and full marks in Portuguese

1874 He helps organise the Liga Operária Baiana (Bahian Workers' League)

1876 His political career begins; the Liga Operária Baiana is officially launched on **November 26**

1877 Querino helps found and build the Academy (later School) of Fine Art, after his teacher and mentor, the Spanish artist Miguel Navarro y Cañizares, breaks with the Liceu

1878-1883 Querino marries Ceciliana do Espírito Santo, sometime between 1878 and 1883.

1880 A list of the founding students of the Congregation of the Bahia Academy of Fine Art (ABAB) is unveiled on 20 May 1880. Querino's name is among them

1881-1884 Querino studies Architecture at the School of Fine Art.

1882 He obtains a teaching certificate in industrial design.

1885 He teaches geometric design at the Liceu de Artes e Ofícios da Bahia and the Colégio dos Órfãos de São Joaquim; becomes a charter member of the Liceu; and joins the abolitionist movement alongside Frederico Marinho de Araújo, Eduardo Carigé and others.

1887 His son Manuel Querino Filho is born on **July 11**.[231]

1887-1888 Querino founds the abolitionist newspaper *A Província*.

1888 Slavery is officially abolished in Brazil on **May 13**. Querino's daughter Maria Anatildes is born on **December 21**.[232]

1888-1895 Querino becomes a civil servant, working at the Public Works Department, and designs the city of Salvador's streetcars.

1889 A coup overthrows Emperor Pedro II and the First Republic is declared.

1889-1890 His son Paulo Querino is born.

1890-1891 Querino's first term as city councillor.

1892 Querino founds and edits the newspaper *O Trabalho* as an outlet for the labour movement.

1894 The Instituto Geográfico e Histórico da Bahia (Geographic and Historical Institute of Bahia; IGHB) is established—Querino is a founding member.

---

[231] "Brasil, Bahía, Registros da Igreja Católica, 1598-2007", database with images, *FamilySearch* (https://www.familysearch.org/ark:/61903/1:1:6XMZ-75WD : 13 March 2022), Manoel Raymundo Querino in entry for Maria Querino, julho de 1899.

[232] "Brasil, Bahía, Registros da Igreja Católica, 1598-2007", database with images, *FamilySearch* (https://www.familysearch.org/ark:/61903/1:1:6XMZ-75WD : 13 March 2022), Manoel Raymundo Querino in entry for Maria Querino, July 1899.

1894—December 19 His daughter Alzira Querino is born (she is christened as "Alzira Crioula" in 1899).[233]

1894-1897 Ceciliana do Espírito Santo dies (year unknown).

1896 Querino works at the State Department of Agriculture until his retirement in 1916.

1897 He marries Laura Barbosa Pimentel.

1897-1899 His second term as city councilman.

1899 Querino leaves politics and devotes himself to the study of Bahia's history and folklore and Black Vindicationism.

1900 Director of the "Pândegos da África" Afro-Carnaval group.

1903 Publication of his first textbook on geometric drawing, *Desenho linear das classes elementaries*.

1908 His son Manuel Querino Filho dies.

1909 Publication of *Artistas bahianos* and *As Artes na Bahia*

1911 Publication of *Elementos de desenho geométrico* and the second edition of *Artistas bahianos*.

1914 *Bailes pastoris* is published.

1916 Publication of *A Bahia de outrora* and *A raça africana e os seus costumes na Bahia*.

1918 Presents *O colono preto como fator da civilização brasileira* at the Sixth Brazilian Geography Conference in Belo Horizonte, Minas Gerais.

1921 His daughter Alzira Querino dies.

1922 Second edition of *A Bahia de outrora*.

1923 The *Revista do Instituto Geográfico e Histórico da Bahia* (no. 48) publishes na article by Querino entitled "Os homens de cor preta na História"; Manuel Querino dies on **February 14,** survived by his widow, Laura, and two of his four children.

1923-1928 Laura Pimentel Querino dies (year unknown).

1928 *A arte culinária na Bahia* is published; on **May 13,** the IGHB unveils his portrait in its gallery.

---

[233] "Brasil, Bahía, Registros da Igreja Católica, 1598-2007", database with images, *FamilySearch* (https://www.familysearch.org/ark:/61903/1:1:66NL-WHJH : Thu Jul 27 01:31:05 UTC 2023), Entry for Alzira Crioula and Alzira, 9 de julho de 1899.

1933 The Frente Negra (Black Front) pays tribute to Manuel Querino, leaving flowers on his tomb in the sacristy of the Church of N. S. dos Homens Pretos in Salvador, Bahia

1938 Artur Ramos edits an anthology of his main works in *Costumes africanos no Brasil*.

1951 The centenary of Manuel Querino's birth is celebrated in Rio de Janeiro and Bahia.

2024 The centenary of Querino's death is commemorated in Salvador, Bahia, with the release of a documentary on his life.

APPENDIX II
"The Education of Freedmen,"
by Harriet Beecher Stowe

The following essay was serialised in Manuel Querino's newspaper O Trabalho *(Labour) in 1892, demonstrating that, although that publication was an outlet for the labour movement—of which Querino had been a leader prior to the abolition of slavery in Brazil in 1888—its editor was deeply concerned with the fate of the people emancipated just four years earlier, who had been denied an education while in bondage and lacked opportunities after Abolition.*

The short period of fourteen years that has elapsed since the late war has been witness of a more wonderful moral and political revolution in these United States than has ever been recorded in history before.

Between four and five million human beings, who had hitherto been deprived of every right of human nature, have been suddenly precipitated into freedom and invested with the rights of republican citizens.

There have been instances before of the sudden emancipations of oppressed masses, but their results have been so fearful as to fill thoughtful minds with a just terror. The French Revolution with its sansculottism, its untold horrors, ended perforce in a despotism, and it was not without cause that an English thinker[234] treated of our emancipation act as "Shooting Niagara." We have shot Niagara, and are alive and well. Our ship of state has been through those mighty rapids and plunged down that awful gulf, while nations held their breath, expecting to see her go to pieces. But lo! She has emerged, stanch and steady, and is now sailing on.

That the passengers have been somewhat tumbled about and shaken, that here and there a timber has cracked or a joint started, that there have been whirlpools and eddies, and uncomfortable sailing, we all know. But the miracle of our day is that *the ship is sailing on*, in better order than ever before—in better order, for that unwieldy stowage of oppression which she was obliged to carry has been thrown overboard, and she sails free!

In order justly to estimate the present state of education and progress among the freedmen of the United States, we must glance back to the condition in which they were under slavery. A slave could hold no property, had *no* rights, could not testify either in a court of justice or a Christian church, could not contract a legal marriage, had no legal rights over his children—in short, was a human being carefully, legally, and systematically despoiled of every right of humanity.

To teach a slave to read and write was forbidden, under heavy penalties. In some States the penalty for teaching him to read was far heavier than for maiming him or putting out his eyes. As the soil in certain States became exhausted, breeding slaves for a more southern market became a systematic process, and was reported upon in agricultural papers and meetings in much the same terms that might apply to the breeding of horses and mules.

In the Northern States, the colored people were generally disfranchised, and, if not forbidden education by law, were repelled from the schools by prejudice, and prejudices apparently far more bitter at the North than at the South.

---

[234] The Scottish essayist Thomas Carlyle.

Appendix II – The Education of Freedmen

In 1832 Miss Prudence Crandall undertook to open a private boarding-school for young colored girls, in Canterbury, Connecticut. The enterprise was denounced in advance, by the people of this place, in a public meeting. When the term opened, with fifteen or twenty young girls from Philadelphia, Boston, New York, and Providence, storekeepers, butchers, milkmen, and farmers, with one consent, refused to sell provisions to the school, and supplies had to be brought from expensive distances. The scholars were insulted in the streets; the door-steps and doors were besmeared with filth, and the well filled with the same; the village doctor refused to visit the sick pupils; and the trustees of the church forbade them to set foot in their building. The house was assaulted by a mob with clubs and iron bars; they broke the glass of the windows and terrified the inmates. Finally, the State Legislature passed an act making this school and illegal enterprise, and under this act Miss Crandall was imprisoned in the county jail.

This apparently unaccountable sensitiveness of the Northern mind become intelligible when we consider that there were as really slaveholders in the Northern as the Southern States. Negro slaves were the assets of every Southern estate, plantation, and firm; they were offered as security for debt, and the large commercial business of the North with the South was carried on upon this basis. There were abundance of rich slaveholders in Northern churches, who felt with the keen instinct of self-interest anything which interfered with their gains, and who did not wish to have trouble of conscience, and they hated the negro because he aroused this uncomfortable faculty. The Northern abolitionist proclaimed that to buy, hold, or sell a human being for gains was a sin against God, and, like all other sins, to be immediately repented of and forsaken. Now, when a New York merchant got a letter from his lawyer, apprising him that he had taken twenty thousand dollars' worth of negroes as security for his debt, and returned answer to sell and remit, it was but natural that he should hereafter be very excitable under such teachings, and denounce them as incendiary and fanatical. The bitterness of Southern slaveholders was tempered by many considerations of kindness for servants born in their houses, or upon their estates; but the Northern slaveholder traded in men and women whom he never saw, and of whose separations, tears, and miseries he determined never to hear.

The great consolatory doctrine that soothed the consciences both of Northern and Southern slaveholders was that the negro was unfit for any other condition than that of slavery; incapable of culture, education, and self-guidance, and therefore, both North and South, efforts to educate him aroused special opposition and resistance.

One of the leaders in this Canterbury affair expressed briefly the sense of the whole pro-slavery party North and South: "We are not merely opposed to *that* school. We mean that there shall *never* be such a school set up anywhere in our State. The colored people *never* can rise up from a menial condition in this country; they ought not to be permitted to rise here. They are an inferior race of beings, and never can or ought to be recognized as the equals of the whites. Let the n****s be sent back to Africa, and there improve themselves as much as they may. The condition of the colored population of our country can *never* be essentially improved on this continent."

This was the vital point of the conflict, briefly stated. The abolitionists set themselves, therefore, to the education of the black race.

Oberlin College, founded in 1835, in Oberlin, Ohio, was the first permanent endowed institution avowedly opened to give impartial privileges of education without regard to color. In our national capital a brave, heroic woman, named Myrtella Miner, consecrated her life to founding a school for the young colored women of the District of Columbia, who had hitherto been left to ignorance and vice. Miss Miner wore out her strength and shortened her life in this cause, but the school she founded still exists, and is doing a good work in Washington. In memory of her heroism the ladies' hall in Howard University is called Miner Hall. Let her memory be blessed!

In 1855 John G. Fee, the son of a Kentucky slaveholder, founded in the little village of Barea, in Madison County, Kentucky, a school in which white and colored were to be admitted to equal privileges.

Appendix II – The Education of Freedmen

Young Fee renewed in his experience the virtues and the persecutions of the primitive Christians. For preaching the duty of emancipation and the sinfulness of slavery in his native Sate, he was disinherited by his father. His whole private patrimony he expended in redeeming a slave woman, whom his father had sold away from her husband into Southern bondage. The woman was a member of the same Christian church with himself. Her ransom left to Fee only a pittance for self-support, and he became a missionary under the care of the American Missionary Society, a society formed on expressly antislavery principles. In his labors young Fee encountered the fury of mob-violence [sic]. Two or three times he was seized, his colored assistant brutally flogged before his eyes, and himself, with rope adjusted round his neck, threatened with hanging, unless he pledged himself to abandon his enterprise and leave the State. With Christian calmness he kneeled down, saying: "I can bear any suffering, but I will give no such pledges"; and today Berea College, with an endowment of between eighty and one hundred thousand dollars, is the monument of his perseverance.

Thus we have seen that until the time of the late war the condition of the African race in these States was, for the most part, a condition of hopeless bondage to ignorance. The efforts for their education were a few twinkling, scattered stars in a night of rayless darkness.

Here we must not omit to do justice to a large class of conscientious Christians among the Southern slaveholders, who felt deeply and oppressively their responsibility to their slaves, and labored sincerely to impart instruction to them within the limits allowed by law. Occasionally individuals were found who took upon themselves the responsibility of disregarding the penalties of law, and teaching their slaves to read and write; but, in the very nature of the case, such instances were exceptional. Yet undoubtedly the kindly relations engendered between servants and masters and mistresses, in these efforts to impart Christian instruction, were the reason why there was no painful uprising or insurrection attending the war. Christianity, however imperfectly apprehended, was a bond of peace between masters and servants.

At last came the war, and in the beginning of that conflict the best political friends of the African race, the antislavery President and Cabinet, and all concerned in the Government, took pains to affirm that emancipation was no part of the object or intention of that war.

But it soon became evident that the liberation of the slave *was* the object and intention of "Him that ruleth in the armies of heaven." The cause of the African was pleaded according to his fashion who hath said, "By fire and sword will the Lord plead with all flesh, and the slain of the Lord shall be many."

The time came when the nation was forced into emancipation as a war measure, and, having liberated the slave, she enrolled him in her armies. Having done this, the national honor became pledged to the protection of the race thus set free, and the right of suffrage and the provisions of the civil-rights bill followed as a necessary consequence.

For years patriots, statesmen, conscientious and Christian men, had toiled and agonized over the inscrutable problem, *How* could slavery be abolished without ruin to the country? Madison, Jefferson, Washington, all had their schemes—all based on the idea that after emancipation it would be impossible for the whites and blacks to live harmoniously together. Sudden emancipation was spoken of as something involving danger, bloodshed, and violence; and yet, as no one could propose a feasible system of preparation, the drift of the Southern mind had come to be toward indefinite perpetuation and extension.

Our emancipation was forced upon us—it was sudden; it gave no time for preparation, and our national honor forced us to give, not only emancipation, but the rights and defenses of citizenship. This was the position in which the war left us. We had four million new United States citizens in our Union, without property, without education, with such morals as may be inferred from the legal status in which they had been kept; they were surrounded by their former

Appendix II – The Education of Freedmen

white owners, every way embittered toward them, and in no wise disposed to smooth their path to liberty and competence.

That in such a sudden and astounding change there should have been struggle and conflict; that the reconstruction of former slave States, in such astonishingly new conditions of society, should have been with some difficulty, wrath, and opposition; that there should have been contentions, mistakes, mismanagements, and plenty of undesirable events to make sensation articles for the daily press, was to be expected.

But wherever upon God's earth was such an unheard-of revolution in the state of human society accomplished with so little that was to be deprecated?

For in this year, 1878, certain propositions of very great significance bear assertion, and can be maintained by ample proof:

1. The cotton crop raised by free labor is the largest by some millions that ever has been raised in the United States. That settles the question as to the free-labor system.

2. The legal status of the negro is universally conceded as a *finality* by the leading minds of the South.

3. The common-school system has been established throughout the Southern States, and recognized in theory by the wisest Southern men as to be applied impartially to whites and blacks.

4. All of the large religious denominations are conducting educational movements among the freedmen on a large scale. There are scattered through the Southern States, under the patronage of different denominations, thirty-nine chartered and endowed institutions for the higher education of colored people as teachers, ministers, physicians, farmers, and mechanics. Besides these, there are sixty-nine schools of a lower grade. It is calculated that in the last sixteen years twenty million dollars has been contributed and invested in the work of educating the freedmen.

5. Leading and influential men at the South are in many cases openly patrons of these educational efforts. Several of these institutions have been generously assisted by the States in which

they are founded. The last reports of all these institutions represent them as in a successful and flourishing condition.

6. The colored race is advancing in material wealth and prosperity.

The bounds of an article are too limited for the abundance of proof that might be cited under these heads.

We shall do our best to select from this abundance, and in the first place we shall consider what is being done for the education of the colored race by the common-school system.

In 1867 Congress created a National Bureau of Education in Washington, to collect statistics upon education and diffuse such information as shall aid the citizens of the United States in the establishment and maintenance of efficient school systems.

The first report of the Commissioner, in 1870, contains this passage (p. 13):

> The information contained in the accompanying papers, in regard to education in the States where emancipation has lately taken effect, contains features in marked distinction from those where freedom has been longer universal. It is gratifying that slavery exists nowhere any longer in the land, to close the door effectually against universal education. It is gratifying to observe the avidity with which those lately slaves have sought the primer and the means of higher instruction. It is gratifying to know that the large-hearted Peabody and many benevolent associations have done so much to facilitate and encourage education among all classes int eh South. It is gratifying to reflect that the Government, through the Freedman's Bureau, has accomplished results so vast in this direction, being able to show that in July last, in *day- and night-schools, regularly and irregularly reported, 149-581 pupils had been in attendance.* It is gratifying to know that under the restoration policy of Congress the reorganized Sate governments have adopted Constitutions making obligatory the establishment and conduct of free public schools for all the children of school age, and that laws have been enacted and the

Appendix II – The Education of Freedmen

work of education so generally commenced under them, organizing superintendence, employing teachers, and building schoolhouses, introducing here and there the germs of systems which have been tried elsewhere and proved most successful.

The report then goes on to mention each Southern State in detail, from which it appears that a movement for common schools had been set on foot in every one of the Southern States, but was meeting with active and powerful resistance. It was a new movement; the States were all poor, embarrassed by the results of the war, and little disposed to submit to any tax for that purpose, and, as usual, those were most opposed who most needed education. The report of 1871 shows the same conflict. It reports an earnest desire on the part of the colored people for education, and in many sections a blind prejudice against any efforts to give it to them. The work of building schoolhouses for the colored people and of supporting teachers was divided between the Freedman's Bureau and the various religious bodies whose missionaries were in the field.

Thus we see that the difficulty of securing common-school provision for the colored population was only part and parcel of the objection to the common-school system itself in the Southern States. The men who have gallantly fought that battle for the whites were the wisest, the most enlightened in their several States, and were fully sensible of the need of education for the colored race; but they had first to conquer the prejudices of an unenlightened community against *any* system of common-school instruction. In February, 1878, a Southern Educational Convention was held in Atlanta, Georgia, with a view to memorializing Congress for aid in popular education. Over a hundred delegates from the eight following States were present, viz., Virginia, South Carolina, Georgia, Florida, Alabama, Louisiana, Tennessee, and Missouri.

A noticeable paragraph in the memorial is the following:

Resolved, That as the educational laws of the several States represented by us make no discriminations in favor of or against the children of any class of citizens, and as those charged with the administration of these laws have endeavored, in the past, to have them carried into effect impartially, so do we pledge ourselves to use our influence to secure even-handed justice to all classes of citizens in the application of any educational funds provided by the national Government.

In another part of their memorial they say:

> In the altered condition of society, brought about by the late war, every man is a voter; and the safety of republican institutions depends upon extending to the masses the benefits of education.

On the ground of the large addition of population to be taught in the persons of the freedmen, and of the losses by depreciation of property consequent on the war, they ask for a larger governmental aid than would be given to the settled Northern States.

What is to be noticed in this appeal is, that it fully assumes on the part of these States the duty of giving equal school privileges to all children of the State, without regard to color or condition. In short, in regard to this branch of the subject, our conviction, based on an examination of the yearly reports submitted to the National Bureau, is that, in the main, the leaders of State education at the South have been well disposed to the colored race; that in theory they regard them entitled to an equal share in State education, and have extended it to them in practice so far as the means have been in their power.

We come now to consider what has been done for the freedmen by the Christian Church in America.

Very early in the war it was decided to receive and protect fugitive slaves, and our armies became cities of refuge for them. "Their advance," says a writer, "was a signal for a rally of slaves from all the country round; they flocked in upon the line of march by bridle-paths and across fields—old men on crutches, babies on their mothers' backs, women wearing cast-off blue jackets of Yankee

Appendix II – The Education of Freedmen

cavalry-men, boys in abbreviated trousers of rebel tray—sometimes lugging a bundle of household goods, sometimes riding an old mule borrowed from 'massa,' but oftener empty-handed, with nothing whatever to show for a lifetime of unrewarded toil. But they were free! And with what swinging of ragged hats, and tumult of rejoicing hearts, and fervent 'God bless you!' they greeted their deliverers!" The year of jubilee, for which they had prayed and waited so many years, was come!

In time, four million of these bondmen were made free by the war power. The same writer from whom we have quoted[235] thus sketches their condition: "They were homeless, penniless, ignorant, improvident; unprepared in every way for the dangers and duties of freedom. Self-reliance they never had had the opportunity to learn, and, suddenly left to shift for themselves, they were at the mercy of knaves ready to cheat them out of their honest earnings. They had been kept all their lives in a school of immorality, so that even church-membership was no evidence that one was not a thief, a liar, or a libertine."

Their former masters were so impoverished by their emancipation and other losses of the war that they had little ability—and were so exasperated that they had less disposition—to help them.

But poor, ignorant, and simple as this emancipated mass were, they differed in one respect from the masses liberated by the French Revolution, and from all other suddenly liberated masses of which we have read in history. Their enthusiasm and impulse was not for plunder or for revenge, or for drink, or any form of animal indulgence, but for *education*. They rushed not to the grogshop but to the schoolroom—they cried for the spelling-book as for bread, and pleaded for teachers as a necessary of life. This enthusiasm to learn on the part of the liberated slaves was met by an equal enthusiasm to

---

[235] Frederick J. Loudin (c. 1836-1904), also quoted in Pike, Godfrey Holden. *From Slave to College President: Being the Life Story of Booker t. Washington.* London, T. Fisher Unwin, 1902.

teach on the part of Northern Christians. Every religious denomination sent its teachers—Unitarians and Orthodox were here of one heart and mind, and their teachers followed the course of the armies, and penetrated wherever they could find protection. Long before the war closed, there were teachers and schools in our camps and in all the region where our armies protected the settlements of fugitive slaves.

The nation took these people as her wards, and appointed a Freedman's Bureau to superintend their affairs—to regulate their wages and work, and to provide for them schoolrooms, schools, and teachers.

We have before us, through the kindness of General Howard, a volume of the reports of this Bureau from January, 1866, to July 1, 1870.

The first report says: "The desire of the freedmen for knowledge has not been overstated. Their freedom has given a wonderful stimulus to all effort, indicating a vitality that augurs well for their future."

The report goes on to say that "all classes, even those advanced in life, are beginning the alphabet—coming to evening and Sabbath schools, and may be seen along railroads, or off duty, as servants on steamboats, or in hotels, earnestly studying their spelling-books. Regiments of colored soldiers are all improving and learning—and the officers deserve great respect for their efforts for the education of their men. The 128th US Colored Troops, at Beaufort, were found gathered into school in a neat camp schoolhouse, erected by the regiment, and taught by regularly detailed teachers from the line officers—the colonel commanding superintending the arrangements with deep interest." The report goes through each Southern State in detail, giving an account in each of the general educational revival. One passage is specially noticeable:

"Through the entire South efforts are being made by the colored people to *educate themselves.*' In the absence of teachers, they are determined to be self-taught, and everywhere some elementary book, or fragments of it, may be seen in the nads of negroes. They

Appendix II – The Education of Freedmen

communicate to each other that which they learn, and with very little learning many take to teaching. Not only are individuals seen at study under the most untoward circumstances, but in many places I have found native schools, often rude and imperfect, but *there they are,* a group of all ages *trying to learn.* Some young man or woman, some old preacher, in cellar, shed, or corner of negro meeting-house, with spelling-book in hand, is their teacher.... Again," says the reporter, "I saw schools of higher order at Goldsboro, North Carolina; two young colored men, who but a little time before had begun to learn themselves, had gathered one hundred and fifty pupils, all quite orderly and hard at study." The report also speaks of schools taught by colored men at Charleston, Savannah, and New Orleans. One in the latter city, he says, would bear comparison with any Northern school; he says that in this school very creditable specimens of writing were shown, and all the older classes could recite or read fluently both in French and English. This was a free school wholly supported by colored people. He says that he gave special pains to ascertaining facts upon this subject, and reports that schools of this kind exist in all the large places, and were making their appearance through the entire Southern country. The Superintendent of Schools in South Carolina assured him that there was no place of any size where such a school was not attempted by the colored people. He remarks, in conclusion: "This is a wonderful state of things. We have just emerged from a terrific war—peace is not yet declared, there is scarcely a beginning of reorganized society at the South—yet here is a people long imbruted by slavery and the most despised of any on earth, whose chains aren o sooner broken than they spring to their feet, an exceeding great army, clothing themselves with intelligence. What other people have shown such a passion for education?"

It must be borne in mind that this is a report in 1866—in the very incipiency of the enterprise. These semi-annual reports to the Freedman's Bureau contain a most wonderful and interesting history of their progress toward education and competence.

In the last report of the Freedman's Bureau, which closed in 1870, they speak of 247,000 children under systematic instruction, with 9,307 teachers and 4,239 schools. They also record in the Freedman's Savings Bank, the total deposits of freedmen, from 1866 to 1870, as $16,960,336.62.

APPENDIX III
Review of *Up from Slavery,* by "Th Bentzon"

The following is a review of Up from Slavery *by Th. Bentzon, the pseudonym of the French journalist, writer, and translator Marie-Thérèse de Solms Blanc (1840-1907). This is an annotated translation of the Portuguese version serialised in the* Diário da Bahia *newspaper in 1902, assisted by a comparison with the original French text and Booker T. Washington's autobiography (in English). Bentzon's review first appeared in a French publication, the* Revue des Deux-Mondes, *in October 1901 (Bentzon 1901; Cook 1955). As the first full translation of Booker T. Washington's best-known memoir was only published in Brazil in 1940, this may have been the first time Manuel Querino and his contemporaries had access to extracts from the book in question.*[236] *Like Graciliano Ramos's version (Washington 1940), this was a "free translation" by Bentzon, and her interpretation and comments revealed her own prejudices.*

---

[236] Unless otherwise noted, footnotes regarding "the translation" are referring to the Portuguese translation from the French original. *Up from Slavery* was first translated into French as *L'autobiographie d'un Negre* in 1903 by Othon Guerlac. As we know that Querino studied and used French in his works, he could have read that edition. Washington's autobiography had also been available in Spanish since 1902 as *De esclavo a catedrático*, translated by Alfredo Elías y Pujol.

Diário da Bahia—Saturday, March 22, 1902, p. 2

"Dear Editor of the *Diário da Bahia*—Based on the report, possibly a transcription, published in this newspaper, entitled "The Black Man with the White Face,"[237] it can be inferred that Booker Washington has only received hostility from the Whites in the northern United States.

That is not precisely true: nor was his only honour from the Presidency of the Republic that of Mr. Roosevelt seating him at his table, which, as a matter of fact, did not scandalize all White Americans, but a number of them, albeit never the majority.

With this in mind and on account of your news of Augustin Leger's[238] critique of Booker Washington's autobiography, I have decided to submit some pages by Th. Bentzon, also reviewing the same work of this illustrious Black man, whose biography is a focus of brilliant examples for the edification of all races.

I will be pleased to see this work published, given the significant interest and utility of the story of this superior Black man."

§§§§§§§§§§§§§§§§§§§§§§§§§§§§§§§§§§§§§

In the Autumn of 1872, a Black man, still young, shabbily dressed, covered in dust, with a bundle on his back, timidly and furtively entered Richmond, the capital of Virginia, the first big city in which he had set foot.

Nowhere are Blacks more numerous than in Richmond, where they make up about half the population. The newcomer was therefore not exposed, as had happened at other points along the way, to being rejected on account of his colour; but if there was more

---

[237] See Appendix IV.
[238] Augustin Léger was the author of *La jeunesse de Wesley*, Paris: Librairie Hachette & Cie, 1910, amd *Journal d'um anarchiste*, 2nd ed. Paris: A. Savine, 1895, among other works. See Cook 1955.

than one inn there for his race, he was not only short of money but he did not know where such inns could be found.

The only thing to do was to wander those streets all night. Despite the late hour, food was still being sold: on the tables, cold meats and pastries that Washington—for that is the name of the traveller who, not having a family name, had boldly taken that one, devoured with his eyes. Hungry, exhausted and ragged, his appearance must have been less than reassuring, and he himself felt uneasy.

Where could he find shelter, where could he sleep? It was past midnight when he noticed a spot where the wooden walkway that bordered the street was much higher than the street level.

He cast a scrutinizing look around, made sure he was completely alone, and found and unexpected refuge, lying down full length, with his traveling bag as a pillow.

This adventure has been compared to that of [Benjamin] Franklin wandering the streets of Philadelphia with nothing but a loaf of bread: parallels have been drawn between the two careers; and the autobiography of Booker Washington has a greater influence on minds today than *Poor Richard's Almanac* had in colonial times. Its first pages are written with almost biblical simplicity: they reveal the first steps of the future educator of a race fast asleep beneath the feet of late passers-by who make the wooden walkway ring in his ears.

Here they are:[239]

I was born a slave on a plantation in Franklin County, Virginia: I am not quite sure of the exact place or exact date of my birth, but at any rate I suspect I must have been born somewhere and at some time. As nearly as I have been able to learn, I was born... [in] 1858 or 1859.[240] *The earliest impressions I can now recall are of the plantation and the slave quarters....*

My life had its beginnings in the midst of the most miserable, desolate, and discouraging surroundings. This was so, however, not

---

[239] Extracts from the original English edition of *Up from Slavery* (Washington 1986) have been adapted to the Portuguese translation of Bentzon's review.
[240] According to the Burroughs family Bible, Booker was born in 1856.

because my owners were specially cruel, for they were not, as compared with many others. I was born in a typical log cabin, about fourteen by sixteen feet square. In this cabin, I lived with my mother and a brother and sister till after the Civil War, when we were all declared free.

Of my ancestry I know almost nothing.... My mother, I suppose, attracted the attention of a purchaser who was afterwards my owner and hers. Her addition to the slave family attracted about as much attention as the purchase of a new horse or cow. Of my father I know even less than of my mother.... I have heard reports to the effect that he was a white man....

Whoever he was, I never heard of his taking the least interest in me...But I do not find especial fault with him. He was simply another unfortunate victim of a disastrous institution....[241]

The cabin had no glass windows; it only had openings in the side which let in the light, and also the cold, chilly air of winter. There was a door to the cabin—that is, something that was called a door—but the uncertain hinges by which it was hung....made the room a very uncomfortable one....

There was no wooden floor in our cabin, the naked earth being used as a floor. In the centre of the earthen floor there was a large, deep opening covered with boards, which was used as a place in which to store sweet potatoes.... While the poorly built cabin caused us to suffer with cold int eh winter, the heat from the open fireplace in summer was equally trying [our house was the plantation kitchen]....[242]

[Occupied by her task as a cook] my mother...had little time in which to give attention to the training of her children [except in the early morning and at night]. One of my earliest recollections is that of my mother cooking a chicken late at night, and awakening her children for the purpose of feeding them. How or where she got it I do

---

[241] The original reads: "He was simply another unfortunate victim of the institution which the Nation unhappily had engrafted upon it at that time" (Washington 1986, 3).

[242] Bentzon added the words in brackets.

not know. I presume, however, it was procured from our owner's farm. Some people may call this theft, If such a thing were to happen now, I should condemn it as theft myself. But taking place at the time it did, and for the reason that it did, no one could ever make me believe that my mother was guilty of thieving. She was simply a victim of the system of slavery [as well...that is all...]

I cannot remember having slept in a bed until after our family was declared free.... [Until then, we] slept in and on a bundle of filthy rags laid upon the dirt floor.

...there was no period of my life that was devoted to play.... [As a small child] I was occupied most of the time cleaning the yards, carrying water to the men in the fields, or going to the mill. [This work I always dreaded. The mill was about three miles from the plantation]: The heavy bag of corn would be thrown across the back of the horse, and the corn divided about evenly on each side; but in some way, almost without exception, on these trips, the corn would so shift as to become unbalanced and would fall of the horse, and often I would fall with it. As I was not strong enough to reload the corn...I would have to wait...till a chance passer-by came along who would help me out of my trouble. The hours while waiting for someone were usually spent in crying.... [By the time I got my corn ground and reached home it would be far into the night]. The road was a lonely one, and often led through dense forests. I was always frightened. The woods were said to be full of soldiers who had deserted from the army, and I had been told that the first thing a deserter did to a Negro boy when he found him alone was to cut off his ears. Besides, when I was late in getting home I knew I would always get a severe scolding or a flogging.[243]

I had no schooling whatever while I was a slave, though I remember on several occasions I went as far as the schoolhouse door with one of my young mistresses to carry her books. The picture of several dozen boys and girls in a schoolroom engaged in study made a

---

[243] Here, Bentzon gives the impression that it was his mother who would punish him for being late and making her worry, thereby softening the harsh reality of enslavement.

deep impression on me, and I had the feeling that to get into a schoolhouse and study in this way would be about the same as getting into paradise...."

(Continues)

Sunday, March 23, 1902

The time would come when Booker Washington would open up the paradise of learning to his peers—teaching them the ways of civilized life which he himself had not known.

In his day, Black children did not sit at the table—they snatched food like irrational creatures, a bit here, another there; some ate from a trough, almost always by hand. He took up that habit, but he never got used to the hideous flax shirt that was the common garment for enslaved people in Virginia. Made with the refuse of the plant, the fabric was an instrument of torture until softened by frequent washing. Washington reckons that one the greatest tokens of affection he received from John, his elder brother, was that he wore new shirts first to break them down. During his childhood, he had no other clothing than this one, which tore his skin like a hair shirt.

He was going through that childhood ordeal when the first rumours of war reached him.

He had a vague idea that he was a slave, and his freedom was in dispute: he understood it one morning, when at daybreak, he woke up hearing his mother's prayer, kneeling over her children, for the success of Lincoln's Afterwards he heard many whispered discussions about it. without the aid of newspapers or books, Southern Blacks were surprisingly informed. They knew that, despite the other reasons which were intentionally given, the cause of the war was their freedom. On this remote plantation, far from the railroad and the towns, word came of every Federal victory and every disaster for the Confederate armies. Sometimes the Blacks had heard of it before the Whites, because, once or twice a week, one of them would go to the post office, and listen discreetly to the comments of the Whites about the latest news. On the way back, he would spread the word before delivering the mail to the "big house." It was called the grape-vine telegraph, comparing information transmitted by word of mouth to the vine that passes from tree to tree. Little Booker—just Booker then—was one of the tendrils of the vine. In the masters' house, moving large paper fans with a pulley to chase away the flies, he paid attention to their conversations.

White people did not live a happy life. *"I think the slaves felt the deprivation less than the whites, because the usual diet for the slaves was corn bread and pork, and these could be raised on the plantation; but coffee, tea, sugar, and other articles which the Whites had been accustomed to use could not be raised on the plantation, and the conditions brought about by the war frequently made it impossible to secure these things. The whites were often in great straits. Parched corn...and a kind of black molasses was used instead of...coffee [sic]."*[244]

They suffered in various ways, and their slaves pitied them instead of hating them.

Later, many Blacks devoted themselves voluntarily to masters who had fallen into poverty. Booker Washington sincerely underscores the mixture of strong devotion to the masters with fervent aspirations for freedom. This feeling was expressed in religious songs to which events gave new meaning: it was no longer a question of being free in heaven, but on earth.

Knowing that the soldiers of the North were fighting for that freedom, the slaves protected from them, with the zeal of loyal dogs, the women and children entrusted to their devotion during their masters' absence.

It would be necessary to go over the slaves' dead bodies before touching the lady, the mistress, who they watched over in the "big house" from which the men were absent, gone far away, perhaps to fight against emancipation. They would give shelter and food to the

---

[244] The original reads: "Parched corn was used for coffee, and a kind of black molasses was used instead of sugar" (1986, 10).

Yankee soldiers, in order to sack the country, but they would never reveal the secret hiding place of the silverware, the jewels, the family's precious objects.

If the master died, did they mourn him; did they bring him back wounded? They treated him tenderly with the same Black hands that might well have served him since childhood. There was not, however, a Black man who mourned slavery or wanted to go back to it. When the hour of emancipation sounded, foreseen by all, because freedom had been in the air for months, the joy was indescribable. Washington tells how things went on the plantation where he lived:

"Early the next morning word was sent to all the slaves, old and young, to gather at the house. In company with the younger ones, I went to the master's house.[245]All of our master's family were either standing or seated on the veranda of the house, where they could see what was to take place and hear what was said. There was a feeling of deep interest, or perhaps sadness, on their faces, but not bitterness. As I now recall the impression they made upon me, they did not at the moment seem to be sad because of the loss of property, but rather because of parting with those whom they had reared and who were in many ways very close to them.

The most distinct thing that I now recall in connection with the scene was that some man who seemed to be a stranger (a United States officer, I presume) made a little speech and then read a rather long paper—the Emancipation Proclamation, I think. After the reading we were told that we were all free, and could go when and where we pleased. My mother...kissed her children, while tears of joy ran down her cheeks....

For some minutes there was great rejoicing...and wild scenes of ecstasy....[246] [but] I noticed that by the time they returned to their

---

[245] Here, *Up from Slavery* reads "In company with my mother, brother, and sister, and a large number of other slaves, I went to the master's house" (1986, 20).

[246] The translation uses the Portuguese word "*selvagens*" for "wild," from the original French word chosen by Bentzon, "*sauvage*," which can also be interpreted as "savage." Othon Guerlac translated "wild scenes of ecstasy" as "*transports*

Appendix III – Review of *Up from Slavery*

cabins there was a change in their feelings. The great responsibility of being free, of having charge of themselves, of having to think and plan for themselves...seemed to take possession of them.

It was very much like suddenly turning a youth of ten or twelve years out into the world to provide for himself. These were the questions of a home, a living, the rearing of children, education, the establishment and support of churches and becoming citizens In a few hours, they had to confront all the great questions that civilization has struggling to resolve for centuries.[247]

Was it any wonder that within a few hours...a feeling of deep gloom seemed to pervade the slave quarters?... There were elderly people who were thenceforth incapable of making a living....[248] *Gradually, one by one, stealthily at first, the older slaves began to wander from the slave quarters to the 'big house' to have a whispered conversation with their former owners as to the future."*

(Continued)

---

frénétiques d'enthusiasm" (1901, 20). The French translation by Florence Carré published in 2021 translates "wild" as *"éclaterant"* (2021, 12).

[247] *It was very much like suddenly turning a youth of ten or twelve years out into the world to provide for himself. In a few hours the great questions with which the Anglo-Saxon race had been grappling for centuries had been thrown upon these people to be solved. These were the questions of a home, a living, the rearing of children, education, citizenship, and the establishment and support of churches.* Bentzon inverts the order of the last two items to read "the establishment and support of churches and citizenship." This is followed by a rendering of the line within brackets, where "civilization" is used instead of "the Anglo-Saxon race."

[248] The original reads "Some of the slaves were seventy or eighty years old; their best days were gone" (1986, 22).

Tuesday, March 25, 1902

Later on, Booker Washington would address the problem of slavery in this broader, more precise fashion:[249] *"[There is no reason to censure Southern white people.] No one section of the country was wholly responsible for its introduction, and, besides, it was recognized and protected for years by the General Government.*

Having got its tentacles fastened on to the economic and social life of the Republic, it was no easy matter for the country to relieve itself of the institution. Then, when we rid ourselves of prejudice, or racial feeling, and look facts in the face, we must acknowledge that, notwithstanding the cruelty and moral wrong of slavery, the ten million Negroes inhabiting his country, who themselves or whose ancestors went through the school of American slavery, are in a stronger and more hopeful condition, materially, intellectually, morally, and religiously, than is true of an equal number of Black people in any other portion of the globe.

This is so to such an extent that Negroes in this country, who themselves or whose forefathers went through the school of slavery, are constantly returning to Africa as missionaries to enlighten those who remained in the fatherland.

This I say, not to justify slavery—on the other hand, I condemn it as an institution, as we all know that in America it was established for selfish and financial reasons...– but to call attention to a fact, and to show how Providence so often uses men and institutions to accomplish a purpose

When persons ask me in these days how, in the midst of what sometimes seem hopelessly discouraging conditions, I can have such faith in the future of my race in this country, I remind them of the

---

[249] This extract comes from the same chapter, prior to Washington's description of his fellow captives' response to emancipation. The original text of the words between brackets reads "I have long since ceased to cherish any spirit of bitterness against the Southern white people on account of the enslavement of my race" (1986, 16).

Appendix III – Review of *Up from Slavery*

wilderness through which and out of which, a good Providence has already led us.

Ever since I have been old enough to think for myself, [I have always told myself that the Black man got the same amount of good and evil from slavery that the White man did.][250]

While still a young man, Booker Washington carried the burdens of recently acquired freedom. To support the family with the addition of a stepfather, he had to toil alongside his brother in the salt factories of Kanawha and the coal mines of Malden. It was in one of those mines that he first heard of a great school established by General Armstrong for people of colour. It was not just a school, said the miners, but poor students could work to pay at least part of their tuition. Moving closer, the young man heard the name of the Hampton Normal and Agricultural Institute in Virginia.

He immediately resolved to go to Hampton, although he had no idea of how far it was or how he would get there. He was obsessed with an idea: he would save up some money to make his wish come true. He earned very little in the mines, but a position opened at the home of General Lewis Ruffner, the mine owner. There was no competition for the job, because Mrs. Ruffner, a Yankee from Vermont, was notoriously strict. It was with trepidation that Washington applied for the job, and was hired for five dollars per month.

It was very little for a house where not a single bit of dust was tolerated on the furniture, nor were lies permitted: intelligent and dedicated, Washington soon understood that his employer's example was worth more than the money they paid her: in her company he acquired the habit of doing things quickly and methodically, and to assess the sense of justice, even in a very strict environment.

---

[250] Here, the original reads "I have entertained the idea that, notwithstanding the cruel wrongs inflicted upon us, the black man got nearly as much out of slavery as the white man did" (1986, 17).

Mrs. Ruffner soon saw that "she could rely on the young Negro." She gave him her absolute trust, and far from criticizing his desire for an education, she encouraged it.

In Winter he was able to attend school for an hour per day, a wretched school for Blacks that had recently opened, and the first time they asked his name, he spontaneously replied, as if with a secret premonition—BOOKER WASHINGTON.[251] At night, he worked alone, absorbed in *his library,* which was an old box fitted with shelves, which he filled with all the printed matter that fell into his hands.

Having prepared in his own way for the great expedition, he got up the courage to speak to his mother.

Although she did not object, she wondered if it wasn't a wild goose chase...

John, his older brother, gave him whatever he could find, but it was the older members of the Black Community of Malden who showed the most sentimental sympathy: they were overcome by the idea that one of their children would go on to higher learning. They all wanted to help in some way: one with some coins, some with a handkerchief, another with an object, they all pitched in to help the traveller.

Despite their help, the satchel that contained Booker Washington's belongings was light.

At the time, the railway did not connect the eastern side [of the state] with West Virginia, where Malden is located: it only went part of the way, [which was] five hundred miles from Malden to Hampton.

The future student's paltry savings did not cover his travel expenses. From time to time, Booker had to look for work, garnering more humiliations than profits.

---

[251] Here, Bentzon changes the order of events. According to Washington, he was still working in the salt-furnace when he announced his surname in school (1986, 34).

After a day's journey on the roof of a bad carriage,[252] he was refused entry at an inn along the way because he was Black: they slammed the door in his face.

The nights are cold in that mountainous region, and so as not to freeze, he walked about until dawn.

There were so many plans accumulated in that soul that there was no place for grudges or resentments. Walking, working, always begging, Booker Washington reached Richmond and took shelter under the sidewalk where we first saw him.

He managed to sleep enough to restore his strength, but the next day he was overcome by hunger. He went to the docks and saw a ship loaded with iron, helped unload it, and got something to eat. His work pleased the captain, who gave him a job for a few days, but to save money he continued to lodge, like a mouse, under the hospitable sidewalk that had been his first friend in Richmond.

After many years, Booker Washington, by then the principal of a celebrated Institute and a notable orator received an enthusiastic reception in that same city; amid the honors he received, his thoughts turned to that famous sidewalk...

However, we are still far from his days of triumph.

So he arrived in Hampton with fifty cents in his pocket, all that he needed to get an education.

(Continued)

Thursday, March 27, 1902

II

The presence of a large, three-story school rewarded the work and efforts required for him to get there. He felt an impulse to kneel: Hampton was the promised land, he was beginning a new life. However, his initial reception was very cold. They did not refuse to

---

[252] Washington merely writes that he travelled across the mountains in a stagecoach (1986, 47).

admit a scruffy-looking Black man, but they let him spend long hours of uncertainty. Finally, one of the head teachers, Miss Mary Mackie, appeared and said, "The recreation room needs cleaning. Take the broom."[253]

He gave heartfelt thanks to the first employer who had trained him in domestic work: he polished the benches so brightly, the tables and decorations were so clean, that after inspecting everything, the arbiter of his fate quietly remarked "I guess you will do to enter this institution."

He was hired as a porter,[254] extremely happy to have reached the first means of paying his tuition. The experience of cleaning was like an entrance examination and gave him more satisfaction than receiving a Harvard diploma.[255] With his characteristic spirit, Booker Washington repeated: *"I have taken [sic] several examinations since then, but I have always felt that this was the best one I ever passed."*[256]

The post of porter [sic] at Hampton was no sinecure. At four a.m., he had to build the fires, and during the day, he cleaned and tidied a large number of rooms. Washington often studied at night, and this kind of courage was not exceptional: about four hundred individuals of both sexes took their desire to learn to the level of heroism. It is notable that none of them entertained thoughts of personal success: they were concerned with their world, which they had a duty to

---

[253] According to Washington, Mackie was the head teacher at Hampton, and she asked him to sweep the "recitation-room" (1986, 52). The error comes from the French translation, *"salle de récréation"* (Bentzon 1901, 766).

[254] Booker T. Washington initially worked at the Hampton Institute as a janitor (1986, 53). Bentzon described his position as a *"portier"* (doorman) in French (1901, 767), which was translated into Portuguese as *porteiro* (porter, doorman, or concierge).

[255] The English original reads: "I was one of the happiest souls on earth. The sweeping of that room was my college examination, and never did any youth pass an examination for entrance into Harvard or Yale that gave him more genuine satisfaction" (1986, 53).

[256] The original reads "I have passed several examinations since then, but I have always felt that this was the best one I ever passed" (1986, 53).

Appendix III – Review of *Up from Slavery*

educate at the right time. Some were nearly forty, and most were at an age when they no longer benefited greatly from lessons in books, but, as Washington repeats, book learning at Hampton was just a small part of their education.

The teachers' example instilled this great truth in the students: the happiest are those who practice the greatest sum of good.

Through attention and dedication, those less gifted with intelligence managed to get some basic instruction, but the most important thing was to learn to live.

General Armstrong had his axioms:—what is commonly called sacrifice is nothing but the best use the individual makes of himself and his resources, the most useful employment of time, strength and money—he who does not sacrifice himself is worthy of pity: he is a pagan, he knows nothing of God. The essential thing in a school is to avoid disputes, maintain close union, get rid of vagabond spirits, whatever their degree of culture—Prayer is the strongest power on earth: it keeps us close to God - first of all God and Country, and then ourselves. –

The general subjected the students to a daily military review, not overlooking the lack of a button or poorly shined shoes.[257]

The obligation to have a good appearance would be an insoluble problem if those interested in Hampton's work did not at least take good care of their clothing.

Daily bathing was mandatory, and this rule[258] was the starting point for a different kind of progress.

Booker Washington wittily celebrated the toothbrush for its moralizing virtue.

---

[257] The original reads: "My anxiety about clothing was increased because of the fact that general Armstrong made a personal inspection of the young men in ranks, to see that their clothes were clean. Shoes had to be polished, there must be no buttons off the clothing, and no grease-spots" (Washington 1986, 60).

[258] The original French reads "*cette extrême propreté*" ("this extreme cleanliness") (Benzton 1901, 769).

When he arrived at the Institute, lacking everything, he was a thousand leagues away from knowing how to use it, and he had never slept on sheets or even knew how to do it, had he not had seven roommates whom he imitated. Surprising revelations came one after another: he learned how to use a tablecloth, a napkin and other objects that he had never known before.

No one expresses better than he the correlation between external care for the body and self-respect. His extreme poverty often made his effort to achieve a good appearance meritorious. The ten dollars monthly board was paid for through his manual labour, and John, his older brother, sent what little he could to help him with the tuition, which was seventy dollars.

However, Booker would never have managed to earn a small part of that amount if General Armstrong had not got him a benefactor, a wealthy citizen of New Bedford, Mr. [Griffiths] Morgan,[259] whose frequent generosity has been so useful to Americans.

Washington devotes a kind of worship to General Armstrong and says somewhere: "The more I appreciate him, the better I am convinced that the whole apparatus of teaching for the success of education does not compare with the effect of everyday relations with good men.... Classes, workshops and teachers could be removed from Hampton, and our education would take place simply through [that] contact."[260]

Aware of the degrading influences he experienced during his childhood and part of his youth, Washington considered General

---

[259] "General Armstrong...very kindly got Mr. S. Griffitts [sic] Morgan of New Bedford, Mass., to defray the cost of my tuition during the whole time that I was at Hampton. After I finished the course at Hampton and had entered upon my lifework at Tuskegee, I had the pleasure of visiting Mr. Morgan several times" (Washington 1986, 59).

[260] *Up from Slavery* reads: "...the more I saw of him the greater he grew in my estimation. One might have removed from Hampton all the buildings, class-rooms, teachers, and industries, and given the men and women there the opportunity of coming into daily contact with General Armstrong, and that alone would have been a liberal education" (1986, 55).

Armstrong just, heroic, superhuman. It is difficult to assess the prestige that this good man exercised over Black students, the blind faith he inspired in them. None believed him capable of failing in any undertaking, and with effortless obedience they fulfilled his slightest wishes.[261] A case in point: when Booker Washington was a student there was no room for new beds, so many applicants were not accepted. The general decides to put up tents, and word spreads that he wants the most robust to stay there as they are more resistant to the cold. The winter was harsh, the wind ripped the poles from the tents and nobody complained. On his morning visit, the general would ask in cheerful tones, How many men woke up frozen? Two hands went up and the owners of those hands laughed.[262]

The helpers were well chosen. One of the most beautiful chapters in the history of the United States is the narrative of the part which teachers from the North played in raising up the Negro.

It was in contrast with the work of politicians who promised much in their own electoral interest and gave little, nourishing with illusions an ignorant people who asked for daily bread for the body and soul.

(Continued)

Friday, March 28, 1902

II (cont.)

Men and women comparable to the great missionaries responded to the appeal for the regeneration of the freedman, because there is

---

[261] *Up from Slavery* reads "It never occurred to me that general Armstrong could fail in anything that he undertook. There is almost no request that he could have made that would not have been complied with" (Washington 1986, 56).

[262] This version of that episode is not included in *Up from Slavery*. Washington writes: "The General would usually pay a visit to the tents early in the morning, and his earnest, cheerful, encouraging voice would dispel any feeling of despondency" (Washington 1986, 57).

more than one kind of apostolate and martyrdom. Washington painted an admirable picture of this compact body of apostles who, inspired by Jesus Christ, participated in a work of redemption, teaching [people] by the hundreds in schools for Blacks founded as if by magic.

At the head of the teachers at Hampton, Washington places the excellent Miss Mackie, his first protector, who, belonging to an old and distinguished Northern family, did not hesitate to throw herself into the school's heaviest tasks, setting the best examples to the students. Despite her delicacy of culture, this Protestant and emancipating sister of charity, washed, swept, and shook things alongside the students, thus convincing them of the dignity of work. Washington owed another teacher his understanding of the sense, beauty and poetic grandeur of Holy Scripture: it was Miss Lord herself who, giving elocution lessons, prepared him for the public role that awaited him. Every Saturday there was an eloquence session at Hampton. Washington was never absent, and, gathering some companions together, he took advantage of a daily twenty-minute break, an excellent prelude to the oratorical talent that lies dormant in every American of any colour.

It was only at the end of the second year, thanks to money from John, that he was able to go to Malden.

The account of the meeting of these brothers who loved each other so much is touching, although one continued to work in the darkness of the mines, while the other competed for university degrees. Washington found his mother on her death bed and lost her shortly afterwards without fulfilling the promise he had made to ensure her a few years of comfort.

He speaks of her death, which happened in painful circumstances, with deep sensitivity. His intellectual superiority over his own [family] did not distance him from any of them.

He visited all the old neighbours, told them in detail about Hampton's hardships, and undertook to speak in church, at Sunday school, and elsewhere. However, his search for work was fruitless—the miners were on strike.

Appendix III – Review of *Up from Slavery*

This accident, he says, regularly occurred as soon as the miners had saved up enough to go on strike for two or three months, so that after the strike they returned to the same wages with a burden of debt on their backs.

Booker Washington is the avowed enemy of strikes and the professional agitators who instigate them.

That year, he was their victim. Without his former employer Mrs. Ruffner, who rehired him, destitution would have reigned in the impoverished home where his mother had just died.

Back at Hampton, he returned to his modest role as a porter [sic], but this did not prevent him from being included in the honour roll of Commencement[263] speakers and finish his course. He views this modestly because, as he repeats: *"The greatest benefits that I got out of my life at the Hampton Institute was: First was contact with...General Armstrong...; Second...I learned what education was expected to do for an individual.... It is not, as many believe, exchanging hard toil for more comfortable and elevated occupations, manual labor for material value, but loving it for the independence and confidence it produces. I finally learned the meaning of a life freed of selfishness."*[264]

He takes pleasure in describing his life:[265] at first, he had to work at a hotel in Connecticut, where his ineptitude brought him many insults and ridicule, but he prevailed by improving himself, and later had the satisfaction of being received as an important and sought-after guest in the same room where he had made such a mediocre debut.

---

[263] Graduation ceremony.

[264] This is a succinct rendering of the original text, in which Washington describes General Armstrong as "the rarest, strongest, and most beautiful character that it has ever been my privilege to meet" (1986, 73).

[265] The original French reads: "Ses degrés, il se plaît a dire, lui furent d'abord fort inutiles...." (His degrees, he likes to say, were at first quite useless to him) (Bentzon 1901, 772).

Washington was appointed schoolmaster in Malden: it was a great joy to help educate, in the fullest sense of the term, the people of his home [town]. The schoolhouse was small: he did not limit himself to the routine of the classes, he attended to the smallest details, taught the children to bathe and dress, preaching his gospel of bathing and the toothbrush, which he called propaganda of high civilization.[266]

He opened a night school for adults who worked in the mines, and it was full. Tireless, he found a way to create a reading room [and] a debating society.

On Sundays he taught two Sunday school classes, one in the afternoon at Malden, and another in the morning three miles away. There were countless private lessons for young men preparing for Hampton. He wasn't worried about being paid, the small official salary as a public-school teacher was enough for him. John was then rewarded for the paternal dedication he had shown: he also entered the Hampton Institute.

Booker Washington says as little as possible about the difficulties he encountered in Malden in 1876 and 1877.

It was a time of heightened activity for the Ku-Klux-Klan, a quasi-fantastic movement [formed] after the Civil War, extending it beyond the illusory declaration of peace. To resist the unbearable abuses of politicians, who were punished with the epithet of carpetbaggers, a White league was formed: sometimes murderous battles were fought between them and the metropolitan police. Unfortunately, the numerous secret societies involved in this hidden war carried too far the terror that was supposed to prevent Blacks from assembling to gain scrutiny. Among the individuals disguised for this policing, there were real bandits: the Ku-Klux mask sheltered many passions, so innocent people were martyred to death and schools were set ablaze because the teachers who put an end to

---

[266] In Washington's words: "In all my teaching I have watched carefully the influence of the toothbrush, and I am convinced that there are few single agencies of civilization that are more far-reaching" (1986, 75).

Appendix III – Review of *Up from Slavery*

Black people's long years of ignorance were more than suspect. Booker Washington avoids dwelling on this dark period of the reconstruction.

"Today," he says, "there are no such organizations in the South: public sentiment would not tolerate it."[267]

Perhaps it is an exaggeration to say that the two races no longer remember this. It must not, however, be forgotten that this autobiography is a work of reconciliation, a book of advice on how to solve the most difficult social problem. In the United States, it is understandable that it finds interpreters and native propagandists in all parties.

To make no further reference, suffice it to say that Kentucky ladies read it to the Negro crowds gathered under the name of members of the Booker Washington class, as English men of letters gather in a Browning Society. The autobiography promises to become the Bible of a race, the star that, in fact, will guide it forward, always prudently and safely.

(Continued)

Tuesday, April 1, 1902

II (cont.)

We left our Malden schoolmaster preparing candidates for the Hampton Institute; we find him pursuing his own studies in Washington [D.C], entrusted with a very important political [mission].[268] The seat of government of West Virginia was going to be

---

[267] The original reads: "Today there are no such organizations in the South, and the fact that such ever existed is almost forgotten by both races. There are few places in the South now where public sentiment would permit such organizations to exist" (1986, 79). Although the Ku Klux Klan ceased to exist in the 1870s (it would reemerge in the early twentieth century), there were similar organizations in the US South – among them, the White League and the Red Shirts, who used violence to prevent Black people from voting or running for office.

[268] The word was missing due to damage to the page of the Brazilian newspaper but retrieved using the French original.

transferred from Wheeling to one of the three cities which the legislature left the citizens to choose. A committee of White people from Charleston asked [Washington] to plead that city's cause in the state.²⁶⁹ He devotes three months to this propaganda and, finally, Charleston beat its rivals and became the state capital.

The reputation as an orator he acquired during this campaign heralded a political career for Booker-Washington [sic]: many intended to guide him in that direction, but his refusal made itself heard:

"[I thought that I could be of greater utility because I feel that the colored population needs, above all, to base itself on education, industry, and property. I could have been successful in politics, but that success took on, in my mind, an aspect of selfishness, it was individual and achieved at the price of duty...

During that time, many individuals of color only studied to become lawyers and enter congress, as nearly all the women only aspired to teach music... They reminded me of an old Black man who wanted to play the guitar and chose one of his young masters as a teacher. To dissuade him, the latter said: Sure, Uncle Jake, I'll give you lessons, but you will pay me three dollars for the first, two for the second, one, and the fourth for twenty-five cents.

Agreed, replied the old Black man, but let's start with the last lesson.

*Future lawyers and pianists were like Uncle Jake.]"*²⁷⁰

---

²⁶⁹ Washington describes his mission as canvassing the state "in the interests of that city" (1986, 92).

²⁷⁰ The original reads: "...I refused, still believing that I could find other service which would prove of more permanent value to my race. Even then I had a strong feeling that what our people most needed was to get a foundation in education, industry, and property, and for this I felt that they could better afford to strive than for political preferment. As for my individual self, it appeared to me to be reasonably certain that I could succeed in political life, but I had a feeling that it would be a rather selfish kind of success – individual success at the cost of failing to do my duty in assisting in laying a foundation for the masses.

Appendix III – Review of *Up from Slavery*

It would be impossible to ridicule such as-yet-inopportune aspirations more aptly.[271]

Washington set the example: after Armstrong and, on [Commencement day], he delivered a memorable speech on the subject—THE FORCE THAT WINS.

In truth, he possessed this force, from Malden to Hampton, on the same road he had travelled five years before on foot to beg for the post of student-porter, he must have thought that never in such a short space of time had such a change been wrought in one man's life.

"The Institute was making progress, meeting the needs of the race."[272]

Washington wastes no opportunity to criticize the ostentatious programs offered by many other colleges for people of colour, because they encourage vanity and multiply illusions.

"These are often their expressions, in matters of evangelization and education, instructors leave the real world, forgetting the individual and the end to be achieved."[273] It was not so at Hampton, nor was it at Tuskegee, later founded by Booker Washington.

At this period in the progress of our race a very large proportion of the young men who went to school or to college did so with the expressed determination to prepare themselves to be great lawyers, or Congressmen, and many of the women planned to become music teachers/ but I had a reasonably fixed idea, even at that early period in my life, that there was a need for something to be done to prepare the way for successful lawyers, Congressmen, and music teachers.

I felt that the conditions were a good deal like those of an old coloured man, during the days of slavery, who wanted to learn how to play on the guitar" (Washington 1986, 93-94).

[271] Here, Bentzon seems to be imposing her own interpretation on a more nuanced message from Washington. It should be noted that his daughter, Portia, became a pianist and studied under a former pupil of Franz Liszt in Germany (Stewart 1977).

[272] The original reads: "I found that during my absence from Hampton the institute each year had been getting closer to the real needs and conditions of our people...." (Washington 1986, 95).

[273] The original reads: "Too often, it seems to me, in missionary and educational work among undeveloped races, people yield to the temptation of doing that which

In the summer of 1897 General Armstrong charged him with the delicate mission of introducing a few Indians [sic] among the students of Hampton against the prevailing opinion that the Redskins [sic] could not be educated. One hundred entirely wild individuals were brought from the Western reservations and entrusted to Booker Washington. The first job was to acquire a kind of paternal sway over them[274] and insensibly fight their prejudices, because the Indian judges himself to be far superior to the White man who works, imagine what it will be like in relation to the Black man marked with the stigma of slavery!...

Washington capably took on this major responsibility. Alone among a hundred individuals who could become hostile, all the more so when their most inveterate tastes and habits were thwarted, he managed to win their trust.

["]Except for the enormous difficulty of learning English, the red men did not seem to me very different from the Black ones. They welcomed us with such cordiality that I wonder if things would be the same among Whites. How many times have I wanted to tell White students that they would educate themselves by helping to educate, and that the unhappier a race is, retarded in civilization, the greater ennoblement it brings to the more civilized one who helps it."[275]

These mild, indirect lessons abound in Booker Washington's evangelical biography. And incidentally, without the least bit of resentment, he recounts an anecdote that took place at the time when he was leading them towards civilization.

---

was done a hundred years before.... The temptation often is to run each individual through a certain educational mould, regardless of the condition of the subject or the end to be accomplished" (1986, 95-96).

[274] Washington describes his role as "house father" (1986, 97).

[275] Bentzon omits Washington's observation that "...no White American ever thinks that any other race is wholly civilized until he wears the White man's clothes, eats the White man's food, speaks the White man's language, and professes the White man's religion" (1986, 98).

Appendix III – Review of *Up from Slavery*

One of his Red disciples was overcome with nostalgia,[276] and as the Secretary of the Interior decided to send him back to his reservation, Washington was charged with accompanying him.

They travelled on a steamboat. At dinnertime, Washington, who was familiar with colour prejudice, waited for most of the White passengers to leave the dining room.

He was immediately told that only his student could be seated at the table. The same adventure was repeated at the hotel in Washington. The Redskin was welcomed warmly but the Black man absolutely rejected. Such incidents are not rare! Frederick Douglass, the coloured man most distinguished for his superior talents, travelled to Pennsylvania in a baggage car, despite having purchased a ticket.

When some Whites expressed regret that such humiliation had been inflicted on him, Douglass got up from the suitcase on which he was sitting and declared: "They cannot degrade Frederick Douglass.

"This insolence only degrades those who practice it."[277]

The same man, to a certain innkeeper who decided [sic] that he could not accommodate him because he only had one room where a White man was already sleeping, replied: "It doesn't matter. I am not prejudiced against color."

In Booker Washington there are no such scathing retorts, he only mentions that train conductors often find themselves greatly perplexed when deciding who is more or less coloured. In the former case, the individual absolutely cannot stay in the White carriage, and if the passenger is not *really coloured* he is offended and asks him if he is Black. Hair, complexion, nose, hands, if nothing betrays the

---

[276] Washington says the Native American student was "taken ill" (1986, 102).

[277] Washington recounts the incident as follows: "When some of the White passengers went into the baggage-car to console Mr. Douglass, and one of them said to him: 'I am sorry, Mr. Douglass, that you have been degraded in this manner,' Mr. Douglass straightened himself up on the box upon which he was sitting, and replied: 'They cannot degrade Frederick Douglass. The soul that is within me no man can degrade. I am not the one that is being degraded on account of this treatment, but those who are inflicting it upon me'" (1986, 100).

colour, the conductor examines the traveller's feet. Depending on the outcome of the inspection, he stays where he is.

Washington was a witness to this, and jokes that his great namesake[278] replied to those who reproached him for responding to a Black man's greeting: "Do you suppose that I am going to permit a Black man to be more polite than I am?"[279]

Social intercourse apart, true Southern gentlemen look kindly on their slaves and their descendants: but it is precisely social intercourse that will become more and more difficult to determine when Whites and Blacks are equally educated, similarly well bred. Washington brushes aside this sensitive issue with exceptional wisdom: but it doesn't matter; sooner or later it will prevail.

Managing his Indians [sic], he helped the general to establish the night school that became characteristic of Hampton. The creation of these classes resulted from the extraordinary demand that could not be met by daytime classes, hence two-hour evening sessions for both sexes for ten hours of work per day.

The students received bed, board, and a small wage that was almost entirely given over to the treasurer to pay their board when the individual took the respective classes. This way, they learned a trade while acquiring indispensable knowledge. When Booker Washington took over the running of the night school, there were a total of twelve students of both sexes working in the sawmill and mill [sic].[280] The night-school students were so enthusiastic that they often asked for lessons to be extended.

"They were called the Plucky Class, and the best achieved a certificate. The class was so popular that now it is attended by three or four hundred students."

(Continued)

---

[278] Here, Bentzon is referring to George Washington.

[279] Booker T. Washington's quotation of the eponymous president has been edited. In *Up from Slavery*, it reads: "Do you suppose that I am going to permit a poor, ignorant, coloured man to be more polite than I am?"

[280] According to Washington, the women worked in the laundry (1986, 104).

Appendix III – Review of *Up from Slavery*

Thursday, April 3, 1902

IV

This is how Washington prepared himself to be the principal of Tuskegee University [sic]. Although originally modest, it was conferred upon him by General Armstrong at the request of two prominent men from Macon who wanted a teacher who would benefit the region as much as possible. They were [George W.] Campbell, an ex-slaveholder, merchant and banker, and Lewis Adam, a freedman who had learned the triple trade of cobbler, harness maker, and tinsmith from the former masters.

"*I visited our Southern cities,*" says Washington, "*and asked who the most honest and influential colored men were in that place. You will know that fifty-percent of cases were Blacks who learned a trade during the days of slavery.*"[281] Thus, he understood that education plans should take into account what Blacks had previously learned. In a way, every large southern plantation was a kind of practical school for farmers, masons, carpenters, cooks, weavers, seamstresses, etc. Their training had a self-serving nature, and intelligence did not develop along with the hand, yet this fragmented education allowed the freedman to earn a living. Therefore, he [Washington] had to improve it, develop it, all the more so because the prosperity of the South depended on the work of Black people, which had been forced labour shortly before. It was a mistake to attempt to build on the bedrock of slavery that which in New England had been built on the foundations of freedom.

After twenty years, the workers on the old plantations began to disappear, and it was clear that there was no one to replace them. Instead of arts and crafts, Blacks acquired a tincture of science and literature that only served to irritate Whites and aggravate prejudice.

---

[281] The original reads: "If one goes today into any Southern town, and asks for the leading and most reliable coloured man in the community, I believe that in five cases out of ten he will be directed to a Negro who learned a trade during the days of slavery" (Washington 1986, 121).

To Booker Washington it seems absurd to say that there is no difference between Blacks and Whites, and that the same kind of education suits both. It may be pleasant for us to think otherwise, but there is strength in recognizing, however, that there is a great difference between the two—which results from the inequality of past conditions.

The new teacher visited the country [sic] to which he had been called: a months' observation left him despondent. It seemed impossible to raise up people whose minimum defect was ignorance. The greater his conviction of their inferiority, the more he was aware of the need to help them with the appropriate aid. It was 1881, the 14th of July, the date set for the opening of the small school in a former church. Whites and Blacks were interested in its success, they discussed it; most ironically assumed that, when educated, Blacks would be less valuable as an economic factor: there would be no more workers on the farms or servants, only educated Blacks with high hats, monocles, walking sticks, presumed to dominate through intelligence...[282]

Washington is not surprised by this summary judgment; many times in his teaching, he had found the type of the poor devil of color intending to follow higher education in a squalid house, letting weeds invade his garden, a lady able to show the Sahara or the capital of China on a map, but without knowing how to lay a tablecloth; the pedant who understood cube roots, but did not know the multiplication table.[283]

---

[282] Bentzon is paraphrasing and giving her interpretation of the original, which reads: "The White people who questioned the wisdom of starting this new school had in their minds pictures of what was called an educated Negro, with a high hat, imitation gold eye-glasses, a showy walking-stick, kid gloves, fancy boots, and what not – in a word, a man who was determined to live by his wits" (Washington 1986, 119).

[283] Again, Bentzon distorts Washington's words and meaning: "Notwithstanding what I have said about them in these respects, I have never seen a more earnest and willing company of young men and women than these students were.... I was determined to start them off on a solid and thorough foundation, so far as their

Appendix III – Review of *Up from Slavery*

That is why he set out to make them unlearn a great deal with the idea of overloading them, willy nilly, with the knowledge of things that were necessary for farming and domestic life.

When the school opened, the enrolment consisted of about thirty students over the age of fifteen, many of whom almost boasted of being teachers.

Some of his students accompanied him, and it was interesting that mere students were admitted to classes higher than those of the teachers.

The complaisance with which these Blacks, who considered themselves educated, spoke of the thick volumes they had already read, of the knowledge they possessed; some boasting of having studied Latin and others of knowing Greek, it was a spectacle more pitiable than ridiculous. However, their poor heads were only burdened with certain grammar rules and many other mathematical formulas, without the sense to apply them. If they intended to expand their education, it was to earn more money. Washington had the courage to force them to start at the beginning; and submissive and persevering, they proved that he could count on them.

Bit by bit, he encouraged the pride that, if misguided, so exposed them to ridicule.

"Big books are not enough: it is necessary to learn to dominate nature, to use air, water, steam, electricity, through new methods; a good education suppresses what is painful and inferior in manual labor. Why do Blacks stay away from factories? It is just that they lack the technical ability and intelligence to compete with Whites. Are you saying that [the White man] refuses to work with a Black man? It matters little in the day when men of color are found who can run a large industry by themselves. Moreover, condition depends on

---

books were concerned. I soon learned that most of them had the merest smattering of the high-sounding things that they had studied. While they could locate the Desert of Sahara or the capital of China on an artificial globe, I found that the girls could not locate the proper places for the knives and forks on an actual dinner-table...." (1986, 123).

character: until there is a new order of things, a good reputation is more necessary for Blacks than the exercise of the vote: when they make themselves valued, they will be better received."[284]

With this skill of addressing men, he added:

"Suppose a Black person carries ten thousand dollars on a railroad, do you think that when he takes the train with his family, they will send him to the Jim Crow car and risk that the company will lose this large sum? No, never; they will open a Pullman for him with the greatest solicitude."[285]

From week to week the number of students grew, and Booker Washington would have been overwhelmed by the rising tide of work, without the help of his wife, Olivia Davidson.[286] Solidly educated in the good schools of Ohio and experienced in teaching, her dedication put to the test during the scourge of yellow fever in a Memphis infirmary, she agreed with Washington that Blacks needed more than what books contain.

Having graduated from Hampton and thanks to the extraordinary philanthropy of a daughter of Boston, Mrs. Mary Hemenway, she had spent two years at Framingham Normal School in Massachusetts. There, they tried to convince her that since she looked White, she could easily disguise her race, and life would be more pleasant for her. Proud and noble, Olivia Davidson rejected the advice, refusing even to engage in silent deception, and made herself respected as who she was.[287]

---

[284] The original reads: "My plan was not to teach [the students] to work in the old way, but to show them how to make the forces of nature – air, water, steam, electricity, horse-power – assist them in their labour" (Washington 1986, 148). The rest of this extract does not come from *Up from Slavery*. It may be from a speech that Bentzon attended.

[285] Another quotation that is not found in *Up from Slavery*.

[286] Olivia Davidson (1854-1889) was Washington's second wife. She helped build the institute when Washington was still married to Fanny Norton Smith Washington, who died in1884. Olivia and Booker married in 1886.

[287] Washington writes: "Before she went to Framingham, some one suggested to Miss Davidson that, since she was so very light in colour, she might find it more

Appendix III – Review of *Up from Slavery*

After graduating from Framingham, she introduced new teaching methods and ideas at Tuskegee, to which she devoted herself.

Her husband confesses, proud of her memory, that her virtues were the cornerstone of that institution, and she died young, the victim of her philanthropic zeal.

Olivia and Washington understood each other perfectly: strengthening character, giving good habits of order, economy, politeness and regularity in family life, imposing an art or craft on one—a kind of breadwinner, instilling the gospel of St. Paul: "Anyone who does not provide for their relatives, and especially for their own household, has denied the faith and is worse than an unbeliever." And in that farming region, encouraging work in the fields, ridding pretentious and fanciful people of the idea of running to the cities, abandoning the farms—that was the first task for both in dealing with the students.

Meanwhile, teachers were trained, and structures were skilfully prepared and went back to the farms to teach how to cultivate the land methodically and develop the moral and intellectual life of their companions.

Washington's constant lesson was against the childish ambition not to work with one's own hands. He repeated the story of the Black man who, when hoeing a cotton field in the heat, fell to his knees exclaiming: "O Lawd, de cotton am so grassy, de work am so hard, and the sun am so hot dat I b'lieve dis darky am called to preach!"

In fact, preaching instead of weeding was the ambition of Tuskegee's first students.

Many who are not Black also share this kind of thinking, which Washington and his worthy companion combated.

(Continued)

---

comfortable not to be known as a coloured woman in this school in Massachusetts. She at once replied that under no circumstances and for no consideration would she consent to deceive any one in regard to her racial identity" (1986, 125).

Saturday April 5, 1902[288]

Three months after the school opened, they could give Tuskegee the size and character they desired. There was an abandoned plantation for sale near the town; Washington purchased it with money generously loaned by General [J. F. B.] Marshall, the treasurer of Hampton, from his own pocket: five hundred dollars.[289] It was a very small sum, but never in his life had he had so much money all at once. The burden of that debt was already crushing him; he lost no time establishing the model farm to which the school was to be annexed, initially housed temporarily in a stable and a henhouse.[290]

The little that remained of the buildings, burnt down during the war, was repaired by the pupils, under their teacher's command. Then they went on to clearing the land. They did so without enthusiasm, making it clear that they had not come to Tuskegee for this; the former schoolteachers were especially afraid of compromising their dignity; but Washington set them an example, axe in hand, and twenty acres of woods were cleared. At the same time, Olivia raised abundant funds in northern cities[291]—she ingeniously organized festivals, sales, to which local families, White and Black alike, lent their support. Everyone showed an interest in a school established on the footing of practical utility; the neighbours, even the poorest, made a small contribution, twenty-five sous [sic], a quantity of sugar cane, a blanket. Washington observes that, of all the gifts, large and small, which arrived at different times, there was one that touched him the most deeply. A woman in her seventies went to see him when the farm was being established. Leaning on a

---

[288] This issue of *Diário da Bahia* is missing from the collections of the Central Library of Bahia and the IGHB. I have translated the instalment published on that date directly from the French (Bentzon 1901, 783-784).
[289] According to Washington, the loan was for $250 (1986, 129).
[290] Washington's version informs us that the stable and henhouse were used as recitation rooms (1986, 130).
[291] Washington observes that Miss Davidson, as he calls her (she was not his wife at the time), raised funds to repay the loan in the town of Tuskegee (1986, 131).

Appendix III – Review of *Up from Slavery*

cane and covered in rags, she said, "Mr. Washington, God knows that I lived in slavery and I don't know anything and I don't have anything, but even so I understand what you want to do; you want to make Black people better. I don't have any money; take these six eggs I've saved, yes, put my six eggs towards the education of those boys and girls."[292] And the humble sacrifices of a poor race bore fruit.

Booker Washington had modelled his institute on Hampton. In 1884, also like Hampton, he founded a night school which now has 457 students and serves as a touchstone for him to judge abilities and good will. Whoever agrees to work with his hands for ten hours a day in exchange for two hours of study deserves to be pushed to the limit. After proving himself in night school, the pupil enters the school proper, where he goes to class four days a week and works two days at his trade. He plies this trade exclusively during the three summer months. Besides, no student, however rich, can be exempted from manual labour at the school. For this, the people of the South, who deem that enormous sums have been wasted on teaching Latin to the Blacks, are grateful to the principal of Tuskegee. [The students] leave their school as carpenters, sawyers, farmers, tailors, etc. Twenty-eight industries are taught. The students themselves raised the buildings that cover their land, they even made the bricks. All good folk, and honouring the moral teachings of their principal. Also, [even] the most obstinate old Southerners esteem and support this. They have not yet called him Mr. Booker Washington, which would establish the recognition of an impossible social equality, but they call him "professor" with a deferential tone, and last year, when the President of the Republic went to visit Tuskegee, these aristocrats

---

[292] Washington's version of the story replicates the woman's speech, as he often does when quoting formerly enslaved individuals: "Mr. Washin'ton, God knows I spent de bes' days of my life in slavery. God knows I's ignorant and poor; but...I knows what you an' Miss Davidson is tryin' to do. I knows you is tryin' to make better men an' better women for de coloured race. I ain't got no money, but I wants you to take dese six eggs, what I's been savin' up, an' I wants you to put dese six eggs into de eddication of dese boys an' gals" (1986, 132).

who call themselves Southern Democrats, perfectly accepted that Washington rode in the same car as Mr. MacKinley [sic] and the Governor of Alabama. This is progress, the importance of which is beyond the ken of us Europeans.

Sunday, April 6, 1902

V

We have seen Booker Washington's work as an educator. Let us now consider him in the role of orator.

It was after a trip North in Tuskegee's interests, in the company of General Armstrong, that he began to stir the crowds with his eloquence. Invited to speak at a meeting of the National Educational Association in Madison, he addressed the difficult problem of "race" for the first time before an audience of four thousand.

The Southerners gathered there in large numbers *"waited in vain to hear this Black man insult the former slaveholding states."*[293] Instead, the speaker praised the South for the good it could do. His line of action has not varied since he settled in Tuskegee and pledged to do justice to Blacks and Whites alike. However, this policy does not prevent him from sincerely denouncing the injuries suffered by people of colour.

The stance between the two races is to employ everything that can unite them, and to avoid what provokes hatred and prejudice.

As for the vote, the Blacks should increasingly consider the interests of the community in which they live, whose future largely depends on them.

---

[293] Washington writes: "Without my knowing it, there were a large number of people present from Alabama, and some from the town of Tuskegee. These White people afterward frankly told me that they went to this meeting expecting to hear the South roundly abused, but were pleasantly surprised to find that there was no word of abuse in my address. On the contrary, the south was given credit for all the praiseworthy things that it had done" (1986, 200).

They must become more and more useful to their city or town, always striving to do better than others, even the most menial tasks, because how they are done makes them lose their menial character. Only then will their colour be forgotten. For example: a Black farmer, a Tuskegee graduate, managed to harvest two hundred and seventy bushels of sweet potatoes on an acre of land that normally produced forty-nine bushels. Soon the White farmers in the neighbourhood turned to his new farming methods, to his knowledge of the chemistry of the soil, and justly recognize that he increased the wealth of the world in which he lived.

This is not to say that Blacks should only plant sweet potatoes, but that if they prosper as sharecroppers, they were establish solid foundations on which their descendants can build.

This was the essence of Booker Washington's first lecture. He concluded by declaring that the hatred he had nurtured in his early youth against those who opposed the progress of Black people had long given way through the development of his intelligence.[294]

"I limit myself to pitying the man capable of this madness, because I know he is wrong and only harms himself. I pity him, because I know that he is trying to stop the progress of the world, whose progress nothing will stop. One might as well try to stop the progress of a mighty railroad train by throwing his body across the track, as to try to stop the growth of the world in the direction of giving mankind more...culture,...and more liberty. Brotherly kindness will be strengthened with further progress."

His robust faith is contagious: in the North, he receives invitations from Whites and Blacks: from the former, he obtains

---

[294] Washington wrote: "In my early life I used to cherish a feeling of ill will toward any one who spoke in bitter terms against the negro, or who advocated measures that tended to oppress the Black man or take from him opportunities for growth in the most complete manner. Now, whenever I hear anyone advocating measures that are meant to curtail the development of another, I pity the individual who would do this. I know that the one who makes this mistake does so because of his own lack of opportunity for the highest kind of growth" (1986, 203).

funds to expand his school; and to the others he vehemently preaches the need for industrial and technical education and the futility of political agitation that will only harm their voting rights. Education and property together are the only elements that give the right to vote.

These two conditions should be rigorously demanded of both races, and the full exercise of political rights would come as a natural, consequently slow, development.

Washington's prudent words do not preclude frankness; it is his principle never to say, for example, in Boston, what he could not repeat in the midst of a tempestuous auditorium in Alabama.

Birth and destiny fixed him in the South shortly before slavery, and nothing shakes his loyalty. A former confederate said recently:

"He never made a specialty of waving a red flag in front of every bull he encountered; in return, however, he achieved what all the books, speeches, incendiary prospectuses, martial law, decrees and amendments to the Constitution could not do... By peaceful methods inspired by Jesus Christ, Booker Washington conquered where Caesar would be defeated."

The most important thing is for Blacks to achieve the esteem and friendship of Southern Whites.

Washington wanted to be heard by an audience of former Confederate slaveholders. The occasion arose in 1893, at an international meeting of Christian workers in Atlanta, Georgia. Then lecturing in Boston, he was invited to speak for "a few minutes." Traveling 2,000 miles to speak for "a few minutes" seemed absurd; however, he made up his mind, and set off immediately, arriving in Atlanta thirty minutes before the appointed time. He put every effort into saying something worthwhile in those five minutes. Speaking before the most influential ranks of White Society, men and women, curious, but generally hostile, he spoke about Tuskegee, its methods and aims, and was applauded. The next day, that brief and substantial speech received favourable comments in the local press: a great victory had been won. Booker Washington extended it, gaining a national reputation when, on October 18, 1895, he gave the famous opening speech at the Atlanta Exposition. His first success: twenty-five of Georgia's most influential citizens were commissioned to ask the orator to accompany them to Washington, DC, and convince Congress to provide government support for the exhibition. And he got all he asked for: with masterful skill, he expressed to Congress his conviction that the best way of freeing the South from the embarrassments resulting from colour prejudice, was to encourage the moral and intellectual progress of the two races together; and the Atlanta Exposition gave them both an opportunity to display the progress they had made after the era of emancipation, and would encourage them to continue.

The exhibition was held with a pavilion devoted to the products of people of colour, with the plan designed by a Black architect and the entire building built by Blacks.

The Whites started out by laughing at the undertaking, but the results showed that their mockery was misplaced

But the greatest success of all was Booker Washington's speech. Never before had a Black person spoken from the same platform as Whites in a national ceremony[.]

(Continued)

Wednesday, April 9, 1902

V

Though no restrictions had been imposed on him, he knew that any word less skilfully used would harm his cause: hence a kind of fear that gripped him: It was the burden of ancestral abjection that weighed on his shoulders. He thought that former slaveholders might be there, and that a few years earlier the first White man present would have had the right to silence him and claim him as a slave. He also had to satisfy his peers—too many were imbued with newfound importance for the intransigent abolitionists of the North and the expropriated Southerners as a whole—an immense people whose disparate elements he was confronting for the first time.

As always, he began by imploring the help of the Most High and committed himself not to speak to anyone in particular, but in the name of what he believed to be truth and justice. The triumph was complete.

Governor Bullock, who had limited himself to introducing him to the gathering as a representative of Black civilization, rushed towards him with an outstretched hand: White and Black were for some time united in a cordial embrace to intense public applause.

With difficulty Washington managed to descend from the platform; the ovation continued loudly in the street, and when he returned to Tuskegee the next day, the crowds applauded him at the [railway] stations.

President Cleveland congratulated him, and has since devoted himself to the Tuskegee School in a way that has benefited it greatly. That was not all.

Dr Gilman,[295] president of Johns Hopkins University of Baltimore, the chairman of the exposition's jury, made Booker Washington a member of that same jury, in the education section, an honour that gave a Black man the unprecedented right to judge the work of White schools and the schools of men of colour.

What is more, the illustrious and uncompromising writer from Virginia, Nelson Page, proposed and was unanimously accepted the nomination of the Black man as secretary of the section. Honors rained down around him.

If there was any dissonance, it was produced by the reaction of his own people, who were unhappy that he had not asked for more extensive rights for Blacks, unhappy to have heard words like these:

["]It is important and right that all privileges of the law be ours, but it is vastly more important that we be prepared for the exercises of these privileges. The opportunity to earn a dollar in a factory just now

---

[295] Daniel Coit Gilman, the first president of Johns Hopkins.

Appendix III – Review of *Up from Slavery*

is worth infinitely more than the opportunity to spend a dollar in an opera-house ["].[296]

Elsewhere:

["]In all things purely mundane, Whites and Blacks can be as separate as the fingers, yet we form a whole in all things essential to mutual progress["].[297]

These were indeed modest claims in the eyes of the radical citizens of colour, but the generosity of Washington's actions excused him from the moderation of his words.

The parents whose children they educated could not deny him recognition, and when the coloured clergy became aware of the events which Booker had the courage to denounce, reconciled with him, when previously some missionaries had declared such a war against him that they advised people not to send their children to the Tuskegee school!

This curious fact is noted, but it is not rare: one of the most radical missionaries had a child in that school when he raged against it.[298]

In every respect, Booker Washington became the guide of his people. After the Atlanta exhibition, some newspapers and certain lecture promoters made him tempting offers. He refused, saying that his mission was Tuskegee, and he spoke freely on matters concerning the race without any commercial gain.

Nevertheless, his autobiography was written bit by bit, on tables in railway waiting rooms and in carriages: he was in demand everywhere, and everywhere he went he drew crowds.

---

[296] From the original Atlanta Exposition speech published in *Up from Slavery* (Washington 1986, 223-224).

[297] The original quote reads: "In all things purely social, we can be as separate as the fingers, yet one as the hand in all things essential to mutual progress" (Ibid., 221-222).

[298] Here, the order of the original paragraph in French has been inverted, possibly for effect, and a new paragraph created (see Bentzon 1901).

Nervous and impressionable, he always felt that he had failed to develop the essential side of his speeches.

In compensation for the preliminary agony, he says, there is the pleasure of mastering the audience, the feeling of intimate communication with the listeners, in a kind of mental and physical enjoyment the idea of which cannot be described.

He hardly bothered with the rules of oratory, he even forgot them in the heat of improvisation and induced the audience to forget them too. Hours spent at banquets and parties are of no concern, and with singular vivacity, he joyfully recalls the small cabin where as a slave he savoured the Sunday molasses sent from the "big house." Nothing ever tasted like that delicacy for him.

He was so active that he gave as many as four speeches per day. In 1898, the trustees of the John [F.] Slater Fund, a generous source of aid for Blacks, voted a sum of money so he could give a series of annual lectures in large Black communities.

In the morning, he speaks to ministers, teachers, and professionals. In the afternoon, Mrs. [Margaret] Murray Washington invites people of her sex to a lecture from the orator. He always notes the White members of the audience.[299]

"*I have never devoted myself,*" he says, "*to work that gave me so much pleasure, and I believe that none has done me as much good. It has enabled my wife and me to go deeply into the conditions of the race, because we make an effort and observe individuals as they are— in churches and in schools, at work and in prisons, even in dens of crime... and my hopes always increase... It is not that I delude myself with what can seem superficial and deceiving in similar meetings: I*

---

[299] The original reads "In the afternoon Mrs. Washington would speak to the women alone, and in the evening I spoke to a large mass-meeting. In almost every case the meetings have been attended not only by coloured people in large numbers, but by the White people" (1986, 248). The discrepancy is due to a mistranslation of the French, which is closer to the original: "Dans l'après-midi, Mrs Washington (née Margaret Murray) convoque les personnes de son sexe, et le soir, l'orateur s'adresse à tous. Il ya toujours beaucoup de blancs dans son auditoire" (Bentzon 1901, 789).

Appendix III – Review of *Up from Slavery*

have enough experience to avoid letting myself be swept away. However, no one could penetrate as I have over these twenty years into the heart of the South, observing the slow but sure progress of the Black race, both from the moral and material standpoint.["]

If we consider the worst scum, we will certainly find examples of infamy, but if we assessed the White man under the same conditions, what conclusion would we reach?[300]

Booker Wasgington [sic] never lost heart. I had the opportunity to see him in 1897, among the notables who had gone to Boston to unveil the monument to Colonel Shaw,[301] the young [White] officer who died heroically at the head of a Black regiment.

After the monument was unveiled, speeches were given in the Music Hall which, despite its size, did not have enough room for the large, hand-picked audience.

The most influential and distinguished people approached the Governor of Massachusetts, and at first glance, the principal of Tuskegee cut an extremely modest figure. The White blood that must flow in his veins had not erased any of the characteristic traits of the race. He is a Black like all the others: prominent lips, flat nose, heavy jaw, yet with an expression of intelligent kindness in his eyes, and his voice was sonorous and confident.[302] The oratorical success of the day fell to him. The Black, in Boston, had been preceded by the legitimate reputation that made him the first of his race to be distinguished with the diploma of an honorary member of Harvard University. When he rose to his full height, everyone felt that they

---

[300] This observation is based on Washington's comment that "One might take up the life of the worst element in New York City, for example, and prove almost anything he wanted concerning the White man, but all will agree that this is not a fair test" (1986, 249).

[301] The monument to Colonel Robert Gould Shaw was erected in the city of Boston in 1897. Today, it stands in the National Gallery in Washington, DC. Booker T. Washington was one of the speakers and, thanks to his talent as an orator, "stole the show" from the eminent White philosopher William James.

[302] Here Bentzon provides a first-hand description of Washington, whose speech she attended, viewed through the filter of her own prejudices.

were in the presence of a force. He spoke of the great military feats of the Civil War, then, turning to the Black soldiers present there, he said: *"To you, to the scarred and scattered remnants of the Fifty-fourth, who, with empty sleeve and wanting leg, have honoured this occasion with your presence, to you, your commander is not dead. Though Boston erected no monument and history recorded no story, in you and in the loyal race which you represent, Robert Gould Shaw would have a monument which time could not wear away."*[303]

Governor Wolcou [Roger Wolcott] enthusiastically raised "Three cheers to Booker Washington!" No one else was applauded with such great enthusiasm. Overcome by the general feeling, the Black sergeant who was the standard-bearer made an overwhelming gesture: it was he who, after the battle where [a large] part of the regiment had fallen, exclaimed "No matter! The old flag never touched the ground."

I repeat, Washington's speech eclipsed all the others who spoke that day.

Years later, amid the general celebrations of the successful conclusion of the Spanish-American War, a party was held in Chicago, and the president of the university[304] invited his colleague from Tuskegee to attend. Washington gave two speeches, one of which, on October 6, 1900, in the immense auditorium where there were approximately 16,000 people, while outside the crowd thronged, interrupting traffic so it was only possible to enter with the aid of law enforcement agents. The guests included President Mac-Kinley [sic],[305] [government] ministers, Navy and Army officers returning from the campaign. Booker Washington described the

---

[303] These are the original words quoted in a newspaper article on the ceremony published in *Up from Slavery* (1986, 252).

[304] William Rainey Harper (1856-1906), the first president of the University of Chicago.

[305] William McKinley (1843–1901), the 25th President of the United States, governed from 1897 to 1901, when he was assassinated. He was succeeded by his vice president, Theodore Roosevelt.

history of Blacks in America, reduced to choosing between slavery and death, and this dilemma taking on duties to the country against their will: Chrispus Attuchs,[306] for example, who shed his blood at the beginning of the revolution to guarantee Whites liberty he could not share. He recalled the valiant conduct of the Blacks of New Orleans under Jackson; the loyalty of Southern slaves to families of masters enlisted under flags that represented the perpetuation of slavery; asserted the bravery of the coloured troops at Port-Hudson, at Fort Wagner, at Fort Pillow, and recently that of the Black regiments who bombed Santiago to liberate another people—In all this, exclaims the speaker, the best part fell to us! He ended the speech with a magnificent appeal to the consciences of his listeners: *["]When they have heard every tale of the valiant conduct of the Negro in the war that just ended; when you have heard it from the mouth of the soldier from the North and the soldier from the South, of the ex-abolitionist and the ex-master, answer your own conscience if a race so willing to sacrifice itself for the Nation, should not have the right to the greatest possibilities of living for it ["].*[307]
(Continued)

Sunday, April 13, 1902

VI

It is natural to wonder how Booker Washington could keep an eye on the school when he always away it. The institute's excellent organization aptly explains this. In the institution's own interests, it

---

[306] Crispus Attucks (ca. 1723 to 1770). Bondsman, sailor, and stevedore, descendant of Africans and Native Americans, hero and martyr of the American Revolution and symbol of the abolitionist movement.

[307] The original reads: "When you have gotten the full story of the heroic conduct of the Negro in the Spanish-American war, have heard it from the lips of the Northern soldier and Southern soldier, from ex-abolitionists and ex-masters, then decide within yourselves whether a race that is thus willing to die for its country should not be given the highest opportunity to live for its country" (Washington 1986, 255).

behoved it not to be dependent on just one man. At Tuskegee, the administration is run by eighty-six people and works like clockwork. Booker Washington found in Warren Logan, the institute's treasurer, his alter ego, and in [Emmett J.] Scott, a faithful secretary who tells him everything takes place there during the principal's absence.[308]

The executive council, composed of nine members who are the heads of the nine sections into which the school is divided, meets twice a week. Furthermore, every week there is a meeting of the financial committee to decide on the week's expenditures, and, lastly, there is a monthly general meeting of the entire faculty.

Hence, Booker Washington knows everything that goes on at the institute, even while he is absent from it.

More than one young Tuskegee graduate voluntarily returns to his hometown, where there are often six Blacks to one White, and what Blacks!!!

[Finding them] in debt, dependent on loans, living in squalid rooms where eight or ten people of both sexes were crowded together, the recent arrival opens the school as a centre of change, organizes clubs, announces lectures, in short, with words and example establishes order and comfort in that miserable group. Towns of that kind are mentioned which quickly became prosperous, provided with well-built houses and inherited in good condition. However, the revolution took place thanks to the influence of one man. The Tuskegee institute has produced great benefits: there, literary, industrial, and religious education unfold in harmony, with a normal school for teachers, a school of arts and crafts, a Bible school to train good preachers, who, in Washington's mind, can play other roles when needed.

The institute has a wonderful annex—it is the lecture hall, which civilizes at great distances. Founded about ten years ago, it was opened with this invocation from an old Black minister: "Lord, we give you thanks for today is our first day of school this year."

---

[308] Washington adds that Scott kept him "informed of whatever takes place in the South that concerns the race" (1986, 259).

Appendix III – Review of *Up from Slavery*

A hundred people came from different parts to attend the opening, which took place under an improvised roof: today the meetings are held in the chapel built by the students, with enough room for two thousand attendees with their respective seats.

Each one recounts his experiences, heard with great interest by the crowd, who thus reap an admirable lesson. Many Blacks of merit, such as the writer Charles Chesmitt [Chesnutt], Professor Bois [W.E.B. du Bois], Bishops Grant, Turner, and Tyrer, Dr Scott and others, take the opportunity to study closely the economic problems on whose solution Black progress depends.

Booker Washington's advice is always the same: only buy as much land as can be farmed; avoid taking out a mortgage; sacrifice to get decent homes, good schools, and a fine clergy.

He encourages the women to devote themselves actively to domestic chores, and this year one of the best reports was written by a Black woman from Texas, the president of the Barnyard [Auxiliary] Societies in her country.[309] In Texas alone, these societies have 2,500 female members whose expertise in home economics, dairy farming, and gardening is well known.

It was in Texas that the Tuskegee-linked societies for progress first emerged. The patron is R. L. Smith,[310] a member of the Texas legislature, certainly the first Black congressman in America to be elected by a majority of White votes.[311]

His last re-election is considered a highlight of the Blacks' upward march.

These societies (*village improvements* [sic]) have a strong educational influence: the press and the most illustrious citizens look

---

[309] https://footnote.wordpress.ncsu.edu/2022/02/28/the-womans-barnyard-auxiliary/
[310] In this final section, Bentzon goes beyond the contents of *Up from Slavery* (most of which are closely paraphrased) to discuss the work of other eminent Black Americans. For more information on R. L. Smith, see https://themetropole.blog/2021/08/24/robert-l-smith-the-farmers-improvement-society-and-black-community-development-in-the-jim-crow-south/
[311] https://lrl.texas.gov/legeleaders/members/memberdisplay.cfm?memberID=3580

favourably on them. The first does not date further back than 1889; it was founded in the small town of [Oakland, Texas] to "provide the Black the first benefit that is lacking"—social security.

Having always relied on their masters, Blacks bear the mark of slavery—spending imprudently and easily falling into debt[.]

The idea of giving them domestic comforts with money spent on gambling and drink was an excellent one. The influence of such associations on their habits was immediate: the accumulation of individual earnings for the necessities of life, and building up capital set aside for new enterprises, proved that the spirit of solidarity [and] fraternity, is the natural result of joint effort.

As far as he could, Smith abolished credit for members of his association, getting them to produce what they needed. Introducing them to cooperative purchases and sales, suggesting voluntary contributions that could produce a mutual aid fund. Oaklands [sic] was transformed to the point where there was no longer any difference between a Black home and a White home, and it soon gained an excellent local reputation.

Today, there are eighty-six such institutions connected with Tuskegee. They meet annually, represented by congressmen, and due to their influence, the number of Black landowners increased by 17% in less than ten years.

The White planters have taken an interest in them, attending lectures or encouraging them, because the former master is usually personally proud of his former slave, and attributes the latter's progress to his own influence.

Notwithstanding all his recognition for northern philanthropists, Booker Washington believes that it is the South that best understands the Blacks and their needs, and facilitates commercial and industrial relations for them. If the opportunity for scientific and literary instruction is still the subject of debate, the applications of Washington's philosophy are absolutely accepted. Nothing is said against the formation of cooperatives established in different parts of Alabama among Blacks who manage to own a pig, feed it, or acquire a plot of land to grow vegetables for domestic use,

Appendix III – Review of *Up from Slavery*

suppressing the traditional idleness of the season and the Sabbath rest. The Black area covers these institutes attached to Tuskegee.

There is no work better than that undertaken by women under the inspiration of Mrs. Booker Washington.

Every Saturday, Tuskegee's female teachers, humble workers, gather in a rented room in the city. Important matters of practical hygiene and morals are discussed, such as the mortality of children, the inconvenience of a single room for the whole family, the duties of women as wives and mothers; the advantages of poultry farming, beekeeping, etc.

In many towns there are lectures along the lines of these.

The need for coloured women to know their duties is extraordinary. The moral sense weakened by prejudices that were aggravated in slavery, left defenceless to the whims of the White man, subject to very powerful temptations, victims of a tacitly organized system that deprives them of the help and sympathy of the White women of the South, always ready to condemn their ways and see them as an ignoble and dangerous rival, women need to educate themselves, because this is the only way for the entire race to rise. They are not, cannot be, inaccessible to culture: this is proven by the considerable number of women who, as models of excellence, have graduated from Tuskegee—instructors with Christian spirit, and devoted to their calling. They usually marry a fellow graduate, and thus form respectable couples.

Booker Washington's example seems to be the secret behind the entire miracle.

His family life is beyond reproach. For him, there is nothing like the joy of spending as much time as possible at his school, in the company of his excellent wife and three children. His rare hours of recreation are spent in conversations and intimate walks, or in gardening and other tasks in which the spirit rests while usefully employed.

Washington only went on holiday once: it was in 1898, when he and his wife paid a rapid visit to Europe. The notes on this voyage are the most unfair and least interesting part of *Up from Slavery*.³¹² He returned three months later.

Booker Washington always repeats these words from the Gospels: "And he had pity on the multitude."

Spare no sacrifice: this could apply to what he said of General Armstrong who, ill and paralyzed, wanted to spend some time at Tuskegee before he died: "no one has ever been as selfless as that man."

(Continued)

Tuesday, April 15, 1902

VII

The powerful influence exerted by Booker Washington's autobiography, published in *The Outlook* magazine, is indisputable. The miraculous rise of a slave, the son of a despised race, takes him to a sphere in which the superior characters of a country of high civilization hover. However, Booker Washington is not the only one. His predestined name is surrounded by the Bruces, Prices, Douglasses, Revelts [sic], Paines, Simmonses, teachers, doctors, lawyers, ministers, Blacks who fill official positions, ably run banks, factories, agricultural enterprises. Unfortunately they are individuals that can be called—exceptional.³¹³

---

³¹² Washington made an observation that must have offended Bentzon profoundly: "In point of morality and moral earnestness I do not believe that the French are ahead of my own race in America.... In the matter of truth and high honour I do not believe that the average Frenchman is ahead of the American Negro; while so far as mercy and kindness to dumb animals go, I believe that my race is far ahead. In fact, when I left France, I had more faith in the future of the Black man in America than I had ever possessed" (1986, 282).

³¹³ Blanche Kelso Bruce (1841-1898), senator; Frederick Douglass (ca. 1818-1895), abolitionist, orator, writer, and diplomat; Hiram Rhoades Revels (ca. 1827-1901), the first Black American US senator; Daniel Alexander Paine (1811-1893), bishop, educator, and author; William J. Simmons (1849-1890), educator, historian, and

Appendix III – Review of *Up from Slavery*

The reports from the administrators of the Slater Fund, an institution that invests one million dollars bequeathed by the philanthropist John Slater in the education of Blacks, give an idea of the progress made and what needs to be done for men [sic] of colour.

It already has thirteen years of experience. Attentive observers exploring the Black belt point out that rapid progress has been made.

By the time of emancipation, Blacks were immersed in profound ignorance; but by the next generation, 40 percent could read, and, from 1878 to 1895, the number of students enrolled in public and private schools rose by 185 percent. The instinct, aptitudes, and interests of the Black man impel him towards agriculture, and his increased tendency is towards the warm lands of the South. His life is shorter than that of the White man, and mortality pursues him more in the cities, where crime also rises because he is eminently sensitive to the influence of the environment.

Above all the Black man need education: when free, left to himself on distant plantations, he does not progress. Curry,[314] the author of one of the reports, notes that the Blacks never made progress in their country of origin: the human development that comes from voluntary energy, the ethnic and political revolutions of civilized nations, do not figure in their history.

In order achieve the civilization they enjoy, it has been necessary for everything to come to them from the outside. Torn from their Africa, subjected to cruel deportation, enslaved under the actions of everything that can degrade an inferior race, the Black man unexpectedly received freedom, the category of citizen, the right to suffrage and electability. However, these were people who, shortly before, had been forbidden by law to learn to read and write, and for whom universities were now opened, along the lines of those who complete the advanced education of Anglo-Saxons.

---

biographer. Price may be a reference to John Price, who escaped re-enslavement due to the Oberlin-Wellington Rescue, which mobilized US abolitionists in 1858.

[314] *The Education of the Negro*, 1896, by J.L.M. (Jabez Lamar Monroe) Curry (1825-1903), secretary of the Slater Fund.

While praiseworthy, northern philanthropy was too hasty and produced harmful results. If anyone wishes to face the ghastly side of the problem can read *The American Negro: What He Was, What He Is, and What He May Become,* a work whose publication coincided with that of [Washington's] autobiography.[315]

The author, W. H. Thomas,[316] is a man of colour who betrayed his race, which he exposes in a dire situation. In his view, Blacks are intelligent but prone to theft, and as for morals, none aged fifteen, lads or lasses, have maintained their innocence. He states that ninety percent of Blacks lead a licentious life in America, and seeks to demonstrate that, until now, the freedman has produced nothing good.

However, Thomaz [*sic*] is in favour of at least elementary education for Blacks, and of agricultural occupations, but this is almost a fait accompli. Based in Boston, he has not followed the evolution of his race in the South. What his book proves is that a higher education may not influence the nobility of character, and that talent is not incompatible with good faith! It seems that Thomaz is one of the politicians who, after emancipation, were elevated to legislative positions by the Black vote. Unfortunately, many people in the North share his opinion of the Black race, and in Philadelphia colour prejudice is extraordinarily violent. The eminent man of colour, du Bois, a graduate of Harvard University, now professor of history and political economy at the University of Atlanta,[317] points to the intensity of this prejudice in his work *The Philadelphia Negro,*

---

[315] Thomas, 1901. The review of *Up from Slavery* published in *The New York Times* on March 9, 1901 (pp. 17, 18) observes that Washington's autobiography "offset" Thomas's book, which it describes as "a fierce arraignment of the American negro [*sic*]". https://nyti.ms/3HVqCOs Artur Ramos cited *The American Negro* as a source on the "Black question" in North America in *O negro brasileiro,* published in 1934 (1988, 7).

[316] William Hannibal Thomas (1843-1935).

[317] W. E. B. du Bois was a professor of History and Economics at Atlanta University (now Clark Atlanta University) from 1897 to 1910, and returned as head of the Sociology department from 1934 to 1944.

which contains observations from his time as an associate professor of sociology at the University of Pennsylvania.

It is well known that Pennsylvania has always been the centre of Negro life in the north. In 1840, that city had 20,000 freedmen, who were being eliminated by European immigration, mainly men who had to look for work elsewhere. There were 6,000 men against 11,000 women. Appreciating the fact with impartiality, Professor du Bois calculates that this imbalance, which persists despite the increase in population, is the cause of the immorality of the life of the Negro in Philadelphia, aggravated by the contempt towards them. However, this contempt affects the innocent much more than the guilty. Among the 40,000 Blacks in Philadelphia, the poor people, including idlers and malefactors, receive public charity; the inferior and worse paid workers, however, find a means of earning a living; but the Black man who, by dint of skill, distinguishes himself in any field, putting himself on a par with the Whites in the arts or industry, does not receive a just reward.

A lawyer or notary will not dare to sit next to his client, the young man in whose veins runs a drop of Black blood, a pharmacist will not employ a suspected descendant of the accursed race, no matter how good his diplomas; a skilled machinist will be dismissed from the workshop where, to his misfortune, the secret of his origin transpires. An inferior situation, a sign of baseness, colour does not allow effort, talent, honour, or work to prevail.

This justifies Booker Washington's advice for Blacks to stay in the South, where, incidentally, when racial hatred erupts, it is appalling. The summary justice applied to Blacks accused of an unpardonable crime—the violation or attempted violation of a White woman—is notorious. In the past two years, there have been several cases: in Leavenworth, Kansas, a Black man was tied to a stake and burned alive without any form of prosecution before a crowd of eight thousand. In Colorado, the same atrocity was carried out with incredibly refined torture and horrible premeditation, inviting journalists and photographers to witness the act. In a town in Georgia, when the authorities prohibited vandalism, they set the prison on fire, resulting in the deaths of two children and injuring twenty men. On the 25th of last May, the Ohio Supreme Court found the entire county responsible, ordering it to pay 5,000 dollars to the heirs of a Black man who had been lynched. And that is fair, because there is no other way to prevent similar acts of violence by the population carried out with the tacit consent of the citizens.

An even more serious case occurred on August 4, 1900, in New Orleans. Robert Charles, a Black activist of herculean strength, put up desperate resistance to the police: he killed some and they only captured him when he was dead.[318]

Several days of revenge followed in the Black quarter: the Whites burned the Thomy Lafon School, which had been donated to the city by a rich philanthropist of colour, along with over thirty houses inhabited by Blacks. These crimes were attributed to the dregs of society, but the part played by White workers, long since enraged by the competence they saw in Blacks, did not go unnoticed. It can be seen, then, that the problem of labour is involved in the question of the Negro in order to poison it, and it is possible to assess the abyss into which the United States will drag itself, if it is not on its guard.

White supremacy in voting is a major concern in the South. Even in Alabama, despite Washington's influence, there is talk of disenfranchising Blacks.

There are, however, a large number of citizens who think like Booker Washington—the right to vote should be denied for lack of ability to those who cannot read and own no property, whether White or Black.

"I cannot believe," he says, "that in addition to the centuries of advantages that education and wealth give to Whites over the Negro, the former still intends [to pass] a special law that will assure him of greater privileges."

The race's demands must centre around material independence, dignity, character, and moral elevation. The great industrial schools

---

[318] Regarding the New Orleans race riot of 1900, see Prince 2017 https://www.jstor.org/stable/44783811

Appendix III – Review of *Up from Slavery*

of Hampton, Turkegee [sic], Spelman, Claflin, and Tongoloo [sic] do more than many conceited universities where the discontented and unqualified multiply: I repeat—the question of social relations will become a threat in the future.

Its varied shades are not perceptible to a European. On the day the Shaw monument was unveiled, Washington was acclaimed, reaching the height of glory and, in the eyes of foreigners, treated as an equal by the Whites of superior status.

However, his biography contains a very suggestive page.

One day he was traveling in the South and happened to enter the saloon car, which is known to be reserved for White society. The most important planters in the region were present, and everyone fell silent. To make matters worse, two female travellers from the North invited him to have tea with them and served him attentively. "Never," says Booker, "was there a meal that seemed to take longer: it was an ordeal from which I fled as soon as I could. As soon as I reached the smoking-room, the same men whose insolence I so feared, when informed of who I was, came to speak to me and earnestly congratulate me on my work."[319]

---

[319] Washington recounts this incident in Chapter XI: "...when I was making a trip from Augusta, Georgia, to Atlanta...I rode in a Pullman sleeper. When I went into the car, I found there two ladies from Boston whom I knew well. These good ladies were perfectly ignorant, it seems, of the customs of the South, and in the goodness of their hearts insisted that I take a seat with them in their section. After some hesitation I consented. I had been there but a few minutes when one of them, without my knowledge, ordered supper to be served to the three of us. This embarrassed me still further. The car was full of Southern White men, most of whom had their eyes on our party.... At last the meal was over; and it seemed the longest one that I had ever eaten. When we were through, I decided to...go into the smoking-room, where most of the men were by that time, to see how the land lay. In the meantime, however, it had become known in some way throughout the car who I was. When I went into the smoking-room I was never more surprised in my life than when each man, nearly every one of them a citizen of Georgia, came up and introduced himself to me and thanked me earnestly for the work that I was trying to do for the whole South" (1986, 170-171).

Everything had gone very well, but there is no denying that the Black's role is more difficult than ever. Once, to be treated humanely, it was enough for him to be an honest and faithful servant; today, if he wants to maintain the role of a free man, he must possess excessive prudence, subtle politics, and the virtues of a saint.

The Booker Washingtons will always be rare, and the development of the race needs thousands of them, as one Black minister candidly said: "Yes, thousands of Washingtons—one at every bend in the road, one on every mountain."

Similarly, we would need them for the crusade of "deploying industry under conditions of morality" and transforming our mediocre graduates into good farmers.

Th. Bentzon

APPENDIX IV
"The Black Man with the White Face"

The following is a translation of "O negro da cara branca," published on page one of the Diário da Bahia *on March 20, 1902:*

"Booker Washington, that illustrious Black man whom President Roosevelt hosted in his palace, as we have reported here, and had him sit at his table, as if he were White, has published some Memoirs, which the author Augustin Leger analyses and appreciates in the *Correspondant*. Booker Washington was a slave, before emancipation. With extreme and moving simplicity, he recounts his sad life during those times, his childhood in a small windowless hut, the clogs that tortured his feet, the harsh cloth shirt that bit his flesh, like a sinapism.... Then, freedom comes and he feels an enormous desire to learn. One day, in that part of Virginia where the family had settled, a young Black man who had learned to read in Ohio appears, and, later, an old soldier "who was said to be immensely learned" also appears in those parts. Then, lessons and night schools are organized. In 1872, Booker, who would have been about fifteen years old (we lack precise records about the time of his birth), set out for the Hampton Agricultural Institute: two hundred leagues away and with a few coppers in his pocket! A terrible odyssey!

"He spends nights out in the open; on foot, or [traveling] for free in any kind of vehicle, he manages to reach the city of Richmond, a hundred kilometres from his Ithaca. Starving, he falls asleep in a corner, and the next morning he manages to get a job as a porter. By dint of energy and patience, engaging in all professions; jumping from porter to valet and from servant to coffee server, he achieves the fullest of educations... And then, he returns home. His reappearance is a pathetic scene: they make him a great man and benefactor! Immediately, we see him get to work. He founds a school, in earnest, on an abandoned plantation; with his followers he begins to build furniture, beds, tables, the essentials, the indispensable. Soon, the school prospers...

"And amid all the indignation and all the revolt that arose in the United States when they learned that he was sitting at the president's table, there is something admirable and truly astonishing: it is to see the passion and ardor this man expends and uses to get them to forgive their fellow men for that dreadful *crime* of possessing, under the epidermis, a regrettable pigment that blackens them against their will, by force."

APPENDIX V
Mentors and Role Models

Booker T. Washington on General Armstrong[320]

General Samuel Chapman Armstrong has been described as Booker T. Washington's "great white father" (Harlan 1975b, title of chapter 3). In this essay, which he wrote for a biography of Armstrong by the general's daughter, Washington defends not only his mentor but his own approach to the education of Black Americans recently emancipated from slavery. As a form of seigneurial control, they had been denied any form of schooling while they were in bondage—except for learning certain trades that were of use to their slaveholders.

The circumstances of its earliest years and the final and permanent outcome of General Armstrong's work for the principle of combined manual labor and mental work are best told by Booker T. Washington:[321]

"When General Armstrong undertook to introduce industrial education at Hampton, the whole subject was new, not only to the

---

[320] Source: Talbot, Edith Armstrong. *Samuel Chapman Armstrong* (1904, 206-210).
[321] Principal of Tuskegee Institute, Tuskegee, Alabama, who at Hampton Institute in its earlier years received the baptism of General Armstrong's spirit and has since his graduation carried on a similar work (footnote in original).

Negro, but to northern and southern white people. The general impression which prevailed among a large number of colored people, especially those who lived in cities in the North and who had received some advantages of education, was that industrial education was something which was meant to retain the Negro in a kind of slavery to limit his sphere of activity. Many of the colored people felt, also, that it was a kind of education that was to be applied to the colored people only. Added to this difficulty was another. The southern white people as a rule approved of industrial education. This made the colored people all the more suspicious of its value and object. They applied in a measure the same rule to this that they applied to politics in the early years of freedom. If a southern white man favored a certain political measure, the colored people usually opposed it. Many felt that if industrial education was a good thing for the Negro the southern white man would not favor it.

"For a number of years after the work was started at Hampton it was misunderstood in the directions to which I have referred, as well as in many others which I shall not take the time to name. General Armstrong, however, went on calmly pursuing the ends that he had in view, seldom stopping to explain himself or to be troubled by misrepresentations. He realized the value of what he had in mind, and felt sure that in the end the whole country would understand him and come around to his position.

"As I have often heard him explain his theory of industrial education—both to me personally and to the school—when I was a student at Hampton, I think I might state his objects briefly as follows:

"First. He was anxious to give the colored people an idea of the dignity, the beauty and civilizing power of intelligent labor with the hand. He was conscious of the fact that he was dealing with a race that had little necessity to labor in its native land before coming to America, and after coming to this country was forced to labor for

Appendix IV – Mentors and Role Models

two hundred and fifty years under circumstances that were not calculated to make the race fond of hard work.[322]

"Second. It was his object to teach the Negro to lift labor out of drudgery and toil by putting thought and skill into it.

"Third. He saw that through the medium of industrial education he could bring the two races in the South into closer relations with each other. He knew that in other matters there were differences which it would take years to change, but he knew that industrially the interests of the two races were identical in the South, and that as soon as he could prove to a southern white man that an educated skilled Negro workman was of more value to the community than an ignorant, shiftless one, the southern white man would take an interest in the education of the black boy.

"Fourth. Through the industrial system at the Hampton Institute it was his object to give the students an opportunity to work out a portion of their boarding expenses. In tis way he meant to prevent the school becoming a hothouse for producing students with no power of self-help or independence. I have often heard him say that the mere effort which the student put forth through the industries at Hampton to help himself was of the greatest value to the student, whether the labor itself was of very much value or not. In a word, he meant to use the industries as a means for building character—to teach that all forms of labor were honorable and all forms of idleness a disgrace.

"The idea of industrial education, beginning for our people at Hampton, has gradually spread among them until I am safe in saying that it has permeated the whole race in every section of the country. There is not a State in the Union where there is any considerable proportion of our race whose influence counts for anything in which they are not interested in industrial education and are manifesting this interest by the establishment of a school or by other substantial

---

[322] Here, while Washington accurately describes the impact of enslavement on the work ethic, he also demonstrates that his image of life in Africa was similar to the stereotype of Indigenous peoples in the Americas.

helps. They now realize, as never before, that the education of the head, the heart and the hand must go together. That while we need classical and professional men, we need a still larger number trained along industrial lines.

"Not only has General Armstrong's belief in industrial education spread among our people in the South, but its influence is felt in the West Indies and Africa and other foreign countries, to such an extent that there are many calls coming from these countries for industrial education.

"The work at the Tuskegee Normal and Industrial Institute is simply one of the results of the work of the Hampton Institute. There are a number of industrial schools, either small or large, in every State where there are any considerable number of our people.

"Perhaps the most interesting thing in connection with the influence of General Armstrong is the rapid growth and spread of industrial education among the southern white people. For a number of years after the Hampton Institute was started the southern white people gave no attention to the subject, and rather took for granted, I think, that it was something in which the Negroes only should receive training. But as they realized from year to year the rapid growth of industrial education among the colored people and the skill and intelligence which they were acquiring, southern white educators here and there began to make investigation and inquire whether or not the same kind of education was not needed for the southern white boy and girl, and very carefully and modestly at first industries were introduced into a white school here and there. These schools, however, were not very popular among the white people at first, but the idea of industrial education among the southern white people has spread until at the present moment I think every southern State has one or more institutions established for tis kind of training for white youths, and the industrial idea has become almost as popular among the white people as among the colored people.

"I think I am not going too far when I make one other suggestion, and that is that the whole country owes General Armstrong a debt not only for the rapid and permanent growth of industrial education among the colored people and white people of the South, but it is to him that all are indebted more than to any one man for the growth of the and training in the northern and western States. It is seldom, in my opinion, that one individual has had the opportunity through a single idea to revolutionize the educational thought and activity of so large a proportion of the world as has been true of the founder of Hampton."

Manuel Querino on Manuel Correia Garcia

Correia Garcia was Querino's guardian. He raised his ward from the age of four, and not only taught him to read and write (which saved him from being sent to the front during the Triple Alliance War) and apprenticed him as a painter and decorator but put Querino in close contact with Bahia's political and artistic circles. The mention of Correia Garcia's visit to the home of the Spanish artist Miguel Navarro y Cañizares (1835-1913)—the founder of the School of Fine Art and another important mentor for Querino—indicates a familiarity that can only have benefited his ward in a society where "who you know" was and still is essential in life. As we can see, there are numerous parallels between Correia Garcia's life and accomplishments, and those of Querino.

Biographical Note on Dr Manuel Correia Garcia

Born in this city [Salvador] on August 15, 1815, he was the legitimate son of the Portuguese merchant of the same name and Leonor Joaquina de Abreu.

He had the misfortune of losing his father when he was three and a half years old: a year later, he began attending primary school, [then,] at the age of nine and a few months he began preparatory school, immediately giving proof of his great intelligence, meriting the highest praise from his teachers and due distinction from his classmates.

When, in 1836, the government of what was then the province [of Bahia] held a competitive examination for candidates wishing to go to Europe to study courses required to found the Normal School of Bahia, Dr Garcia was one of those who passed the exams.

His test results during that competition were the most brilliant of all, confirming his good standing among his teachers and classmates, which was justified by his excellent recommendations.

He went to Europe, fulfilling the noble mission of acquiring pedagogical knowledge and teaching it to the studious and hardworking youths of his time.

When he arrived in France together with the distinguished Bahian, João Alves Portella, his colleague happened to fall ill. On the day set for the entrance exam, Dr Garcia was quizzed by a committee of three members of the Institute, three sages, therefore, who were so enthusiastic about the young man from Bahia's performance, masterfully handling the language which Racine had so greatly enriched, that they decided to exempt him and his colleague Portella (who did not sit the exam) from being tested in the other subjects, and both were admitted.

[Correia Garcia's] academic experience firmly and robustly expressed his talent and his unsurpassed devotion to study, proof of which is that he obtained a first-class teacher's diploma from the École Normale de Paris. Upon returning to his homeland, as a reward for his merits, he was appointed as a lecturer at the Normal School.

He devoted all his activities to the love of science, of which he was a fervent devotee.

He married, and after his beloved consort passed away in the flower of her youth, in 1847 he wed his second wife, Maria Izabel Brandão Garcia, who is still living, and with whom he had seven children, five of whom survived him. In 1851, he wrote an essay entitled: *Idéias de um monarquista constitucional* (Ideas of a Constitutional Monarchist), in which he stressed, with the fine language unique to him, the disadvantages of republican Brazil at that time, fighting against the revolutionary movement of 1848 in

Appendix IV – Mentors and Role Models

Pernambuco [the Praieira Revolt], giving scintillating examples, from the Roman Republic to the United States of North America.

A little-known circumstance about him is worth mentioning here. He was the powerful secret hand that directed the pacification of Pernambuco. A close friend of Colonel Pedro Antônio Velloso da Silveira, father of the revolutionary Pedro Ivo, according to the President of the Province, the Brazilian who was the incarnation of patriotism, of venerable memory, Francisco Gonçalves Martins, later Viscount of S. Lourenço, arranged for Colonel Pedro Antônio to confront the revolutionary forces. [Pedro Antônio] was seriously wounded by the forces led by his son. When [Pedro Ivo] heard the news, he went to his father, who demanded that his son surrender his arms out of filial love, and thus ended a struggle that was already very harmful to the country.[323]

[Correia Garcia] distinguished himself greatly as an orator, a notable lawyer, a *repentista*,[324] and a fluent speaker—[his words] honed by the useful and conscious handling of his reading of the classics.

He was a poet of some merit, as some of the works he left us in that genre attest, particularly in satire, which was his predilection.

An excellent writer of prose, in close contact with privileged minds, such as Agrário de Menezes, Silva e Almeida, Álvares da Silva, Raposo de Almeida, and many others, he effectively contributed to elevating the name of Bahia in the republic of letters. He was a firm devotee of the fine arts.

Incidentally, when Professor Lellis Piedade was explaining the fine arts of Egypt to his students at Professor Cañizares's house, Dr Garcia came in and gave an aside; absent-mindedly, he went on and finished the lesson, withdrawing apologetically when he had concluded, [but] in the end everyone was pleased.

---

[323] This version of events differs greatly from the official history of the Praieira Revolt.

[324] A singer of improvised verses.

As a provincial deputy, the records attest to his competence in various fields of knowledge, particularly regarding public education and jurisprudence.

A superb polemicist, he collaborated with nearly all the newspapers of his time.

The editor the *Correio Mercantil* and the *Jornal da Bahia*, and editor-in-chief and owner of *Nova Epocha*, he rendered remarkable services as a co-founder of the Instituto Histórico da Bahia (Historical Institute of Bahia) and a staunch fighter on behalf of the homeland's literature. On May 13, 1844, he was appointed captain-prosecutor of the Hunters' Battalion of the 1st Legion of the National Guard, and Deputy Chief Constable of the Sé district in 1857; in 1861 he was arbitrarily forced to retire due to political circumstances, by virtue of the *Organizational Regulations*. Elected Provincial Deputy in two legislatures, and Salvador City Councilman in 1868, he performed these roles with noble character and elevated views.

In recognition of the important legal services which he provided for the Portuguese—16th of September Society, the King of Portugal saw fit to invest [Correia Garcia] with the regalia and title of a knight of the order of Conceição de Villa-Viçosa on September 3, 1872; and on May 29, 1879, he became a Commander of the same order. He was a teacher at the Colégio dos Órfãos de São Joaquim, a member of the Higher Council for Public Education, and a corresponding member of the Sociedade Propagadora das Bellas-Artes (Society for the Propagation of Fine Art).[325] A full member of the Dramatic Conservatory, and corresponding member of the Special Religious Institute, he wrote several short books, some unpublished, among them: *Aplicação da moral à política* (The Application of Morals to Politics), and the *Biografía de D. Romualdo, como parlamentar e politico* (Biography of D. Romualdo, as a Lawmaker and Politician).

In 1871, according to qualified opinions, he wrote an important thesis on the death penalty in Latin, which was submitted to the

---

[325] Manuel Querino was a founding member of that society.

University of Tubingen, Germany, earning him the degree of Doctor of Philosophy.

He made politics a mission, and for that reason was never appreciated as much as his undeniable merit deserved. Biting satire often wounded his self-esteem, for he was seen as being immoderate; but he was compensated for this with consideration of his real merits, which even his enemies recognized.

He died poor—naturally, as that is the fate of the hardworking man—on February 23, 1890, bequeathing his family an honourable name, crowned by the bright flashes of his robust talent, well known to the apostles of letters.

He was one of the greatest stars of journalism and jurisprudence of his time.

He had the advantage of combining talent and enlightenment with a love of work.

Bahia, September 7, 1896.[326]
Manuel Querino
(Founding Member of the Instituto Geográfico e Histórico da Bahia)

Querino, Manuel. "Notícia biográfica do Dr Manuel Correia Garcia" In: Garcia, Manuel Correia. *História da Independência da Bahia.* Salvador: Bahia Typ. e Encadernação—Empreza Editora, 1900.

---

[326] The date on which Brazil celebrates its independence from Portugal.

BIBLIOGRAPHY

ARCHIVES CONSULTED

Arquivo Público do Estado da Bahia
Centro de Documentação (Cedoc) A Tarde
Biblioteca Pública do Estado da Bahia - Periódicos
Booker T. Washington Papers, Manuscript Division, Library of Congress
Hemeroteca Digital Brasileira—Fundação Biblioteca Nacional
Instituto Geográfico e Histórico da Bahia (IGHB)

BRAZILIAN PERIODICALS CONSULTED

A Tarde — Salvador, Bahia
Almanaque Brasileiro Garnier
A Noite—Rio de Janeiro, RJ
Correio da Manhã—Rio de Janeiro, RJ
Correio Paulistano—São Paulo, SP
Diário da Bahia—Salvador, Bahia
Diário Nacional—São Paulo, SP
Gazeta de Notícias—Rio de Janeiro, RJ
Imprensa Popular—Rio de Janeiro, RJ
O Clarim d'Alvorada—São Paulo, SP
O Imparcial—Rio de Janeiro, RJ
O Paiz—Rio de Janeiro, RJ
O Trabalho—Salvador, Bahia

Pharol—Juiz de Fora, Minas Gerais
Quilombo—Rio de Janeiro, RJ
Renascença—Salvador, Bahia

A Tarde (Salvador, BA). "Centenário de Manoel Quirino: as homenagens da Bahia." July 28, 1951.

A Tarde (Salvador, BA). "Encerradas as comemorações do centenário de Manuel Querino." July 29, 1951.

Agassiz, Louis, and Elizabeth Cary Agassiz. *Viagem ao Brasil: 1865-1866.* Translated and annotated by Edgar Süssekind de Mendonça. Brasília, DF: Senado Federal, 2000.

Agassiz, Louis, and Elizabeth Cary Agassiz. *A Journey in Brazil.* Release date: December 12, 2017. https://www.gutenberg.org/files/56171/56171-h/56171-h.htm

Aguiar, Pinto de. Foreword to *A raça africana e os seus costumes*, by Manuel Querino, 5-11. Salvador: Livraria Progresso, 1955.

Aguiar, Ronaldo Conde. *O rebelde esquecido: tempo, vida e obra de Manoel Bomfim.* Rio de Janeiro: Topbooks, 2000.

Alberto, Paulina Laura, George Reid Andrews, and Jesse Hoffnung-Garskof, editors and translators. *Voices of the Race: Black Newspapers in Latin America, 1870-1960.* Cambridge and New York: Cambridge University Press, 2022.

Albuquerque, Wlamyra Ribeiro de. "Esperanças de Boaventuras: construções da África e africanismos na Bahia (1887-1910)." *Estudos afro-asiáticos,* Rio de Janeiro, 24, no. 2 (2002): 215-245. http://www.scielo.br/scielo.php?script=sci_arttext&pid=S0101-546X2002000200001.

Albuquerque, Wlamyra Ribeiro de. *O jogo da dissimulação*: *Abolição e cidadania negra no Brasil.* São Paulo: Companhia das Letras, 2009.

Albuquerque, Wlamyra Ribeiro de. "Esperanças de Boaventuras: construções da África e africanismos na Bahia (1887-1910)." In *Política, instituições e personagens da Bahia (1850-1930),* edited by Jeferson Afonso Bacelar and Cláudio Luiz Pereira, 93-124. Salvador: EdUFBA, 2013.

Albuquerque, Wlamyra R. de and Walter Fraga Filho. *Uma história do negro no Brasil.* Salvador: Centro de Estudos Afro-Orientais; Brasília: Fundação Cultural Palmares, 2006.

Alix-Garcia, Jennifer, Laura Schechter, Felipe Valencia Caicedo, and S. Jessica Zhu. "Country of Women? Repercussions of the Triple Alliance War in Paraguay." *Journal of Economic Behavior & Organization* 202 (October 2022): 131-167.

Alves, Marieta. *Intelectuais e escritores baianos: breves biografias.* Salvador: Prefeitura Municipal: Fundação Museu da Cidade, 1977.

Amado, Jorge. *Tenda dos milagres.* 36th ed. Rio de Janeiro: Record, 1987.

Amado, Jorge. *Tenda dos milagres.* São Paulo: Companhia das Letras, 1969.

Amado, Jorge. *Navegação de cabotagem.* Rio de Janeiro: Record, 1992.

Amado, Jorge. *Tent of Miracles.* Madison: University of Wisconsin Press, 2003.

Anderson, Benedict. *Nação e consciência nacional.* São Paulo: Editora Ática, 1989.

Anderson, Benedict. *Imagined Communities. Reflections on the Origin and Spread of Nationalism.* London: Verso, 2016.

Appiah, Kwame Anthony. *In My Father's House: Africa in the Philosophy of Culture.* New York and Oxford: Oxford University Press, 1992.

Appiah, Kwame Anthony. *Na casa de meu pai: a África na filosofia da cultura.* Translated by Vera Ribeiro. Rio de Janeiro: Contraponto, 1997.

Appiah, Kwame Anthony. "Racial Identity and Racial Identification." In *Theories of Race and Racism: A Reader,* edited by Les Back and John Solomos, 606-615. London and New York: Routledge, 2000.

Araújo, Emanoel, ed. *A mão afro-brasileira: significado da contribuição artística e histórica.* São Paulo: Tenenge, 1988.

Araújo, Emanoel, ed. *A mão afro-brasileira: significado da contribuição artística e histórica.* 2nd ed. São Paulo: Museuafrobrasil, 2010.

Araújo, Emanoel, ed. *Eu tenho um sonho: de King a Obama, a saga negra do Norte*. São Paulo: Museuafrobrasil, 2011.

Armistead, Wilson. *A Tribute for the Negro: Being a Vindication of the Moral, Intellectual, and Religious Capabilities of the Coloured Portion of Mankind; with Particular Reference to the African Race*. Manchester: William Irwin, 1848. http://docsouth.unc.edu/neh/armistead/armistead.html

American Sociological Association. *Robert Ezra Park*. Washington, DC [n.d.] https://www.asanet.org/robert-e-park/?hilite=robert+ezra+park

Ascoli, Peter Max. *Julius Rosenwald: The Man Who Built Sears, Roebuck and Advanced the Cause of Black Education in the American South*. Bloomington, Indiana: Indiana University Press, 2006.

Ayoh'Omidire, Felix, and Alcione O. Amos. "O Babalaô Fala: A Autobiografia de Martiniano Eliseu do Bomfim." *Afro-Ásia* 46 (2012): 229-26. https://doi.org/10.9771/aa.v0i46.21267.

Azevedo, Célia Maria Marinho de. *Abolicionismo: Estados Unidos e Brasil, uma história comparada (século XIX)*. São Paulo: Annablume, 2003.

Azevedo, Célia Maria Marinho de. *Onda negra, medo branco: o negro no imaginário das elites, século XIX*. 2nd ed. São Paulo: Annablume, 2004.

Azevedo, Thales de. Introduction to *Costumes africanos no Brasil*. 2nd ed. expanded and annotated, by Manuel Querino, 7-9. Edited, foreword, and annotations by Raul Lody. Recife: Fundação Joaquim Nabuco: Editora Massangana, 1988.

Bacelar, Jeferson Afonso, and Carlos Alberto Dória. "Creator of Bahian Folk Cuisine." In *Manuel Querino (1851-1923): An Afro-Brazilian Pioneer in the Age of Scientific Racism*, 149-175. Crediton: Editora Funmilayo Publishing, 2021.

Bacelar, Jeferson Afonso, and Cláudio Pereira. *Bahia negra na coleção Museu Tempostal*. Coleção Etnobahia. Salvador: P555 edições, 2006.

Bacelar, Jeferson Afonso. "Resenha de São Luís. Biografia [de Jacques Le Gof]." Unpublished manuscript, 1990.

Bacelar, Jeferson Afonso. "Itinerários intelectuais e o debate sobre as desigualdades étnico-raciais." Unpublished manuscript, 1998.

Bacelar, Jeferson Afonso. *A hierarquia das raças: negros e brancos em Salvador*. Rio de Janeiro: Pallas, 2001.

Bacelar, Jeferson Afonso. *Mário Gusmão: um príncipe negro na terra dos dragões da maldade*. Rio de Janeiro: Pallas, 2006.

Bacelar, Jeferson Afonso. "De candomblés a negros ilustres." In *Manuel R. Querino: seus artigos na* Revista do Instituto Geográfico e Histórico da Bahia, edited by Jaime Nascimento and Hugo Gama, 177-183. Salvador: Instituto Geográfico e Histórico da Bahia, 2009.

Bacelar, Jonildo. "Carlos Ott: 1908-1997." *Guia Geográfico História da Bahia*. https://www.historia-brasil.com/bibliografia/carlos-ott.htm

Bahia Ilustrada. "Propaganda indigna." Salvador, vol. 5, no. 39, June 1921.

Baker, Lee D. *From Savage to Negro: Anthropology and the Construction of Race, 1896-1954*. Berkeley and Los Angeles: University of California Press, 1998.

Baker, Ray Stannard. *Following the Color Line: An Account of Negro Citizenship in the American Democracy*. New York: Doubleday, Page & Company, 1908. Kindle.

Baldwin, James. "A Talk to Teachers." *Saturday Review* (December 21, 1963): 1-6. http://richgibson.com/talktoteachers.htm

Banta, Melissa, and Curtis M. Hinsley, with Joan Kathryn O'Donnell. *From Site to Sight: Anthropology, Photography, and the Power of Imagery*. Thirtieth Anniversary Edition. New introduction by Ira Jacknis. Cambridge, Mass.: Peabody Museum Press, Harvard University, 2017.

Barbash, Ilisa, Molly Rogers, and Deborah Willis, eds. *To Make Their Own Way in the World: The Enduring Legacy of the Zealy Daguerreotypes*. Foreword by Henry Louis Gates, Jr. Cambridge, Mass./New York: Peabody Museum Press/Aperture, 2020.

Barreto, Lima. *Contos completos de Lima Barreto*. Edited with a foreword by Lília Moritz Schwarcz. São Paulo: Companhia das Letras, 2010.

Barros, José Teixeira. "Manuel R. Querino. Apresentação." In *A Bahia de outr'ora: Vultos e factos populares*, 2nd ed. expanded, by Manuel Querino, iii-vii. Bahia: Livraria Econômica, 1922.

Barros, José Teixeira. "Manuel R. Querino. Apresentação." In *A Bahia de outrora*. 3rd ed., by Manuel R. Querino. Foreword and annotated by Frederico Edelweiss. Salvador: Livraria Progresso, 1946.

Barthes, Roland. *A câmara clara*. Rio de Janeiro: Nova Fronteira, 1984.

Barthes, Roland. *Camera lucida: Reflections on Photography*. S.l.: Lulu.com, 2022. Kindle.

Becker, Howard S. "The Chicago School, So-called." http://web.archive.org/web/20080203122901/http://home.earthlink.net/~hsbecker/chicago.html.

Becker, William B. "Cabinet Cards." In *Encyclopedia of Nineteenth-Century Photography*, edited by John Hannavy, vol. 1, 233-234. New York: Routledge, 2008.

Benbow, Mark E. "Birth of a Quotation: Woodrow Wilson and 'Like Writing History with Lightning.'" *The Journal of the Gilded Age and Progressive Era* 9, no. 4 (October 2010): 509-533. https://www.jstor.org/stable/20799409

Bennett, Drake. "Questions for Kwame Anthony Appiah: The Trouble with Identity." *Boston News*, no. 6, February 6, 2005. http://archive.boston.com/news/globe/ideas/articles/2005/02/06/the_trouble_with_identity?pg=full

Bennett, William J. *America: The Last Best Hope*. Vol. 2, *From a World at War to the Triumph of Freedom, 1914-1989*. Nashville, Tennessee: Thomas Nelson, 2008.

Bentzon, Th. [Marie-Thérèse de Solms Blanc]. "L'autobiographie d'un nègre." *Revue des Deux Mondes* (1829-1971), Cinquième période 5, no. 5 (October 15, 1901): 759-801.

Bentzon, Th. [Marie-Thérèse de Solms Blanc]. "*A autobiografia de um negro* (resenha)." Serialized in *Diário da Bahia* from March 22 to April 15, 22 1902.

Biddiss, Michael D. *Father of Racist Ideology: The Social and Political Thought of Count Gobineau.* New York: Weybright and Talley, 1970.

Bieze, Michael. *Booker T. Washington and the Art of Self-Representation.* New York: Peter Lang, 2008.

Blanchard, Pascal, Nicolas Bancel, Gilles Boetsch, Éric Deroo, and Sandrine Lemaire, eds. *Human Zoos: Science and Spectacle in the Age of Colonial Empires.* Translated by Teresa Bridgeman. Liverpool: Liverpool University Press, 2008.

Bomfim, Manoel. *A América Latina: Males de origem.* Rio de Janeiro: Topbooks, 2005.

Bontemps, Arna. *Young Booker: Booker T. Washington's Early Days.* New York: Dodd, Mead & Company, 1972.

Booker Washington Institute of Liberia. *National Alumni Association of North America.* Liberia, West Africa, 2018. https://www.bwitigers.org/bwi-history

Bosi, Alfredo. *Literatura e resistência.* São Paulo: Companhia das Letras, 2002.

Bourdieu, Pierre; Wacquant, Loïc. "On the Cunning of Imperialist Reason." *Theory, Culture & Society* 16, no. 1 (1999): 41-58.

Bourdieu, Pierre. *Razões práticas: Sobre a teoria da ação.* Campinas: Papirus, 1996.

Bourdieu, Pierre. *A distinção: Crítica social do julgamento.* Porto Alegre and São

Paulo: Zouk/Edusp, 2006.

Bourdieu, Pierre. *A economia das trocas simbólicas.* 6th ed. São Paulo: Perspectiva, 2009.

Bracey, Christopher A. *Saviors or Sellouts: The Promise and Peril of Black Conservatism, from Booker T. Washington to Condoleezza Rice.* Boston: Beacon Press, 2008.

Braga, Julio Santana. *Sociedade Protetora dos Desvalidos: Uma irmandade de cor.* Salvador: Ianamá, 1987.

Branch, Taylor. *Pillar of Fire: America in the King Years, 1963-65*. New York: Simon & Schuster, 1998.

Brasil. Código penal de 1890. Brasília, DF, 1890. http://www.scribd.com/doc/55636995/Codigo-Penal-de-1890-Completo.

Brookshaw, David. *Race and Color in Brazilian Literature*. Metuchen, N.J. & London: The Scarecrow Press, 1986.

Brundage, W. Fitzhugh, ed. *Booker T. Washington and Black Progress: Up from Slavery 100 Years Later*. Gainesville: University Press of Florida, 2003.

Bundles, A'Lelia. *Self Made: The Life and Times of Madam C. J. Walker*. London: John Murray, 2020. Kindle.

Burke, Peter. *Testemunha ocular: História e imagem*. Bauru, SP: EdUSC, 2008.

Burke, Peter. *Eyewitnessing: The Uses of Images as Historical Evidence*. London: Reaktion Books, 2011. Kindle.

Burnett, Lonnie A. *Henry Hotze Confederate Propagandist: Selected Writings on Revolution, Recognition, and Race*. Tuscaloosa, Alabama: University of Alabama Press, 2008. Google Books/Kindle.

Burns, E. Bradford. "Bibliographical Essay: Manuel Querino's Interpretation of the African Contribution to Brazil." *The Journal of Negro History*, Chicago 59, no. 1 (January 1974): 78-86.

Burns, E. Bradford. "A interpretação de Manuel Querino à contribuição africana no Brasil." *Revista de Cultura da Bahia*, Salvador 9 (January-December 1974): 61-72.

Burns, E. Bradford. *A History of Brazil*. 3rd ed. New York: Columbia University Press, 1993.

Burrell, Tom. *Brainwashed: Challenging the Myth of Black Inferiority*. Carlsbad, CA: Smiley Books, 2010.

Butler, Kim D. *Freedoms Given, Freedoms Won: Afro-Brazilians in Post-Abolition São Paulo and Bahia*. New Brunswick: Rutgers University Press, 2000.

Bibliography

Calmon, Jorge. *Manuel Querino, o jornalista e o político*. Ensaios/Pesquisas, 3. Salvador: Centro de Estudos Afro-Orientais, UFBa, 1980

Calmon, Jorge. *O vereador Manuel Querino*. Salvador: Câmara Municipal de Salvador, 1995.

Calmon, Pedro. *História da literatura bahiana*. 2nd ed. Rio de Janeiro: Livraria José Olympio Editora, 1949.

Montalembert, Charles Forbes Comte de. *De l'avenir politique de l'Angleterre*. Paris: Didier, 1857. Google Books. https://www.google.co.uk/books/edition/De_l_avenir_politique_de_l_Angleterre_pa/frHdISJsoIAC?hl=en

Carnegie, Andrew. *The Autobiography of Andrew Carnegie and The Gospel of Wealth*. S.l.: Seven Treasures Publications, 2010. Original edition: London: Constable & Co. Limited, 1920.

Carnegie, Andrew. *The Autobiography of Andrew Carnegie*. Delhi: General Press, 2022. Kindle.

Carneiro, Edison, and Aydano de Couto Ferraz, eds. *O negro no Brasil: Trabalhos apresentados ao 2º Congresso Afro-Brasileiro (Bahia)*. Rio de Janeiro: Civilização Brasileira, 1940.

Carneiro, Edison. *Ladinos e crioulos: Estudos sobre o negro no Brasil*. Rio de Janeiro: Civilização Brasileira, 1964.

Carroll, Rebecca, ed. *Uncle Tom or New Negro? African Americans Reflect on Booker T. Washington and Up from Slavery One Hundred Years Later*. New York: Broadway Books: Harlem Moon, 2006.

Carvalho, José Murilo de. *Os bestializados: O Rio de Janeiro e a República que não foi*. 3rd ed. São Paulo: Companhia das Letras, 1991.

Carvalho Jr., Álvaro Pinto de. *O Barão de Jeremoabo e a política de seu tempo*. Salvador, BA: SECT, 2006.

Castellucci, Aldrin A. S. "Flutuações econômicas, crise política e greve geral na Bahia da Primeira República." Poder: Tramas e Tensões. *Revista Brasileira de História* 25, no. 50 (December 2005) https://doi.org/10.1590/S0102-01882005000200006

Castellucci Junior, Wellington. *Pescadores e roceiros: Escravos e forros em Itaparica na segunda metade do século XIX, 1860-1888.* São Paulo: Annablume: Fapesp; Salvador: Fapesb, 2008.

Certeau, Michel de. *A invenção do cotidiano: artes de fazer.* 2nd ed. Petrópolis: Vozes, 2000.

Chaves, Miguel. "Manoel Querino e o Lyceu." *O Democrata.* February 14, 1923, 2.

Chiacchio, Carlos. "Homens & Obras—Resenha bibliográfica." *A Tarde.* June 3, 1932, 3.

Coleman, James Smoot. *Nigeria: Background to Nationalism.* Berkeley, Los Angeles and London: University of California Press: 1971.

Cook, Mercer. "Booker T. Washington and the French." *The Journal of Negro History,* Chicago 40, no. 4 (October 1955): 318-340. http://www.jstor.org/stable/2715657.

Cooper, Donald B. "The New 'Black Death': Cholera in Brazil, 1855-1856." *Social Science History* 10, no. 4 (Winter 1986): 467-488.

Costa e Silva, Alberto da. "Portraits of African Royalty in Brazil." In *Identity in the Shadow of Slavery,* edited by Paul E. Lovejoy, 129-136. London: Continuum, 2000.

Couve, Antenor Boaventura. "Meu avô Rei Ossurumis: narrativa de um descendente de um rei africano escravo na Bahia." *Revista Almanaque do Mensageiro da Fé,* Salvador (1964): 96-99. In *Bahia Textos* (blog). May 24, 2010. http://bahiatextos.blogspot.com/2010/05/meu-avo-rei-ossurumis.html.

Cruz, Itan. "Saraiva, Dantas e Cotegipe: Baianismo, escravidão e os planos para o pós-abolição no Brasil (1880-1889)." PhD thesis, Faculdade de Filosofia e Ciências Humanas, Programa de Pós-Graduação em História, Universidade Federal da Bahia, 2022. https://ppgh.ufba.br/sites/ppgh.ufba.br/files/cruz_itan._saraiva_dantas_e_cotegipe_baianismo_escravidao_e_os_planos_para_o_posabolicao_no_brasil_1880-1889_0.pdf

Cunha, Manuela Carneiro da. "Olhar escravo, ser olhado." In *Escravos brasileiros do século XIX na fotografia de Christiano Jr.,* edited by Paulo Cezer de Azevedo and Mauricio Lissovsky, xxiii-xxx. São Paulo: Ex Libris, 1988.

Cunha, Manuela Carneiro da. *Negros, estrangeiros: os escravos libertos e sua volta à África*. 2nd edition revised and expanded. São Paulo: Companhia das Letras, 2012.

Cunnigen, Donald, Rutledge M. Dennis and Myrtle Gonza Glascoe, eds. *The Racial Politics of Booker T. Washington*. Amsterdam: Elsevier, 2006.

Dagbovie, Pero Gaglo. "Exploring a Century of Historical Scholarship on Booker T. Washington." *The Journal of African American History* 92, no. 2 (Spring, 2007): 239-264.

DaMatta, Roberto. *Relativizando: uma introdução à Antropologia Social*. Petrópolis: Vozes, 1981. Kindle.

Daniel, Pete; Smock, Raymond. *A Talent for Detail: The Photographs of Miss Frances Benjamin Johnston 1889-1910*. New York: Harmony Books, 1974.

Davis, Deborah. *Guest of Honor: Booker T. Washington, Theodore Roosevelt, and the White House Dinner that Shocked a Nation*. New York: Atria Books, 2012.

Degler, Carl. *Neither Black nor White: Slavery and Race Relations in Brazil and the United States*. Madison, Wisconsin: The University of Wisconsin Press, 1971.

Degler, Carl. *Nem preto nem branco: escravidão e relações raciais no Brasil e nos E.U.A*. Rio de Janeiro: Editorial Labor do Brasil, 1976.

De la Fuente, Alejandro, and George Reid Andrews, eds. *Afro-Latin American Studies: An Introduction*. New York: Cambridge University Press, 2018.

Deutsch, Stephanie. *You Need a Schoolhouse: Booker T. Washington, Julius Rosenwald, and the Building of Schools for the Segregated South*. Evanston, Illinois: Northwestern University Press, 2011.

Domingues, Petrônio, and Flávio Gomes. "Printing Ideas: Intellectuals and Racial Mobilization in Post-War Brazil (1945-1955)." Translated by H. Sabrina Gledhill. *Journal of Latin American Communication Research* 3, no. 2 (2013): 116-134.

Dória, Carlos Alberto, and Jeferson Afonso Bacelar. *Manuel Querino: criador da culinária popular baiana.* Salvador: P55 Edição, 2020.

Dorsey, Carolyn A. "Olivia Davidson Washington." In *Notable Black American Women,* edited by Jessie Carney Smith, 1221-24. Detroit/London: Gale Research Inc., 1992.

Dosse, François. *O desafio biográfico: escrever uma vida.* Translated by Gilson César Cardoso de Souza. São Paulo: EdUSP, 2005.

Douglass, Frederick. *Narrative of the Life of Frederick Douglass, an American Slave, Written by Himself.* Boston: Anti-Slavery Office, 1845.

Douglass, Frederick. "Narrative of the Life of Frederick Douglass, An American Slave." In *Narrative of the Life of Frederick Douglass, An American Slave and Incidents in the Life of a Slave Girl,* by Frederick Douglass. Introduction by Kwame Anthony Appiah. New York: Modern Library, 2004.

Drinker, Frederick E. *Booker T. Washington, The Master Mind of a Child of Slavery.* Facsimile edition. London: Forgotten Books, [1915].

Du Bois, David G. "Washington e Du Bois: duas opções de liberdade." In *As almas da gente negra,* by W. E. B. Du Bois Rio de Janeiro: Lacerda, 1999.

Du Bois, W. E. B. "William Monroe Trotter." In *W.E.B. Du Bois: A Reader,* edited by David Levering Lewis,135-137. New York: Henry Holt and Company, 1995.

Du Bois, W. E. B. *The Souls of Black Folk.* Centennial edition. New York: W.W. Norton & Company, 1999a.

Du Bois, W. E. B. *As almas da gente negra.* Translated by Heloísa Toller Gomes. Rio de Janeiro: Lacerda, 1999b.

Du Bois, W. E. B. *The Souls of Black Folk.* New York: Barnes & Noble, 2003.

Du Bois, W. E. B. *The Souls of Black Folk.* N.p.: G&D Media, 2019. Kindle.

Du Bois, W. E. B. *The Suppression of the African Slave-Trade to the United States of America, 1638-1870.* New York: Oxford University Press, 2007a. Kindle.

Du Bois, W. E. B. "The Talented Tenth." In *The Negro Problem*, edited by Booker T. Washington. New York: James Pott & Company, 1903. https://archive.org/details/negroproblemseri00washrich/page/2/mode/2up

Dugrivel, C. M. A. *Des bordes de la Saône à la baie de San Salvador ou promenade sentimentale en France et au Brésil*. Paris: Lacour, 1843.

Duncan, Russell. *Where Death and Glory Meet: Colonel Robert Gould Shaw and the 54th Massachusetts Infantry*. Georgia: University of Georgia Press, 1999.

Dyer, Thomas G. *Theodore Roosevelt and the Idea of Race*. Baton Rouge and London: Louisiana State University Press, 1980.

Earl Castillo, Lisa. "Icons of Memory: Photography and its Uses in Bahian Candomblé." *Stockholm Review of Latin American Studies* 4 (March 2009): 11-23.

Earl Castillo, Lisa. *Entre a oralidade e a escrita: a etnografia nos candomblés da Bahia*. Salvador: EdUFBA, 2010.

Earl Castillo, Lisa. "A nação 'Ketu' no contexto histórico: subgrupos iorubás na Bahia oitocentista." In *África, margens e oceanos: perspectivas de história social*, edited by Lucilene Reginaldo and Roquinaldo Ferreira, chapter 8. Campinas: Editora Unicamp 2021a.

Earl Castillo, Lisa. "The 'Ketu Nation' of Brazilian Candomblé in Historical Context." *History in Africa* 0 (2021b): 1–41.

Edelweiss, Frederico, foreword to the third edition of *A Bahia de outrora*, by Manuel Querino. Salvador: Livraria Progresso, 1946.

Elias, Norbert, and John L Scotson. *Os estabelecidos e os outsiders*. Translated by Vera Ribeiro. Rio de Janeiro: Zahar, 2000.

Eller, Jack D. and Reed M. Coughlan. "The Poverty of Primordialism." In *Ethnicity*, edited by John Hutchinson and Anthony D. Smith, 45-51. Oxford and New York: Oxford University Press, 1996.

Ellis, Charlesetta Maria. "Robert S. Abbott's Response to Education for African-Americans Via the Chicago Defender, 1909-1940"

(1994). *Dissertations.* 3431. https://ecommons.luc.edu/luc_diss/3431

Ellison, Ralph. *Invisible Man.* New York: Vintage International, 1995.

Engs, Robert Francis. *Educating the Disfranchised and Disinherited: Samuel Chapman Armstrong and Hampton Institute, 1839-1893.* Knoxville: University of Tennessee Press, 1999.

Ermakoff, George. *O negro na fotografia brasileira do século XIX.* Rio de Janeiro: George Ermakoff, 2004.

Evans, Lucy. "*The Black Atlantic:* Exploring Gilroy's Legacy." *Atlantic Studies* 6, no. 2 (August 2009): 255-268.

Fanon, Frantz. *Black Skin, White Masks.* Translated by Richard Philcox. Foreword by Kwame Anthony Appiah. New York: Grove Press, 1967.

Fanon, Frantz. *Peau noire, masques blancs.* Paris: Points-Essais-Seuil, 1971.

Fausto, Boris. *História concisa do Brasil.* 2nd ed. São Paulo: EdUSP, 2008.

Firmin, Anténor. *The Equality of the Human Races: Positivist Anthropology.* Translated by Asselin Charles. Champaign, Illinois: The University of Illinois Press, 2002.

Fisher, Dorothy Canfield. "The Washed Window." *American Heritage* (December 1955). https://www.americanheritage.com/washed-window

Fisher, Isaac. "Funeral of Booker T. Washington." *Negro History Bulletin* 48, no. 1 (1985): 13–15. http://www.jstor.org/stable/44176616

Flory, Thomas. "Race and Social Control in Independent Brazil." *Journal of Latin American Studies,* Cambridge 9, no. 2 (1977): 199-224.

Foner, Eric, ed. *Freedom's Lawmakers: A Directory of Black Officeholders During Reconstruction.* Revised edition. Baton Rouge: Louisiana State University Press, 1996. Google Books.

Foner, Eric. *Reconstruction: America's Unfinished Revolution.* New York: Harper, 2011 Kindle.

Fonseca, Luís Anselmo da. *A escravidão, o clero e o abolicionismo.* Facsimile of the 1887 edition. Recife: Fundação Joaquim Nabuco: Editora Massangana, 1988.

Fonseca, Maria Nazareth Soares. "Retratos em preto e branco: o negro no imaginário cultural brasileiro." In *Ardis da imagem: exclusão étnica e violência nos discursos da cultura brasileira*, edited by Edimilson de Almeida Pereira and Núbia Pereira de Magalhães Gomes, 15-27. Belo Horizonte: Mazza Edições: Editora PUC, 2001.

Fraga, Myriam. *Luiz Gama.* "A Luta de Cada Um" Collection. São Paulo: Editora Callis, 2005.

Francisco, Flávio Thales Ribeiro. "Aurora negra: afro-paulistas e afro-americanos na modernidade." In *Retratos e espelhos: raça e etnicidade no Brasil e nos Estados Unidos*, edited by Vinícius Rodrigues Vieira and Jacquelyn Johnson, 55-75. São Paulo: FEA, USP, 2009.

Franklin, Benjamin. *Franklin's Arrival in Philadelphia*, 1846. https://www.ushistory.org/franklin/essays/franklinarrives.htm

Franklin, John Hope. "The Dilemma of the American Negro Scholar." In *Soon, One Morning: New Writing by American Negroes (1940-1962)*, edited by Herbert Hill. New York: Alfred A. Knopf, 1969.

Franklin, John Hope. *Reconstruction after the Civil War.* 2nd ed. Chicago and London: University of Chicago Press, 1994.

Franklin, John Hope, and Alfred A. Moss, Jr. *From Slavery to Freedom: A History of African Americans.* 7th edition. New York: McGraw-Hill, Inc., 1994.

Freire, Fabiana Silveira de Andrade. "Modelagem em 3D aplicada ao desenho de espirais." In Simpósio Nacional de Geometria Descritiva e Desenho Técnico, 21. Santa Catarina, Florianópolis, 2013. Presentation for Graphica '13, 2013, Santa Catarina. https://silo.tips/download/modelagem-em-3d-aplicada-ao-desenho-de-espirais

Freire, Luiz Alberto Ribeiro. "Descuido corrigido." *Perfil retocado.* Caderno Cultural, *A Tarde*, December 17, 2005, 2-4.

Freire, Luiz Alberto Ribeiro. *A talha neoclássica na Bahia.* Rio de Janeiro: Versal, 2006.

Freire, Luiz Alberto Ribeiro. "A história da arte de Manuel Querino." Encontro da Associação Nacional de Pesquisadores em Artes Plásticas, 19. Cachoeira, BA. 2010. https://anpap.org.br/anais/2010/pdf/chtca/luiz_alberto_ribeiro_freire.pdf

Freyre, Gilberto. *Perfil de Euclides e outros perfis.* 2nd ed. Rio de Janeiro: Record, 1987.

Gale, Robert L. "Marie-Thérèse de Solms Blanc." In *A Sarah Orne Jewett Companion,* by Robert L. Gale, 28-29. Westport, Conn.: Greenwood Publishing Group 1999.

Garcia, Manuel Correia. *História da Independência da Bahia.* Salvador: Bahia Typ. e Encadernação—Empreza Editora, 1900.

Gates, Jr., Henry Louis. *Black in Latin America.* New York and London: New York University Press, 2011.

Gatewood, Willard B. "Booker T. Washington and the Ulrich Affair." *The Journal of Negro History* 55, no. 1 (January 1970): 29-44. https://doi.org/10.2307/2716543.

Garvey, Marcus. "The Negro's Greatest Enemy." In *Selected Writings and Speeches of Marcus Garvey,* edited by Bob Blaisdell, 1-10. Mineola, NY: Dover Publications, 2004.

Geertz, Clifford. "Primordial Ties." In *Ethnicity,* edited by John Hutchinson and Anthony D. Smith, 40-45. Oxford and New York: Oxford University Press, 1996.

Gilfrancisco (Gilberto Francisco dos Santos). "Carlos Ott: professor e historiador anônimo na Bahia. Sergipe," *Literature & Cultura Brasileira.* (blog), September 18, 2012. http://professorgilfrancisco.blogspot.com.br/2012/09/carlos-ott-professor-e-historiador.html.

Gilroy, Paul. *The Black Atlantic: Modernity and Double Consciousness.* Cambridge, Mass.: Harvard University Press, 1993.

Gilroy, Paul. O *Atlântico negro: modernidade e dupla consciência.* Translated by Cid Knipel Moreira. São Paulo: Ed. 34; Rio de Janeiro: UCAM: Centro de Estudos Afro-Asiáticos, 2001.

Gimonet, Jean Claude. *Praticar e compreender a pedagogia da alternância dos CEFFAS*. Petrópolis: Vozes, 2007.

Gledhill, Sabrina. "Afro-Brazilian Studies before 1930: Nineteenth-Century Racial Attitudes and the Work of Five Scholars." MA Paper (Latin American Studies)—University of California, Los Angeles (UCLA), 1986.

Gledhill, Sabrina. "Manuel Raimundo Querino." In *Manuel R. Querino: seus artigos na* Revista do Instituto Geográfico e Histórico da Bahia., edited by Jaime Nascimento and Hugo Gama, 225-238. Salvador: IGHB, 2009.

Gledhill, Sabrina. "'Velhos respeitáveis': notas sobre as pesquisas de Manuel Querino e as origens dos africanos na Bahia." *História Unisinos*, São Leopoldo, RS, 14, no. 3 (September-December 2010): 340-344.

Gledhill, Sabrina. "Reflexões sobre retratos de Manuel Querino." *Sœculum: Revista de História*, João Pessoa, 25, (July-December 2011): 131-140. 2011a. http://periodicos.ufpb.br/ojs/index.php/srh/article/view/13997/7919.

Gledhill, Sabrina. "Representações e respostas: táticas no combate ao imaginário racialista no Brasil e nos Estados Unidos na virada do século XIX." *Sankofa: Revista de História da África e de Estudos da Diáspora Africana*, São Paulo, 4, no. 7 (July 2011): 44-72. 2011b.

Gledhill, Sabrina. "Manuel Querino e a luta contra o 'racismo científico.'" In *Personalidades negras: trajetórias e estratégias políticas*, edited by Jaime Nascimento and Hugo Gama, 17-51. Salvador: Quarteto, 2012.

Gledhill, Sabrina. "Expandindo as Margens do Atlântico Negro: Leituras Sobre Booker T. Washington no Brasil." *Revista de História Comparada*, Rio de Janeiro, 7, no. 2 (2013): 122-148. https://revistas.ufrj.br/index.php/RevistaHistoriaComparada/article/view/682 2013a.

Gledhill, Sabrina. "Manuel Querino: operários e negros diante da desilusão republicana." In *Política, instituições e personagens da*

Bahia (1850-1930), edited by Jeferson Afonso Bacelar and Cláudio Luiz Pereira, 125-143. Salvador: EdUFBA, 2013b.

Gledhill, Sabrina, ed. *Manuel Querino (1851-1923): An Afro-Brazilian Pioneer in the Age of Scientific Racism.* Crediton, UK: Editora Funmilayo Publishing, 2021.

Gledhill, Sabrina. "A Pioneering Afro-Brazilian Ethnologist: The Life and Work of Manuel Querino." *Bérose - Encyclopédie internationale des histoires de l'anthropologie*, Paris, 2023. https://www.berose.fr/article2797.html?lang=en

Gobineau, Joseph Arthur Compte de. *Essai sur l'inégalité des races humaines.* 1884. In *Œuvres* by Joseph Arthur Compte de Gobineau. Editions La Bibliothéque Digitale. Kindle.

Goings, Kenneth W. and Eugene M. O'Connor. "Lessons Learned: The Role of the Classics at Black Colleges and Universities." *The Journal of Negro Education* 79, no. 4 (Fall 2010): 521-531.

Gomes, Flávio, Jaime Loriano, and Lilia Moritz Schwarcz, eds. *Enciclopédia Negra: Biografias afro-brasileiras.* São Paulo: Companhia das Letras, 2019.

Gould, Stephen Jay. *The Mismeasure of Man.* New York and London: W.W. Norton, 1996.

Gould, Stephen Jay. *A falsa medida do homem.* São Paulo: Martins Fontes, 2003.

Graham, Lawrence O. *Our Kind of People: Inside America's Black Upper Class.* New York: Harper Collins, 1999.

Green, Toby. *A Fistful of Shells: West Africa from the Rise of the Salve Trade to the Age of Revolution.* London: Penguin Books, 2020.

Grinberg, Keila. "Manuel Pinto de Souza Dantas." In *Dicionário do Brasil Imperial (1822-1889)*, edited by Ronaldo Vainfas, 517-518. Rio de Janeiro: Objetiva, 2002.

Guimarães, Antônio Sérgio Alfredo. "Manoel Querino e a formação do 'pensamento negro' no Brasil, entre 1890 e 1920." 2004. https://www.scribd.com/document/138237337/Manuel-Querino-e-a-formacao-do-pensamento-negro-no-Brasil-de-A-S-A-Guimaraes

Guridy, Frank. *Forging Diaspora*: *Afro-Cubans and African Americans in a World of Empire and Jim Crow*. Chapel Hill: The University of North Carolina Press, 2010.

Hall, Stuart. *A identidade cultural na pós-modernidade*. 11th ed. Rio de Janeiro: DP&A, 2006.

Harlan, Louis R, ed. *The Booker T. Washington Papers*: *Autobiographical Writings*. v. 1. Chicago: Illinois University Press, 1972a.

Harlan, Louis R, ed. *The Booker T. Washington Papers: 1860-89*. v. 2. Chicago: Illinois University Press, 1972b.

Harlan, Louis R, ed. *The Booker T. Washington Papers*: 1889-95. v. 3. Chicago: Illinois University Press, 1974.

Harlan, Louis R, ed. *The Booker T. Washington Papers*: 1895-98. v. 4. Chicago: Illinois University Press, 1975a.

Harlan, Louis R. *Booker T. Washington: The Making of a Black Leader, 1856-1901*. Oxford: Oxford University Press, 1975b.

Harlan, Louis R. *Booker T. Washington*: *The Wizard of Tuskegee, 1901-1915*. Oxford: Oxford University Press, 1983.

Harlan, Louis R. "Sympathy and Detachment: Dilemmas of a Biographer." In *Booker T. Washington in Perspective*: *Essays of Louis R. Harlan*, edited by Raymond W Smock. Jackson, Mississippi and London: University Press of Mississippi, 1988. Kindle.

Harlan, Louis R. and Raymond W. Smock, eds. *The Booker T. Washington Papers: 1899-1900*. v. 5 Chicago: University of Illinois Press, 1976.

Harlan, Louis R. and Raymond W. Smock, eds. *The Booker T. Washington Papers: 1901-02*. v. 6 Chicago: University of Illinois Press, 1977.

Harlan, Louis R. and Raymond W. Smock, eds. *The Booker T. Washington Papers: 1903-04*. v. 7. Chicago: University of Illinois Press, 1977b.

Harlan, Louis R. and Raymond W. Smock, eds. *The Booker T. Washington Papers: 1904-06*. v. 8. Chicago: University of Illinois Press, 1979.

Harlan, Louis R. and Raymond W. Smock, eds. *The Booker T. Washington Papers: 1906-08.* v. 9. Chicago: University of Illinois Press, 1980.

Harlan, Louis R. and Raymond W. Smock, eds. *The Booker T. Washington Papers: 1909-11.* vol. 10. Chicago: University of Illinois Press, 1981a.

Harlan, Louis R. and Raymond W. Smock, eds. *The Booker T. Washington Papers: 1911-12.* v. 11. Chicago: University of Illinois Press, 1981b.

Harlan, Louis R. and Raymond W. Smock, eds. *The Booker T. Washington Papers: 1912-14.* v. 12. Chicago: University of Illinois Press, 1982.

Harlan, Louis R. and Raymond W. Smock. eds. *The Booker T. Washington Papers: 1914-15.* v. 13. Chicago: University of Illinois Press, 1984.

Hawkins, Hugh. *Booker T. Washington and His Critics: The Problem of Negro Leadership.* Boston: Heath. 1974.

Heider, Karl G. "The Rashomon Effect: When Ethnographers Disagree." *American Anthropologist,* New Series, London, 90, no. 1 (March 1988): 73-81. https://www.jstor.org/stable/678455.

Hellwig, David J., ed. *African-American Reflections on Brazil's Racial Paradise.* Philadelphia: Temple University Press, 1992.

History, Art & Archives, United States House of Representatives. *Black Americans in Congress, 1870–2007.* Washington, U.S.: Government Printing Office, 2008. https://history.house.gov/baic/

History, Art & Archives. United States House of Representatives. *The Negroes' Temporary Farewell: Jim Crow and the Exclusion of African Americans from Congress, 1887–1929.* Washington, U. S.: Government Printing Office, 2008. https://www.gpo.gov/fdsys/pkg/GPO-CDOC-108hdoc224/pdf/GPO-CDOC-108hdoc224.pdf

Hoffnung-Garskof, Jesse. "The Migrations of Arturo Schomburg: On Being *Antillano,* Negro, and Puerto Rican in New York 1891-1938." *Journal of American Ethnic History* 21, no. 1 (Fall, 2001): 3-49.

Hofstadter Richard. *Social Darwinism in American Thought*. Boston: Beacon Press, 1992.

Holmes, Richard. *Footsteps: Adventures of a Romantic Biographer*. London: Harper Perennial, 2005. Kindle.

Holt, T. C. "Du Bois." In *Harlem Renaissance Lives: From the African American National Biography*, edited by Henry Louis Gates, Junior, and Evelyn Brooks Higginbotham. Oxford: Oxford University Press, 2009.

Horne, Gerald. *The Deepest South: The United States, Brazil and the African Slave Trade*. New York: New York University Press, 2007.

Horne, Gerald. *O sul mais distante: os Estados Unidos, o Brasil e o tráfico de escravos africanos*. Translated by Berilo Vargas. São Paulo: Companhia das Letras, 2010.

Horton, James Africanus Beale. *West African Countries and Peoples, British and Native: And a Vindication of the African Race*. Cambridge and New York: Cambridge University Press, 2011 [1868].

Hubbell, John T. "Abraham Lincoln and the Recruitment of Black Soldiers." *Journal of the Abraham Lincoln Association*, Michigan, 2, no. 1 (1980): 6-21. http://hdl.handle.net/2027/spo.2629860.0002.103.

Hunt, James. "On the Negro's Place in Nature." *Journal of the Anthropological Society of London* 2 (1864): xv-lvi. https://doi.org/10.2307/3025197

Ianni, Octávio. "Research on Race Relations in Brazil." In *Race and Class in Latin America*, edited by Magnus Mörner. New York: Columbia University Press, 1970.

Instituto Geográfico e Histórico da Bahia. "Inventário." *Revista do Instituto Geográfico e Histórico da Bahia*, Salvador, 85 (1972-1975): 183-283.

Jackson, Jr., David H. *Booker T. Washington and the Struggle against White Supremacy*. New York: Palgrave Macmillan, 2008.

Jaspin, Elliot. *Buried in the Bitter Waters: The Hidden History of Racial Cleansing in America*. New York: Basic Books, 2007.

Jayawardena, Chandra. Review of *Old Societies and New States: The Quest for Modernity in Asia and Africa* de Clifford Geertz, *American Anthropologist*, London, 66, no. 4, Part 1 (August 1964): 906-908. http://www.jstor.org/stable/668194.

Jefferson, Thomas. *Notes on the State of Virginia*. Chicago, 1784. http://press-pubs.uchicago.edu/founders/documents/v1ch15s28.html.

King, Reyahn, Sukhdev Sandhu, James Walvin, and Jane Girdham. *Ignatius Sancho: An African Man of Letters*. Foreword by Caryl Phillips. London: National Portrait Gallery, 1997.

Kowarick, Lúcio. *Trabalho e vadiagem: a origem do trabalho livre no Brasil*. 2nd ed. Rio de Janeiro: Paz e Terra, 1994.

Kraay, Hendrik. "'Em outra coisa não falavam os pardos, cabras, e crioulos: o 'recrutamento' de escravos na guerra da Independência na Bahia." *Revista Brasileira de História*, São Paulo, 22, no. 43 (2002): 109-126.

Kraay, Hendrik. "Os companheiros de Dom Obá: os Zuavos Baianos e outras companhias negras na Guerra do Paraguai." *Afro-Ásia*, Salvador, 46 (2012): 121-161.

Kramer, David. "Booker T. Washington Visit a Surprise for George Eastman." *Democrat and Chronicle* (Rochester, NY), February 5, 2012.

Kremer, Gary R. ed. *George Washington Carver: In His Own Words*. Columbia and London: University of Missouri Press, 1987.

Kremer, Gary R. *George Washington Carver: A Biography*. Santa Barbara, Denver and Oxford: Greenwood, 2011.

Kytle, Ethan J. "Trading an African Dashiki for Union Blue." *The New York Times* http://opinionator.blogs.nytimes.com/2013/10/04/trading-an-african-dashiki-for-union-blue/?smid=pl-share.

Lapouge, Georges Vacher de. *Les Sélections Sociales: Cours libre de science politique professé a l'universitè de Montpellier (1888-1889)*. Paris: Librairie Thorin & Fils A, 1896. https://archive.org/stream/lesselectionssoc00vach.

Le Goff, Jacques. *São Luis: biografia*. Rio de Janeiro: Editora Record, 1999.

Leal, Maria das Graças de Andrade. "A arte de ter um ofício: Liceu de Artes e Ofícios da Bahia (1872-1972)." Thesis (MA in History). Universidade Federal da Bahia School of Philosophy and Human Science, 1996.

Leal, Maria das Graças de Andrade. *Manuel Querino: Entre letras e lutas, Bahia: 1851-1923*. Dissertation (PhD in History), Pontifícia Universidade Católica de São Paulo, São Paulo, 2004.

Leal, Maria das Graças de Andrade. *Manuel Querino: entre letras e lutas, Bahia, 1851-1923*. São Paulo: Annablume, 2009.

Leite, José Roberto Teixeira. *Pintores negros do oitocentos*. Published by Emanoel Araújo. São Paulo: Edições K, 1988.

Levine, Robert M. *Images of History: Nineteenth and Early Twentieth Century Latin American Photographs as Documents*. Durham: Duke University Press, 1989.

Lewis, David Levering. *W. E. B. Du Bois: Biography of a Race 1868-1919*. New York: Owl Books, 1993.

Lewis, David Levering. *W. E. B. Du Bois: The Fight for Equality and the American Century 1919-1963*. New York: Owl Books, 2001a.

Lewis, David Levering. Introduction. *W.E.B. Du Bois: An Encyclopedia*, edited by Gerald Horne and Mary Young. Santa Barbara, CA: Greenwood, 2001b.

Lima, Vivaldo da Costa. "Sobre Manuel Querino." In *A anatomia do acarajé e outros escritos* by Vivaldo da Costa Lima, 87-97. Salvador: Corrupio, 2010.

Lody, Raul. "Prefácio à 2ª ed." *Costumes africanos no Brasil* by Manuel Querino, 2nd ed. expanded and annotated, 11- 12. Foreword, annotated and edited by Raul Lody. Recife: Fundação Joaquim Nabuco: Massangana, 1988.

Lody, Raul. Introduction. "Memórias e permanências de uma Bahia africana em receitas e sabores." *A arte culinária na Bahia*, by Manuel Querino. São Paulo: Martins Fontes, 2011, p. 11-19.

Long, Carolyn Morrow. *A New Orleans Voudou Priestess: The Legend and Reality of Marie Laveau.* Gainesville: University of Florida Press, 2006.

Lopez, Adriana, and Carlos Guilherme Mota. *História do Brasil: uma interpretação.* 2nd ed. São Paulo: Ed. Senac, 2008.

Losch, Paul S. "Dr Henry W. Furniss: cônsul afro-norte-americano na Bahia, 1898-1905." *Afro-Ásia,* Salvador, no. 40 (2009): 223-258.

Luker, Ralph E. *The Social Gospel in Black and White: American Racial Reform, 1885-1912.* Chapel Hill: University of North Carolina Press, 1998.

Machado, Maria Helena Pereira Toledo, and Sasha Huber. *(T)races of Louis Agassiz: Photography, Body and Science, Yesterday and Today.* São Paulo: Capacete Entretenimentos 2010.

Mainzer, Klaus. *Symmetries of Nature: A Handbook for Philosophy of Nature and Science.* Translated by Barbara H. Mohr and Thomas J. Clark. Berlin; New York: de Gruyter, 1996.

Mamigonian, Beatriz. *Africanos livres: a abolição do tráfico de escravos no Brasil.* São Paulo: Companhia das Letras, 2017.

Mamigonian, Beatriz. "The Rights of Liberated Africans in Nineteenth-Century Brazil." In *Current Trends in Slavery Studies in Brazil,* edited by Stephan Conermann, Mariana Dias Paes, Roberto Hofmeister Pich, and Paulo Cruz Terra, 71-100. Berlin: De Gruyter, 2023.

Marable, Manning. *Malcolm X: A Life of Reinvention.* New York: Viking, 2011.

Marx, Anthony W. *Making Race and Nation: A Comparison of the United States, South Africa, and Brazil.* Cambridge: Cambridge University Press, 1998.

Mathews, Basil. *Booker T. Washington: Educator and Interracial Interpreter.* Cambridge: Harvard University Press, 1948.

Mattos, Wilson Roberto de, and Marluce de Lima Macêdo. Foreword to the 3rd ed. *Costumes africanos no Brasil,* by Manuel Querino. Salvador: EdUNEB, 2010.

Mattoso, Kátia M. de Queirós. *Bahia: A cidade de Salvador e seu mercado no século XIX.* Salvador: HUCITEC, 1978.

Mattoso, Kátia de Queirós. *Ser escravo no Brasil*. Translated by James Amado. 3rd ed. São Paulo: Brasiliense, 2003.

Maxell, Anne. "Montrer l'Autre: Franz Boas et les soeurs Gerhard." In *Zoos humains: de la Vénus hottentote aux reality shows*, edited by Pascal Blanchard, Nicolas Bancel, Gilles Boetsch, Éric Deroo, and Sandrine Lemaire, 331-339. Paris: La Découverte, 2002.

McGill, Ralph. "W. E. B. Du Bois." *The Atlantic Monthly*. November 1965. http://www.theatlantic.com/past/docs/unbound/flashbks/black/mcgillbh.htm.

McNab, Kaitlyn. "Why the Myth that Dark Skin is Harder to Photograph Persists." November 2, 2021. https://www.allure.com/story/photographing-darker-skin-tones

Meier, August. *Negro Thought in America, 1880-1915: Racial Ideologies in the Age of Booker T. Washington*. Ann Arbor: The University of Michigan Press, 1988.

Mendonça, Joseli M. Nunes. *Entre a mão e os anéis: a lei dos sexagenários e os caminhos da abolição no Brasil*. 2nd ed. Campinas, SP: Editora da Unicamp, 2008.

Mendonça, Renato. "O negro e a cultura no Brasil: breve histórico dos estudos afro-brasileiros de linguística, etnografia e sociologia." In *O negro no Brasil. Trabalhos apresentados ao 2º Congresso Afro-Brasileiro (Bahia)*, edited by Edison Carneiro and Aydano do Couto Ferraz. Rio de Janeiro: Civilização Brasileira, 1940.

Menezes, Jaci Maria Ferraz de. "Abolição no Brasil: a construção da liberdade." *Revista HISTEDBR*, Campinas, no. 36 (December 2009): 83-104.

Meréje, [João] Rodrigues de. *O problema da raça*. São Paulo: Casa Editorial Paulista, 1934.

Mirzoeff, Nicholas. *Bodyscape: Art, Modernity and the Ideal Figure*. London: Routledge, 1995.

Monasta, Attilio. *Antonio Gramsci*. Translated by Paolo Nosella. Ministério da Educação/Fundação Joaquim Nabuco, 2010. Kindle.

Montagner, Miguel Ângelo. "Trajetórias e biografias: notas para uma análise bourdieusiana." *Sociologias*, Porto Alegre, 9, no. 17 (January-June 2007): 240-264.

Monteiro, Filipe. "Carlos Ott (1908-1997)." *Revista de História da Biblioteca Nacional*, Rio de Janeiro (September 17, 2007).

Moore, Jacqueline M. *Booker T. Washington, W. E. B. Du Bois, and the Struggle for Racial Uplift*. Wilmington, DE: Scholarly Resources, 2003.

Moraes, Denis de. *O velho Graça: Uma biografia de Graciliano Ramos*. Rio de Janeiro: José Olympio, 1996.

Moses, Wilson J. *Black Messiahs and Uncle Toms: Social and Literary Manipulations of a Religious Myth*. Revised edition. University Park: The Pennsylvania State University Press, 1993.

Moses, Wilson J. *Creative Conflict in African American Thought: Frederick Douglass, Alexander Crummell, Booker T. Washington, W. E. B. Du Bois, and Marcus Garvey*. Cambridge: Cambridge University Press. 2004.

Mostern, Kenneth. *Autobiography and Black Identity Politics: Racialization in Twentieth-Century America*. Cambridge: Cambridge University Press, 1999.

Muller, Maria Lúcia Rodrigues. *A cor da escola: Imagens da Primeira República*. Cuiabá, MT: EdUFMT: Entrelinhas, 2008.

Myrdal, Gunnar. *An American Dilemma: The Negro Problem and Modern Democracy*. vol. 1. New Brunswick: Transaction Publishers, 2007.

Myrdal, Gunnar. *An American Dilemma: The Negro Problem and Modern Democracy*. vol. 2. New Brunswick: Transaction Publishers, 2008.

Nascimento, Abdias do. *Quilombo: Vida, problemas e aspirações do negro*. Facsimile edition. Rio de Janeiro, no. 1-10, December 1948-July 1950. São Paulo: Editora 34, 2003.

Nascimento, Abdias do. *O genocídio do negro brasileiro: Processo de um racismo mascarado*. Rio de Janeiro: Paz e Terra, 1978.

Nascimento, Abdias do. "Teatro experimental do negro: trajetória e reflexões." *Estudos avançados*, São Paulo, 18, no. 50 (April 2004): 209-224. http://www.scielo.br/scielo.php?script=sci_arttext&pid=S0103-40142004000100019&lng=en&nrm=iso

Nascimento, Abdias do. *Biografia detalhada*. Salvador, 2013. http://www.abdias.com.br/biografia/biografia.htm

Nascimento, Jaime, and Hugo Gama, eds. *Manuel Querino: seus artigos na Revista do Instituto Geográfico e Histórico da Bahia*. Salvador: IGHB, 2009.

Nascimento, Jaime, and Hugo Gama, eds. *Personalidades negras: trajetórias e estratégias políticas*. Salvador: Quarteto, 2012.

Nasaw, David. *Andrew Carnegie*. New York: Penguin Books, 2006.

National Association for the Advancement of Colored People. *NAACP: Celebrating a Century: 100 Years in Pictures*. Layton, Utah: Gibbs Smith, 2009.

National Association for the Advancement of Colored People. *NAACP History: W.E.B. Du Bois*. Layton, Utah: Gibbs Smith, 2014.

National Park Service. *Alabama: Tuskegee Institute National Historic Site* Washington, DC, https://www.nps.gov/places/tuskegee-institute-national-historic-site.htm#:~:text=Tuskegee%20Institute%20National%20Historic%20Site%2C%2040%20miles%20east%20of%20Montgomery,African%20Americans%20founded%20in%201881

New York Times. Dr B. T. Washington, Negro Leader, Dead. November 15, 1915. https://archive.nytimes.com/www.nytimes.com/learning/general/onthisday/bday/0405.html#:~:text=%2D%2DBooker%20T.,Washington%20arrived%20from%20New%20York.

Nobrega, Cida, and Regina Echevarria. *Mãe Menininha do Gantois*. Salvador: Corrupio, 2006.

Nogueira, Oracy. "Preconceito racial de marca e preconceito racial de origem: sugestão de um quadro de referência para a interpretação do material sobre relações raciais no Brasil." In

Tanto preto quanto branco: estudos de relações raciais, by Oracy Nogueira. São Paulo: T. A. Queiroz, 1985.

Nogueira, Oracy. *Negro político, político negro*. São Paulo: Edusp, 1992.

Norell, Robert J. *Up from History: The Life of Booker T. Washington*. Cambridge: Harvard University Press, 2009.

Northup, Solomon. *Twelve Years a Slave*. Introduction by Ira Berlin. New York: Penguin, 2012 1853. Kindle.

Nunes, Antonietta d'Aguiar. "As leis orçamentárias provinciais baianas (1835-1889) como instrumento de política educacional." *Gestão em ação*, Salvador, 8, no. 3 (September-December 2005): 329-340.

Nunes, Eliane. "Manuel Raimundo Querino: o primeiro historiador da arte baiana." *Revista Ohun*, Salvador, 3, no. 3 (September 2007): 237-261.

Oates, Stephen B. *Biography as History: The Twelfth Charles Edmondsen Historical Lectures*. Waco, Texas: Markham Press Fund, 1990.

Oliveira, Ana Cristina Audebert Ramos de. "O conservadorismo a serviço de memória: tradição, museu e patrimônio no pensamento de Gustavo Barroso." Thesis (M.A. in Social History of Culture) Pontifícia Universidade Católica do Rio de Janeiro, Rio de Janeiro, 2003. http://www.maxwell.lambda.ele.puc-rio.br/5077/5077_3.PDF

Oliveira, Waldir Freitas de. "Terá sido Manuel Querino um biógrafo?" In *Manuel R. Querino: seus artigos na* Revista do Instituto Geográfico e Histórico da Bahia, edited by Jaime Nascimento and Hugo Gama, 201-210. Salvador: IGHB, 2009.

Ortiz, Renato. *Cultura brasileira & identidade nacional*. São Paulo: Editora Brasiliense, 1985.

Ott, Carlos. "Noções sobre a procedência d'arte de pintura na Província da Bahia." *Revista do Patrimônio Histórico e Artístico Nacional*, Rio de Janeiro, 11 (1947): 197-213.

Painter, Nell Irvin. *The History of White People*. New York: W. W. Norton & Company, 2010. Kindle.

Park, Robert E. *Race and Culture: Essays in the Sociology of Contemporary Man*. London: The Free Press of Glencoe, 1950.

Pereira, Baptista. *O Brasil e a raça: conferência feita na Faculdade de Direito de São Paulo a 19 de junho de 1928*. São Paulo: Emp. Graphica Rosetti, 1928.

Pereira, Edimilson de Almeida, and Núbia Pereira de Magalhães Gomes. *Ardis da imagem: Exclusão étnica e violência nos discursos da cultura brasileira*. Belo Horizonte: Mazza Edições: Editora PUC, Minas, 2001.

Pereira, Gonçalo de Athayde. *Prof. Manuel Querino: Sua vida e suas obras*. Bahia: Imprensa Oficial do Estado, 1932.

Petruccelli, José Luis. "Raça, etnicidade e origem nos censos de EUA, França, Canadá e Grã-Bretanha." *Estudos Afro-Asiáticos*, Salvador, 24, no. 3 (2002): 533-561.

Phillips, Tom. "A Story Brazil Never Wanted to Tell': The Podcasts Reclaiming the Country's Black History." *The Guardian* October 6, 2022. https://www.theguardian.com/world/2022/oct/06/brazil-history-african-brazilians-tiago-rogero-querino-project

Pierson, Donald. *Negroes in Brazil: A Study of Race Contact at Bahia*. Chicago: University of Chicago Press, 1942.

Pinto, Ana Flávia Magalhães. *De pele escura e tinta preta: a imprensa negra do século XIX (1833-1899)*. Thesis (MA in History) Universidade de Brasília, Departamento de História, Brasília, DF, 2006.

Prado Junior, Caio. *Formação do Brasil contemporâneo*. São Paulo: Brasiliense, 2000.

Prince, K. Stephen. "Remembering Robert Charles: Violence and Memory in Jim Crow New Orleans". *The Journal of Southern History* 83, no. 2 (May 2017): 297-328. https://www.jstor.org/stable/44783811

Quadros, Andrea Novais Soares de. "Vieira, Severino." Fundação Getúlio Vargas CPDOC. N.d. https://cpdoc.fgv.br/sites/default/files/verbetes/primeira-republica/VIEIRA,%20Severino.pdf

Querino, Manuel Raimundo. *Artistas bahianos (indicações biographicas)*. Rio de Janeiro: Imprensa Nacional, 1909.

Querino, Manuel Raimundo. *Artistas bahianos: indicações biográficas*. 2nd ed., improved and carefully revised. Bahia: Officinas da Empresa "A Bahia," 1911.

Querino, Manuel. *As artes na Bahia*. 2nd ed. Bahia: Officinas do "Diário da Bahia," 1913.

Querino, Manuel. *A raça africana e os seus costumes: memoria apresentada ao 5º Congresso de Geographia*. Bahia: Imprensa Official do Estado. 1917.

Querino, Manuel. *O colono preto como factor da civilização brazileira*. Bahia: Imprensa Official do Estado, 1918.

Querino, Manuel. *A Bahia de outr'ora: vultos e factos populares*. 2nd ed. Bahia: Livraria Econômica, 1922.

Querino, Manuel Raimundo. "Os homens de côr preta na Historia." *Revista do Instituto Geográfico e Histórico da Bahia*, Salvador, no. 48 (1923): 353-363.

Querino, Manuel Raimundo. *Costumes africanos no Brasil*. Edited, foreword, and annotated by Artur Ramos. Rio de Janeiro: Civilização Brasileira, 1938.

Querino, Manuel Raimundo. *A Bahia de outrora*. 3rd ed. Foreword and annotated by Frederico Edelweiss. Salvador: Livraria Progresso, 1946.

Querino, Manuel Raimundo. *A Bahia de outrora*. Republication of the 3rd ed. Foreword and annotated by Frederico Edelweiss, illustrated by Carybé and Ligia. Salvador: Progresso, 1955.

Querino, Manuel Raimundo. *Costumes africanos no Brasil*. 2nd ed. Foreword, annotated, and edited by Raul Lody, introduction by Thales de Azevedo. Recife: Massangana, 1988.

Querino, Manuel Raimundo. "Notícia biográfica do Dr Manuel Correia Garcia (1896)." In *O Instituto Histórico da Bahia e seu Periódico (1856-1877)*, 33-36. Facsimile edition. Fundação Cultural do Estado da Bahia: Salvador, 2001.

Querino, Manuel Raimundo. *A arte culinária na Bahia*. Salvador: P555 Edições: Theatro XVIII, 2006a.

Querino, Manuel Raimundo. *A raça africana e seus costumes na Bahia.* Salvador: P555 Edições: Theatro XVIII, 2006b.

Querino, Manuel Raimundo. "Os homens de côr preta na História." In *Manuel R. Querino: seus artigos na* Revista do Instituto Geográfico e Histórico da Bahia, edited by Jaime Nascimento and Hugo Gama, 187-199, 2009a.

Querino, Manuel Raimundo. "Um baiano ilustre: Veiga Muricy." In *Manuel R. Querino: seus artigos na* Revista do Instituto Geográfico e Histórico da Bahia, edited by Jaime Nascimento and Hugo Gama, 219-224, 2009b.

Querino, Manuel. *Costumes africanos no Brasil*, 3rd ed. Edited by Wilson Roberto de Mattos and Marluce de Lima Macêdo. Salvador: EdUNEB, 2010.

Manuel Querino. "The African Race and its Customs in Bahia." *Art in Translation* 14, no. 1 (2022): 8-72 DOI: 10.1080/17561310.2022.2046517

Raeders, Georges, ed. *D. Pedro II e o Conde de Gobineau (correspondência inédita).* São Paulo: Companhia Editora Nacional, 1938.

Ramos, Artur. "Prefácio." In *Costumes africanos no Brasil,* by Manuel Querino. Foreword and annotated by Artur Ramos, 5-16. Rio de Janeiro: Civilização Brasileira, 1938.

Ramos, Artur. *O negro brasileiro*: Etnografia religiosa e psicanálise. Recife: Fundação Joaquim Nabuco: Massangana, 1988. Google Books.

Ramos, Graciliano. *Linhas Tortas.* 7th ed. Rio de Janeiro: Record, 1979.

Ramos, Ricardo. *Graciliano: retrato fragmentado.* Foreword by Silviano Santiago. 2nd ed. São Paulo: Editora Globo, 2011

Rauner Library. "A Curious Choice." Friday, May 13, 2022. Blog. https://raunerlibrary.blogspot.com/2022_05_08_archive.html

Rego, Waldeloir. *Capoeira Angola: Ensaio sócio-etnográfico.* Salvador: Editora Itapuã, 1968.

Reed, Ishmael. "Booker vs. the Negro Saxons" [Introduction]. In *Up from Slavery*, by Booker T. Washington, vii-xxii. New York: Signet Classic, 2000.

Reis, João José. *Slave Rebellion in Brazil: The Muslim Uprising of 1835 in Bahia*. Translated by Arthur Brakel. Baltimore: Johns Hopkins University Press, 1995.

Reis, João José. *Rebelião escrava no Brasil: A história do Levante dos Malês em 1835*. São Paulo: Companhia das Letras, 2003.

Reis, João José. *Domingos Sodré: um sacerdote africano*. São Paulo: Companhia das Letras, 2008a.

Reis, João José. "Posfácio" (Afterword). "Raça política e história na tenda de Jorge." In *Tenda dos milagres*, by Jorge Amado, 293-302. São Paulo: Companhia das Letras, 2008b.

Reis, João José. *Divining Slavery and Freedom: The Story of Domingos Sodré, an African Priest in Nineteenth-Century Brazil*. Translated by H. Sabrina Gledhill. New York: Cambridge University Press, 2015.

Reis, Meire Lúcia Alves dos. "A cor da notícia: discursos sobre o negro na imprensa baiana, 1888-1937." Thesis (MA in History) Universidade Federal da Bahia, Salvador, 2000.

Ribeiro Francisco. "Aurora negra: afro-paulistas e afro-americanos na modernidade." In *Retratos e espelhos: Raça e etnicidade no Brasil e nos Estados Unidos*, edited by Vinicius Rodrigues Vieira and Jacquelyn Johnson, 55-75. São Paulo: FEA/USP, 2009.

Richardson, Heather Cox. *The Death of Reconstruction: Race, Labor, and Politics in the Post-Civil War North, 1865-1901*. Cambridge, Mass.: Harvard University Press, 2004.

Riley, Benjamin Franklin. *The Life and Times of Booker T. Washington*. New York: Fleming H. Revell. 1916. Kindle.

Ringlingdocents.org. History of Ringling Bros. and Barnum & Bailey. http://ringlingdocents.org/history.htm

Rodrigues, Raimundo Nina. *Os africanos no Brasil*. 8th ed. Brasília: Universidade de Brasília, 2004.

Rodrigues, Raimundo Nina. *As raças humanas: a responsabilidade penal no Brasil*. Bahia: Imprensa Popular, 1894.

Rodrigues, Tadeu Luis Maciel. "Hemetério José dos Santos: educador, homem de letras e sua obra. Cuiabá." Trabalho apresentado no VII Congresso Brasileiro de História da Educação—SBHE, 2013.

Rosen, Jeffrey. "The Web Means the End of Forgetting." *New York Times Magazine.* July 19, 2010 http://www.nytimes.com/2010/07/25/magazine/25privacy-t2.html.

Rosenberg, Emily S. "The Invisible Protectorate: The United States, Liberia, and the Evolution of Neocolonialism, 1909-1940." *Diplomatic History*, Oxford, 9, no. 3 (July 1985): 191-214.

Sampaio, Consuelo Novais, ed. *Canudos: Cartas para o Barão.* 2nd ed. São Paulo: Edusp, 2001.

Sampaio, Consuelo Novais. *Pinto de Aguiar: Audacioso inovador.* Salvador: Press, 2011.

Sampaio, Moiseis de Oliveira. "O coronel negro: Coronelismo e poder no norte da Chapada Diamantina." Thesis (MA in Regional and Local History), Universidade Estadual da Bahia, Salvador, 2009.

Santos, Flávio Gonçalves dos. "Os discursos afro-brasileiros face às ideologias raciais na Bahia (1889-1937)." Thesis (MA in History), Universidade Federal da Bahia - UFBA, Salvador, 2001.

Santos, Mariana de Mesquita. "O Rosário e suas contas: Redes associativas e cidadania de membros da Irmandade de Nossa Senhora do Rosário do Pelourinho (Salvador, 1880-1930)." *Crítica Histórica* 12, no. 23 (2021): 222-265. Dossiê Escravidão e Pós-Abolição no Brasil. https://doi.org/10.28998/rchv12n23.2021.0010

Santos, Sivaldo dos Reis. " 'O nobre educador' da Bahia: Trabalho, cidadania e sociabilidades (1870-1922)." *Trilhas da História* 10, no. 19 (August-December 2020). https://trilhasdahistoria.ufms.br/index.php/RevTH/issue/view/627

Saunders, John. "Class, Color and Prejudice: A Brazilian Counterpoint." In *Racial Tensions and National Identity*, edited by Ernest Q. Campbell, 141-165. Nashville: Vanderbilt University Press, 1972.

Schapochnik, Nelson. "Cartões-Postais, Álbuns de Família e Ícones da Intimidade." In *História da vida privada no Brasil 3: República da*

Belle Époque à Era do Rádio, edited by Nicolau Sevcenko, 9th printing, 423-512. São Paulo: Companhia das Letras, 1998.

Schwarcz, Lília Moritz. *O espetáculo das raças: Cientistas, instituições e questões raciais no Brasil (1870-1930)*. São Paulo: Companhia das Letras, 1993.

Scott, Emmett J., and Lyman Beecher Stowe. *Booker T. Washington: Builder of a Civilization*. Garden City, N.Y.: Doubleday, Page & Company, 1916. Kindle.

Sealy, Mark, and Gaëtane Verna, eds. *Sasha Huber: YOU NAME IT*. Milan: Mousse Publishing, 2022.

Seleções. Reader's Digest announces in *A Noite*, that its March 1 issue will contain " A Janela Lavada" ["The Washed Window," by Dorothy Canfield Fisher"]. New York: Reader's Digest Magazine, 1956.

Seigel, Micol. *Uneven Encounters: Making Race and Nation in Brazil and the United States*. Durham: Duke University Press, 2009.

Sena, Consuelo Pondé de. "Necrológio: Frederico Edelweiss." *Revista de História* no. 111 (1977): 183-187 https://doi.org/10.11606/issn.2316-9141.v0i111p183-187

Shaw, Gwendolyn Du Bois. *Portraits of a People: Picturing African Americans in the Nineteenth Century*. Andover, Massachusetts: Addison Gallery of American Art; Seattle: University of Washington Press, 2006.

Shelby, Tommie. "Cosmopolitanism, Blackness, and Utopia, a Conversation with Paul Gilroy." *Transition*, Indiana, no. 98 (2008): 116-135. https://doi.org/10.2979/trs.2008.-.98.116

Silva, Aldo José Morais. "Instituto Geográfico e Histórico da Bahia: Origem e estratégias de consolidação institucional, 1894-1930." Dissertation (PhD in History), Universidade Federal da Bahia, 2006.

Silva, Eduardo. *Dom Obá II d'África, o príncipe do povo: Vida, tempo e pensamento de um homem livre de cor*. São Paulo: Companhia das Letras, 1997.

Silva, James Roberto. *Doença, fotografia e representação: Revistas médicas em São Paulo e Paris, 1869-1925*. São Paulo: EdUSP, 2009.

Silva, Kátia Maria de Carvalho. *O Diário da Bahia e o século XIX*. Rio de Janeiro: Ediçoes Tempo, 1979.

Silva, Sérgio Antônio. "Papel, penas e tinta: A memória da escrita em Graciliano Ramos." Dissertation (PhD in Literature) Universidade Federal de Minas Gerais, Minas Gerais, 2006.

Silva, Viviane Rummler da. "Miguel Navarro y Cañizares e a Academia de Belas Artes da Bahia: relações históricas e obras." *Revista Ohun*, Salvador, 2, no. 2 (October 2005): 219-261.

Silva, Viviane Rummler da. "Pintores fundadores da Academia de Belas Artes da Bahia: João Francisco Lopes Rodrigues (1825-1892) e Miguel Navarro y Cañizares (1843-1913)". Thesis (MA in Visual Arts), Universidade Federal da Bahia, Salvador, 2008.

Skidmore, Thomas E. *Black into White: Race and Nationality in Brazilian Thought*. New York: Oxford University Press, 1974.

Skidmore, Thomas E. *Preto no branco: Raça e nacionalidade no pensamento brasileiro*. Translated by Raul de Sá Barbosa. São Paulo: Paz e Terra, 1976.

Skidmore, Thomas E. "Bi-Racial U.S.A. vs. Multi-Racial Brazil: Is the Contrast Still Valid?" *Journal of Latin American Studies*, Cambridge, 25, no. 2 (May 1993): 373-386.

Skidmore, Thomas E. *Uma História do Brasil*. 4th ed. São Paulo: Paz e Terra, 2003.

Smith, Anthony D. *The Ethnic Origins of Nations*. Oxford: Blackwell Publishers, 1986.

Smith, Gina. *The Genomics Age: How DNA Technology Transforms the Way We Live and Who We Are*. New York: AMACOM, 2004.

Smith, Shawn Michelle. "Photographing the 'American Negro': Nation, Race and Photography at the Paris Exposition of 1900." In *With Other Eyes: Looking at Race and Gender in Visual Culture*, edited by Lisa Bloom, 58-87. Minneapolis and London: University of Minnesota Press, 1999.

Smith, Shawn Michelle. *Photography on the Color Line: W.E.B. Du Bois, Race, and Visual Culture*. Durham and London: Duke University Press, 2004.

Smithsonian Institution. *Soldiering: Zouave Uniform*. New York, 1861. http://www.civilwar.si.edu/soldiering_zuoave.html.

Smock, Raymond W. *Booker T. Washington: Black Leadership in the Age of Jim Crow*. Chicago: Irvin R. Dee, 2009.

Smock, Raymond W, ed. *Booker T. Washington in Perspective: Essays of Louis R. Harlan*, Jackson, Mississippi and London: University Press of Mississippi, 1988. Kindle.

Sodré, Jaime. *Manuel Querino: Um herói da raça e classe*. Salvador: [n.p.], 2001.

Sollors, Werner, Caldwell Titcomb, and Thomas A. Underwood, eds. *Blacks at Harvard: A Documentary History of the African-American Experience at Harvard and Radcliffe*. New York: NYU Press, 1993. Kindle.

Sollors, Werner. *Neither Black nor White Yet Both: Thematic Explorations of Interracial Literature*. Oxford: Oxford University Press, 1997.

Souza, Bernardino de. Apendice (Appendix). In *Prof. Manuel Querino: Sua vida e suas obras* by Gonçalo de Athayde Pereira, 33-34. Bahia: Imprensa Oficial do Estado, 1932.

Souza, Bernardino de. "À guisa de um prefácio. Em torno da geografia da alimentação," in *A arte culinária na Bahia*, by Manuel Querino, 9-20. Salvador: Editora Progresso, 1951.

Souza, Jessé de. "Por uma teoria da ação social da modernidade periférica: Um diálogo crítico com Florestan Fernandes." In *A invisibilidade da desigualdade brasileira*, edited by Jessé de Souza. Belo Horizonte: Editora UFMG, 2006.

Spivey, Donald. *Schooling for the New Slavery: Black Industrial Education, 1868-1915*. Eritrea: Africa World Press, 2007.

Steele, Shelby. "Pride and Compromise" (review of *Up from History*, by Robert Norrell). https://www.nytimes.com/2009/02/15/books/review/Steele-t.html.

Stewart, Ruth Ann. *Portia: The Life of Portia Washington Pittman, the Daughter of Booker T. Washington*. Garden City, NY: Doubleday & Company, Inc., 1977.

Stowe, Harriet Beecher. *Uncle Tom's Cabin.* New York: Barnes & Noble Classics, 2003.

Stowe, Harriet Beecher. *A cabana do Pai Tomás.* Translated by Carline Ramos Kurukawa. São Paulo: Madras, 2004.

Stucke, Maurice E. "Better Competition Advocacy." *St. John's Law Review* 82, no. 3 (Summer 2008): 951-1036. https://scholarship.law.stjohns.edu/cgi/viewcontent.cgi?referer=&httpsredir=1&article=1081&context=lawreview

Szwako, José. "Identidades liquidadas." *Revista de Sociologia e Política*, Curitiba, no. 27 (2006): 215-218.

Talbot, Edith Armstrong. *Samuel Chapman Armstrong: A Biographical Study.* New York: Doubleday, Page & Company, 1904.

Tavares, Luís Henrique Dias. *História da Bahia.* 10th ed. Salvador: EdUFBA; São Paulo: Unesp: FEU, 2001.

Tavares, Luís Henrique Dias. *História da Bahia.* 11th ed. revised and expanded. São Paulo: Ed. da UNESP; Salvador: EdUFBA, 2008.

Tavares, Luis Henrique Dias. Apresentação. In: SAMPAIO, Consuelo Novais. *Pinto de Aguiar: Audacioso inovador.* Salvador: Press Color, 2011.

The Bennington Evening Banner. "Leader of Negro Race is Dead at Tuskegee." Bennington, USA, 1, November 15, 1915.

The Crisis. "Booker T. Washington" [unsigned obituary by W. E. B. Du Bois]. 11, no. 2 (November 1915): 82.

The Crisis. Men of the Moment. "A Photographer" (May 1917): 31.

Thomas, William Hannibal. *The American Negro: What He Was, What He Is, and What He May Become.* New York: The Macmillan Company, 1901.

Thomson, Thos. E. Watson. *Sketches: Historical, Literary, Biographical, Economic, Etc.* Ga.: Jeffersonian Pub. Co. Date of Original: 1916. https://dlg-staging.galib.uga.edu/record/dlg_zlgb_gb0290/fulltext.text

Thompson, Robert Farris. *Flash of the Spirit: African & Afro-American Art & Philosophy.* [no place]: Vintage eBooks, 1983. Kindle edition.

Tiédé, Lívia Maria. "Race United: Frederico Baptista de Souza and the Black Activism in São Paulo in Post-Abolition Brazil 91875-1960)."

Article summary of PhD thesis. Rice University, Houston, Texas, November 2022.

Tiéde, Lívia Maria. "União da Raça: Frederico Baptista de Souza e a Militância Negra Paulista no Brasil Pós-Abolição (1875-1960)." PhD Dissertation, Institute of Philosophy and Humanities, Universidade Estadual de Campinas (UNICAMP), Campinas, 2023.

Tocqueville, Alexis de. *De la démocratie en Amérique*. Paris: Pagneere, 1848. Kindle.

Torres, Alberto. *O problema nacional brasileiro*. Rio de Janeiro: Imprensa Nacional, 1914.

Trachtenberg, Alan. *Reading American Photographs: Images as History, Mathew Brady to Walker Evans*. New York: Hill and Wang, 1990.

Trinchão, Gláucia Maria Costa, and Suely dos Santos Souza, eds. *Os saberes em desenho do professor Manuel Raimundo Querino*. Coleção Ação Referência, Volume 3. Salvador/Feira de Santana: EdUFBA/UEFS Editora, 2021.

Trouillot, Michel-Rolf. *Silencing the Past: Power and the Production of History*. Boston: Beacon Press, 1995.

Tuchman, Barbara W. "Biography as a Prism of History." In *Biography as High Adventure: Life-Writers Speak on their Art*, edited by Stephen B. Oates, 93-103. Amherst: University of Massachusetts Press, 1986.

Turazzi, Maria Inez. *Poses e trejeitos: A fotografia e as exposições na era do espetáculo (1839-1889)*. Rio de Janeiro: Funarte: Rocco, 1995.

Valladares, Lícia do Prado. "A visita do Robert Park ao Brasil, o 'homem marginal' e a Bahia como laboratório." *Caderno CRH*, Salvador, 23, no. 58 (April 2010). https://www.scielo.br/j/ccrh/a/Wn7N5ck5VBthSHLcv3wZvKb/?lang=pt.

Vandiver, Frank E. "Biography as an Agent of Humanism." In *Biography as High Adventure: Life-Writers Speak on their Art*, edited by Stephen B. Oates, 50-64. Amherst: University of Massachusetts Press, 1986.

Vasconcellos, C. "O circuito social das fotografias da Gente Negra: Salvador 1860-1916." Thesis (MA in Social History), Universidade Federal da Bahia, Salvador, 2006.

Vasconcellos, Christianne. "A fotografia da Gente Negra no discurso científico de Manuel Querino." Lecture given during the "Manuel Querino: Vida e Obra" seminar at the Instituto Geográfico e Histórico da Bahia (IGHB). Salvador, August 28, 2008.

Vasconcellos, Christianne. "O uso de fotografias de africanos no estudo etnográfico de Manuel Querino." *Sankofa*: Revista de História da África e de Estudos da Diáspora Africana, São Paulo, no. 4 (December 2009): 88-111.

VeraCidade. "Foi isso que eu fiz na vida: fazer História" (Interview with Cid Teixeira). *VeraCidade* Revista da Secretaria Muncipal de Desenvolvimento Urbano, Habitação e Meio Ambiente—SEDHAM (Salvador, BA) V, no. 6 (December 2020). http://www.veracidade.salvador.ba.gov.br/v6/index.php?option=com_content&view=article&id=8&Itemid=3

Vianna, Antonio. "Manoel Querino (conferência)." *Revista do Instituto Geográfico e Histórico da Bahia*, Salvador, no. 54 (1928): 305-316.

Vilas Boas, Sergio. *Biografias & biógrafos: Jornalismo sobre personagens*. São Paulo: Summus, 2002.

Vilas Boas, Sergio. *Biografismo: Reflexões sobre as escritas da vida*. São Paulo: Ed. da UNESP, 2007.

Villaça, Antonio Carlos. *O nariz do morto*. Rio de Janeiro: Civilização Brasileira, 2006.

Wallis, Brian. "Black Bodies, White Science: Louis Agassiz's Slave Daguerreotypes." *American Art*, Washington, DC, 9, no. 2 (Summer 1995): 39-61.

Wantuil, Zeus. *Grandes Espíritas do Brasil*. Salvador: Federaçao Espírita do Brasil, 2002.

Washington, Booker T. "Address by Booker T. Washington, Principal Tuskegee Normal and Industrial Institute, Tuskegee, Alabama, At Opening of Atlanta Exposition," 18 September 1895. https://history.iowa.gov/history/education/educator-resources/primary-source-sets/reconstruction-and-its-impact/booker-t

Washington, Booker T. recording of an excerpt from "Address by Booker T. Washington, Principal Tuskegee Normal and Industrial Institute, Tuskegee, Alabama, At Opening Of Atlanta Exposition." https://history.iowa.gov/history/education/educator-resources/primary-source-sets/reconstruction-and-its-impact/booker-t

Washington, Booker T. *Après l'esclavage: Up from slavery, l'autobiographie de Booker T. Washington.* Translated by Florence Carré. N.p.: Editions Bagourd, 2021.

Washington, Booker T. *Autobiographie d'un nègre.* Translated by Othon Guerlac. Third edition. Paris: Librairie Plon, 1904.

Washington, Booker T. *De esclavo a catedratico.* Translation of *Up from Slavery* by Alfredo Elías y Pujol. New York: D. Appleton & Co., 1902.

Washington, Booker T. *Frederick Douglass.* N.p..: General Books, 2009.

Washington, Booker T. *Memórias de um negro.* Translation of *Up from Slavery* by Graciliano Ramos. São Paulo: Companhia Editora Nacional, 1940.

Washington, Booker T. *My Larger Education: Being Chapters from My Experience.* Garden City, NY: Doubleday, Page. 1911.

Washington, Booker T. *My Larger Education.* Radford, VA.: Wilder Publications, 2008. Kindle.

Washington, Booker T. "My View of Segregation Laws." *New Republic*, Hampton, p. 113-114, Dec. 5, 1915. https://newrepublic.com/article/103513/my-view-segregation-laws

Washington, Booker T. *The Story of My Life and Work.* Cincinnati, Ohio: W. H. Ferguson Company, 1900. E-book.

Washington, Booker T. *Up from Slavery.* Harmondsworth, Middlesex: Viking Penguin, 1986.

Washington, Booker T. *Up from Slavery.* New York: New American Library, 2000.

Weber, Bruce. "Abdias do Nascimento, Rights Voice, Dies at 97." *New York Times*, New York, May 30, 2011.

http://www.nytimes.com/2011/05/31/world/americas/31nasciment o.html?smid=pl-share

Weber, Max. *Economy and Society: An Outline of Interpretive Sociology*, edited by Guenther Roth and Claus Wittich.. Berkeley: University of California Press, 1978.

Weber, Max. *Economia e sociedade: Fundamentos da sociologia compreensiva*. Translated by Regis Barbosa and Karen Elsabe Barbosa; technical editor, Gabriel Cohn. Brasília: Editora Universidade de Brasília, 1991.

Weiss, Ellen. Robert R. *Taylor and Tuskegee: An African American Architect Designs for Booker T. Washington*. Introduction by Robert Louis Gates, Jr. Montgomery: New South Books, 2012.

Werneck, Maria Helena. *O homem encadernado: Machado de Assis na escrita das biografias*. Rio de Janeiro: EdUERJ, 2008.

West, Michael R. *The Education of Booker T. Washington: American Democracy and the Idea of Race Relations*. Columbia University Press, 2006.

Westerbeck, Colin L. "Frederick Douglass Chooses His Moment." *Art Institute of Chicago Museum Studies* 24, no. 2 (1999): 145–262. https://doi.org/10.2307/4112966.

Wetherell, James. *Brazil: Stray Notes from Bahia*. Liverpool: Webb and Hunt, 1860.

Wetherell, James. *Brasil: apontamentos sobre a Bahia*. Salvador: Edição Banco da Bahia S/A, 1964.

Williams, Clarence G. "From 'Tech' to Tuskegee: The Life of Robert Robinson Taylor." January 13, 1998. https://wayback.archive-it.org/7963/20190702041158/https://libraries.mit.edu/archives/mit history/blacks-at-mit/taylor.html

Willis, Deborah, ed. *Picturing Us: African American Identity in Photography*. New York: The New Press, 1994.

Willis, Deborah. *Reflections in Black: A History of Black Photographers, 1840 to the Present*. New York: W.W. Norton & Co., 2000.

Wilkerson, Isabel. *The Warmth of Other Suns: The Epic Story of America's Great Migration.* New York: Vintage Books, 2011. Kindle.

Woodward, C. Vann. *The Origins of the New South, 1877-1913.* Baton Rouge: Louisiana State University Press, 1951. Kindle.

Woodward, C. Vann. *Reunion and Reaction: The Compromise of 1877 and the End of Reconstruction.* Oxford: Oxford University Press, 1966. Kindle.

Woodward, Kathryn. "Identidade e diferença: uma introdução teórica e conceitual." In *Identidade e diferença: a perspectiva dos estudos culturais,* edited by Tomaz Tadeu da Silva. Petrópolis: Vozes, 2009.

Wormser, Richard. *National Negro Business League.* South Burlington, 2002. https://www.thirteen.org/wnet/jimcrow/stories_org_business.html

Zimmerman, Andrew. *Alabama in Africa: Booker T. Washington, the German Empire, and the Globalization of the New South.* Princeton: Princeton University Press, 2010.

ILLUSTRATIONS

Front cover: Booker T. Washington, ca.1903. Photograph by C. E. Cheyne; Manuel R. Querino (Leite 1988, 89)

Back cover: Detail of illustration from *Artistas baianos* (Querino 1909)

Fig. 2-1. Teodoro Sampaio. Source: Wikimedia Commons https://commons.wikimedia.org/wiki/File:Teodoro_F_Sampaio.jpg

Fig. 3-1. W. E. B. Du Bois's unsigned obituary of Booker T. Washington *(The Crisis* 1915, 82)

Fig. 4-1. Detail of the "Shaw Memorial"—plaster cast in the collection of the National Gallery of Art, Washington, DC (photo by Sabrina Gledhill)

Fig. 4-2. Olivia Davidson. Washington University of Texas UTOPIA Portrait Gallery Original source: Booker T. Washington, The Story of My Life and Work. Cincinnati: W.H. Ferguson, 1901 http://www.lib.utexas.edu/photodraw/portraits/index.html

Fig. 4-3. Portrait of Severino dos Santos Vieira, in the IGHB gallery (photo by Sabrina Gledhill)

Fig. 4-4. Centennial postage stamp, issued in 1956. Source: https://postalmuseum.si.edu/collections/object-spotlight/booker-t-washington-postage-stamp

Fig. 5-1. Booker T. Washington, ca. 1903. [Booker T. Washington sitting and holding books] C. E. (Christopher Ethelbert) Cheyne.

Library of Congress Prints and Photographs Division Washington, D.C. 20540 USA http://hdl.loc.gov/loc.pnp/pp.print

Fig. 5-2. Manuel R. Querino, *Artistas baianos*, 2nd ed. (1911). Frontispiece

Fig. 5-3. Ladislau dos Santos Titára, *Artistas baianos*, 2nd ed. (1911)

Fig. 5-4. Portrait of Manuel Querino Unveiled in the IGHB Gallery in 1928 (Calmon 1995).

Fig. 5-5. Portrait of Manuel Querino by Graça Ramos (2005) Oil on canvas (photo by Rosa França)

Fig. 5-6. Reading Room at the Tuskegee Institute Library, ca. 1902. [Interior view of library reading room with male and female students sitting at tables, reading, at the Tuskegee Institute] digital file from original glass neg. Frances Benjamin Johnston. Library of Congress Prints and Photographs Division Washington, D.C. 20540 USA http://hdl.loc.gov/loc.pnp/pp.print

Fig. 5-7. Faculty of the Tuskegee Institute with Andrew Carnegie, 1906. [Tuskegee Institute faculty with Andrew Carnegie, Tuskegee, Alabama]. Frances Benjamin Johnston. Library of Congress Prints and Photographs Division Washington, D.C. 20540 USA http://hdl.loc.gov/loc.pnp/pp.print

Fig. 5-8. Portrait of Booker T. Washington, ca 1917. [Booker T. Washington, half-length portrait, standing, against white background] digital file from original photo. C. M. Battey. Library of Congress Prints and Photographs Division Washington, D.C. 20540 USA http://hdl.loc.gov/loc.pnp/pp.print

Figs. 5-9 to 5-25. Illustrations from *Costumes africanos no Brasil* (Querino 1938)

Fig. 5-26. Illustration from *Artistas baianos* (Querino 1909)

Fig. 5-27. Portrait of Manuel Querino (Leite 1988, 89)

Fig. 5-28. Book cover with retouched photograph of Manuel Querino (Nascimento and Gama 2009)

ABOUT THE AUTHOR

Sabrina Gledhill is an independent scholar, publisher, writer, and translator. After 28 years in Salvador, Bahia, Brazil, where she raised a family and earned a PhD in Ethnic (Brazilian) and African Studies from the Federal University at Bahia, she returned to the UK in 2015. Dr Gledhill also holds an MA in Latin American Studies from UCLA.

Her research focusses on Brazilian and US race relations, with a particular emphasis on Black Atlantic intellectuals, notably Manuel Querino. She is the author of *Travessias no Atlântico Negro: Reflexões sobre Booker T. Washington e Manuel Querino*, which she has translated and updated to produce *Black Atlantic Crossings*.

Expanding on her studies of Querino, Dr Gledhill edited and co-authored *Manuel Querino (1851-1923): An Afro-Brazilian Pioneer in the Age of Scientific Racism*, published in 2021, and, in 2024, published two edited volumes based on his work: *The Need for Heroes: Black Intellectuals Dig Up Their Past* and *Heroes Sung and Unsung: Black Artists in World History*.

As a translator, she has provided English speaking readers access to over 40 books, including such notable works as *Death is a Festival: Funeral Rites and Rebellion in Nineteenth-Century Brazil*, by João José Reis, *The Story of Rufino: Slavery, Islam and Freedom in the Black Atlantic*, by João José Reis, Flavio Gomes, and Marcus de Carvalho, and *Francisco de Paula Brito: A Black Editor in Brazil*, by Rodrigo Camargo de Godoi.

www.ingramcontent.com/pod-product-compliance
Lightning Source LLC
Chambersburg PA
CBHW071808230426
43670CB00013B/2394